Celebrating the Third Decade and Beyond

New Challenges to ASEAN-India Economic Partnership

Prabir De and Suthiphand Chirathivat

Editors

KNOWLEDGE WORLD

KW Publishers Pvt Ltd
New Delhi

ISBN 978-93-86288-00-4
e-book ISBN 978-93-86288-01-1

Published in India by Kalpana Shukla

KNOWLEDGE WORLD

KW Publishers Pvt Ltd
4676/21, First Floor, Ansari Road, Daryaganj, New Delhi 110002
Phone: +91 11 23263498/43528107
Email: knowledgeworld@kwpub.com • www.kwpub.com

2011 FPBA BEST PUBLISHERS AWARD (ENGLISH)

Printed and Bound by Bhavish Graphics.

CONTENTS

FOREWORD

Ambassador Shyam Saran
Chairman, RIS

ASEAN-India economic integration has made substantial progress in recent years. At the ASEAN-India Commemorative Summit 2012 in New Delhi, ASEAN-India relations had been elevated to the Strategic Partnership level. The Act East Policy has imparted new momentum to ASEAN-India relations, and the stage is now set for the deepening of collaboration across a range of political, economic, commercial, cultural and people-to-people links. There is specific focus on issues relating to connectivity, trans-national terrorism, and maritime security. The proposed Regional Comprehensive Economic Partnership (RCEP) Agreement, when concluded, will be the key to promoting political stability and economic prosperity in our shared region.

ASEAN and India will be celebrating 25 years of their dialogue relations in 2017. This book entitled "Celebrating the Third Decade and Beyond: New Challenges to ASEAN-India Economic Partnership" is, therefore, a timely initiative to review the past and suggest the ways to further strengthen all round relations in the future. A collaborative effort of the ASEAN-India Centre (AIC), New Delhi and ASEAN Studies Centre (ASC), Bangkok, this book deals with some of the challenges being faced by the ASEAN-India economic integration process. Each chapter in this book explores the outstanding issues and attempts to draw some policy implications. I would like to record my appreciation of the efforts that have been put by Prof. Prabir De and Prof Suthiphand Chirathivat in putting together this volume. I also congratulate all the authors who have contributed to this volume.

I am sure this book will provide new ideas and suggestions in deepening the ASEAN-India Economic Partnership. I trust it will be a valuable reference for policymakers, academics and practitioners.

September 2016 **Shyam Saran**
New Delhi

PREFACE

Two and half decades passed away since India undertook the Look East Policy (LEP) as an effort to strengthen its economic and strategic relations with Southeast and East Asian countries. The impetus in regional integration received through LEP has gained new momentum through the Act East Policy (AEP). India's proactive role in building a common market with an ambitious but realistic connectivity programme has increased her footprint in Southeast and East Asia considerably.

The India-ASEAN relationship is passing through its third decade. India became a sectoral partner of ASEAN in 1992, a dialogue partner in 1996, and a summit-level partner in 2002. The ASEAN-India strategic partnership—the elevated relationship that began at the 2012 Commemorative Summit—gives a greater hope in delivering stronger bilateral relations. ASEAN and India will be celebrating 25 years of their dialogue relations, 15 years of summit level relations and five years of strategic partnership in 2017.

ASEAN has embraced the ASEAN Economic Community (AEC) on 1st January 2016, albeit on a smaller scale. In parallel, ASEAN has undertaken series of initiatives to achieve the AEC 2025 milestones. AEC comprises four pillars: a single market and production base, a highly competitive economic region, a region of equitable economic development, and a region fully integrated into the global economy, each has strong implications for India and other dialogue partners of ASEAN.

The relationship is set to deepen in coming days as ASEAN and India step up their collaboration across a range of economic and strategic issues. For example, ASEAN and India (along with other countries) have been working towards establishing a Comprehensive Free Trade Area through Regional Comprehensive Economic Partnership (RCEP) Agreement. India's deeper cooperation with ASEAN and vice versa would positively influence the future course of regional integration in Asia-Pacific.

Time is ripe for India to establish a strong economic partnership with ASEAN. While this will reinforce India's security, it would also gradually remove economic isolation of India's North East Region (NER). At the same time, both ASEAN and India have been facing several challenges.

To discuss the challenges and prospects of economic integration between India and ASEAN, the ASEAN Studies Centre (ASC) of the Chulalongkorn

University, the Research and Information System for Developing Countries (RIS) and Indian Embassy in Thailand organised an International Conference to Commemorate the 20th Anniversary of ASEAN-India Cooperation titled "Seamless Integration into the Third Decade: Building on Two Decades of ASEAN-India Partnership" in Bangkok on 20-21 September 2012. Some of the papers presented at this Conference were updated later and added in this volume. In a way, origin of this book belongs to this Conference. We are thankful to students, research assistants and administrative staff of Chulalongkorn University for their kind support to this Conference. We also thank the Thai Government and Chulalongkorn University for extending financial support to organise this Conference.

There is a need to review the past and undertake new strategies to help us achieve a new paradigm of ASEAN-India relations. This book makes an attempt to fulfil this objective through its regional integration narratives. It has 12 chapters and each chapter tries to capture essential features of the cross-cutting issues and attempts to draw some policy implications.

The subject of this book will be of special interests to regional cooperation and integration specialists, government officials, researchers and the students. The volume would certainly help them in formulating strategies and advancing knowledge in this field.

We would like to thank all the contributors, authors and partners for the enthusiasm, hard work and support that made this volume possible. In particular, we are grateful to Ambassador Shyam Saran for his guidance and encouragement. We are thankful to Prof. Sachin Chaturvedi, Director-General, RIS for his support in publication of this volume. We also acknowledge the comments from experts, policymakers, research scholars, and government officials.

We are especially thankful to Ambassador Anil Wadhwa, former Secretary (East), Ministry of External Affairs (MEA), Government of India; Ambassador Suresh K Reddy, Indian Ambassador to ASEAN and EAS; Ms. Pooja Kapur, Joint Secretary (ASEAN-ML), Ministry of External Affairs (MEA), Government of India for their support and cooperation.

We have benefitted from discussions with several scholars at Chulalongkorn University such as Sineenat Sermcheep, Chayodom Sabhasri, Surat Horachaikul, Piti Srisangnam, among others. We acknowledge the editorial support extended by Anupama D Masali. We are also grateful to Opinder Kaur for her sincere editorial assistance. Durairaj Kumarasamy assisted us in finalisation phase of the manuscript. The support of ASEAN Studies Centre (ASC) of Chulalongkorn University and ASEAN-India Centre (AIC) at RIS in carrying out the project and this publication is gratefully acknowledged. Mr Jose Mathew of KW Publishers helped in the production of the book.

Views expressed in this publication are those of the authors and not the views of the ASEAN-India Centre (AIC) at Research and Information System for Developing Countries (RIS), ASEAN Studies Centre (ASC) of Chulalongkorn University, or the ASEAN Secretariat. Usual disclaimers apply.

New Delhi and Bangkok
September 2016

Prabir De and **Suthiphand Chirathivat**

LIST OF TABLES, FIGURES, MAPS, BOXES

Chapter Four

Chapter Five

Chapter Six

Chapter Seven

Chapter Eight

Chapter Nine

Chapter Ten

Chapter Eleven

ABBREVIATIONS

ACCC	ASEAN Connectivity Coordinating Committee
ADB	Asian Development Bank
AEC	ASEAN Economic Community
AEP	Act East Policy
AFAS	ASEAN Framework Agreement of Services
AFTA	ASEAN Free Trade Area
AGE	Applied General Equilibrium
AHN	Asian Highway Network
AIEPG	ASEAN-India Eminent Persons Group
AIFTA	ASEAN-India FTA
AITGA	ASEAN-India Trade in Goods Agreement
AMM	ASEAN Ministerial Meeting
APEC	Asia-Pacific Economic Cooperation
APT	ASEAN plus Three
ARF	ASEAN Regional Forum
ASEAN	Association of Southeast Asian Nations
ASI	Archaeological Survey of India
AYUSH	Ayurveda, Yoga and Naturopathy, Unani, Siddha and Homoeopathy
BIMSTEC	Bay of Bengal Initiative for Multi-Sectoral and Technical Cooperation
BTILS	BIMSTEC Transport Infrastructure and Logistics Study
CECA	Comprehensive Economic Cooperation Agreement
CEPA	Comprehensive Economic Partnership Agreement
CEPEA	Comprehensive Economic Partnership in East Asia
CEP	Cultural Exchange Programme
CERT	Computer Emergency Response Team
CGE	Computable General Equilibrium
CII	Confederation of Indian Industry
CSIR	Council of Scientific and Industrial Research
CTC	Comprehensive Trade Costs
E&E	Electrical and Electronic Equipment
EAFTA	East Asian Free Trade Area
EAS	East Asia Summit

EHS	Early Harvest Scheme
EIU	Economist Intelligence Unit
EPA	Economic Partnership Agreement
EWEC	East-West Economic Corridor
FDI	Foreign Direct Investment
FTAAP	Free Trade Area of the Asia-Pacific
GATS	General Agreement on Trade in Services
GVCs	Global Value Chains
GMS	Greater Mekong Subregion
GTAP	Global Trade Analysis Project
GUPES	Global Universities Partnership for Education for Sustainability
GVA	Gross Value Added
HSL	Highly Sensitive Lists
ICCR	Indian Council for Cultural Relations
ICT	Information and Communication Technology
ICWA	Indian Council of World Affairs
IGNCA	Indira Gandhi National Centre for the Arts
IPN	International Production Network
ITA	Information Technology Agreement
IWT	Inland Water Transport
KMTTP	Kaladan Multimodal Transit Transport Project
KSFS	Karimganj Steamer and Ferry Station
LCSs	Land Custom Stations
LDCs	Least Developed Countries
LEP	Look East Policy
MDA	Market Develop Assistance
MEA	Ministry of External Affairs
MGC	Mekong-Ganga Cooperation
MIEC	Mekong-India Economic Corridor
MNCs	Multinational Corporations
MPAC	Master Plan on ASEAN Connectivity
NDA	National Democratic Alliance
NER	North Eastern Region
NHDP	National Highways Development Project
NMCC	National Manufacturing Competitiveness Council
NSEC	North-South Economic Corridor

PC	Parts and Components
PSR	Product Specific Rules
RCEP	Regional Comprehensive Economic Partnership
REER	Real Effective Exchange Rate
S&T	Science and Technology
SAARC	South Asian Association of Regional Cooperation
SARDP-NE	Special Accelerated Road Development Programme in Northeast
SEC	Southern Economic Corridor
SEOM	Senior Economic Officials Meeting
SEZ	Sittwe Economic Zone
SITC	Standard International Trade Classification
SKRL	Singapore-Kunming Rail Link
SOM	Senior Officials' Meeting
TAB	Trading Across Borders
TAC	Treaty of Amity and Cooperation
TBSE	Technology Bureau for Small Enterprises
TH	Trilateral Highway
TIFTA	Thailand-India Free Trade Agreement
TISTR	Thailand Institute of Scientific and Technological Research
TiVA	Trade in Value Added
TNC	Trade Negotiating Committee
ToT	Terms of Trade
TPP	Trans-Pacific Partnership
UNEP	United Nations Environment Programme
UNESCAP	United Nations Economic and Social Commission for Asia and the Pacific
WTO	World Trade Organization

CONTRIBUTORS

ANDREW KAM JIA YI, Fellow, Institute of Malaysian and International Studies (IMIS), Kuala Lumpur

ANUPAMA D. MASALI, Research Fellow, Faculty of Economics, Chulalongkorn University, Bangkok

BISWAJIT NAG, Associate Professor, Indian Institute of Foreign Trade (IIFT) New Delhi

CHANDRIMA SIKDAR, Associate Professor, School of Business Management, Narsee Monjee Institute of Management Studies (NMIMS), Pune

DURAIRAJ KUMARASAMY, Consultant, ASEAN-India Centre (AIC), Research and Information System for Developing Countries (RIS), New Delhi

IMDADUL ISLAM HALDER, Research Associate, ASEAN-India Centre (AIC), Research and Information System for Developing Countries (RIS), New Delhi

ISHANI NASKAR, Associate Professor, Rabindra Bharati University (RBU), Kolkata

LAWRENCE SURENDRA, Chairman, The Sustainability Platform (TSP), Bengaluru

NUANPAN THAMANOVANISH, Officer for Intelligence Monitoring and Early Warning Unit (IMEU), Mission of Thailand to the European Union, Royal Thai Embassy, Brussels

P K H SINGH, Adviser (Transport), North East Council (NEC), Shillong

PITI SRISANGNAM, Assistant Professor, Faculty of Economics, Chulalongkorn University, Bangkok

PRABIR DE, Coordinator, ASEAN-India Centre (AIC) and Professor, Research and Information System for Developing Countries (RIS), New Delhi

SINEENAT SERMCHEEP, Assistant Professor, Faculty of Economics, Chulalongkorn University, Bangkok

SOPHIE BOISSEAU DU ROCHER, Senior Research Associate, Center for Asian Studies, institut francais des relations internationales (IFRI), Paris

SUTHIPHAND CHIRATHIVAT, Chairman, Chula Global Network and Executive Director, ASEAN Studies Center (ASC), Chulalongkorn University, Bangkok

THAM SIEW YEAN, Professor, Institute of Malaysian and International Studies (IMIS), Kuala Lumpur

ONE

INTRODUCTION

Prabir De and Suthiphand Chirathivat

India and Southeast Asian countries are striving for greater regional integration. Despite geographical proximity and cultural affinity, trade and investment between ASEAN and India are substantially lower than the potential. The Free Trade Agreement (FTA) in goods, implemented in 2010, and the services trade and investment agreement in 2015 between ASEAN and India represent an important effort to enhance regional integration. While ASEAN and India are celebrating the third decade of partnership, the relationship of both partners is not a merely recent product. They have indeed a long experience of interactions, an association made of exchanges, and peaceful interactive influences.

India shares both land and maritime boundaries with ASEAN. Civilisational and cultural links between India and the Southeast Asia date back thousands of years. Probably no other country has such strong links with the Southeast Asia region as much as India by way of religion, language, culture and civilisation. People in Southeast Asia, by nature, seem to enjoy and treasure the feelings of this closeness. India is perceived by Southeast Asian countries as a benevolent power. Despite deep and structural influence of India on Southeast Asia, the region has nevertheless been able to transform into its own version of Indianisation as it is rooted in the constructive and rich landscape and melting pot of culture and history.

India's "Look East Policy" (LEP) was in force for more than two decades, and thereafter, has been replaced by the "Act East Policy" (AEP). The ASEAN-India relations have gained a constant momentum throughout this period. The LEP was devised as a strategy to boost trade and foster economic cooperation with East and Southeast Asian countries. But, the incentive to intensify political dialogue was not there.

Regional integration, if done correctly, can work. It is often claimed that the regional integration process in Southeast Asia has been driven by market forces, with little support from formal institutional arrangements. However, the situation began to change when the ASEAN Free Trade Area (AFTA) was launched in 1993. The integration has gained momentum with implementation of various FTAs with the dialogue partners including the ASEAN-India FTA, which came into effect in 2010. Furthermore, ASEAN has taken a further step forward, transforming itself from a mere free trade area into the ASEAN Economic Community (AEC), which could enhance the free movement of goods, services, investment, capital and skilled labour, and could contribute to the formation of single market as well as a single production base. ASEAN has embraced the AEC on 1st January 2016, albeit on a smaller scale. In parallel, ASEAN has undertaken series of initiatives to achieve the AEC 2025 milestones. AEC comprises four pillars: a single market and production base, a highly competitive economic region, a region of equitable economic development, and a region fully integrated into the global economy, each has strong implications for India and other dialogue partners of ASEAN (Mikic, 2016).

The ASEAN-India economic integration has made substantial progress in lowering trade costs, economic integration seems to advance further (AIC-RIS, 2015). However, both of them have been facing several challenges that cover a number of areas and which call for concerted efforts by ASEAN member states and India. Some serious challenges at present are declining trade between ASEAN and India; incomplete physical connectivity projects; a near stagnation of bilateral FDI flows, to mention a few.

This book deals with the economic integration between ASEAN and India. Each chapter in this volume tries to capture essential features of the cross-cutting issues and attempts to draw some policy implications. Following introduction, it has 11 chapters; each is unique in dealing with important cross-cutting issues relating to ASEAN-India integration.

The potential for a constructive political relation between India and ASEAN remains largely untapped. There is an urgent need to take the political relations to the next level as India is serious about engagement with the Asia-Pacific; ASEAN is undoubtedly a first-choice partner. Chapter 2 discusses how to reinforce a much needed pillar of political cooperation between ASEAN and India, and puts forward a list of recommendations if political relation is to achieve full potential from this participation.

Chapter 3 reviews the historical and cultural links in the region that are core elements in India's cultural diplomacy. This in turn is expected to harness India's potential to emerge as a soft power in the region. This chapter briefs about the concepts of cultural diplomacy and soft power before moving to historical and cultural links between India and Southeast Asia. It suggests that it would be useful to cultivate the cultural links and engage with the countries in their specific historic and contemporary contexts. A calibrated approach would perhaps help India to reap the benefits of cultural diplomacy and help her emerge as an important neighbour to ASEAN.

In the contemporary period, while ASEAN continues to enhance and facilitate economic cooperation as it moves toward the attainment of an ASEAN Economic Community by 2025, the region has also cultivated economic cooperation with its key trading partners from outside the region, including India. ASEAN-India FTA represents an important first step towards fostering closer economic ties among the member countries of this agreement. Chapter 4 reviews the trade relations between ASEAN and India, analyses the impact of ASEAN-India FTA on ASEAN's exports of manufactured goods to India and India's exports of manufactured goods to ASEAN, and presents suggestions to further enhance ASEAN-India trade in goods.

Chapter 5 takes the discussion further ahead. The opening up of trade between India and the ASEAN region did not quite explain the increase in the two-way trade between them. India's trade with these countries in general has been greater in years after 2009 irrespective of the countries implementing the FTA. This chapter provides an in-depth analysis using the computable general equilibrium (CGE) modelling framework of the Global Trade Analysis Project (GTAP), and indicates that India's two-way trade with the region is likely to increase substantially (almost 53 per cent) by December 2021, when the tariff liberalisations, as per the commitments of all the partner countries, are completed. Increase in India's imports from the region would be much greater than its exports to the region. Initially, Malaysia and Thailand become the largest markets for Indian goods. But, when the relatively smaller ASEAN countries intensify their tariff liberalisations, the Lao PDR and the Philippines emerge as the most important markets, followed by Cambodia, Vietnam and the rest of ASEAN. This chapter indicates that as the FTA proceeds in phases, India's trade with the ASEAN region increases consistently, with imports rising more than exports and the trade basket gradually becoming more intensive in secondary products than in primary products.

The welfare effect of ASEAN–India Free Trade Agreement (AIFTA) too varies widely for India. It is dependent on the nature of liberalisation. At the initial stages of the opening up, India's welfare position is negative mainly due to worsening terms of trade. But, as the scope of the FTA widens with smaller ASEAN countries joining in, India's welfare turns positive. It gains both allocative efficiency and large endowment. India is likely to benefit from the FTA as more of the smaller countries from the region liberalise their trade with India. Particularly, notable would be the endowment effect, which is likely to increase manifold as the phased tariff liberalisation process proceeds. This is mainly brought about by the increase in demand for unskilled labour mostly in the expanding export intensive sectors in the country. Chapter 5 also illustrates that the ASEAN-India FTA will provide more internal benefit to India as it unfolds gradually. However, bilateral trade deficit of India is bound to rise and we should not have a myopic view towards the trade deficit only. The ASEAN FTA is bound to increase economic activities within India leading to more employment and income generation. With reduction in trade cost alongside tariff liberalisation, the employment gains to India will increase further. The success of ASEAN-India FTA also depends very much on the structured implementation path of mega-regionals in Asia viz. Regional Comprehensive Economic Partnership (RCEP), Trans-Pacific Partnership (TPP) and Free Trade Area of the Asia-Pacific (FTAAP). In other words, the emergence of the idea for a broader regional economic integration in East Asia represents a real challenge for ASEAN. Chapter 6, therefore, analyses the emerging architecture of FTAs in Asia, and suggests that ASEAN's regional integration will only be successful if linkages are broadened with regional and global partners through proper framework of region-wide trading arrangements.

To strengthen the regional integration, bilateral relations among the member countries play a critical role. Chapter 7 presents a case study of India-Thailand bilateral relations to justify the need for greater cooperation between ASEAN and India. The cultural relations between India and Thailand could be traced back through histories. The strong cultural and economic ties between the two countries illustrate a key stepping stone to build efficient and seamless connections for a more competitive, prosperous, and integrated region. This chapter indicates that to unlock the economic potential of the eight North Eastern states of India and gain the maximum utilisation of the ASEAN production network in Thailand and the Greater

Mekong Subregion (GMS) countries, the connectivity between ASEAN and India has to be improved. An improved connectivity is must in order to facilitate the production networks between them.

Chapter 8 takes the discussion of ASEAN-India production networks further ahead. This chapter discusses those policies that are required to synchronise the functions of Indian SMEs with international production networks (IPN) governance models. Automobile, pharmaceutical, machinery are the sectors which can be promoted to develop relational model with the lead firms, thereby strengthening the production networks between ASEAN and India. To facilitate the production networks, free flow of investment and movement of skilled labourers across the region are must. Services trade between ASEAN and India is the next step forward.

Services trade is an area which offers complementarities. Chapter 9 attempts to shed light on the trends in services trade, identifies the barriers to trade in selected products, and presents a set of recommendations to facilitate the services trade between India and ASEAN. The chapter concludes that both ASEAN and India have to ease restrictions to cross-border trade in services and allow for majority foreign ownership in services trade area.

India connects Southeast Asia with Southwest and Central Asia, whereas Myanmar represents an important gateway for India to Southeast Asia and vice versa. The opening up of Myanmar represents a further scope of strengthening the partnership. Chapter 10 discusses the connectivity agenda between ASEAN and India. It explains the ASEAN-India physical connectivity initiatives in connection with the strategies of Master Plan on ASEAN Connectivity (MPAC), and presents the a set of recommendation to deal with the emerging challenges in connectivity.

The North Eastern Region (NER) of India is the bridgehead of India's connectivity with Southeast Asia. The NER is also central to India's AEP. Chapter 11 analyses current scenario of NER's domestic infrastructure (also known as backend infrastructure), discusses the challenges faced by NER, and finally, presents a set of policy implications.

Finally, with the advent and advancement of technology, the knowledge economy has gained a growing importance of innovation, not only competitiveness enhancing features but also innovation for coping with the social, ecological, environmental and economic impacts of increasing cross-border trade flows and ties. Chapter 12 explores the possibility of and the enabling conditions needed for knowledge institutional cooperation in the Asian regional context, specifically between India and ASEAN. This chapter concludes that innovative cooperation can be built, and it can contribute to virtuous cycles of innovation and social benefit through the process of mutual learning, if priority is given in such cooperation not purely in an inward looking institutional sense, but looking outward to society and forward to the future, anticipating the challenges that our societies commonly face in terms of ecological sustainability, economic growth with justice and equity and quality of life for all citizens in our nations.

Next Steps

Unless the high external protection levels are dismantled across the board, regional tariff liberalisation at the ASEAN-India level (or for that matter within RCEP) could lead to substantial trade diversion. This has been happening in the ASEAN-India region, where firms are taking shelter of such protections and getting into less efficient production process (Sally, 2013). On the issue of how to make ASEAN-India FTA itself as effective as possible, the sensitive goods lists should be minimised. Liberal rules of origin need to be negotiated between the two partners. Trade facilitation by means of harmonisation of standards and customs procedures and cooperation in transport infrastructure is very important. MRAs have to be signed in services trade sectors. It would be worth logical to undertake a review of the ASEAN-India FTA and monitor problems and obstacles relevant to both tariff and non-tariff measures (NTMs) in order to promote and increase the FTA utilisation. These reforms and liberalisation will contribute to strengthen the integration process even if all bilateral FTAs are subsumed into RCEP. However, success would depend how strongly ASEAN and India are getting integrated with the world economy (AIC-RIS, 2015).

Implementation matters, mere signing of the FTA is not enough. In implementing FTAs, we need to keep in mind that regional integration can only be successful if it unleashes new competition that lowers prices, introduces new technology and gains productivity. At the same time, FTA may give rise to negative effects, including rise in poverty and inequality. These effects should be identified and appropriate measures should be taken to address them. Coordinated efforts are necessary to realise sustainable growth and development in India and Southeast Asia.

Until recently, political cooperation was the weak link of the relation between ASEAN and India. Twenty five years after the establishment of the ASEAN-India dialogue relations, ASEAN-India cooperation needs a new impulsion, or, more precisely, a real, substantive beginning to go beyond wishful thinking level.

The ASEAN-India relations have achieved much over the last 25 years. But its success has given rise to new challenges. It will continue to play a central role in promoting economic integration and inclusive development over the next 25 years.

References

AIC – RIS (2015) *ASEAN-India Development and Cooperation Report 2015*, ASEAN-India Centre (AIC) - Research and Information System for Developing Countries (RIS), New Delhi: Routledge.

Mikic, Mia (2016) "Trade Implications of the ASEAN+ Agreements for Other Asian Countries", in Mia Mikic and Bruno Jetin (eds.) *ASEAN Economic Community: A Model for Asia-wide Regional Integration?* New York: Palgrave Macmillan

Sally, Razeen (2013) "ASEAN FTAs: State of Play and Outlook for ASEAN's Regional and Global Integration", in Sanchita Basu Das, Jayant Menon, Rodolfo C Severino, Okmar Lal Shrestha (eds.) *The ASEAN Economic Community: A Work in Progress*, Singapore and Manila: Institute of Southeast Asian Studies (ISEAS) and Asian Development Bank (ADB)

TWO

ASEAN-INDIA POLITICAL COOPERATION: HOW TO REINFORCE A MUCH NEEDED PILLAR?

Sophie Boisseau du Rocher

Introduction

Twenty five years after the establishment of the ASEAN-India Dialogue relations and fifteen years after the beginning of the Summit Partnership, political cooperation between ASEAN and India needs a new impulsion, or, more precisely, a real, substantive beginning to go beyond wishful thinking level.

Until recently, political cooperation was the weak link of the relation between ASEAN and India. Since the launching of the Look East Policy (LEP) in 1991, the most often cited impetus for cooperation is the converging economic interest, and, then, the security interest. This reality is indeed worrying as the concern is that between rising economic and security imperatives, there is no room, no time and no investment for a much needed constructive political dialogue. The basic argument is that this missing link might be detrimental to the whole package, and may even be risky.

If there is a potential for a more substantial political relation, it is not yet clear when and how this potential will be fully exploited. Indeed, we observe two main contradictory trends: on one side, if there are foundations and incentives to deepen and have a well-balanced political relation that is waiting to be more efficiently exploited, while on the other side, the perception that this relation, because it is perceived as a "non-threatening" relation, does not deserve priority, is also palpable. The current international political context might bring a new sense of urgency to propel this much needed pillar in order, as it was said during the 10th ASEAN-India Ministerial Meeting at Phnom Penh (July 2012), "to achieve the full potential of the partnership".

To do so, India and ASEAN have some assets to exploit. First, their relation is a well-constructed relation. India and Southeast Asia are not recent partners. They have indeed a long experience of interaction, an association made of exchange and peaceful interactive influence. Southeast Asia has been deeply and structurally influenced by India. As demonstrated by Lucian Pye in his master book on the cultural dimension of political authority (Pye, 1985), the conceptualisation of political space, political rules and mechanisms has been inspired by India. Therefore, there is a common political background and a deep understanding that links both partners. Other scholars, such as Robert Heine-Geldern, have also extensively written on this process of Indianisation (Geldern, 1956). Undoubtedly, the Indian footprint on political culture in Southeast Asia has created an implicit political affinity, which defines and justifies in itself the India-ASEAN relation. Nonetheless, this asset has been neglected until now because India has not yet assumed its role and responsibility as a source of political inspiration for its neighbours. Second asset is historical coexistence with an alternation of proximity and distant periods. Civilisational and cultural links date back thousands of years, perhaps even in the prehistoric period. Probably no other country has influenced the region as much as India by way of religion, language, culture and civilisation. Ancient Indian classical works such as the Ramayana became reference parts of Southeast Asia, while Indian merchants began bringing Hinduism and Buddhism by the 1st century AD, influencing the development of kingdoms and empires like Srivijaya in Sumatra and Majapahit in Java, Bali and the Philippine archipelago. Indian influence is still visible in Southeast Asian architecture, food, music, language and religion. There is also historical evidence to suggest that these flourishing economic and cultural relations did not end in the pre-colonial era or even during the colonial interlude. Because of the British policy of large scale migration to support the plantation and mining sectors, this interlude brought many Indians into Southeast Asia and the "Indian" community in the region could be considered as another asset in terms of political rapprochements. There is certainly no doubt that Singapore emerged as an important bilateral partner of India since it used its highly skilled diplomats of Indian origin to boost the bilateral link and support India's case for increased cooperation with ASEAN. Post-World War II (WWII) and post-independence period of India brought again many opportunities to strengthen the links. The common fight against colonialism allowed India to express its support to its neighbours; for instance, India convened the Asian Relations Conference in New Delhi in March 1947 primarily to express solidarity with the freedom struggles all across Southeast Asia. Equally important was the Special Conference on Indonesia held in January 1949, which was attended by 15 nations to express support to the Sukarno-led armed struggle against the Dutch colonial rule. Some years later, the participation to the new global order, notably through the Non-aligned movement, was another cause for rapprochement. Indeed, after independence, by virtue of its geopolitical location and its position during the freedom struggles India was expected to play the role of a stabiliser and peacemaker: its neutralist/non-aligned policy had considerable appeal in Southeast Asia. Due recognition was accorded to India's stature as a regional power when it was made the Chairman of International Control Commission that was set up under the 1954 Geneva Accord on Vietnam. The Afro-Asian Conference (also called the Bandung Conference) in April 1955, which India had co-sponsored and actively participated, is a major turning point as a striking signal: the importance of this conference on the creation of ASEAN is recognised.

At this stage, two points can be observed. First, India was, and still is, perceived by Southeast Asian countries as a benevolent power. Unlike Japan or China, it does not have to worry about its past with the region. Second, India and ASEAN share certain diplomatic practices (such as consensus, non-interference in domestic affairs and power-balancing pragmatism) that definitely contribute to a softer mode of understanding. These two points could reinforce political cooperation as a common ground.

The Cold War marked the start of a period of distancing and introduced suspicion and mutual mistrust. As India went to fight with China (1962) and Pakistan (1965 and 1971), it mechanically granted a lesser attention to Southeast Asia. Even, this context drove Indian diplomacy to a much more pragmatic and less idealistic position in world politics. Its appeal on Southeast Asian countries decreased and the region itself was caught into the polarisation process induced by ideological security rivalry, notably with the Vietnam War.

The end of the Cold War provided the opportunity to reconsider and propel the relation into stronger economic and security ties. After three decades, the founding members of ASEAN have gone through tremendous transformations: it was time for India to correct its own neglect. With this ambition, Prime Minister P. V. Narasimha Rao conceived the "Look East Policy" to restore its relations with its eastern neighbours, and most notably with Southeast Asia (Grare and Amitabh, 2001). ASEAN was one of the focal points of the LEP. Institutional rapprochements were encouraged. Today, ASEAN is a major partner of India, and this dense network of political links might serve as a support to boost the partnership. In 2016, India is a Dialogue Partner of ASEAN[1], has implemented an FTA with ASEAN in 2010, attends the post-ministerial conferences, is a member of ARF, has instituted an annual ASEAN-India Summit since 2002, has signed the Treaty of Amity and Cooperation (ASEAN TAC) in 2003, has signed ASEAN-India Partnership for Peace, Progress and Shared Prosperity in 2004 (at the third ASEAN-India Summit in Vientiane), is a participant of the East Asia Summit (EAS) since its very beginning in 2005 (even if some countries still question the coherence of having India into East Asia) and organized the Commemorative Summit in 2012. The Delhi Dialogue was inaugurated in 2009 and has become a regular event at track 1.5 level (with the eighth series in February 2016). To foster this institutional network, the Indian Foreign Office set up an ASEAN ML Division in August 2011.

This multi-faceted institutional dialogue did not impede bilateral relations with each member of ASEAN. Some, like Singapore (which train troops on Indian soil) or Indonesia, have a particularly close relation, while others, like the Philippines or Cambodia, have an insignificant level.

Apart from the motivation to regain some influence with this fast expanding region, to boost trade relations and strengthen security ties, India needed to affirm its interest in being considered as a full participant of Asian new balances. Outside South Asia, India considered Southeast Asia as an obvious space for cooperation since geo-strategic, political and economic conditions offered an opportunity to play a role. Therefore, it was time to carve a suitable place for its influence as Southeast Asia was going under growing pressure from China. On the political front, India did progress in these last 20 years in absolute terms but not in relative terms because of the phenomenal activity and programmes launched by China, and therefore, this needs assessment. This trivial assessment puts into question the efficiency of its diplomatic tools. To reposition itself, it might take advantage of the current search for friends and support expressed by Southeast Asia: ASEAN appears as an obvious candidate. The objective of closer ASEAN-India ties here would not be to contain Beijing, but to jointly manage its rising profile

1. India became a Sectoral Dialogue Partner of ASEAN in 1992 and a Full Dialogue Partner at the 5th ASEAN Summit in Bangkok, Thailand on 14-15 December 1995.

in the region in a peaceful, inclusive and constructive way: it is not a minor challenge in the current context.

A Strategic Relation, Yet Lacking Centrality

Why is this relation strategic for both partners and why is it necessary to give it a new impulsion when celebrating the 25th anniversary?

The second part of the question is easier to answer: a new impulsion is necessary because there is growing disappointment from the ASEAN side. Indeed, ASEAN thought India would play a much more active role after the experience of China and the United States, both of which have launched plenty of political initiatives and supported them by a constant stream of visits by political leaders of all levels. Indian Prime Minister's visits to Southeast Asia have been rare, nothing to say about Parliament's members, federal or local representatives. Now, fifteen years after the launching of the Summit meetings, after a period of adjustment and mutual knowledge, it is time for more political affinity. "ASEAN-India relation" as a concept has been a reality in the economic realm, but not yet in the political one.

Rationale: The Importance of a Political Dialogue

As regard to the first part of the question, political arguments are obvious. First argument relates to the current structural change in the global balance of power, a change of paradigm that needs to be discussed, understood and managed since it will have lasting consequences on the development (economic as well as political) and performance of East Asia and on each of its members. The current evolution of global as regional geopolitics calls for consultation and dialogue. The evolving flow of power in East Asia has created all the more turbulences that it happens in a global context characterised by uncertainty (mostly due to the decline of a world order that was dominated by the West). For more than a decade, East Asia has been considered as the rising region in global balances: this shift of power has introduced new challenges, especially concerning the distribution of power (with increasing pressure of China which overtook Japan as the world's second largest economy and the "return" of a pro-active America, which has bet both on India and ASEAN). And, if it is not difficult to observe an increasing inter-connectedness as economies are less dependent on Western markets, the rationale for a stronger political cooperation still appears elusive and has to be worked out.

One major question still needs to be addressed by the Asian countries: what kind of Asia do we want to build and transfer to the next generations? Of course, the basic spontaneous answer will be a prosperous Asia. But, is it enough as a political future? Because the answer is loaded with political content, it can not be addressed by China or the United States alone as they might be immediately accused to promote their own national interests in defining the political contours of the region. Yet, because this central question is not debated, by default, the most vocal define it and set the rules: the price to pay for alignment, for secondary actors such as ASEAN and India could appear very high. The failure of ASEAN Phnom Penh meeting (July 2012) sent an alarming signal for the Association as it raised questions about its ability to preserve its autonomy and much-vaunted centrality amidst Great powers with the potential to dominate the region. This setback revealed the weakness of the Association, and its absence of resilience, when taken into the trap of competing and overwhelming external interests.

Therefore, there is a strong political incentive to engage in a debate on what kind of political governance would be most appropriate for Asia's future in a polycentric world. And, how to embed it? What appears clearly is that if India wants to be a part of the region as it has proclaimed and does not want to be left out or stay at its margins, it must contribute to the debate. For all the reasons presented in the introduction, Southeast Asia and India might find a constructive support in each other's position to engage in the discussion and enlarge it to other participants in an inclusive way emphasising political cooperation and not competition. Because of the diversity of its members and its tradition of "comfortable and goodwill diplomacy", ASEAN is a dialogue partner of choice. This debate might be a big, and a risky one, but certainly a necessary and strategic one if India and ASEAN do not want to miss the present opportunity. India and ASEAN should support the rise of complementary and alternative poles of soft power in Asia and the creation of a network of like-minded partners.

Second correlated incentive relates to the unfinished regional architecture. The main challenge posed by this elusive political cooperation scheme is to make it more coherent, more concrete and efficient and not just a potential tool for Great powers' ambitions and projections. There is a need to find as to what kind of political regional order India and ASEAN would like to have. Major players have their own agenda and long-term strategies, while India and ASEAN, for different reasons, would more favourably adopt a flexible and inclusive approach to this essential question for the political order to work. The next set of question is: What kind of common vision/ambition do India and ASEAN share for the current regional construction and to what extent do they consider each other as leading forces behind this regional project, and What kind of rules are needed to secure political cooperation? Both the partners want to promote regional grouping and not only the functional side of the regional grouping. To implement the common vision, both partners need to be clear on the identity, and the substance of this identity. The challenge for the next generation is to transform this economic and trade architecture into a substantive and consistent political grouping. Regionalisation is not only a matter of money and trade agreements; it is first and foremost a matter of future co-existence, the essence of political action. Ambivalence on this issue of identity might lead to misunderstanding of goals and exploitation of an implicit competition for national interests. As India has consistently supported ASEAN as the driving force in further evolution of the undergoing regional processes, their cooperation in shaping the future of Asia, a matter of concern for the years to come, appears only natural. Furthermore, it will be of mutual benefit as it will reinforce ASEAN's much needed centrality and will offer India a non-threatening platform to exchange with other regional powers. This common vision presents a high strategic value in a climate of growing implicit tensions, to work and engage on a revisited, but consensual, political vision for the future.

Third reason to enhance this dialogue is political convergence and it is a major strategic issue. Here too and whether it admits it or not, India offers an alternative political model to the existing models within the East Asia Community. Often qualified as the biggest democracy in the world, India can not neglect this parameter. Its symbolic value – as proof that democracy and development are not incompatible – may have a spill over effect on countries that are still struggling in the turbulences of political transition. To say it bluntly, its democratic credentials are major differences with other Asian powers, and yet, it never presents them as an asset in its political dialogue with its ASEAN partners. Even, India's perceived lack of enthusiasm for democracy promotion is cited by critics as a hurdle in its claim to global leadership. Of course, India is committed to the principle of non-interference in domestic affairs, but there are plenty of ways to contribute to political consolidation such as support to institution-building, political pluralism or freedom of expression. Myanmar might provide the opportunity for further engagement.

Fourth reason is common security interests and the imperative to secure common security challenges such as terrorism, sea-lane protection and maritime security or non-traditional security challenges (climate change, disaster relief, food security, etc). Much has already been accomplished in terms of bilateral cooperation, yet much needs to be improved to go beyond a functional cooperation to protect the stability of a political community. As India chooses to embark on a benign projection of its rising power, it has become imperative to chalk out common goals with its neighbours. Southeast Asia has always been a place of geostrategic interest for external partners. To find countervailing forces in the new Southeast Asia strategic landscape is a priority for ASEAN members. For India, these security rapprochements appear like a basis to secure the ASEAN-India plan of action for a strategic partnership.

A Second Rank Relation

India's Look East Policy has been in force for more than two decades now and the ASEAN-India relation has gained a constant momentum. Originally it was devised as a strategy to boost trade and foster economic cooperation with ASEAN and Southeast Asian countries. It has succeeded in this field, but failed to evolve from a peripheral position to a central one. Most probably, because the political side of this LEP is light and not perceived as a priority. Both the sides are reserved. Though there have been some initiatives from both sides, but they have been inefficient till now. The incentive to intensify political dialogue is not there.

Indeed, India's Look East policy of engagement with the region has not given its full potential on the political and security sides and India, as a potential political leader, structured along clear political lines, has a low visibility in ASEAN member states. There is no strong political initiative or dialogue that can be associated with this political relation. The network for political dialogue has been implemented, but remains under-utilised: there is little political substance in the so said common political declarations. Political cooperation is viewed through functional cooperation such as building roads, bridges or organising a car rally, but apart from having a prosperous future, the choice of societal and political values or the building of institutions to protect them are not debated.

The ASEAN-India Eminent Persons Group (AIEPG), as an epistemic community, was pivotal in changing this perspective[2] and helped to forge a rationale and incentive to boost this facet of cooperation.

This lack of progress and limited political clout can be explained by several interrelated factors:

- India's political stance often appears tentative and not well thought out. In fact, India has not decided which seat it wants to occupy in Asia. On a short to medium term basis to compete with China might be out of reach and exhausting (and if India had some pretention to serve as a counterweight to China the pro-active Chinese political initiatives have put a very high level of potential comparison in these last few years and this will stress India's limited capacity);
- India has failed to spell out its interests, concerns and strategic stakes clearly, which often results in considerable confusion, especially in Southeast Asia, notably when compared with countries like South Korea or Australia, not to speak of China;
- Indian domestic problems (which sometimes question the coherence of its discourse and its ambition to be considered as a candidate for a Great power status) and sometimes poor administration;
- Other priorities (instability in Pakistan and Afghanistan for instance) or lack of priority; and
- The willingness of not to antagonise other players.

Basically, India does not yet have any precise political agenda with ASEAN and maintains a declaratory diplomacy. It often acts in a non-methodological way that creates disappointment and frustration. The management of the Human Rights issue is a case in point. ASEAN has made these rights more visible in its Charter, and since 2009 has adopted an ASEAN Inter-Governmental Commission on Human Rights. If India does not share the same concern and priority, it has decided to avoid this "sensitive" issue in the Plan of Action, a move that has been even accepted by China. What about the sharing of identity, values and experiences? If

2. The AIEPG was set up to draft a new ASEAN-India Vision Document which was adopted at the Commemorative Summit in 2012. All the meetings of the AIEPG have been held. First was held in Phnom Penh on 2-3 August 2011, second in New Delhi on 20-21 October 2011, third in Kuala Lumpur on 9-10 March 2012 and the fourth and final meeting was held in Kochi on 16-17 September 2012.

India wants to have world or regional power status, it should not be reluctant to assert its political status.

On the other side, ASEAN too has its own set of difficulties. The Association did not express enough interest in this political dialogue. As was said in the introduction, ASEAN-India relation is perceived as a "non-threatening" relation, and therefore, coming second after more urging issues. Coveted by China and the United States, and also approached by second-rank partners such as Japan, South Korea or Australia, ASEAN did not dedicate enough time and resources to deepen the new partnership. The Association has also to go through its own limits, including persistent nationalism and mutual mistrust, thus reducing the Association's capacity to project itself as a united front abroad, articulate policy and enhance collective leverage. As a result, intra-ASEAN discords and domestic turbulences make it difficult for outsiders to conduct negotiations with an Association still lacking collective authority despite the implementation of its charter. The "ASEAN Way", a set of functioning norms and principles, is more operational in reacting to initiatives rather than in launching new policies. Furthermore, ASEAN public does not know much about India and would not support any specific measure.

Myanmar as a Showcase of Limited Cooperation

Myanmar is the place where the spheres of influence of ASEAN, China and India overlap. It is the country that links South and Southeast Asia sharing borders with Bangladesh and India to the West, and China, Laos and Thailand in the North and East. Myanmar is India's front door to Southeast Asia. Its location is central to strengthen India's Look East-Act East Policy and counterbalance China's influence in the region. The recent political opening is a cause for optimism and an incentive to reconsider cooperation. It is, therefore, the perfect case study for measuring the degree of political connectivity between India and ASEAN.

The political interest is of course not the only one. Myanmar's geostrategic positioning at the entrance of the Malacca Strait (1,930 km of coast on the Bay of Bengal with some 800 islands) and close to the Indian Ocean shipping lanes gives this country an indisputable strategic value. Other than the strategic location, the country is richly endowed with natural resources (wood, hydrocarbons, copper, zinc, uranium, gold, precious stones) and is also become one of the major suppliers of energy for Asia. In a resource-intensive economic context (especially with regard to energy), the supply/demand argument outweighs many other considerations. Access to Myanmar's oil and gas reserves is probably the most important consideration in Indo-Burma relations. Myanmar's five main trading partners are from Asia, accounting for 70 per cent of its exports and 90 per cent of its imports, respectively.

Gateway to Southeast Asia and ASEAN, Myanmar can be considered as a showcase of India's policy with the region. And on this ground too, the record is poor; until now, Myanmar has not been a bridge to India-ASEAN political cooperation. But, if we see it with an optimistic view, Myanmar might be the space of a new active rapprochement between ASEAN and India.

No Public Political Cooperation

Since the stakes are high for both, one might have expected Myanmar to be an easy and natural focus of cooperation between India and ASEAN. This is not the case and very little can be found on this issue. Therefore, it is interesting to analyse the reasons of this diplomatic posture that certainly cannot be neglected.

Two basic principles support India and ASEAN's policy towards Myanmar. First is non-interference in domestic affairs, and second is flexible transformation by invitation. Through these principles, both partners share some basic convictions that explain their convergent approach and their reluctance to cooperate in a public political front. First, India and ASEAN never believed that domestic change in Myanmar would come by force or confrontational diplomacy. They were very uncomfortable with Western pressure (and ASEAN paid a heavy price for its position (Boisseau du Rocher, 2012)); indeed, they felt much more comfortable to discuss with the *junta* than with any other political actor in order "to change the system from inside". Second, strategic imperatives were predominant for them as they both needed to avoid driving Myanmar into China's arms. Third, the concept of a "pariah state" introduced by the United States and the European Union was perceived as illusory by both partners as Myanmar was a participant in Asian power games and a member of ASEAN; to further ostracise it was leading to a dead-end.

ASEAN initiated its policy of "constructive engagement" at the end of the 1980s to open a dialogue with the "legitimate" political actors in Myanmar.

This policy was mostly driven by ASEAN member-states' willingness to exploit untapped resources and investment opportunities (Bachoe and Stothard, 1997). Rangoon was then invited to join the Association in the early 1990s, an entry that was finalised in July 1997 and this admission made India ASEAN's contiguous neighbour sharing a long border of 1,600 kms. During this phase, and in order to engage and socialise the *junta* – thus giving preference to stability – ASEAN's approach was governed by a strict adherence to its non-interference doctrine as "the sanctity of national sovereignty is ASEAN most sacred corporate value" (Leifer, 1989). Yet, much of the so-called engagement was economic dealings by individual ASEAN members with the government in Burma/Myanmar. Political persuasion was not considered as an aggressive feat but rather as a process of conviction; the "constructive engagement" policy was thus replaced by the "flexible engagement" policy, with no better results (Jones, 2008). The 1997 financial and following socio-political crisis in the different member-states of ASEAN contribute to explain this failure: little was done because each member, from Thailand to Indonesia, had already much to do at home. Furthermore, ASEAN was torn between new and founding members, thus unable to pursue the reforms advocated by some members (Thailand and the Philippines). The Depayin killing[3]and the ASEAN chairmanship crisis[4] were additional events that further put ASEAN in the spotlights. Criticized for its contradictions and its inability to influence the *junta*, ASEAN was not ready to launch any new policy on Myanmar. Some experts demonstrated that its "critical disengagement" policy, coupled with the writing of the ASEAN charter, was indeed another attempt to cautiously influence Myanmar's junta through "quiet diplomacy" (Jones, 2008). However, most of them agreed on ASEAN's risk-adverse posture on this issue. It was only after cyclone Nargis in May 2008 that the Association adopted a more exposed position and called for further cooperation with the international community, including India.

On its side, India's policy towards Myanmar was driven by three motivations: (i) access to natural resources, (ii) combat insurgencies

3. On 30 May 2003, a NLD (National League for Democracy) motorcade was attacked at Depayin, thus killing 4 of Aung San Suu Kyi bodyguards: this dramatic incident signaled a return of the hard-liners to power, a shift confirmed by Khin Nyunt's demotion of his post as Prime Minister in August 2003.

4. After tough discussions within the Association, Myanmar decided not to assume the rotating chairmanship in 2006 "in order not to affect ASEAN's solidarity and cohesiveness."

(in the Northeast region), and (iii) balance against growing Chinese influence. After a virulent criticism of the 1988 events, India abandoned its political ambitions with Myanmar early, in 1993, when it realised the growing Chinese influence in the country and the consequent potential threat to its territorial security. This strategic parameter constitutes a permanent feature of Indian policy towards Myanmar, irrespective of the nature of the Myanmar regime. Initially, India strongly supported the prodemocracy movement in Burma and Aung San Suu Kyi, who was given the Jawaharlal Nehru Award in 1993. However, in the mid 1990s, realpolitik contingencies prevailed and India changed course to a "velvet diplomacy", giving itself the tools to discuss with the regime. The support to the "representatives of Burmese democracy" was perceived as counterproductive to India's interests and security. But, even after this shift, Myanmar has never been at the forefront of Indian interest except when the Burmese generals played one off against the other to "raise the bids"[5] because when Sino-Indian energy interests compete, Myanmar benefits in some form.

The important point to stress here is that even if India decided purposely to neglect the political side of its bilateral dialogue with the *junta*, it was not rewarded. The local power struggle was unfavourable to India as it does not have a permanent seat at the Security Council as China has, therefore, no veto right. Of the two sides, oil policy and political dialogue, the choice made by India proved disappointing. As a consequence, dialogue with ASEAN was a way to build a new policy approach. Furthermore, closer engagement of Myanmar with ASEAN could give a boost to the "Look East Policy".

It is important to realise that for different reasons, including divergent positions within public opinion or amongst members, India and ASEAN did not invest much on Myanmar; no one believed in a prompt change in the country and refused to antagonise with the *junta*. They both considered economic sanctions as meaningless and counterproductive and even after dramatic events such as the Depayin massacre or the Saffron Revolution of

5. More often than not, Beijing has stumped India on the energy front, which was most visibly demonstrated in 2006 when Chinese state-owned company Petro China beat India's OVL (Oil and Natural Gas Corporation Videsh Ltd.) and GAIL (Gas Authority of India Limited) in securing a deal to access natural gas in an offshore block in the Shwe field in the Bay of Bengal. Naypyidaw's decision to sell China the gas from the fields where India has made an investment has been a major disappointment for India. Recently, extensive natural gas found in three fields in the Gulf of Bengal has become a new contentious issue in China-India relations.

2007[6], sanctions as a means to pressurise the *junta* were not even mentioned. Indeed, they systematically refused to be associated with Western pressure. As long as China was giving the *junta* resources and revenues, India and ASEAN thought it was more productive to engage the generals because, by virtue of the Chinese cooperation, these generals were not isolated. It was not an ideological stance but a pragmatic observation.

To create a constructive and non-vehement relation that could drive a change was a common tactic but it was never considered to take collective measures in order to prompt developments. So, India and ASEAN followed their own soft engagement policy, mostly dedicated to economic issues, without much fanfare,[7] but with the implicit ambition to contribute to a political transition through moderate pressure and incentives to policy change. In this perspective, India and ASEAN welcomed the seven-point Roadmap to Democracy (2003), which secured a role for the military, therefore reassuring the *junta* of its position in the future Burmese political landscape. Today, most observers date the emergence of the ongoing political change with this Roadmap. Therefore, if political cooperation was limited to the lowest level, India and ASEAN worked for the same goal.

A Call for Rapprochement? Myanmar as an Appropriate Showcase of Political Cooperation

The current political transition of Myanmar is one of the most important and positive developments in Southeast Asian and Asian affairs. It is a process of strategic and symbolic significance for both India and ASEAN, which are major, and obvious, stakeholders in the transformation. This transition is greeted as a common success (India and ASEAN consider that their policy of engagement paid off), and could be exploited as the beginning of a new cooperation programme to concretely support a transition still hampered by

6. After the Saffron revolution, ASEAN Foreign ministers expressed their "revulsion" in a common statement while India did not condemn the repression but merely issued anodyne statements such as "it is our hope that all sides will resolve their issues peacefully through dialogue. India has always believed that Myanmar's process of political reform and national reconciliation should be more inclusive and broad-based" (26 September 2007).
7. Nevertheless, it is interesting to note that both India and ASEAN allowed Burmese political activists or dissidents with the freedom of expression. Declarations were made against the military regime in those countries but couldn't be attributed to local authorities.

many uncertainties. More than any other players[8], India and ASEAN are directly concerned by the impact and consequences of the Burmese return to "the international community".[9]Both appear as reliable and legitimate partners as they have been efficient contributors in the last decade in the establishment of an atmosphere conducive to meaningful international dialogue. But, there is an obvious upshot of convergence of interests. India's strengthening interactions with the individual countries and the regional body at large are mutually reinforcing. Does it mean they might try to engage in some kind of cooperation to jointly comfort and encourage this political process?

Some arguments speak in favour of deepened "political connectivity". In the current transformation of the balance of power in East Asia, India needs a stronger ASEAN. ASEAN needs to regain some legitimacy before it launches its Community and Myanmar needs to enhance its credentials as a "normal" member-state of ASEAN and a "normal" participant to regional security. This change suits the interest of both India and ASEAN, which will certainly benefit from a stable, prosperous and predictable Myanmar. They both have offered to help strengthen Myanmar's political transition to keep Myanmar on track with reform and this will provide them with new opportunities, a more stable environment and access to the national and local political network. New areas of cooperation could be tapped such as capacity building, strengthening of democratic institutions and engagement with civil society. Both are key providers of expertise and training (institution-building, reconciliation process, elections, etc.) and, as long-term benevolent partners they can play the role of facilitator and collaborators in policy formulation and basic social development.

Working together on some focused projects in an interactive relationship, without expectation for any immediate rewards but long term stability for the region, will send a confidence-building message to the regime. But much

8. And first and foremost, because of the Chinese pressure on the region, cf Johannes Dragsbaek Schmidt, 'India/China Rivalry and Competition in Southeast Asia', international conference 'India in International Relations: European and Indian perspectives', 27-29 April 2011, New Delhi, organised by Jawaharlal Nehru University, Delhi and Centre for Contemporary India Research and Studies, Institute of International Relations, and University of Warsaw.

9. Myanmar, as a buffer between India and ASEAN, is either a point of contention of a point of rapprochement, cf Myint-U (2011).

still needs to be done to instil trust and good-will in the implementation of a community of "caring and sharing societies". The Rohingya crisis of summer 2012 (communal violence in the Rakhine State that degenerated and caused some 90 deaths and the displacement of an estimated 90,000 people), though concerning both India and ASEAN (because of refugees), did not lead to a joint declaration that could have helped in finding the solution. Indeed, there was not even an attempt after the Burmese Foreign Minister Wunna Maung Lwin categorically rejected an ASEAN proposal to call for an "emergency meeting" because of the humanitarian crisis. The question is still on the table as whether the transition will lead to a change of behaviour of the Burmese regime.

To engage in a lasting cooperation with the Burmese regime, India and ASEAN do have some arguments:

- First, the contrasting political systems between China on one side, India and ASEAN on the other one, do call for different forms of governance.
- Second, the willingness of the regime to decrease its dependence on China without shifting mechanically to the United States.
- Third, their own experience with a fast growing process (the founding members of ASEAN have all similar experiences of attracting and managing FDI for long term growth and can transfer their pool of knowledge and experience in their developmental trajectory).
- Fourth, same can be said with their own political transition.
- Fifth, the fact that, because of their policy in these last 15 years, neither ASEAN nor India can be accused of being in favour of one or the other political actors.
- Sixth, the existence of different fora, ASEAN of course, but also BIMSTEC (Bay of Bengal for Multi-Sectoral and Technical Cooperation) and MGC (Mekong Ganga Cooperation) that might help to create political networks.

The added value of their cooperation to nurture Burmese political opening might be of interest to all parties. Former ASEAN Secretary-General Surin Pitsuwan urged Myanmar to take advantage of the ASEAN family, and avoid the pitfalls and mistakes which others have made. "We are all working towards the common dream of improving a lot of the people, and I assure you of the fullest support from the (ASEAN) Secretariat, and the ASEAN family," said the former Secretary-General (ASEAN Secretariat, 2012).

India should use Myanmar's increasing weight in ASEAN to reinforce ties with the Association and produce a win-win situation for the three partners. India-ASEAN political cooperation has the potential to bring all the countries of the region into a (still potential) community of "political destiny", an ambition that is still a gamble for some countries of ASEAN.

Indeed, for ASEAN as a group, the good news could come from Myanmar. What Myanmar has done is considered a milestone under the ASEAN Charter (which champions democracy and human rights' promotion) and the ASEAN Political and Security Community (Chongkittavorn, 2012). If the country continues on its path without taking a reverse, it will prove the rightness of the Association's methods and the mutual benefit. "After years of being chastised as the black sheep of the ASEAN family since it joined in 1997, now the time has come for the Thein Sein government to make his country a showcase for ASEAN" (Chongkittavorn, 2012). Myanmar's chairmanship of ASEAN, after Brunei, gave the region an energising wake-up by choosing the promotion of freedom and democratic stability in ASEAN as one of its theme; in this perspective, the support of India was much appreciated.

Last but not the least, the international community is following Myanmar's recent democratisation with attention. A common policy to help Myanmar to achieve a "sustainable development" would certainly have a positive impact on the perception of their capacity to join forces to improve the political future of the country. Indeed, Myanmar could become the showcase of an efficient political cooperation. Furthermore, following India and ASEAN's policy of engagement, the US and European Union already pay greater attention to this region, thus opening new windows of opportunities.

Cooperation a Premium Option in Difficult Times

The year 2012 marked 20 years of Dialogue Partnership between India and ASEAN and 10 years of Summit Partnership. Time of maturity has come as demonstrated by the India-ASEAN Commemorative Summit in December 2012. India and ASEAN will be celebrating their 25 years of Dialogue Partnership and 15 years of Summit Partnership in 2017. And, with maturity comes responsibility. The challenge is to justify that ASEAN and India have become pivotal for each other (as declared) and to translate this ambition into a political asset.

Difficult Times

ASEAN, 49 years in 2016, is going through difficult times. Some experts have even predicted "the end of its centrality" (Acharya, 2012) as the Association is facing challenging deadlines.

The implementation of an ASEAN Community by 2015 is the first of those. There are several reasons behind meeting the deadlines: member-states are not doing enough to get ready for the ASEAN market; ASEAN as a regional institution is not well equipped to deal with its new responsibilities; nationalist discourses are more frequent and some governments are less convinced of the interest of such a community and put it in the balance. Indeed, the ASEAN Community might illustrate the deep diverging trends that penalised the Association; it might also widen the gap between the founding members and the last comers. The challenge is not only of economic nature; it is mostly a political challenge, which calls into question the members' intrinsic willingness to cooperate.

Of course, the Phnom Penh Ministerial Meeting (9-13 July 2012) was a watershed and a wrong signal in this critical juncture. For the first time in its history, the ASEAN Ministerial Meeting (AMM) did not end up in a common declaration because of the refusal of Cambodia (which was handling the ASEAN chairmanship in 2012) to include the positions of the Philippines and Vietnam regarding their dispute with China over the South China Sea. The traditional norm of consensus building has not been respected, thus putting aside the ASEAN spirit and putting in doubt the famous ASEAN way. After this unprecedented failure, and since there are still plenty of tensions within the Association, Surin Pitsuwan, the 12th Secretary General of the ASEAN, called for an ASEAN "soul searching" (Lee-Brago, 2012). The ambition is to regain some cohesion and coordination, efficiency and legitimacy around a common identity before the 2015 deadline.

The situation is all the more critical for the Association that it will have to solve its problems in an evolving environment with more powerful neighbours. Therefore, there is a strong incentive, for its own survival, to forge closer political partnerships with those neighbours. The support of India and enhanced political cooperation might be encouraging signs.

India has to show not only solidarity but creativity. It has to express more loudly the political values that are found in its community, the democratic management of diversity, in order to go beyond a utilitarian relation with ASEAN.

Some general observations might be of some value to redirect its policy towards ASEAN:

- India should get rid of the mistaken assumption that GDP, trade or even connectivity automatically translates into political or geopolitical influence. Economic and political powers are complementary, but economy alone does not make a preeminent player.
- India should also not overestimate the influence of its strategic partnership with the US if the European Union on its own influence in Southeast Asia. India is neither an intermediary nor a balancer in the region. It has its own assets and should exploit them.
- When focusing on the political declarations issued by the Indian Foreign Ministry, one notices that there is little political substance and that economy serves as a political message, so allowing India not to redefine the substance of its political message. But, what does India have to offer of its own? What is its added value? In the 1950s, India had a strong influence on Southeast Asia in forging choice (either domestic policy or foreign policy); Southeast Asia's new independent countries were inspired by Nehru's vision as a blend of realism and idealism. What is the specificity of India's message today? What kind of power does India aspire to? These questions need to be analysed.

The basic argument here is that the 1997 crisis has illustrated the limits of the Anglo-Saxon liberal model for Southeast Asian societies. What has been observed during the last 15 years is the rising interest for the Chinese model of governance based on the power of its economy and a unique style of government. But this model, which is not presenting benefits for Southeast Asian societies and which itself is in a process of self-introspection and doubt, might not be the premium choice for Southeast Asia's future.

The argument lies in India's strength and resilience in its being the world's largest non-Western democracy. India has successfully integrated pluralism and diversity with institutional democracy. There is need to find answers to questions like: How can India share its experience with ASEAN member states? How can it bring something new in the debate? Because the process of acculturation is already done, India should find an advantage to express more clearly its policy and values when cooperating with ASEAN. In a context of competing models of governance and modernities, it should define and use its soft power and think about the ways its plural political system can inspire Southeast Asian countries. Its political values and institutions are assets when deepening its political relation with ASEAN. India has to convince its partners of the interest of its model of modernity, and of its benefits on long term socio-political stability.

India has a special responsibility to support a collective commitment to participatory political systems. It has the legitimacy to do so since the resilience of its democracy speaks about itself. Political cooperation is not about prosperity and trade; it is about engaging in a debate on political values, political identity and the choices for societies.

Proposals

To adopt a realist middle way of engagement and strengthen "political connectivity", India and ASEAN should launch different initiatives that could be associated with people and with their "special relationship".

- With the perspective of the launching of the ASEAN socio-political community, to launch a debate on political values and political identity would be of interest. Questions like: what will be the foundations of this political community? how to build it, and how do manage a plural community? will need be thought about? India should use its own experience to push for its advantage of having a political trajectory perceived as complementing rather than challenging ASEAN.
- ASEAN will need support and assistance. India, which has already provided aid to the new members in terms of institution-building, human skills or technical expertise, could extend this assistance in the preparation of the Community. To act through functional support might be considered as a convenient step towards deepening of the political dialogue.
- Establishing of an ASEAN-India institute for the future to deal with long-term issues like demography, food security, ecology, etc., which have a direct impact on stability. Economic as well as political developments have to be sustainable for coming generations, and it is a common ground where ASEAN and India could position themselves together. It is the responsibility of "knowledge intermediaries" to provide arguments and facts for debate. This institute may be located within the Nalanda University.

- An exchange of "good services" to demonstrate confidence in each other's capacity, the refusal of any alignment and their involvement to contribute to a peaceful political architecture across Asia would be a good idea. This mutual support would also help them to comfort their self-image (a much appreciated move when ASEAN is under harsh critics). ASEAN could support India's permanent membership at the UN Security Council (when China is boxing India in the corner on this topic), while India could support the ASEAN nuclear free zone initiative.

The potential for a constructive political relation between India and ASEAN remains largely untapped. India and ASEAN have set up the framework. They now have to fill the substance. There is an urgent need to take the political relation to the next level, and if India is serious to engage with the Asia-Pacific region, ASEAN is undoubtedly a first-choice partner.

References

Acharya, Amitav. (2012). *The End of ASEAN Centrality?*. Asia Times Online 8. Available at: http://www.atimes.com/atimes/Southeast_Asia/NH08Ae03.html

ASEAN Secretariat. (2012). *Myanmar to Tap the ASEAN Secretariat to Prepare for 2014 Chair, Business Group Call for Level Playing Field, and Lifting of Sanctions Will Help Clear the Road to Better Livelihood for the People.* 22 February. Available at: http://www.aseansec.org/26799.html

Bachoe, Ralph & Stothard, Debbie (Eds). (1997). *From Consensus to Controversy: ASEAN's Relationship with Burma's SLORC.* Alternative Asean Network on Burma (ALTSEAN-BURMA), Bangkok, cf p: 37.

du Rocher, S. B. (2012). *The European Union, Burma/Myanmar and ASEAN: A challenge to European norms and values or a new opportunity?*. Asia Europe Journal, 10(2-3), 165-180.

Chongkittavorn, Kavi. (2012). *Burma Shaking up Media Reform in ASEAN Countries.* Mizzima, 1 October. http://www.mizzima.com/edop/commentary/8138-burma-shaking-up-media-reform-in-asean-countries.html

Geldern, Robert Heine. (1956). *Conceptions of State and Kingship in Southeast Asia.* Ithaca: Cornell University Press.

Grace, F., & Mattos, A. (2001). *Indian and ASEAN: the politics of India's look east policy*. Manohar. New Delhi. IN.

Jones, L. (2008). *ASEAN's albatross: ASEAN's Burma policy, from constructive engagement to critical disengagement.* Asian Security, 4(3), 271-293.

Leifer, Michael. (1989). *ASEAN and the Security of Southeast Asia.* London: Routledge.

Lee-Brago, Pia. (2012). *ASEAN Should do Some Soul-searching.* The Philippine Star. 15 July.

Myint-U, Thant. (2011). *Where China meets India: Burma and the New Crossroads of Asia.* New York: Farrar, Straus and Giroux.

Pye, Lucian. (1985). *Asian Power and Politics: The Cultural dimensions of Authority.* Cambridge: Harvard University Press.

THREE

ACT EAST POLICY AND INDIA'S CULTURAL DIPLOMACY WITH ASEAN

Ishani Naskar

Introduction

The National Democratic Alliance (NDA) government that has been in power since 2014 has shown an active interest in India's immediate neighbours – within and beyond the confines of the subcontinent. India's relation with her eastern neighbourhood is believed to have received a new impetus after being catapulted from the incrementally maturing Look East Policy (LEP) to the newly conceived Act East Policy (AEP). The qualitative difference that hinges on the terms 'Look' and 'Act' is underlined by the conviction of the present government that India's relations with her neighbours should be marked by action and dynamism rather than confining to the sobriety of gaze towards them. In this spirit, it is perhaps not too much of a coincidence to see that in 2015, Prime Minister Narendra Modi explained the Act East Policy in Singapore, where twenty-two years ago, Prime Minister P.V. Narasimha Rao introduced India's Look East Policy.[1]

Now the Act East Policy is based on three robust areas indicated by the three 'Cs' – Commerce, Culture, and Connectivity. These three domains earmark the contours of India's engagement with the East. Commerce and trade, as well as connectivity have remained the foci of attention in Look East Policy (LEP), especially gaining momentum in AEP. Moreover, at the India-ASEAN Commemorative Summit, held in New Delhi in 2012, the Vision Statement had reiterated the need for multi-sectoral engagement to implement the pledge of India-ASEAN Partnership for Peace, Progress,

1. In 2014, Prime Minister Modi used the 24th ASEAN Summit platform at Naypyidaw, Myanmar, to unveil his Act East Policy. This was preceded by Indian Foreign Minister Sushma Swaraj's visit to Myanmar, Vietnam and Singapore where she did the homework for the launching of the Act East Policy by arguing that Look East Policy is not adequate, it was time for Act East.

and Shared Prosperity. In keeping with the dynamics of this enhanced engagement, socio-cultural interactions between ASEAN and India are expected to not only broaden but also deepen the relations in terms of people-to-people contacts and historical and cultural links.

Culture, in particular, has the vast potential in identifying the civilisation and historical links that go beyond the parameters of modern day state-to-state relations and can help inter-state relations like that between India and her eastern neighbours take a qualitative leap. Particularly, the Act East Policy has its own strong point in being able to encourage the element of culture and guide Indian foreign policy towards evolving an active component of cultural diplomacy. In fact, one of the defining points of India's attempt to project the country as an emerging soft power is activating her cultural assets and stringing them with her history in the region. Concepts like Project *Mausam* have been launched along this line to rediscover the old civilisation links, and trade routes (especially, maritime routes) between India and her eastern neighbours, particularly Southeast Asian neighbours, and thus also reviving the cultural contacts between the two sides.

This chapter takes a modest look at historical and cultural links in the region that are core elements in India's cultural diplomacy. This in turn is expected to harness India's potential to emerge as a soft power in the region. The chapter briefs about the concepts of cultural diplomacy and soft power before moving to historical and cultural links between India and Southeast Asia.

Cultural Diplomacy – the Emerging Dimension of Soft Power

A basic understanding of cultural diplomacy would mean, using a country's culture as an instrument in its foreign policy, precisely foreign policy objectives. The volume of literature on cultural diplomacy is still to research up to work in the other fields of diplomacy. A substantial section of the research on cultural diplomacy has been region or country specific, mostly concentrating on the West. One of the well-known contributions in this field is by Robert Fox. He tries to understand the dynamics of culture as one of the drivers of diplomacy, wherein he brings to light the difficulties of trying of define cultural diplomacy because of what he calls the 'semantic baggage', indicating a lack of unanimity in accepting the term (Fox, 1999). He mentions that the notion of cultural diplomacy depends on various factors like resources, culture, education of practitioners and government policies particular to the country, etc. (Fox, 1999). In the same line, Lending (2000) has shown the differences in research works undertaken by different countries because of the semantic differences in what is understood by them as cultural diplomacy. There is also a lack of unanimity on how to relate cultural diplomacy with general diplomacy and especially with public diplomacy; a general tendency is to see cultural diplomacy as a subset of public diplomacy.[2] Yet, Cummings Jr. (2003) has defined cultural diplomacy as "the exchange of information, ideas, art and other aspects of culture among nations and their peoples to foster mutual understanding", which is in any case seen as a part of public diplomacy, the way a nation presents itself to the others. Another aspect of this discussion on cultural diplomacy is the ability of a nation to deploy culture in its foreign policy formulation to project itself as a soft power.

Diplomacy as a constituent of state craft is perhaps older than the nation state, but as a concept soft power is a new entry. The term was exported from the west following the famous work by Joseph Nye, *Soft Power: The Means to Success in World Politics* (Nye, 2004). He has introduced soft power as the ability to get things done through ways and means of attraction rather than applying coercive means. More precisely, he defines it as "A country may obtain the outcomes it wants in world politics because other countries – admiring values, emulating its example, aspiring to its level of prosperity and openness – want to follow it." One of the selling points of soft power is culture. Western countries especially influential ones like the United States and the UK have considered culture as an important tool for reaching out to the international society; it has been slowly incorporated into their public diplomacy. With the resurgence of Asia, prominent Asian countries especially ancient civilisations like India and China have also used culture to project a favourable image of them. Subsequently, these prominent Asian countries are at present giving serious attention to cultural diplomacy. Yet, the fact is that for countries like China and India, culture has been a medium of exchange of ideas, values, and opinions from times preceding modern history. In the case of India, there are abundant evidences of her ancient contacts with the West like Rome and Mesopotamia as much as with the East – China and Southeast Asia. Especially with Southeast Asia, India has maintained ancient contacts primarily through trade, pilgrimage,

2. See, Mulcahy (1999)

and political expansion, but with limited continuity in the colonial and the immediate post-independence period. In the contemporary times, with the launch of the Look East Policy, rediscovering of the old historical and cultural contacts has gained relevance within the foreign policy discourse of the country. The following sections look at some of the aspects of India's ancient cultural links with the region.

India's History in Ancient Southeast Asia – Bricks of the Cultural Network

India's contacts with Southeast Asia have been traced largely through archaeological sources, literary works, and narratives even though some of them were Chinese. The general perception is that a substantial part of ancient Southeast Asia had come under India's influence to the extent that it has been claimed that many provinces and kingdoms of the region have been *Indianised.* It implies a spontaneous acceptance of Indian culture and values as a way of life; this was especially prevalent in the elite and kings, but may have permeated in other sections of the society too. The process had started around the beginning of the first millennium, but the impact has continued till the 20th century AD and beyond.[3] The research on tracing this process of Indianisation has brought about debates among historians, which in a way helps one understand the roots of Indian culture in the region. Prominent Indian historians like R.C. Majumdar have argued that Indian culture spreaded in the region during the prehistoric times primarily in two ways – trade and emigration (Majumdar, 1991). The argument was that following trade contacts, movement of people from India and settlements started taking place; the gradual absorption of Hindu religion and culture resulted in Indianisation. Later, with the beginning of the Christian era, Indian expansion and colonisation took place parallel to the rise of Hindu kingdoms and empires in North, Central and, later, in South India. Thus, the concept of *Greater India* was advocated that was the foundation of Indian cultural expansion in the region. Such a theory has been supported by Coedes (1968), who has provided almost similar reasons for the expansion of Indian influence – through invasion, elite travellers and commerce. Coedes agrees to the extensive cultural influences from India that can be traced in contemporary times through language, influence over contemporary legal

3. For details see, Coedes (1968), Kulke (2003) and Majumdar (1991).

and administrative systems and in the presence of architectural evidences. In contrast, Wolters's works stressed the role of various Southeast Asian agencies in accepting and adopting elements of Hindu cultural influences in the region (Wolter, 1999). He has argued that even trade expansion around the Indonesian archipelago had no relations with Indian maritime trade and was a rather indigenous process (Wolter, 1967). Paul Mus has explained the prevalence of common beliefs and cults in both Southeast Asia and the adjacent regions of India, which he believes existed before the arrival of the so- called colonisation influences from India. Thus, the basic argument was that when the Indian influence arrived in Southeast Asia, the ground was already there for the easier acculturation with the local cultures.[4] Perhaps, the acceptance of Indian cultural traits was also selective. In another case, there has been substantial research on the nature of Indian influence that tries to probe the role of the Indian agencies (castes) in expanding towards the Greater India concept – the warrior (*Kshatriya*) class, the tradesman (*Vaishya*) class and the priestly (*Brahmin*) class. Ian Mabbet sees an eclectic infusion of the role of all the three castes as none could have an overwhelming role in the Indianisation process. Subsequently, the Indian cultural traits evident in the region do not constitute a monolith but a plurality based on various traditional heritages (Mabbet, 1977). Thus, there seemed a sense of convergence between the cultural elements of the Indian classes and the local cultures such that every local culture would have some element of Indianisation or the greater Indian cultural influence.

In all this, it is important to understand that, travel to the region especially for trade has been extremely important in the whole discourse on India-Southeast Asia exchange networks. Maritime routes have been important here. A substantial amount of work is evident in tracing the routes. Coedes (1968) has mentioned two routes to Southeast Asia. The first route could have started from the South of India either through the 10° channel crossing the Andaman and Nicobar Islands and leading to Takuapa in Thailand or South of the 10° channel crossing the Nicobar Islands heading towards the headland of Aceh and reaching Kedah in Malaysia. On the second route, ships sailed along the coast of Martaban and Tavoy in Burma then took the caravan route crossing three Pagodas and other passes reaching Menam

4. For details see, Paul Mus, "Cultes indiens et indigenes au Champa", BEFEO, 33 (1933), translated into English as *"Indian seen from the east – Indian and indigenous cults in Champa", Monash Papers on Southeast Asia*, number three, 1975.

Chao Phraya delta by way of Kanchanaburi and Ratchaburi. The wind currents were extremely important in controlling the maritime navigation; needless to say, navigators had to be conversant with the oceanic wind cycles, especially over the Bay of Bengal.[5]

One of the earliest accounts of maritime trade that also reflects the ways the Indian cultural has spread is available in the ancient Buddhist texts of the *Jatakas*. They mentioned long distance journeys over land, river, and sea, wherein Indian traders are described as venturing into *Suvarndvipa* (Southeast Asia) and *Ratnadvipa* (Srilanka). There are mentions of important ports like *Bharukaccha* from where merchants travelled to Southeast Asia, specifically *Suvarnabhumi*.[6] Further, they revealed of group formations across classes for maritime ventures, but most important they also revealed that Buddhists were actively involved in trade and travelled across the Bay to Southeast Asia. The *Pali* texts like *Mahaniddesa,* or *Milinda panha* and *Divyavadana* also mentioned Suvarnbhumi as the most important and active trade centre and port. The *Arthashastra* mentioned about sea-borne trade and the variety of gems and ornaments. Other literary sources include the *Sangam* literature of the South that mentions of trading along the coastline through rivers that open up in the Bay waters. They also found mention of *Yavanas* (Greek speakers) arriving in boats at the Coromondel coast before leaving for Southeast Asia (Ruangsup, 2013). Accounts of foreign travellers more famously, Fa Hsien mentioned travels from *Madhyadesa* to the East (Ruangsup, 2013). Most of the accounts of ancient maritime trade mentioned the kinds of items involved in trade between India and Southeast Asia, which included cotton textile, sandal wood, silk, fine muslin, horses, camels, elephants and steel weapons. These came from several parts of country. Important ports on the east coast included Tamralipti, Palur, Kalingapatnam, Dharanikota, Arikamedu, Poompuhar Chandrketugarh, to mention a few.

The spread of the Indian network is also evident through the archaeological evidences available along the coast and even in the interiors. Graves and the burial materials are some of the archaeological sources that give information about ancient contacts and links. Graves in the peninsular region of India give an idea that there was trade along the eastern coast that stretched to Sri Lanka and to Southeast Asia because the kind of metals

5. A crisp explanation of the wind cycles over the Bay of Bengal is provided in Tripati (2011).

6. See, *Sussondi Jataka* No. 360, available at, http://www.sacred-texts.com/bud/j3/j3061.htm.

found in such ancient graves were common all along the coast. These included copper, iron, high quality garnets and also pearl. That the Indian goods were popular among the prehistoric communities of Southeast Asia is evident from the archaeological items found in the region – stone and glass beads, nephrite pendants and bronze drums. These were also found in grave complexes, which could be read as the increasing acceptance of Indian elements in the indigenous milieu (Gupta, 2005). Similarly, the spread of pottery of various kinds across the Bay is reflective of not only widespread trade but also assimilation of their usage, practices and methods into local cultures.[7] Rock edicts also mentioned in maritime trade, especially during the Mauryan period. In particular, Ashoka's edicts mentioned in sea borne activity for both trade and the spread of religion *aka dhamma* (Ruangsup, 2013).

Apart from the trade benefits, maritime exchanges were also introducing consistent social exchange especially around the regions and centres, where trade activities were taking place, or, were located along the trade routes. The social interaction ensured the gradual transition of Indian cultural elements that took place as a result of the settlement of Indian emigrant communities. Besides the trading communities, the arrival of Brahmins led to the spread of Brahminical rituals. Hinduism gradually found acceptance. The ruling class sponsored and accepted the religion, especially with the spread of Hindu kings. Buddhism added another dimension to the cultural matrix of ancient Southeast Asia. The absorption of Indian cultural elements was possible with the formation of the first generation of states in the Southeast Asia around the first millennium BC, followed by the rise of Indic rulers and kingdoms.[8] The evolution of the early state system involved several cultural aspects like art, crafts, literature, language, architecture and ways of social organisation along with sophisticated rituals as a testimony to the superior position of the royalty.[9]

7. For details see, Tripati (2011), pp.1080-1081.

8. Indic Civilisation was the term used by French archaeologists like Sylvain Levy and Jean Przyluski from the Ecole de l'Extreme Orient.

9. A rather rich and engrossing piece of work that covers several elements of this complex historical India- Southeast Asia continuum is *Cultural Relations between India and Southeast Asian Countries* by H.B. Sarkar.

Evidence of Continuing Indian Cultural Influence in Contemporary Southeast Asia – Basis to Build Bridges

The history of Southeast Asia has clear associations with India. The previous section has provided a concise idea of the historical connect between India and Southeast Asia that premises the Indian cultural expanse in the region. This cultural connect has continued in the contemporary cultural mosaic of the region. Consistent cultural influences are evident in Southeast Asian heritage – both tangibles and intangibles. Intangibles include language, literature, palaeography, mythology, law, philosophy and religion, which are part of everyday life of Southeast Asia. Tangibles include art and architecture, scriptures and inscriptions. As Sanskrit and Pali had reached Southeast Asia quite early and had become the language in administration and cultural activities, the presence of Indian names even in modern Southeast Asia is common. From names of towns to individuals many bear the Indian touch; they have a mythological connect or follow names of Indian deities. The name of the ancient capital of Thailand, *Ayuthia,* may have been derived from the ancient Ramayana capital of *Ayodhya*. Again, *Khambuja,* – the ancient name of Cambodia, was perhaps derived from similarly named ancient town in Kabul Valley. The Sultan of Brunei bears the title *Seri Bhagwan,* which was drawn from the Indian words *Shree Bhagwan,* thus giving the head a divine sanction. Perhaps, the Thai province of Aranya Prathet in Thailand is simply the jungle province or Aranya Pradesh. *Bahasa Indonesia* has many Sanskrit words – *Garuda Airways* (Indonesian national airline), *Yuddha Griha* (for defence ministry), *Sinta* (Indonesian version of Sita), to name a few. In Burma, the name of one of the main rivers the *Irrawaddy*, comes from the word *Irawati*, the Vedic name of one of the tributaries of Indus, Ravi (Jha, 2014). Again, the early area of the Thai people in Yunnan was known as Gandhara in Indo-China, a part of which was called *Videharajya*, the capital was Mithila.[10] 'Pur' in Kuala Lumpur, the capital of Malaysia, means town in Sanskrit. Another town *Seramban* is actually *Sri Ram Ban* (Lord Ram's Bow). The Commander-in-Chief is known as Lakshmana, which reminds one of the roles played by Ram's brother Lakshman in the battle at Sri Lanka. In the context of the Indian influence, Eliot (1954) observes: "In Ceylon, Burma, Siam, Camboja, Champa and Java, religion,

10. For more details see, D.C. Sircar, "Indian Influence on the Geographical Names of Southeast Asia", *Voice of Aryas*, 29 February 2016. Available at: http://voiceofaryas.com/2016/ancient-technology/indian-in%EF%AC%82uence-on-the-geographical-names-of-south-east-asia/.

art, the alphabet, literature, as well as whatever science and political organization existed, were the direct gift of Hindus, whether Brahmans or Buddhists...." A good amount of work has been carried out in trying to understand Sanskrit as a dominant *lingua franca*, as the language of political and aesthetic expression in the polities that had clear Indian influence.[11] A strong relationship between the development and spread of Sanskrit and the Brahmins has been examined and confirmed by scholars like Johannes Bronkhorst (Bronkhorst, 2011). However, as a caveat, one needs to add that the activities and agenda of Brahmins in the region stretched beyond Hindu religious rituals. They rather evolved as a service provider for a social order and for rituals albeit political, that provided the local community a sense of unity and established their position in the social milieu.[12]

Indian epics like *Ramayana* and *Mahabharata* have had a lasting effect on Southeast Asian societies. In some places, irrespective of the state or majority religion, *Ramayana* stories have been adapted into the education curriculum (Sarkar, 1985). Many countries of Southeast Asia have adopted and adapted the *Ramayana* into their own belief system. In Buddhist-majority Thailand, *Ramayan* is prevalent as *Ramakein* or *Ramakirti*, and has been embraced by the nobility as much as by the general masses because apart from preaching morality, it also speaks of the divine sanction of the King. Even till this day, the Thai King bears the title of *Rama*. The *Ramakriti* is a purely adapted version of the original *Ramayan* with purely Thai touch and has resulted in a parallel belief among the Thais about the originality of that text. *Ramayan* stories are found depicted on the walls of the funeral temple of the Royalty and on the walls of the temple of the Emerald Buddha (Jha, 2014). The *Nang Yai*, the shadow art performance is believed to have been drawn from India and has some exclusive portions from the Indian *Ramayana*. In Laos too, Ramayana has taken an art form – depicted through paintings (mural) and dance forms. The *Phra Lak Phra Lam*, which is known as *Ramayana* in Laos, is painted on the walls of the Vat Oup Muong temple (Sarkar, 1985). This Laotian *Ramayana*, has been mixed with *Panchatantra* (known as *Nithan Nang Tantai*) for a didactic effect in passing the moral message(s). In Myanmar, *Ramayana* started as an oral tradition. It is believed

11. Sheldon Pollock uses the term 'Sanskrit Cosmopolis' to emphasise the importance of Sanskrit as a language for both political and aesthetic expression especially in the polities with strong Indian influence both in South and Southeast Asia. See Pollock (1996).

12. See Casparis and Mabbett (1993).

to have started during the reign of King Anawrahta (1044-77), the founder of the first Burmese Empire at Pagan. This form of oral narration was known as *Rama Zatdaw* in Burmese, which continued till the 16th Century, and, later, Ram got adopted into Buddhism as much as the oral tradition got transformed into songs called *Rama Thagyin*. Subsequently, the Buddhist version of *Ramayana – Jataka –* got transformed into the popular art form of *Yama zat pwe*, which is popular even at present.[13] *Ramayana* has taken on to popular art forms in Malaysia (*Wayang Kulit*), and, in Indonesia, it is presented through the puppet show called the *Wayang*. In Indonesia, the famous *Kakawin Ramayana* is considered to be one of the oldest testaments of Indo-Javanese literature. Yet, there is a different Balinese *Ramayana – Rama Kidung*, which has some distortions from the original *Ramayana* but the *Ramkavaca* has lot of similarities with the *Valmiki Ramayana* (Jha, 2014). *Ramayana* is present in both Cambodia and Vietnam in the form of art and murals. In Cambodia, the walls of magnificent Angkor Wat temple and the Ba Poun Temple are adorned with paintings from the *Ramayana*. In Vietnam, in 600 BC, an image of *Valmiki* was installed at Tra Kien in Champa. There are scriptural references to the *Uttarakhand* episode of *Ramayana* in the *Mi-Son* inscription of King Prakasdharman around the same time (Tapaswi, 1986). A number of literary creations, namely, *Amaramala*, *Arjuna Vivaha* and *Bharata Yuddha*, the *Wajang Kulit* are based on the *Ramayana* and the *Mahabharata* themes. The Indian *Ramayana,* in whatever form, has become a part of Southeast Asian cultural mosaic accentuating the literary, artistic treasures and is also quite embedded in the religious beliefs and political structures of the region.

Architectural remnants in some countries of Southeast Asia also reflect the spread of Indian culture, especially through the dominant role of religion – Hinduism and Buddhism. Brahmanism accepted as a cult also strengthened the religious fervour of the region resulting in the proliferation of temples and stupas. In Hinduism, *Shiva* (known as *Siva* in Southeast Asia) has been represented in the male reproductive organ form, the phallus or the *Linga* in several temples across the region. There are claims that this form of worshipping the phallus seems to have been quite ancient before

13. For a vivid idea of the *Ramayana* in Myanmar see, "The Ramayana in Southeast Asia: (3) Burma", *British Library Asian and African Studies Blog*, 5 May. Available at: http://britishlibrary.typepad.co.uk/asian-and-african/2014/05/the-ramayana-in-southeast-asia-3-burma.html.

the creation of Hindu architectures. *Siva* has been found in various forms in different Southeast Asian countries with the maximum number in Siam, where he was worshipped since 6th AD. Several forms of *Siva* like the dancing *Siva* or the five-headed Siva have been found in Thailand. In Java, Prambanan or the Lara Jonggrang temple is considered by some scholars as superior to Borobudur (Coomarswamy, 1926). Bali is home to thousands of big and small temples of which a number of them belong to *Siva*. In other countries like Vietnam (ancient *Champa*), the phallus is complemented by the female reproductive organ, the *Yoni*. The *My-Son* and *Po* Nagar in ancient *Champa* were known as *Shaivaite* towns (Vasudevan *et al.,* 2012). *Vishnu* is also worshipped in Southeast Asia. The largest *Vishnu* temple in Southeast Asia is in Cambodia – the *Angkor Wat* that was built by King Suryavarman II. The architectural structure is based on Indian mythology of the *Meru*, while the walls are adorned by the stories of *Rama* and *Siva* (Jha, 2014). *Vishnu* is also worshipped in Thailand; the *San Phra Kal* in Lopburi is a *Vishnu* temple, other temples are in Nakhon Sithammarat, Pimay, Bangkok and Takua Pah (Jha, 2014). *Garuda*, *Vishnu's* vehicle is also found in modern day architecture in Bangkok. It is also found in Bali, Indonesia. In Bali, the *Vishnu* temples are known as Pura Puseh (Jha, 2014). The famous Batu Caves temple of Lord Murugan in Malaysia is also evidence of the continuing Indian influence in the country.[14] Indian art forms like the Amaravati, the Pallava and Pala have had a strong impact on the holy structures – Hindu or Buddhists, and art and architectures of Southeast Asia in general (Sarkar, 1985). Buddhism has had transcendental effects on Southeast Asia, thus enriching culture through its contributions. Various forms of Buddhist statues are available across Southeast Asia – Thailand, Vietnam and Indonesia. The artistic forms of these statues are claimed to be of Indian origins.[15] A very resourceful exposition about the Buddhist and Hindu architectural links between India and Southeast Asia is provided by John Guy in *Lost Kingdoms: Hindu Buddhist Sculpture of Early Southeast Asia* (Guy, 2014). Southeast Asia is home to both Therveda and Mahayan Buddhism; while Buddhism in most parts of Southeast Asia is influenced

14. The temple in the Batu Caves was, however, established much later in the late 1800s in the name of Lord Murugan (*Kartika)* and not an exact equivalent to ancient Indian temple architecture. Nonetheless, it is testimony to continuing Indian cultural influence in Southeast Asia.

15. They bear a similarity to the *Amaravati* style in India. For details see, Coedes (1968: p.43).

by Theraveda Buddhism. Vietnam follows Mahayana Buddhism and is largely influenced by Chinese culture. Thus, Vietnamese follow Chinese inscriptions and are an exception in the region. Yet, the Duong Buddhist Sanctuary at Bin Dinh village in Quang Nam province is believed to have been built by King Indravarman (Vasudevan *et al.,* 2012). Myanmar is a land beset with the influence of Buddhism assumably from India and is the home of stupas at Bago Thanton, Pagan, Mrauk U in the Rakhine region.[16]

Apart from these evidences, inscriptions that reflect the acceptance of *Sanskrit*, *Pali* and even *Tamil* as language are found in different texts of Southeast Asia. Since 12th Buddhist Era, various Southeast Asian languages[17] have been influenced the texts of the region. The Indonesian Sarasamuccaya is an important work in this category with a generous use of *Sanskrit* (Sarkar, 1985). Inscriptions in Malaysia are in *Sanskrit,* even *Tamil* version of *Sanskrit* is found in Bali, Indonesia. Ancient scripts of Bali are found to be in *Sanskrit* and in ancient Bali. Perhaps later, *Sanskrit was* incorporated into Bali language. The language has also found a place in early inscriptions of the Cham region. Verses in ancient *Sanskrit* like *Vasantatilaka and Sarudlavikririta* are representative of the use of the Sanskrit language previous to the appearance of Cham language (Vasudevan *et al.,* 2012). Interestingly, the influence of Indian languages had also reached the Philippines. Several scholars have shown how *Sanskrit* permeated Filipino language, thereby enriching the language. [18] *Sanskrit* inscription belonging to early 5th AD was found in Sithep, Thailand and the language has been given a lot of respect. It is now a part of Thai cultural practices and rituals. In all this, it becomes evident that Indian languages have not remained confined to courts and nobility only. Through the gradual incorporation and acceptance in the region, they have either created the base of vernacular language or enriched it. As Lamb (1975) observed, many Southeast Asian languages contain an important proportion of words of Sanskrit or Dravidian (Lamb, 1975). In McFarland's the Siamese-English Dictionaries, out of the total vocabulary of about 40,000 words, 1362 are Pali and Sanskrit words (Basham, 1954).

---

16. A good detailed discussion of the architectural similarity between stupas of Southeast and Indian architecture is available in, Thabrew (2014).
17. A good discussion of the influence of Indian languages – Sanskrit Pali and Tamil has been made by, Mesangrutdharakul (2015).
18. For details, see T. H. Pardo de Tavera (1887), "El Sanscrito en La langua Tagalog" Paris; D. N. Roy (1929), "The Philippines and India," Manila; and Buddha Prakash (1964), "India and the World", cited in Jha (2014).

India's Cultural Diplomacy towards Southeast Asia: Culture as an Asset for Contemporary Diplomatic Outreach

India's cultural and historical heritage could increase her growing acceptance in her immediate eastern neighbourhood. This argument is not too far-fetched if one looks at the contemporary history of India. India's idealist approach towards formulating foreign policy in the post-independence period was reflective of India's belief in philosophy of tolerance and peace. India's belief of *Vasudheva Kutumbkam* (the world is one family) underlines her understanding of the world as a whole family. Emperor Asoka's emissaries sent the message of peace to large parts of Asia. In modern times, Swami Vivekananda's messages had strong philosophical underpinnings that helped reveal India's image as a rich civilisation with deep cultural roots. His messages speak for not only tolerance but also complementarities and plurality. This is also reflected in Nobel laureate Tagore's works and philosophy of a global village. His *Crisis of Civilisation* is a concerning piece about the conflicts and confrontations that challenge the global family concept. Such rich philosophical and cultural heritage helped Nehru mould a befitting unique foreign policy for the country. It was transferred into the unique policy of Non-Alignment that renounced power, conflict and allegiance to groups and more importantly the rejection of colonialism. Based on India's belief in full freedom of countries and sovereign equality, India organised the first Asian Relations Conference, held under the auspices of the Indian Council of World Affairs (ICWA) in March 1947. This Conference was also an expression of India's interest in international affairs. Along the same lines, India's conference on the Dutch crisis was driven by India's rejection of colonialism. One of the issues, which was highlighted through the conference, was the need for understanding the importance of culture as a bonding force and an avenue to reach out to countries.[19] This idea has been institutionalised with the establishment of the Indian Council for Cultural Relations (ICCR). Over the period of time, other institutes and agencies have been adding substance to India's cultural diplomatic drives. These include the India International Centre, the Indira Gandhi National Centre for the Arts (IGNCA) and the three Academies – *Sangeet*

---

19. See Speech delivered by Pandit Jawaharlal Nehru at the 1st Asian Relations Conference held in New Delhi on 24 March 1947. Available at: http://icwadelhi.info/asianrelationsconference/images/stories/jawaharlalnehru.pdf

Natak Academy, *Lalit Kala Academy* and the *Sahitya Academy,* whose job is to promote their respective areas across various countries, especially in the neighbourhood. The ICCR, along with these institutions and other agencies, is assisted by the government in creating friendship circles, offering scholarships, organising festivals seminars, conferences and cultural programmes, facilitating academic interactions and undertaking other promotional activities.

India's cultural drive(s) towards Southeast Asia has been based primarily on cultural agreements. India has had cultural agreements at a bilateral level for quite some time – Indonesia (29 December 1965), the Philippines (6 September 1969), Vietnam (18 December 1976), Thailand (29 April 1977), Malaysia (3 March 1978), Laos (17 August 1994), Cambodia (31 January 1996) and Myanmar (25 January 2001). India signed a Memorandum of Understanding with Singapore on 5 February 1993 (Sahai, n.d.). Various Cultural Exchange Programmes (CEPs) were held among many of the ASEAN countries, namely, Indonesia, Laos, Malaysia, the Philippines, Singapore, Thailand and Vietnam. Education has gradually emerged as an important tool of cultural diplomacy. The ICCR sponsors a number of Chairs for Indian Studies. The idea is to develop interest in Indian studies; India has also set up Indian Chairs of Studies at various universities in Southeast Asia. These Chairs exist at the Preah Sihanouk Raja Buddhist University, Phnom Penh (Cambodia); Mahendradatta University, Bali; Gadja Madah University, Jogjakarta (Indonesia); University of Malaya, Kuala Lumpur (Malaysia); National University of Singapore (Singapore); and University of Social Sciences and Humanities, Ho Chi Minh City (Vietnam). Cultural centres exist at Kuala Lumpur (Malaysia) and Bangkok (Thailand). Student exchanges have been taking place that have resulted in strengthening the people-to- people contact as well as help promote India's image in the region. Student exchange programme was conceived by the erstwhile Prime Minister of India, Dr. Manmohan Singh as a familiarisation tool to build greater economic and cultural understanding between the two dynamic Asian regions. The programme invites young graduate and post-graduate students from the 10 ASEAN member states with academic interest in India. There have been six such visits so far, and these ASEAN-India Students Exchange Programmes showcasing Indian culture provide them new insights on the vast diversity and give an idea into the way the country manages variegated issues.[20] A look at the government websites reveals that the Government of India offers various international scholarships for students from abroad. Some of these include General Cultural Scholarship Scheme, Cultural Exchange Programme Scheme (scholarship through the ICCR for foreign students' based on bilateral agreements), Technical Cooperation Scheme of the Colombo Plan (applicable for Asian students only), and ICCR scholarships for students of performing and visual arts.[21] The ASEAN-India Centre (AIC) has been constantly encouraging people-to-people contact. The ASEAN-India Eminent Person's Lecture Series is also a step towards bringing the two sides closer and introducing various angles of Indian spectrum to Southeast Asia. Eminent historians like Romila Thapar have spoken on ancient Indian history, revealing the rich heritage of the country. At an International Conference on India's Civilizational Links in 2015, the Keynote Address delivered by Secretary (East) of the Ministry of External Affairs (MEA) touched on almost all the parameters of India's cultural connect with Southeast Asia. The speech also highlighted India's interest in protecting the Indian ancient cultural symbols and structures in Southeast Asia that are part of the rich history between the two sides.[22] The Archaeological Survey of India (ASI) has undertaken restoration projects of Angor Wat, the Ta Prohm Temple (Siem Reap, Cambodia),

---

20. The Ministry of External Affairs India, in collaboration with the Confederation of Indian Industry (CII), hosted the seventh ASEAN-India Students Exchange Programme during 9-18 November 2014. 250 students from the 10 ASEAN countries of Brunei, Cambodia, Indonesia, Lao PDR, Malaysia, Myanmar, Philippines, Singapore, Thailand, and Vietnam participated in the programme. For details see, *ASEAN-India: Building Youth Partnerships through Culture and Entrepreneurship*, CenPEG.org, 8 January 2015. Available at: http://cenpeg.org/events/jan2015/ASEAN-India=Building_Youth_Partnerships_through_Culture_and_Entrepreneurship.html. A year by year coverage of the Student Exchange Programme is also available with the Ministry of External Affairs, Government of India, at: http://mea.gov.in/aseanindia/sep.htm.

21. For more information see, "Government of India Scholarships for International Students." Available at, http://www.archive.india.gov.in/overseas/study_india/studyinindia.php?id=10

22. For more details see Keynote address by Secretary (East) at the Inaugural Session of the International Conference on "ASEAN-India Cultural Links: Historical and Contemporary Dimensions" held in New Delhi on 23 July 2015. Available at: http://mea.gov.in/Speeches-Statements.htm?dtl/25502/Keynote_address_by_Secretary_East_at_the_Inaugural_Session_ofthe_International_Conference_on_ASEANIndia_Cultural_Links_Historical_and_ContemporaryDi

the Ananda Temple (Bagan, Myanmar).[23] In 2012, following a two-day international conference on the Cham Civilisation, the Government of India pledged a US$ 3 million to the conservation project at My Son Sanctuary in Quang Nam Province, Vietnam (Viet Nam News, 2012). The importance of culture has been also highlighted as a part of the growing strategic partnership between ASEAN-India Partnership. At the 2nd ASEAN-India Think-Tank Roundtable, Prof. Du Thu Ha from Vietnam indicated the importance of culture and educational exchanges between India and the ASEAN countries to take the strategic relationship forward.[24] India has built strong socio-cultural relations with Vietnam by helping them in capacity building and training as well as organising cultural festivals in the country.[25]

Two other important factors also constitute India's strive towards cultural diplomacy – the role of the Indian Diaspora and the importance of religion, especially Buddhism. Considering the long history of emigration from India to neighbouring Southeast Asia, the Indian Diaspora has been prominent, though not spread uniformly. Especially, the generations that have moved in during the colonial period have been quite noticeable. They continue to act as the cultural bridge between India and ASEAN countries both in terms of tangible (temples and such places of worship) and intangibles (rituals, cuisines and lifestyles). It is because of them Indian films and entertainment industry has entered the region, which have also become immensely popular amongst the locals. Popular Bollywood movies and movie stars have become household names in many of the Southeast Asian countries like Malaysia, Indonesia and other Southeast Asian countries. Some countries are also looking at business possibilities, thanks to Bollywood's constant search for foreign locations and high-end technology (Singh, 2008). The First Indian Film Festival in the region was organised in Vietnam in 2015. Indian songs and films are now being adapted and copied, which indicates the transnational popularity of Indian entertainment. Indian superstar Shahrukh Khan had been conferred with the title of '*Datuk*', which is a title of respect there. Indian Government has considered the Diaspora and the film and

23. Different publications on the restoration works and conservation strategy of the ASI are available.

24. For details see Ha (2013).

25. See, "Overview of India-Vietnam Bilateral Relations", Embassy of Hanoi, Vietnam, June 2016. Available at: http://indembassy.com.vn/cms.php?id=8

entertainment industry as strategic assets in promoting India's image. They are expected to play an important role in establishing the connectivity.[26] The powerful Indian Diaspora is expected to not only forward India's interests but also add to the country's growth and development. Prime Minister Narendra Modi in his spirited speech to the Indian Diaspora in Malaysia emphasised that India is not confined to its territory, thus underlining the need for an active Diaspora of the region (The Hindu, 2015). Another important idea conceived by the present government is *Yoga* as a tool of outreach to the people of other countries. Prime Minister has taken interest in not only promoting yoga by convincing the UN to declare the International Yoga Day, he has also set-up the Ministry of Ayurveda, Yoga and Naturopathy, Unani, Siddha and Homoeopathy (AYUSH).

Buddhism has spread all over Asia. One of the reasons that India has been associated with the philosophy of peace and tolerance is because of her close association with Buddhism. Buddhism as a messenger of peace and plurality, and, because of the geographical spread, it has found global appeal. India as the fountainhead of Buddhism is seen as an emerging force. Buddhism has become an important element of the Act East Policy (AEP). The Government promotes Buddhist tourism. The Ministry of Tourism has identified three tourist circuits along with other funding and popularisation projects to promote tourism. Conclaves and Conferences supplement the tourist potential of the country.[27] To showcase and project the Buddhist Heritage of India, International Buddhist Conclaves have been organised by the Ministry of Tourism since 2004, but, not in continuity. Prime Minister Narendra Modi attended the 2015 Conclave in Bodhgaya and is expected to attend the upcoming one in October 2016. One of the leading projects of Buddhist diplomacy is the revival and re-establishment of the Nalanda University as an ancient seat of Buddhist learning and heritage. It allows the Buddhist schools all across the world to trace their lineage. The Ministry of Tourism has recently announced boosting of the Buddhist circuit under

26. Connectivity transcends physical connectivity and extends to digital and even cultural connectivity. Activities reflecting the physical connectivity included the INS *Sudarshini,* tracking the ancient monsoon route across Indian Ocean to Southeast Asia and the Commemorative India-ASEAN Car Rally across nine of the 10 ASEAN states. The commemorative trip by *INS Sudarshini* is a symbolic trip to trace the India's cultural roots in Southeast Asia.

27. For details see, "Development of Buddhist Tourism." *Press Information Bureau, Ministry of Tourism, Government of India, 10*February 2014. Available at: http://pib.nic.in/newsite/PrintRelease.aspx?relid=103310

the *Swadesh Darshan* scheme and already Rs. 10 billion have been released for this purpose. Perhaps, the government is also looking forward towards the private-public partnership to promote Buddhist tourist circuits (Divya, 2016).

Conclusions

The discourse on India's relations with Southeast Asia through the prism of foreign policy falls flat if one would accept the fact that the concept of delimiting territory of Asia into regions is an offshoot of following the Western scholarship. The drive to establish the cultural connect between the regions is perhaps a testimony to the fact that there is an attempt to free oneself from the regional stereotypes. India's Act East Policy (AEP) with its objective of identifying and threading the cultural tangibles and intangibles to place, India in their cultural mosaic must be understood in the light of the attempt to create an alternate discourse to the predominant Western ones. The influences of ancient civilisations like India or for that matter China have to be understood in the light of continuity rather than through time periods or historical epochs. The Act East Policy (AEP) seeks to trace the historical continuity of the relationship that is embedded in the cultural links between the two sides – India and ASEAN countries. Human relations have preceded structural relations. One could refer to the border states of India in the Northeast, where communities have continued to maintain relationships, interactions irrespective of modern state formations. Suryanarayan (2013) refers to the interaction with a Naga student who had come from Myanmar for higher studies without a visa. There may be several such unrecorded stories of continuous human interactions and intermingling between the peoples across the 'borders'. The border markets (*haats*) that have been self-sustaining in their own way are yet another fact that the governments of both sides are now reconciling and institutionalising the border trade. Similarly, trade connections across the region have been developed since early times and they made use of the maritime continuum of the Indian Ocean. Culture harnessed onto this connectivity and bonded Indian culture with indigenous ones. The Act East Policy (AEP) of India is building upon this continuum of history trying to enliven the contacts and points of convergence. This is expected to have spill over effects on the strategic relationship evolving between India and the ASEAN members.

The other point that is part of the discourse on Indian foreign policy is the ability to turn its investments in cultural communications into India's emergence as a soft power. However, how soft power projection is transferred into foreign policy dividends is something that is yet to be understood in all its approaches. One must accept a few facts here. First, soft power is not easy to measure empirically except that it will help India to gain strategic leverage in the region and create an enabling environment that would help her achieve strategic goals. Second, India's soft power entrepreneurship has had a late start, compared to other major states, and, there seems to be a slow capitalisation on the soft power potentials. In Southeast Asia, India will have to face the tough challenge from China, who seems to have moved in leaps and bounds in showcasing its own history and culture. Third, it is necessary to take note of the fact that only soft power projection is of less appeal until backed by hard power abilities – economic strength, military prowess and political influence. In this also, India finds stiff competition from China. It is no wonder that the AEP has been rigorously pursuing military and defence cooperation with Southeast Asia.[28] Fourth, India's domestic picture also affects its ability to sell its story convincingly. Income inequality, lack of infrastructure, corruption, religious intolerance, and perception of social security, all eat into India's drive for 'Make in India'. Last but not the least, India's move in cultural diplomacy is not a smooth one. It is also important to understand the fact that there are some itchy issues that await some form of attention. For example, there is the question of homeless Indians struggling in some countries of Southeast Asia, namely, Myanmar, Malaysia and in the Philippines, which awaits solution for long. Again Shahrukh Khan's *Datukship* was not without some opposition from within. Moreover, India should not try to over-subscribe the historical theory of Indianisation as an excuse to either detoxify effects of Westernisation or to essentially compete with the Chinese. The ASEAN countries are quite conscious of their own cultural heritages and apprehend being belittled by the major civilisations whether Chinese or Indian. Moreover, the ASEAN countries individually have respective perceptions about India or China or both, and, it is not useful to paint them with the same brush. What would be useful is to

28. See, Kasturi (2016).

cultivate the cultural links and engage with the countries in their specific historic and contemporary contexts. A pragmatic approach would be to have consistent academic exchange between the institutions. This could be followed up by interactions with policy makers. A calibrated approach would perhaps help India reap the benefits of cultural diplomacy and help her emerge as a well-meaning neighbour to ASEAN.

References

Basham, A.L. (1954). *The Wonder That Was India*. New Delhi, p.400.

Bronkhorst, J. (2011). The Spread of Sanskrit in Southeast Asia. In Manguin, P. Y., Mani, A., & Wade, G. (Eds.). *Early Interactions between South and Southeast Asia: Reflections on Cross-Cultural Exchange.* (pp. 263-75). Singapore: Institute of Southeast Asian Studies.

De Casparis, J. G., & Mabbett, I.W. (1993). Religion and Popular Beliefs of Southeast Asia before c 1500. In Tarling, N. (ed), *The Cambridge History of Southeast Asia, Volume 1*, *from Early Times to C. 1800.* (pp. 276-339). Cambridge University Press.

Coedes, George. (1968). *The Indianized States of Southeast Asia*. Honolulu: University of Hawaii Press.

Coomaraswamy, A. K. (1926). *History of Indian and Indonesian Art*. New York: Dover Publications, p.49.

Cummings, M. C. (2003). *Cultural diplomacy and the United States government: A survey*. Center for arts and culture. Available at: http://www.americansforthearts.org/sites/default/files/MCCpaper.pdf.

Divya, A. (2016). *On the anvil, trans-national Buddhist circuit from India to Nepal.* The Indian Express. 31 May.

Eliot, C. (1954). *Hinduism and Buddhism: All Historical Sketch*, VoL I. Boston. (p.4).

Fox, R. (1999). *Cultural Diplomacy at Crossroads. Cultural Relations in Europe and the Wider World*. London: The British Council. (p.2).

Gupta, S. (2005). The Bay of Bengal Interaction Sphere (1000 BC – 500 AD). In *Indo-Pacific* Pre *History Association Bulletin,* 25, (Taipei Papers Vol.3), 26-27.

Guy, J. (2014). *Lost Kingdoms: Hindu and Buddhist Sculpture of Early Southeast Asia.* New York: Metropolitan Museum of Art.

Ha, Do Thu. (2014). Cultural and Educational exchange between India and Vietnam. In *Dynamics of ASEAN-India Strategic Partnership,* Proceedings of the Second Round Table on ASEAN-India Network of Think-Tanks (AINTT) held in September 2013. Available at: http://aic.ris.org.in/wp-content/uploads/2014/05/Do-Thu-Ha-paper.pdf.

Jha, Pankaj Kumar. (2014). *Indian Cultural Diffusion in Southeast Asia: A Case Study of Thailand.* Jawaharlal Nehru University, 86-90.

Kasturi, C. S. (2016). *All roads lead to SE Asia*. The Telegraph, 6 June 2016.

Kulke, H. (2001). *Kings and Cults: History of State Formation and Legitimation in India and Southeast Asia.* New Delhi: Manohar Publishers.

Lamb, A. (1975). Indian Influence in Ancient Southeast Asia. In Basham, A. L. (ed.) *A Cultural History of India*, New Delhi: Oxford University Press. (pp. 442-443).

Lending, M. (2000). Change and Renewal: Norwegian Foreign Cultural Policy 2001-2005. Topical Foreign Policy Issues Report 2. Policy Planning and Evaluation Unit. The Royal Norwegian Ministry of Foreign Affairs. Oslo.

Mabbet, I. (1977). *The Indianization of Southeast Asia, Reflections on the Historical Sources.* Journal of Southeast Asian Studies, Vol. 8, no.2, 157-160. September.

Majumdar, R.C. (1991). *Hindu Colonies in the Far East*. Calcutta: Firma KLM Private Ltd.

Mesangrutdharakul, W. (2015). *Pali Sanskrit and Tamil words in South East Asia: A case study of the Thai, Lao, Malaysia Language*. Review of Integrative Business and Economics, Vol 4. (NRRU), 2015, 158-165.

Mulcahy, K.V. (1999). *Cultural Diplomacy and Exchange Programmes.* Journal of Arts, Society and Management, Vol 29, No.1, 7-28.

Nye, J. S. (2004). *Soft Power: The Means to Success in World Politics.* New York: Public Affairs. (p.5).

Pollock, S. (1996). The Sanskrit Cosmopolis, 300-1300: Transculturation, Vernacularization and the Question of Ideology. In Houben, J. E. (Ed.). *Ideology and Status of Sanskrit: Contributions to the History of Sanskrit Language.* Leiden: Brill. (pp. 197-247).

Ruangsup, W. (2013). *The Cultural Relationship between India and Southeast Asia from the Beginning of the Christian Era.* Thesis chapter. (P.50). Available at: shodhganga.inflibnet.ac.in/bitstream/10603/35965/3/chapter%203.pdf

Sahai, Paramjit S. *India's Cultural Diplomacy in Southeast Asia: A New Thrust*. Available http://www.academia.edu/14698180/Vietnam_Conference_-_Final_Paper-Indian_Cultural_Diplomacy-Southeast_Asia

Sarkar, H.B. (1985). *Cultural Relations between India and Southeast Asian Countries*. New Delhi: Indian Council of Cultural Research and Motilal Banarasidass.

Singh, Y. (2008). *Bollywood in Southeast Asia.* IPCS Articles #2734. 19 November. Available at: http://www.ipcs.org/article_details.php?articleNo=2734

Suryanarayan, V. (2013). *India and Southeast Asia: a Personal Narrative from Chennai.* The IPCS Special Report 139, March.

Tapaswi, A. (1986). *Popularity of the Rama-legend in Southeast Asia.* Journal of Asian Studies, Vol. 4, No. 4, October-December. (p.11). cited in Jha (2014).

Thabrew, W. V. (2014). *Buddhist Monuments and Temples of Myanmar and Thailand*. Bloomington Author House UK Ltd.

The Hindu. (2015). *India not confined to its territory: Modi.* The Hindu, 22 November. Available at: http://www.thehindu.com/news/national/prime-minister-narendra-modis-twoday-malaysia-visit-modis-address-at-the-indian-diaspora/article7905548.ece

Tripati, S. (2011). *Ancient maritime trade of eastern Indian littoral*. Current Science, Vol. 100, No.7, 10 April, 1079-1080.

Vasudevan, H. *et al.* (2012). *India-Southeast Asia Cultural Interactions. The Challenge of Common Heritage Enterprise*. A Report of the IFPS Special Group. Institute of Foreign Policy Studies, University of Calcutta, Kolkata.

Viet Nam News. (2012). *Cham form cultural link to India.* Viet Nam News, 27 June 2012. Available at: http://vietnamnews.vn/Life-Style/226629/cham-form-cultural-link-to-india.html.

Wolters, O.W. (1967). *Early Indonesian Commerce: A study of the origins of Srivijaya.* Ithaca: Cornell University Press. (p. 247).

Wolters, O.W. (1999). *History, Culture and Region in Southeast Asian Perspectives*. South East Asia Program and Institute of Southeast Asian Studies.

FOUR

REASSESSING THE IMPACT OF THE ASEAN-INDIA FREE TRADE AGREEMENT

Tham Siew Yean and Andrew Kam Jia Yi

Introduction

Since the institutionalization of the Association of Southeast Asian Nations (ASEAN) in 1967, the Southeast Asia region has initiated numerous economic cooperation initiatives, including the ASEAN Free Trade Area (AFTA). Intra-ASEAN trade has progressively increased from approximately 19 per cent in 1993 to 25 per cent in 2010 to 24 per cent in 2015 (Thangavelu and Aekapol, 2009; ASEAN Secretariat, 2012). The growth in intra-regional trade is largely fostered by regional production networks that have emerged as a result of the region's relative openness to foreign direct investment (FDI), especially in the older ASEAN-5 countries. Hence, to a large extent, the region's growing intra-regional trade has been led by the private sector's search for profit maximization through production fragmentation and locating each stage of production at where its cost of production is the lowest.

Despite the growth in intra-regional trade, ASEAN's trade is still dominated by trade partners that are from outside the region. For example, the EU, Japan, and USA contributed a total of 49 per cent, 29 per cent, and 27 per cent, respectively, to ASEAN's total trade in 1998, 2010 and 2015. The increasing importance of China is seen in the escalation of her share in ASEAN's total trade from a mere 3.5 per cent in 1998 to 11.3 per cent in 2010 to 14.8 per cent in 2015. This is also associated with China's integration with the regional production networks in ASEAN due to the shift in MNC production to China in search of lower labour cost of production for labour-intensive products in the late 1990s and 2000s.

The importance of trade partners from outside the region and the need to forge economic alliances, especially with the large countries, has motivated

ASEAN to sign several extra-regional trade agreements, such as with China, Japan, Australia-New Zealand, South Korea and India (Medalla and Mantaring, 2009). As a result, ASEAN serves as a "hub" for these ASEAN+1 agreements. Of all the extra-ASEAN partners, India has the smallest share of ASEAN's total trade, comprising 2.6 per cent in 2015. Nevertheless, India's share has grown from a mere 1.2 per cent in 1998 to 3.4 per cent[1] in 2013 with the enforcement of the ASEAN-India FTA (AIFTA). Since it is the first multilateral FTA that India has negotiated to date, it is not surprising that numerous scholars have examined the AIFTA and its impact, particularly on the Indian economy. However, these studies have not focussed on the impact on exports of manufactured goods nor has there been a critical look at the role of tariff liberalization compared with other variables in the export of these goods between ASEAN and India. In view of this, the first objective of this chapter is to compare the impact of the AIFTA on ASEAN's exports of manufactured goods to India and India's exports of manufactured goods to ASEAN. This chapter focuses on the manufacturing sector as it reflects ASEAN's comparative advantage compared to India. It is also expected that ASEAN will gain more from the scheduled tariff reduction as India's tariffs are relatively higher than ASEAN's in this sector. The second objective is to compare the role of tariff liberalization to other variables in the export of manufactured goods between ASEAN and India.

The chapter is organised as follows. After the introduction, Section 2 reviews the literature on the AIFTA, while salient features of ASEAN-India trade and the AIFTA are highlighted in Section 3. The model, data and estimation methods are explained in Section 4, while the results are explained in Section 5. The conclusion in Section 6 summarizes key findings of this paper and some suggestions to further enhance ASEAN-Indian trade in goods.

Literature Review

The literature on the ASEAN-India FTA (AIFTA) can be categorized into three main groups. In the first group, the literature examined the prospects and possible coverage of an agreement before the agreement was signed in 2009, based on the characteristics of ASEAN-India trade and economic ties (see, for example, Sen *et al.*, 2004, Ariff and Lim, 2004). Lee, *et al.* (2007), however, used time series analysis to test for the possible impact of

1. Author's calculations based on UNCOMTRADE data.

a prospective FTA. They found that liberalization in the prospective FTA would have a substantial effect in the goods and services markets as these markets were already relatively integrated based on existing economic ties of both economies.

The second group used analytical narratives to examine the impact of the agreement on India, after the agreement was signed. Pal and Dasgupta (2008) concluded that India would not benefit from the agreement in the short run as the two partners of the agreement are not natural trading partners. But, they agreed that the agreement made strategic sense in the long-run, especially since India aspires to be a hub for services exports. Likewise, Francis (2009) and Harihal (2010) also concluded that the agreement would increase ASEAN's access to the Indian market for semi-processed and processed agricultural goods, to the detriment of India's agricultural sector due to the competitive strength of ASEAN producers in this sector.

The third group used different quantitative techniques to investigate the impact of the agreement after it was signed. Based on trade specialization and trade intensity indicators, Ohlan (2012) found that India is less competitive than ASEAN, and the agreement may not benefit India, unless the country enhances its competitiveness. The SMART and gravity models were used by Veeramani and Saini (2010), Ahmed (2010), and Mondal *et al.* (2012) to measure the trade and welfare impact of the FTA. Specifically, the findings of Veeramani and Saini support the negative trade impact of the agreement on India's plantation commodities, although a net welfare gain is obtained as the gain in consumer surplus outweighed the loss in tariff revenue. But in the case of dairy trade, Mondal *et al.* (2012) found that India, being the largest milk producer in the world, would be able to increase its exports with tariff liberalization in the Philippines, Myanmar and Vietnam, based on simulations with the SMART model. ASEAN, on the other hand, would not be able to gain much in terms of its dairy exports to India, as India has kept most of the dairy product tariff lines in its exclusion list. Ahmed (2010) used both the Global Trade Analysis Project (GTAP) and SMART models to examine the welfare and trade impact of the agreement. His main findings indicate welfare gains for both India and ASEAN, although the terms of trade for India will deteriorate. However, the increase in ASEAN's exports of processed food items, agricultural products and fisheries to India may have an adverse impact on the trade balance and revenue of India.

Sikdar and Nag (2011) also used a GTAP model to analyse the impact on India and ASEAN based on the final scheduled tariff liberalization in the agreement. Their simulation results indicate that India's exports to ASEAN and ASEAN's exports to India will increase with tariff liberalization. However, there will be a welfare loss for India due to allocative inefficiency and negative terms of trade. ASEAN, on the other hand, will have a welfare gain due to improvements in their terms of trade.

Based on the above literature review, it can be seen that previous studies have focussed mainly on the welfare impact of the agreement as well as its impact on trade in agricultural products or overall trade. But, ASEAN's existing comparative advantage in trade lies in manufactured goods as opposed to India's strength in services (Ariff and Lim, 2004; Sen *et al.*, 2004). There is also a concern in the literature from India that the scheduled liberalization will only increase ASEAN's exports of manufactured goods to India, but not vice versa. Moreover, how important is the scheduled tariff liberalization in the agreement for ASEAN and India's exports of manufactured goods compared to other factors that can also influence this trade? The World Bank's data from the *Doing Business* indicates that the cost of importing[2], is relatively higher in India, compared with the ASEAN-5, and the impact of bringing down tariffs to zero can be easily negated if the movement of goods between countries face bottlenecks in terms of both hard and soft infrastructure.

In view of the above, the first objective of this study seeks to examine and compare the impact of the AIFTA on the exports of manufactured goods from ASEAN to India and India's exports of manufactured goods to ASEAN. The second objective is to ascertain the relative importance of the scheduled tariff liberalization compared with other contributory factors in the export of manufactured goods between ASEAN and India. Based on these objectives, the study uses an augmented gravity model as this type of model allows for the control for other trade related variables and to quantify any changes in a country's trade due to the FTA (Plummer *et al.*, 2010).

2. Cost measures the fees levied on a 20-foot container in U.S. dollars. All the fees associated with completing the procedures to export or import the goods are included. These include costs for documents, administrative fees for customs clearance and technical control; customs broker fees, terminal handling charges and inland transport. The cost measure does not include tariffs or trade taxes. Only official costs are recorded.

Salient Features of ASEAN-India Trade and the ASEAN-India Free Trade Agreement (AIFTA)

Salient Features of ASEAN-India Trade

Based on the availability of data and the relative importance of the different economies in ASEAN's trade with India, we focus on the ASEAN-5 economies, namely, Indonesia, Malaysia, the Philippines, Singapore and Thailand. Although the share of ASEAN's trade with India to ASEAN's total trade is relatively small, trade between these economies and India have witnessed an upward trend (Figure 1).

The ASEAN-5 have benefited from foreign direct investment (FDI) inflows in the second half of the 1980s and early 1990s to become different nodes of production for the goods produced in the region. Consequently, the share of exports of manufactured goods in the total exports of the ASEAN-5 economies comprised 78 per cent in 2000, followed by an equally high share of imports of manufactured goods, amounting to 78 per cent also for the same year[3]. The shares of exports and imports of manufactured goods have fallen progressively over time with the decline in competitiveness of the region and increasing competition from other countries in the region. It is, therefore, not surprising that manufactured exports to and imports also hold a significant share in the ASEAN-5's total exports to and imports from India, although this also had faced a downward trend, as shown in Figure 2, with some upturn in the share of manufactured goods imported in total imports from India from 2011 to 2013.

The relative importance of manufactured exports to each ASEAN-5's total exports with India is shown in Figures 3. Resource-rich countries such as Malaysia and Indonesia understandably have a lower share as they also export palm oil to India, given that these two countries are the largest producers and exporters of palm oil in the world. In contrast, manufactured exports constitute a large share of export of the Philippines, Thailand and Singapore to India as they export considerably less primary commodities to India (Figure 3).

3. Sourced from UNCOMTRADE undated

Figure 1: Share of ASEAN-5 Exports and Imports with India to Total Trade

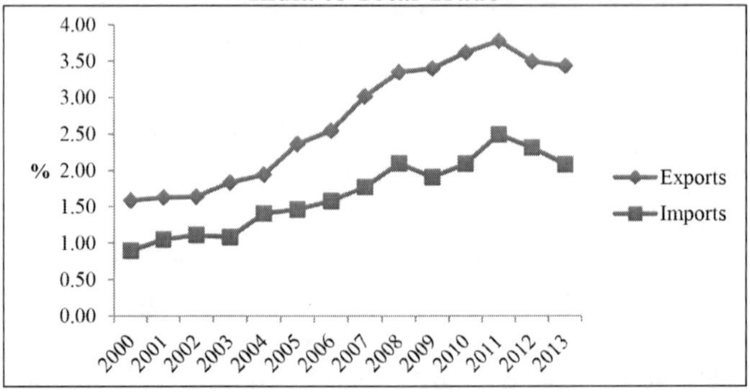

Source: UNCOMTRADE

Figure 2: Share of Exports and Imports of Manufactured Goods in Total Exports and Imports of the ASEAN-5 with India

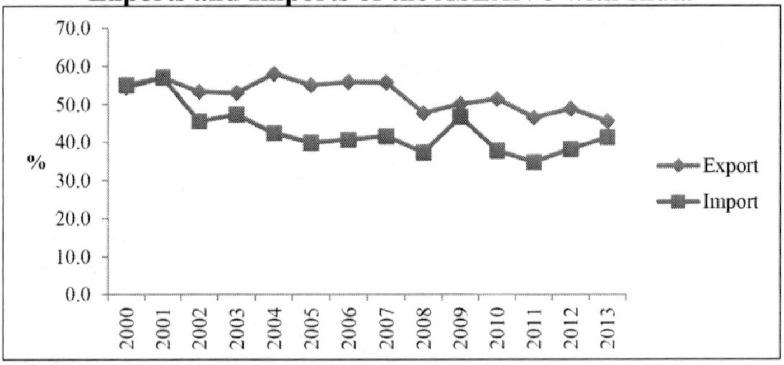

Source: UNCOMTRADE

Figure 3: Share of Manufactured Exports as a Percentage of Total Exports to India

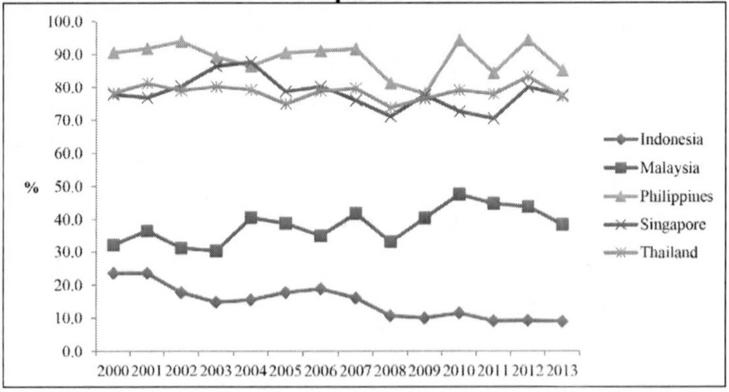

Source: UNCOMTRADE

Table 1: India's Exports to ASEAN Compared to ASEAN's Exports to India

Year	India's Manufactured Export to ASEAN / Total Indian Manufactured Exports (%)	Total Manufacturing Export to ASEAN (US$ billion)	Total Manufactured Exports to World (US$ billion)	ASEAN's Manufactured Import from India / Total ASEAN Manufactured Import (%)	ASEAN's Manufactured Import from India (US$ billion)	Total ASEAN's Manufactured Import from World (US$ billion)
2000	5.0	1.3	26.0	0.71	1.9	272.8
2001	5.9	1.6	27.0	0.85	2.1	244.5
2002	5.5	1.6	30.1	0.78	2.0	257.3
2003	5.7	2.1	36.5	0.79	2.2	284.6
2004	6.0	2.8	46.6	0.99	3.5	350.8
2005	6.4	3.8	58.6	1.64	6.4	390.6
2006	6.2	4.3	69.1	1.04	4.5	432.1
2007	5.8	4.6	79.3	1.21	5.7	475.5
2008	7.1	6.9	98.0	1.38	7.4	537.1
2009	8.4	8.4	100.3	1.49	6.5	437.9
2010	7.2	8.3	115.4	1.26	7.2	567.9
2011	8.2	12.5	151.7	1.49	9.3	627.3
2012	7.7	12.2	157.4	1.40	9.6	682.0
2013	7.6	13.0	172.0	1.38	9.3	673.6

Source: UNCOMTRADE

Table 1 compares the share of India's manufactured exports to ASEAN as a percentage of total India's manufactured exports to the world with the share of ASEAN's manufactured import from India as a percentage of ASEAN's total manufactured imports. In value terms, India's manufactured exports to ASEAN increased progressively from US$ 1.3 billion in 2000 to US$ 13 billion in 2013, and its share in terms of total India's total manufactured exports increased from 5.0 per cent in 2000 to 7.6 per cent in 2013. Similarly, ASEAN's manufactured imports from India increased steadily from US$ 1.9 billion to US$ 9.3 billion over the same period. The share of ASEAN's manufactured imports from India as a share of total ASEAN manufactured imports to the world increased from 0.7 per cent to 1.4 per cent for the same period. Overall, India only contributes less than two per cent of ASEAN's total manufactured imports. This may imply that India is yet to participate significantly in ASEAN's production networks.

While ASEAN is well known for its parts and components trade in electronics, ASEAN's parts and components (PC) exports to India as a share of total manufactured exports to India is small, averaging less than 19 per cent for the period shown in Table 2. Similarly, the share of these goods to India's total manufactured exports to ASEAN is also quite small, averaging 5 per cent for the period shown. This indicates that the production network trade in electronics for ASEAN pertains more to the ASEAN and Northeast Asia rather than with India. This is despite the fact that both ASEAN and India are signatories of the WTO's Information Technology Agreement (ITA), where the tariff for these goods were brought down to zero in 1997.

Table 2: Parts and Components (PC) Trade in Information, Communication and Technology (ICT) Products between ASEAN and India, 2000-2013

Year	ASEAN PC Exports to India/Total ASEAN Manufactured Exports to India (%)	India PC Exports to ASEAN/India Manufactured Exports to ASEAN (%)
2000	24.5	8.5
2001	25.6	14.7
2002	24.1	4.5
2003	25.3	4.4
2004	26.4	5.1
2005	22.5	1.8
2006	24.4	2.9

2007	10.2	3.4
2008	14.2	3.2
2009	12.4	11.4
2010	14.0	4.5
2011	11.6	4.2
2012	9.7	2.7
2013	10.8	2.5
Average (2000-13)	18.3	5.28

Source: Computed based on UNCOMTRADE

Salient Features of ASEAN-India Free Trade Agreement (AIFTA)

After six long years of negotiations, the ASEAN-India FTA (AIFTA) was finally inked in 2009. The ASEAN-India Comprehensive Economic Cooperation Agreement (CECA) consist of a Trade in Goods Agreement (AITIGA) that became effective in January 1, 2010. In 2015 agreement for trade in services and investment was added. The significance of the agreement lies in the fact that it has created one of the world's largest trade blocs, and it represents the most ambitious preferential trading arrangements that India has ratified thus far (Harilal, 2010).

Tariff liberalization in AITIGA is divided into five groups of products, namely, Normal Track, Sensitive Track, Special Products, Highly Sensitive List and Exclusion List, as summarized in Table 3.

Table 3: Proportion of Tariff Lines under Different Categories

Country	Categories of Products								
	EL	NT-1	NT-2	SP	ST	HSL-A	HSL-B	HSL-C	Total
India	10.7	63.9	10.3	0.3	14.8	Nil	Nil	Nil	100.0
Brunei	12.8	68.6	11.3	Nil	7.4	Nil	Nil	Nil	100.0
Cambodia	2.0	80.4	4.1	Nil	13.2	0.2	Nil	Nil	100.0
Indonesia	7.6	41.8	4.7	Nil	39.5	Nil	0.1	6.3	100.0
Lao PDR	2.8	69.5	8.6	Nil	19.2	Nil	Nil	Nil	100.0
Malaysia	9.9	59.2	14.6	Nil	15.1	Nil	0.3	0.9	100.0
Myanmar	14.1	64.4	7.5	Nil	14.0	Nil	Nil	Nil	100.0
Philippines	13.0	58.9	17.0	Nil	6.8	Nil	Nil	Nil	100.0
Vietnam	18.3	60.3	8.9	Nil	7.0	0.4	1.2	4.0	100.0
Thailand	12.2	67.0	8.9	Nil	11.7	0.2	Nil	Nil	100.0

Notes: EL: Exclusion List; NT-1; NT-2: Normal Track 1 and 2; SP: Special Products; HSL- A, B, C: Highly Sensitive Lists A, B, and C (see Appendix 1 for a description of the modalities). Singapore is excluded from the above because of its near zero tariff status.

Source: Harilal (2010)

Given that India's tariffs are relatively higher than the tariffs of ASEAN countries, the liberalization of tariffs under AITIGA is expected to benefit ASEAN more than India (Francis, 2009; Harilal, 2010; CUTS-CITEE, 2010). For example, based on the scheduled liberalization for India, the average reduction in non-agricultural products for Normal Track-1 and 2 amount to 1.8 per cent and 2.5 per cent, respectively, from 2007 to 2010 (Francis, 2009). In 2013, all tariffs in NT-1 non-agricultural goods became zero, while has been dropped by another 4.5 per cent for NT-2. Automobiles have the largest tariff reduction, with its tariffs dropped from an average MFN tariff rate of 17 per cent in 2007 to 9.1 per cent in 2010 for products in NT-1 and subsequently reduced further to zero. In the case of NT-2 automobile products, tariffs were reduced from an average MFN rate of 10 per cent to 7.5 per cent from 2007 to 2010. Electrical and electronic equipment (E&E) have a more modest tariff reduction, falling from an average MFN rate of 6.1 per cent to 4.4 per cent from 2007 to 2010 for NT-1 products. The average tariff rate for E&E products in NT-2 also reduced from 9.2 per cent to 6.7 per cent in the same period.

However, trade in manufactured goods in the ASEAN countries is facilitated by the regional production networks of the multinationals (MNCs) operating in the region. It is unclear if India's scheduled tariff reduction will lead to significant increase in ASEAN's exports to India. This is because the region's trade in intermediate goods is dominated by trade between the affiliates of the MNCs. India's manufacturing sector is not yet a significant part of this region's production network as evidenced by the data shown in Table 2. It would appear that trade in manufactured goods between ASEAN and India, especially trade in intermediate goods, is dependent on whether the AITIGA will attract more FDI into India. If the AITIGA serves to attract more efficiency-seeking FDI into India's manufacturing sector, it may possibly integrate India's manufacturing sector into the MNCs' production network in ASEAN, thereby increasing intra-industry trade between India and the ASEAN economies.

Model, Data and Analysis

Augmented Gravity Model

In line with the objectives of the study, two models are used to examine and compare the impact of the AIFTA on the exports of manufactured goods from ASEAN and India to the partner country of this agreement. The first model examines the impact of AIFTA and other controlled variables from ASEAN's perspective, while the second model examines the impact from India's experience. The basic gravity model of bilateral trade posits that trade is positively determined by the economic mass of the trading partner(s), but adversely affected by the distance between them (Tinbergen, 1962; Anderson, 1979). The general specification of an augmented gravity model consists of additional exploratory variables that explain distance attributes and other variable of interests that may affect bilateral trade. Following this structure, the augmented gravity model for this paper is specified as follows:

Model 1: The ASEAN Model

$$\ln X_{i,India,t} = \alpha + \beta_1 \ln GDP_{i,t} + \beta_2 \ln GDP_{India,t} + \beta_3 \ln \text{Distance}_{i,India,t}$$

$$+ \beta_4 colony + \beta_5 Tariff_{India,t} + \beta_6 REER_{i,t} + \gamma_1 \ln FDI_{i,(t-1)} + \varepsilon_{i,India,t} \cdots\cdots\cdots (1)$$

Model 2: The Indian Model

$$\ln X_{India,i,t} = \sigma + \theta_1 \ln GDP_{India,t} + \theta_2 \ln GDP_{i,t} + \theta_3 \ln \text{Distance}_{India,i,t}$$

$$+ \theta_4 colony + \theta_5 Tariff_{i,t} + \theta_6 REER_{i,t} + \gamma_2 \ln FDI_{India,(t-1)} + \varepsilon_{India,i,t} \cdots\cdots\cdots (2)$$

where subscripts *i* represents the individual ASEAN-5 country and their market destination, India in the year *t*. Therefore, $X_{i,India,t}$ denotes the real exports of manufactured goods from the *i*th ASEAN country to India in year *t*. Model 2 explains the relationship from India's perspective. For example, in Model 2, $X_{India,i,t}$ represents the real exports of manufactured goods from India to the *i*th ASEAN country.

$GDP_{i,t}$, $GDP_{India,t}$ and $Distance_{i,India,t}$ are the basic elements of the gravity model. $GDP_{i,t}$, $GDP_{India,t}$ are real GDP of the exporter, *i* and India (the partner country). The variables represent the economic masses or market depth of the countries. Real GDP indicates the income strength or the production capacity of the exporter. Conversely, it also represents the consumption power of the trade partner. Therefore, β_1 (or θ_1) and β_2 (or θ_2) > 0.

Although many have argued that geographical distance is increasingly irrelevant with increasing advancements in communications technology (Cairncross, 1997), distance in our model implies the risks dimensions in trade such as ignorance of foreign legal, administrative, customs and business practices. It also measures trade costs associated with time lags such as spoilage, logistics costs and fuel-oriented price shocks. Thus, *Distance* inversely affects exports, that is, β_3 (or θ_3) < 0. To control for cultural distances (disparities) between the trading nations, the model also includes a common coloniser indicator, *Colony*. A prior, the assumption is that countries with similar coloniser may share similar administrative and economic and institutional settings – all of which mitigate the uncertainties in forming trading partnerships. Therefore, it is expected that β_4 (or θ_4) > 0.

The important variable for this study is the tariff indicator (*Tariff*), where it examines the significance of India's trade liberalisation schedule under the AIFTA on ASEAN's exports to India. Trade theory postulates an inverse relationship between trade and tariff barriers, β_5 (or θ_5) < 0. The difference in coefficient values provides a relative comparison on the impact of the AIFTA on the exports of manufactured goods from ASEAN and India to each other. If $\beta_5 > \theta_5$, it, therefore, justifies the concern in the Indian literature that the scheduled liberalization has increased ASEAN's exports of manufactured goods to India to a greater extent compared to the converse case of India's exports of manufactured goods to ASEAN (but, not vice versa - it is also negative, but not significant).

The gravity model is further augmented with the exporter country's competitiveness indicator proxy by the real effective exchange rate (*REER*)[4]. Since the indicator is a weighted average of a country's currency relative to an index or basket of other major currencies adjusted for the effects of inflation, a decrease in REER means a depreciation of domestic currency (an appreciation in competitiveness which may be attributed to increased productivity), thus, encouraging exports and discouraging imports β_7 (or θ_5) < 0.

The final variables represent for the investment-trade nexus in India and the ASEAN countries. To prevent the problem of endogeneity due to the possible dual causality between FDI and trade, we employ a common practice by imposing one period lag for both indicators (see Kawai and Zhai, 2009; Xuan and Xing, 2008). Earlier section of the paper emphasised

4. The REER is an indicator that measures the "relative price and cost". It aims to assess a country's price or cost competitiveness relative to its principal competitors in the international markets (European Commission, undated). The movements in real effective exchange rates provide an indication of a country's aggregate external price competitiveness and can be interpreted as changes in technology progress that leads to productivity improvement in goods commonly traded (Catão, 2007).

on the significance of FDI-driven exports of the ASEAN countries within the regional production networks. However, since India is not a part of the regional production network, we postulate $\gamma_1 < 0$, if inflows of FDI into ASEAN divert exports into India by focussing on intra-regional trade. On the other, the impact of FDI into India, γ_2, is ambiguous since it hinges on whether AITIGA will attract more efficiency seeking FDI into India's manufacturing sector that integrates into ASEAN's production networks.

The detailed construction and sources of the variables are available in Appendix 2.

Estimation Method

This study uses a panel regression of the ASEAN-5 and India, over time (from 2000 to 2010). The Hausmann test is insignificant, suggesting that the errors are not correlated with the regressors while the Breusch-Pagan Lagrange Multiplier (LM) test indicates that there are no significant differences in variances across countries. Therefore, the Pooled-OLS estimator is most appropriate for this model[5]. The Levin-Lu-Chu (LLC)[6] test for panel unit root confirms that the variables are generally stationary (Appendix 3). The mean variance inflation factor (vif) test indicates non-severe multicollinearity problems in the models. To control for heteroskedasticity, the estimation is done using the heteroskedasticity-robust standard errors estimator.

Empirical Results and Discussion

Table 4 shows the estimation results. The basic gravity variables, *GDP* and *Distance* exhibit the expected coefficient signs. An increase in 1 per cent of the GDP of ASEAN countries will result in a 1.5 per cent increase of ASEAN's exports to India. An increase in the India's GDP will induce an increase in ASEAN export as well - but with a smaller magnitude in terms of impact. Similarly in Model 2, the rise in both GDP indicators increases India's exports to ASEAN. This shows that mutual economic prosperity between the countries will increase bilateral manufactured exports. In

5. If the error terms represent trade policies across ASEAN countries, it may be the case that ASEAN countries are equally similar in terms of openness regime and structure (e.g. AFTA has been well established in ASEAN countries since the 1990s).

6. LLC method is suitable for strongly balanced dataset, which fits the representation of our dataset (STATA has verified that our dataset is strongly balanced). In addition, the regression model focuses on ASEAN as a single unit of analysis. Therefore, the assumption that all panels share a common autoregressive parameter is reasonable.

addition, similar colonial history has a positive impact on exports as well. The impact of colonial history is stronger for ASEAN countries. This result suggests that ASEAN exporters placed more importance on cultural similarities, compared to their Indian counterparts.

Reduction in tariffs will induce an increase in ASEAN's exports to India by less than 1 per cent. This is an indication that the AITIGA has the potential to strengthen trade in manufactured goods between ASEAN and India. On the other, the results from Model 2 suggests that tariff liberalisation under the AIFTA is insignificant for India. It is important to note that the period of tariff liberalization covered in this study only pertains to the first year of liberalization alone under the AITIGA and the results may change with a longer period of liberalization. Nevertheless, the different impact of tariff reduction obtained for ASEAN and India can be inferred from the extent of tariff liberalization from 2009 to 2010. In 2009, 49.9 per cent of ASEAN's tariff lines were already at 5 per cent and below and the number of tariff lines in this category increased merely to 55.3 per cent in 2010. This indicates only a modest increase in tariff liberalization since the tariffs were already low in 2009. However, the number of tariff lines in India that fell to 5 per cent increased from 11.4 per cent to 41.8 per cent from 2009 to 2010. This contributed to the significant impact of India's tariff reduction on ASEAN's exports to India even for just one year of liberalization.

More importantly, the overall result solidifies our hypothesis that there are other contributory factors that warrant further attention. Model 1 show that distance or trade cost is the most important factor affecting ASEAN manufactured exports to India. An increase in 1 per cent of trade cost reduces almost 3 per cent of manufactured exports to India. In comparison with Model 2, the impact of trade cost on India's export to ASEAN is smaller. This finding is important because it shifts the attention to a more pressing issue beyond the AITIGA tariff liberalisation commitments. Trade costs and non-tariff barriers could potentially be the main elements that determine the success of the AIFTA and not tariff liberalisation per se.

The FDI indicator is insignificant for ASEAN countries. This may due to the absence of production network linkages with India (refer Table 1). MNCs operating in ASEAN countries have yet to explore trade opportunities with India. Similar phenomenon can be explained in Model 2, where an increase in FDI inflows to India insignificantly affects India's exports of manufactured goods to ASEAN countries. It is possible that the results may change if additional data in terms of bilateral FDI flows are made available, but there is no published data on these bilateral flows at the point of this study. Finally, improvement in competitiveness is important for penetrating both markets as the REER shows expected signs in both models.

Table 4: Estimated Results

Variables	ASEAN (Model 1)	Variables	India (Model 2)
	$lnX_{i,India}$ = Dependent Variable		$lnX_{India,i}$ = Dependent Variable
$lnGDP_{i,t}$	1.509***	$lnGDP_{i,t}$	1.062***
	(15.97)		(12.81)
$lnGDP_{India,t}$	0.791***	$lnGDP_{India,t}$	0.805***
	(4.92)		(3.75)
lnDistance	-2.954***	lnDistance	-0.264*
	(-16.84)		(-1.96)
colony	1.307***	colony	0.655***
	(18.95)		(7.28)
Tariff	-0.00288***	Tariff	-0.000810
	(-5.13)		(-0.64)
REER	-0.0103***	REER	-0.00555***
	(-10.38)		(-4.76)
$\ln FDI_{i,(t-1)}$	0.0276	$\ln FDI_{India,(t-1)}$	0.0147
	(0.99)		(0.23)
cons	28.15***	cons	7.293**
	(16.09)		(3.45)
N	56	N	59
Hausmann Test	Prob > χ^2 = 0.0892		Prob > χ^2 = 0.6157
LM test	Prob > χ^2 = 0.1215		Prob > χ^2 = 0.1045
Model Selection	Pool OLS		Pool OLS
Mean VIF	2.78 < 10		3.09 < 10

*** $p<0.01$ ** $p<0.05$ *$p<0.10$

Conclusions

While ASEAN continues to enhance and facilitate its economic cooperation as it moves toward the attainment of an ASEAN Economic Community by 2025, the region has also cultivated economic cooperation with its key trading partners from outside the region, including India. AIFTA represents an important first step forward towards fostering closer economic ties between the member countries of this agreement.

The main findings of this paper show that while lowering tariff barriers will improve ASEAN's manufactured exports to India, its impact is relatively smaller than the impact of other variables in the model. Reducing trade costs in India is another important factor to address, if the ASEAN-5 seeks to improve its manufactured exports to India and vice versa. While both the Framework Agreement and the AITIGA contain provisions that address import costs such as different trade facilitation measures[7], including non-tariff barriers or non-tariff measures, these provisions lack specificity, and, hence, they are difficult to monitor. Adopting, monitoring and setting targets for specific trade facilitation measures need to be considered to enhance ASEAN's exports to India (Wong and Pellan, 2012). Similarly, while the connectivity improvement is going to reduce trade costs, monitoring its implementation, especially the Mekong-India Economic Corridor (MIEC), and the connectivity between Myanmar-Northeast India and rest of India is of the utmost importance.

Collecting better and more accurate data on trade costs between ASEAN and India will also facilitate researchers to refine their tests on the role of trade costs in facilitating trade between the partner countries of the AIFTA. Currently, there is not enough data to test this important role in a more rigorous fashion.

Similarly, it is also equally important to implement the services and investment agreement. More importantly, ASEAN's implementation of the ASEAN Framework Agreement of Services (AFAS) and investment initiatives within ASEAN must be monitored and implemented for the impending agreements on services and investment with India to be meaningful.

At the same time, the ASEAN-5 cannot afford to be complacent and need to improve the competitiveness of the exports through suitable domestic measures that can address their respective needs for structural transformation.

---

7. Article 3 in the Framework Agreement for example, addresses NTBs, customs procedures, rules and regulations. Similarly, articles 8 and 14 in the AITIGA also address NTBs and customs procedures.

Malaysia, for example, has been losing its competitiveness in manufacturing and needs to restructure its economy. Increased opportunities to export to India through the AIFTA only opens doors for ASEAN exporters but these doors of opportunities cannot be seized without improved competitiveness on the part of ASEAN producers.

[An earlier version of the paper was published by the authors in *Jurnal Ekonomi Malaysia* Vol. 48, No. 2, 2014. Authors have received the approval from the journal authority for this publication.]

References

Ahmed, S. (2010). *India-ASEAN Trade Agreement: A Sectoral Analysis*.

Available at http://ssrn.com/abstract=1698849 Accessed 15 October 2012. http://dx.doi.org/10.2139/ssrn.1698849

Anderson, J. E. (1979). *A Theoretical Foundation for the Gravity Equation*. American Economic Review, 69(1). 106-116.

Ariff, M., & Lim, C.C. (2004). *ASEAN-India FTA: Issues and Prospects*. Paper presented at the ASEAN-India Forum on ASEAN-India Economic Relations: The Road Ahead, 9-10 February 2004. Singapore.

ASEAN Secretariat. (2012). *ASEAN Community in Figures 2011*.

Cairncross, F. (1997). *The Death Of Distance : How The Communications Revolution Will Change Our Lives*. Boston: Harvard Business School Press.

Catão, L. A. V. (2007). *Why Real Exchange Rates? Finance and Development*. A Quarterly Magazine of the IMF, 44(3). Available at: http://www.imf.org/external/pubs/ft/fandd/2007/09/basics.htm. Accessed 28 August 2012.

Consumer Unity and Trust Society – Centre or International Trade, Economics and Society (CUTS-CITEE). (2010). *India-ASEANFTA: A Move towards Multilateral Free Trade Agreements?* Briefing Paper 1/200. Available at: www.cuts-citee.org Accessed 28 August 2012.

European Commission, undated. Available at: http://ec.europa.eu/economy_finance/db_indicators/competitiveness/index_en.htm. Accessed 28 August 2012.

Francis, S. (2009). *The ASEAN-Free Trade Agreement: A Sectoral impact analysis of increased trade integration in goods*. Available at: www.networkideas.org/ideasact/dec09/pdf/smitha_francis_paper.pdf Accessed 28 August 2012.

Harilal, K.N. (2010). *ASEAN-India Free Trade Area: Noises of Dissent from Deep South*. Occasional Paper 2010:01, Kerala State Planning Board, Government of Kerala, Thriuvanathapruam. Available at: www.unitedworld.in/.../State%20planning%20board%20research%20. Accessed 28 August 2012.

Lee, H.H., Lee H.A. & Liew, K.S.V. (2007). *India-ASEAN-5 Economic Integration: Impact of Liberalization*. The IUP Journal of Applied Economics, VI (6), 7-20.

Masahiro, K. & Zhai, F. (2009). *PRC-Latin America Economic Cooperation: Going Beyond Resource and Manufacturing Complementarity*. ADBI Working Paper Series (137): 1-28.

Medalla, E. M., & Mantaring, M. C. (2009). *On free trade agreements (FTAs): the Philippine perspective (No. DP 2009-35). Philippine Institute for Development Studies*. Manila, Philippines.

Mondal, B., Sirohi, S. & Thorat, V. (2012). *Impact of ASEAN-India Free Trade Agreement on Indian Dairy Trade: A Quantitative Approach*. Munich Personal RePEc Archive (MPRA), 20 August 2012. http://mpra.ub.uni-muenchen.de/40790/MPRA Paper No. 40790, posted 21 August 2012. Accessed 15 October 2012.

Ohlan, R. (2012). *ASEAN India Free Trade Agreement in Goods: An Assessment*. African Journal of Social Sciences, 2(3), 66-84.

Pal, P., & Dasgupta, M. (2008). *Does a Free Trade Agreement with ASEAN Make Sense?* Economic and Political Weekly, 43(46) (Nov. 15-21): 8-12.

Plummer, M.G., Cheong, D. & Hamanaka, S. (2010). *Methodology for impact assessment of free trade agreements*. Manila: Asian Development Bank (ADB).

Randveer, M., & Rell, M., (2002). *The Relationship between Competitiveness and Real Exchange Rate in Estonia*. Bank of Estonia Research Paper.

Sen, R., Asher, M.G. & Rajan, R.S. (2004). *ASEAN-India Economic Relations: Current Status and Future Prospects*. Paper presented at the ASEAN-India Forum on ASEAN-India Economic Relations: The Road Ahead, 9-10 February 2004, Singapore.

Sikdar, C. & Nag, B. (2011). *Impact of India-ASEAN Free Trade Agreement: A cross-country analysis using general equilibrium modelling*. Asia Pacific Research and Training Network on Trade (ARTNeT) Working Paper Series, No. 107, November. Bangkok: UNESCAP.

Thangavelu, S. & Aekapol, C. (2009). *Free Trade Agreements, Regional Integration and Growth in ASEAN*. Available at: www.paftad.org/files/33/Thangavelu%20&%20Chongvilaivan.pdf Accessed 30 August 2012.

Tinbergen, J. (1962). *Shaping the World Economy; Suggestions for an International Economic Policy*, (Appendix VI). New York: The Twentieth Century Fund.

Xuan, N. T., & Xing, Y. (2008). *Foreign Direct Investment and Exports: The Experiences of Vietnam*. Economics of Transition, 16(2), 183-197.

United Nations Commodity Trade Statistics (Comtrade). http://comtrade.un.org/db/ Accessed 28 August 2012.

World Bank undated. Available at: http://www.imf.org/external/pubs/ft/fandd/2007/09/basics.htm Accessed 28 August 2012.

Wong, M.H. & Pellan, M.I. (2012). *Trade Facilitation: The Way Forward for ASEAN and Its Partners*. Economic Research Institute for ASEAN and East Asia (ERIA) Policy Brief, No. 2012-04, July 2012. ERIA.

Veeramani, C., & Saini, G.K. (2010). *Impact of ASEAN-India FTA on India's Plantation Commodities: A Simulation Analysis*. Working Paper (WP)-2010-004. Indira Ghandi Institute of Development Research, Mumbai, April 2010. http://www.ididr.ac.in/pdf/publication/WP-2010-004 Accessed 15 October 2012.

Appendix 1: Modalities for Tariff Liberalization under the AIFTA

Modalities	Description
1. Normal Track	Gradual reduction and subsequent elimination of custom tariffs on 4000 products that account for 80 per cent of traded goods.
1.1 Normal Track 1 (January 01, 2010 to December 31, 2013 1.2 Normal Track 2 (January 01, 2010 to December 31, 2016)	Tariffs will be eliminated on 3,2000 products under 7,788 tariff lines, These are mostly products with 7.5-10 per cent duties and the average reduction rate will be 1.5-2 per cent per year. Tariffs will be eliminated on 800 products under 1,252 tariff lines. These are mostly products with 7.5-10 per cent duties and the average reduction rate will be 1-1.5 per cent per year
2. Sensitive Track	Tariffs will be reduced on about 560 products that account for 10 per cent of trade goods. Applied MFN tariff rates above 5 per cent will be reduced to the level of 5 per cent.
2.1 Structure 1 (January 01, 2010 to December 31, 2016) 2.1 Structure 2 (January 01, 2010 to December 31, 2016) 2.3 Structure 3 (January 01, 2010 to December 31, 2019)	Duties on items with MFN applied tariffs of more than 5 per cent will be reduced to 5 per cent. This can be maintained up to 50 tariff lines. For remaining products from tariff lines beyond 50, duties on products with MFN applied tariff rates higher than 5 per cent will be reduced to 4.5 per cent and then eventually to 4 per cent. For products with 4 per cent duty rates in the sensitive list (products to be identified), tariffs will be eliminated in a phased manner.
3. Special Products (January 01, 2010 to December 31, 2019)	Tariff reduction for products such as crude and refined palm oil, coffee, black tea and pepper phased over ten years for India.
4. Highly Sensitive List: 4.1 Category 1 4.2 Category 2 4.3 Category 3	Reduction of tariffs for products in a phased manner for ASEAN countries. Reduction of applied MFN tariff rates to 50 per cent of the base rate. Reduction of applied MFN tariff rates by 50 per cent of the base rate. Reduction of applied MFN tariff rates by 25 per cent of the base rate.
5. Exclusion List	List contains 489 items out of which 302 are from the agriculture sector, 81 from textiles, 52 items from machinery and auto, 17 from chemical and plastics.

Source: CUTS CITEE (2010)

Appendix 2: Data Used in Models 1 and 2

Variable	Variable Construction	Data Source
X	• Value of bilateral manufacturing exports in US$ at constant (2005) price. Deflated by the export price index. • Manufacturing products are based on UNCTAD definition – (SITC 5 to 8, excluding 667 and 6)	UnComtrade, Prices are taken from the Economist Intelligence Unit (EIU) database
GDP	• Gross domestic product (GDP) at constant market prices, rebased to 2005 constant prices and translated into US$ using the LCU: $ exchange rate in 2005.	EIU database
Distance	• The great-circle or orthodromic distance is the shortest distance between any two points on the surface of a sphere measured along a path on the surface of the sphere (as opposed to going through the sphere's interior).	BACI dataset, http://www.cepii.fr/anglaisgraph/bdd/baci.htm
Colony	• 1 if the ASEAN country was under the British Colony (Malaysia and Singapore), 0 if otherwise.	
Tariff	• 2000 – 2009, Tariff rate, most favoured nation, simple mean, manufactured products (per cent). Simple mean most favoured nation tariff rate is the unweighted average of most favoured nation rates for all products subject to tariffs calculated for all traded goods. Data are classified using the Harmonized System of trade at the six- or eight-digit level. Tariff line data were matched to Standard International Trade Classification (SITC) revision 3 codes to define commodity groups. Manufactured products are classified using SITC revision 3. SITC (5-8 excluding division 68).	World Bank, http://data.worldbank.org/indicator/TM.TAX.MANF.SM.FN.ZS ASEAN Secretariat,

	• 2010 – 2011, simple average from AIFTA schedule of Tariff Commitments. The HS codes are matched with the SITC codes. Manufacturing products are defined as HS 11 to HS 97 excluding HS 71, 74 to 81. • Since the Philippines have a different schedule, we normalised the tariff rates and created a tariff index with 2007=100. This is to create a consistent cross country indicator. The trend shows that the index dropped after 2010.	
REER	• Real effective exchange rate index (2005 = 100) • Real effective exchange rate is the nominal effective exchange rate (a measure of the value of a currency against a weighted average of several foreign currencies) divided by a price deflator or index of costs. • CPI-based REER is used because it contains more information about real variables (trade flows and investment) than other REER indices (Randveer and Rell, 2002)	International Monetary Fund, International Financial Statistics.
FDI	• FDI as a share of GDP	EIU database

Source: Authors

Appendix 3: LLC and IPS Test Results (Adjusted t)*

$\ln X_{i,India}$	-2.8133 (0.0025)	$\ln X_{India,i}$	-3.0553 (0.0011)
$\ln GDP_{i,t}$	-1.8861 (0.0296)	$\ln GDP_{i,t}$	-1.8861 (0.0296)
$\ln GDP_{India,t}$	-6.2648 (0.0000)	$\ln GDP_{India,t}$	-6.2648 (0.0000)
Tariff	-3.7701 (0.0001)	Tariff	-3.4153 0.0003
REER	-3.3520 0.0004	$\ln FDI_{India,(t-1)}$	-3.6819 (0.0001)
$\ln FDI_{i,(t-1)}$	-2.7878 (0.0027)		

*Time invariant variable (Distance) and dummy variable (colony) not included.
P-value in the parentheses

FIVE

WILL INDIA GAIN FROM INDIA-ASEAN FTA? ANALYSIS OF SIMULATED SCENARIOS BASED ON PHASED IMPLEMENTATION

Chandrima Sikdar and Biswajit Nag

Introduction

The ASEAN-India Free Trade Agreement (AIFTA) came into effect on January 1, 2010 with respect to Malaysia, Singapore and Thailand. For the remaining ASEAN members, it is expected to come into force by 2016 after the countries complete their internal requirements. Of the ten countries, India's trade with ASEAN has been mainly concentrated in Indonesia, Malaysia, Singapore and Thailand before AIFTA came into force. In the years immediately before the implementation of AIFTA, Singapore was the largest destination for Indian goods (38 per cent of total exports to ASEAN in 2009) and also the largest source of imports for India for most of these years except in 2009, in which imports from Indonesia surpassed Singapore (26 per cent of India's total imports from ASEAN in 2009 came from Singapore and 31 per cent came from Indonesia).[1]

As has been mutually agreed, the tariff liberalization under the India-ASEAN FTA would gradually cover 75 per cent of the two-way trade between India and ASEAN countries starting from January 2010. The FTA will lead to the elimination of tariff for about 4000 products including electronics, chemicals, machinery and textiles. Of these 4000 products, 3200 products had duties reduced by end of the year 2013, while duties on remaining 800 products would be lowered to zero or near zero by end of 2016. Under the Trade in Goods Agreement, the Schedules of Tariff Commitments have been drawn by all the member countries indicating product-wise tariff concessions or no concessions. One important observation about the tariff cuts under this agreement is about the base rates, which are the applied rates (not the bound

1. Sourced from WITS

rates) as of 1 July 2007, except for products identified as Special Products. Implications of taking applied rates as base rates are quite far-reaching for product lines and countries where there is considerable difference between bound and applied rates.

The schedule of tariff reduction commitments undertaken by the AIFTA members varies significantly among them. For example, India's commitments to the Philippines are quite different from her commitments to the rest of the ASEAN countries. This is true for each ASEAN member also as each one of them has separate tariff reduction schedule vis-à-vis India. In spite of the variability among the tariff schedules, they share certain common features as outlined in Article 4 and Annexure 1 of the Agreement (goods section). The tariff lines are divided into five broad categories (see Table 1), viz., Normal Track, Sensitive Track, Special Products, Highly Sensitive Lists and Exclusion List according to the intensity of tariff reduction or elimination commitments (Harilal, 2010).

Table 1: Proportion of Tariff Lines under Different Categories by ASEAN Members and India

Country	Categories								
	EL	NT-1	NT-2	SP	ST	HSL - A	HSL - B	HSL - C	Total
India	10.7	63.9	10.3	0.3	14.8	Nil	Nil	Nil	100.0
Brunei	12.8	68.6	11.3	Nil	7.4	Nil	Nil	Nil	100.0
Cambodia	2.0	80.4	4.1	Nil	13.2	0.2	Nil	Nil	100.0
Indonesia	7.6	41.8	4.7	Nil	39.5	Nil	0.1	6.3	100.0
Lao PDR	2.8	69.5	8.6	Nil	19.2	Nil	Nil	Nil	100.0
Malaysia	9.9	59.2	14.6	Nil	15.1	Nil	0.3	0.9	100.0
Myanmar	14.1	64.4	7.5	Nil	14.0	Nil	Nil	Nil	100.0
Philippines	13.0	58.9	17.0	Nil	6.8	Nil	Nil	4.4	100.0
Vietnam	18.3	60.3	8.9	Nil	7.0	0.4	1.2	4.0	100.0
Thailand	12.2	67.0	8.9	Nil	11.7	0.2	Nil	Nil	100.0

Note: EL refers to Exclusion List; NT-1 and 2 to Normal Track 1 and 2; SP to Special Products; ST for Sensitive Track and HSL – A, B and C to Highly Sensitive Lists A, B and C;
Singapore is not included in the analysis for it follows near perfect free trade policies.
Source: Harilal (2010)

While India keeps around 10.7 per cent of her tariff lines in the exclusion list, Vietnam keeps nearly 18.3 per cent of the tariff lines under this category. Considering all ASEAN members together, they have kept around 10 per cent of the tariff lines in the exclusion list. It follows from the above that nearly 90 per cent of the tariff lines are subject to reduction commitments. It is also important to note that there are no tariff reduction commitments under exclusion list vis-à-vis the base rates, i.e., applied rates as on 1 July 2007. But, these base rates, which are the upper limits to which tariffs can be raised in the AIFTA regime and they are much lower than their corresponding WTO bound rates in case of India. The proportion of tariff lines kept under the Highly Sensitive Lists (HSL) also varies significantly among members. India does not keep any tariff line under these lists. Indonesia has nearly 6.4 per cent of the tariff lines kept under the HSL. Malaysia (1.2 per cent), the Philippines (4.4 per cent), Vietnam (5.6 per cent) and Cambodia (0.2 per cent) are the other members using the HSL facility. Instead, India has kept 14.8 per cent tariff lines in the sensitive category, which includes some spices, products of animal origin, chemical products including pharmaceutical products, specific plastic, polymer, rubber and leather products, some cotton woven etc. Apart from this, India's list consists of special products, which are not there in the list of other countries who are party to this agreement. This constitutes only around 0.3 per cent of India's tariff lines. Special Product is an exclusive group designed for the five product groups viz., crude and refined palm oil, coffee, black tea and pepper. There is hardly any uniformity in the reduction commitments among these five product groups (see Table 2).

Table 2: Reduction Commitment by India of Special Products under India-ASEAN FTA

Tariff Line	Base Rate	Not later than 1st January				As on
		2010	2013	2016	2021	31.12.2021
Crude Palm Oil	80	76	64	52	40	37.5
Refined Palm Oil	90	86	74	62	50	45
Coffee	100	95	80	65	50	45
Black Tea	100	95	80	65	50	45
Pepper	70	68	62	56	51	50

Note: The original table gives rates for all the years between 2010 and 2021
Source: Harilal (2010)

The rest of the paper is organized as follows. Section 2 presents the scenario of India's trade with ASEAN. A discussion on literature is provided in Section 3. Section 4 discusses the methodology and Section 5 presents the data. The impact of the FTA on the partner countries, particularly India, as revealed by the GTAP modelling framework are presented in Sections 6 and 7. Finally, conclusions are drawn in Section 8.

India's Trade with ASEAN

ASEAN as a group is an important trade partner of India. In the years immediately succeeding the implementation of the FTA almost 11.5 per cent of India's exports have been going to ASEAN and India imported almost 9 per cent of its total imports from these countries together. India's exports increased by leaps and bounds in countries like Singapore, Malaysia, Indonesia, Thailand and Vietnam, etc. During 2014 and 2015, India's imports from Indonesia, Singapore and Lao PDR have also grown rapidly. Table 3 provides export import data with respect to bilateral trade between India and ASEAN members for the five years succeeding the implementation of the FTA.

Table 3: India's Trade with ASEAN Countries (2011 – 2015)

ASEAN members	Exports (US$ million)					Imports (US$ million)				
	2011	2012	2013	2014	2015	2011	2012	2013	2014	2015
Brunei	870.61	33.40	40.25	42.48	30.39	704.93	939.26	766.06	942.65	607.78
Cambodia	6400.25	6021.92	5557.94	4444.76	2868.88	13964.66	14068.29	14984.08	15184.88	13902.02
Indonesia	89.57	110.08	136.77	154.07	145.35	8.41	10.13	12.79	16.42	42.99
Lao PDR	13.97	27.31	61.31	63.61	51.26	70.17	143.73	111.33	59.63	142.95
Malaysia	455.86	526.85	742.87	868.53	859.97	1262.04	1346.18	1366.24	1392.76	1016.30
Myanmar	3798.82	3791.20	5496.82	4642.23	4892.06	9106.22	10494.09	9330.74	10928.50	9559.92
Philippines	1006.62	1119.25	1469.07	1436.90	1304.35	450.28	494.19	408.79	400.69	518.19
Singapore	15627.48	13552.71	14189.02	9676.62	7805.08	8155.30	7797.33	7026.64	7069.42	7396.00
Thailand	2767.92	3454.13	4203.81	3438.52	3113.56	5055.56	5499.27	5475.44	5680.94	5650.14
Vietnam	3466.53	3658.16	5987.61	6526.52	5357.21	1554.28	1945.49	2826.67	2781.69	2680.09
Share in India's total exports (%)	11.44	11.15	11.25	9.86	10.00					
Share in India's total imports (%)						8.72	8.74	9.08	9.68	10.62

Source: UNCOMTRADE

It is important to note that India's exports to smaller ASEAN countries such as Cambodia, Lao PDR, and Myanmar increased substantially in the last few years. India's import of mineral fuels and mineral oils from Brunei jumped substantially in these years. In 2015, Brunei occupied 1.5 per cent of India's imports from ASEAN. Figure 1 provides a snapshot of the importance of individual ASEAN countries as India's export destination and import sources.

Figure 1: Share (per cent) of Individual Country in India's Trade with ASEAN

(a) India's Exports to ASEAN in 2015

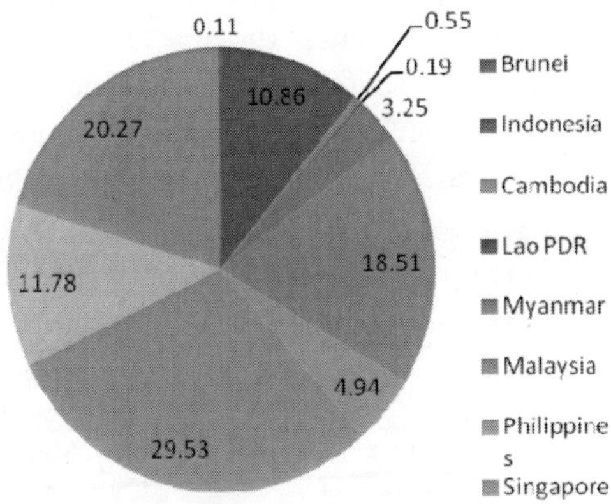

(b) India's Imports from ASEAN in 2015

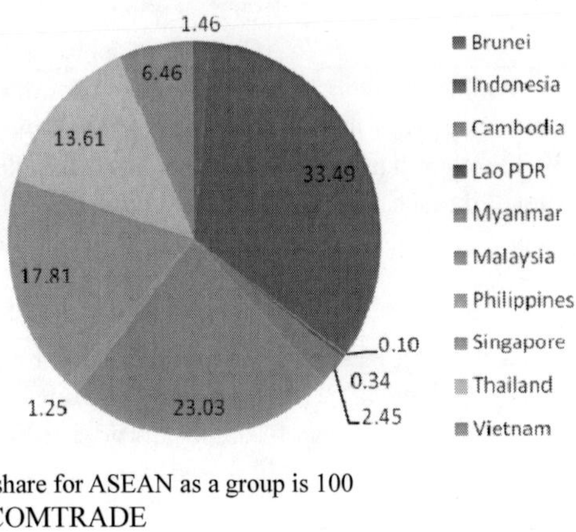

Note: Sum of share for ASEAN as a group is 100
Source: UNCOMTRADE

The main exports of India to the ASEAN region have been meat, edible vegetables and fruits, cereals, cotton, tobacco, salt, sulphur, organic chemicals, pharmaceutical products, iron and steel, copper, electrical & electronic equipments, machineries, etc. The main imports of India from the ASEAN region have been the items like mineral fuels, animal and vegetable fats, chemicals, pharmaceutical products, rubber products, wood products, electronic equipments, machineries, ships, boats and floating structures, optical, photopgraphic, musical instruments, etc. However, for individual countries it is widely different. For example, in Cambodia, Lao PDR, Myanmar, India's one of the major exportable is medicines and pharmaceutical products, but in Singapore, Malaysia and Thailand, machinery, accessories, precious stones, meat and animal products occupy primary position. Similarly, India imports mineral fuel from Brunei, Indonesia and Malaysia, and electronic products from Singapore and Thailand, wood products from Myanmar, etc. Table 4 provides a summary of major tradable products between India and ASEAN countries.

Table 4: Top Exporting / Importing Items of India to / from ASEAN Countries, 2013

Partner Name	Export	Import
Brunei	Meat and edible meat, Edible vegetables and certain roots, Vehicles other than Railway or Tram, Cereals, Nuclear Reactors, Boilers, Machinery,	Mineral fuels, Mineral oils, Organic Chemicals, Raw Hides and Skins, Electrical Machinery and equipment, Optical, Photographic and Cinematographic
Cambodia	Pharmaceutical products, Cotton, Man-made staple fibres, Raw hides and skins, Vehicles other than Railway or Tram, Oil seeds and Oleaginous fruits	Wood and Articles of wood, Animal/veg fats & oils, Edible fruit and nuts, Miscellaneous chemical products, Art of apparel & clothing access, Pharmaceutical products, Rubber and articles thereof
Indonesia	Mineral fuels, oils, Nuclear Reactors, Boilers, Machinery, Organic chemicals, Iron and steel, Vehicles other than Railway or Tram, Oil seeds and Oleaginous fruits	Animal/veg fats & oils, Mineral fuels, oils, Ores, slag and ash, Rubber and articles thereof, Organic chemicals

Lao PDR	Vehicles other than Railway or Tram, Nuclear Reactors, Boilers, Machinery, Pharmaceutical products, Electrical mchy equip, Optical, photo, cine, meas, Aluminium and articles thereof, Articles of iron or steel, Meat and Edible meat	Ores, slag and ash, Wood and articles of wood, Lead and Articles thereof, Nuclear Reactors, Boilers, Machinery, Articles of Iron & Steel, Natural/cultured pearls, prec stone
Malaysia	Ships, boats and floating structure, Mineral fuels, oils, Organic chemicals, Electrical mchy equip parts, boilers, mechanical machineries, Meat and Edible meat Copper and Articles thereof, Nickel and Articles thereof.	Mineral fuels, oils & product, Animal/veg fats & oils, boilers, mchy, Electrical mchy equip parts, Nuclear Reactors, Boilers, Machinery, Wood and articles of wood, Organic Chemicals
Myanmar	Sugar and Sugar Confectionary, Pharmaceutical products, Iron and steel, Electrical mchy equip parts, Mineral fuels, oils & product, Cotton, Vehicles other than Railway or Tram, Nuclear Reactors, Boilers, Machinery	Edible vegetables and certain roots, Wood and articles of wood, Edible Fruit and Nuts, Coffee, tea and spices, Oil seeds and Oleaginous fruits
Philippines	Vehicles other than Railway or Tram, Nuclear Reactors, Boilers, Machinery, Rubber and Articles thereof, Meat and edible meat, Electrical mchy equip parts, Iron and steel, Vehicles, Pharmaceutical products	Electrical mchy equip parts, Nuclear Reactors, Boilers, Machinery, Mineral fuels, oils & product, Optical, Photographic and Cinematographic, Vehicles other than Railway or Tram.
Singapore	Mineral fuels, oils & product, Ships, boats and floating structure, Natural/cultured pearls, prec stone, Nuclear Reactors, Boilers, Machinery,Organic Chemicals, Electrical mchy and equipments	Electrical mchy equip parts, Nuclear Reactors, Boilers, Machinery, Mineral fuels, oils & product, boilers, mechanical machineries, Organic chemicals, Ships, boats and floating structure, Optical, Photographic and Cinematographic, Plastics and articles thereof
Thailand	Natural/cultured pearls, prec stone, Nuclear Reactors, Boilers, Machinery, Vehicles other than Railway or Tram, Electrical mchy equip parts, Residues & waste from the food, Organic chemicals, Iron and steel	Nuclear Reactors, Boilers, Machinery, Electrical mchy and equip, Plastics and articles thereof. Organic chemicals. Rubber and articles thereof, Vehicles other than Railway or Tram.

Vietnam	Residues & waste from the food, Meat and edible meat, Electrical mchy equip parts, Cereals, Iron and steel, Cotton, Vehicles other than Railway or Tram, Coffee, Tea, matï and Spices, Nuclear Reactors, Boilers, Machinery	Electrical mchy equip parts, Coffee, tea, matï and spices, Salt, Nuclear Reactors, Boilers, Machinery, Mineral fuels, oils & product, Inorganic Chemicals.

Source: Derived from UNCOMTRADE

Objectives and Motivation

So far among all FTAs in which India is involved, AIFTA constitutes the biggest trade volume. Hence, the impact of this agreement is expectedly large enough to influence many of the important trade related variables such as trade volume, prices of traded goods, terms of trade as also trade related issues like welfare, production efficiency, resource distribution, factor prices and income. Against this backdrop the present study seeks to analyse the impact of this trade agreement and the consequent free entry of a large number of goods from the ASEAN countries to the Indian economy.

It is six years into the FTA and India and the three big ASEAN countries of Malaysia, Singapore and Thailand have completed the tariff liberalization with respect to the products in their Normal Track 1. Thus, the study at the outset begins by assessing if the FTA implementation has increased the two-way trade between India and ASEAN. For this a regression exercise is done. Thereafter, to analyse in detail the impact of the FTA on the various trade variables and trade related aspects in the partner countries the study does an applied general equilibrium (AGE) analysis. It uses the Global Trade Analysis Project (GTAP) and does several simulations through GTAP data to understand the impact of the AIFTA by calibrating various liberalization scenarios. The AIFTA will progress gradually and there will be phased liberalization of the tariffs by the countries. Accordingly, this study analyses the impact of this phased liberalization through modifying simulation framework. The computable general equilibrium (CGE) model through GTAP helps us in this direction by accommodating all the necessary changes.

The studies used various models to analyse the possible impact of this agreement. Pal and Dasgupta (2008, 2009) and Harilal (2010) used tariff and trade data extensively through partial equilibrium framework. On the other hand, Sen *et al.* (2004) and Karmakar (2005) used descriptive framework and Lee and Liew (2007) used time series analysis to study the possible impact. Veeramani (2010) used SMART and gravity model for the same. Few studies such as Kawai *et al.* (2007) and Sasatra and Prasopchoke (2007) used CGE framework. Kawai *et al.* (2007) highlighted that the consolidation at the ASEAN+6 level would yield the largest gains to East Asia among plausible regional trade arrangements. The study by Sasatra and Prasopchoke (2007) indicated that ASEAN-5 would achieve greater benefits from the FTAs if they fully liberalized trade among themselves. Veermani (2010) argued that AIFTA will cause significant increase of imports of plantation commodities into India. The increase in imports will be mostly driven by trade creation rather than trade diversion. The proposed tariff reduction as per the India-ASEAN trade agreement may lead to significant tariff revenue loss to the Indian government. However, the gain in consumer surplus (due to the fall in domestic price and the consequent reduction in dead-weight loss) outweighs the loss in tariff revenue leading to net welfare gain.

Ahmed (2010) investigated the sectoral dimensions of India–ASEAN Free Trade Agreement as a result of tariff liberalization. Using a GTAP and SMART model, this study revealed that both India and ASEAN gain in terms of welfare, while the terms of trade for India deteriorates. The study revealed that in case of India, processed food products, grain crops, textile and wearing apparel, light manufacturing and heavy manufacturing are the sectors expected to be affected significantly. ASEAN's exports of processed food items, agricultural products and fisheries are likely to increase, which might result in adverse impact on employment and wages of Indian working class. This study also revealed that the present FTA will affect India's trade balance adversely and cause revenue losses for India. To understand the impact on unskilled workers the study considered sticky wage and allows factors of production to adjust accordingly. Francis (2011) analyzed the implications of India's tariff reduction commitments under the AIFTA for its agricultural and non-agricultural sectors and concluded that ASEAN countries will gain significant market access in India in many semi-processed or processed agricultural products, thus adversely affecting the domestic agricultural sector. Indian SMEs in agriculture-related products and food products, as also in some intermediate goods and light manufacturing products, are likely to be negatively affected. But, import liberalization in intermediate goods is likely to lead to India's deeper integration in production networks in some industries such as machinery, chemicals and transport equipment.

Sikdar and Nag (2011) also analyzed the impact of tariff liberalization commitments by India and the ASEAN members, but looks at the overall impact on India as well as ASEAN members under the phased liberalization schedule as agreed in the FTA. Using the CGE modeling framework of the Global Trade Analysis Project (GTAP) database, several simulations are undertaken, involving different scenarios of India's trade liberalization with the ASEAN region.

The results of the simulations reveal that post-FTA, India's exports to ASEAN increase substantially, with the largest accesses gained in Thailand, Cambodia, Vietnam, Malaysia, the Philippines and the Lao PDR. The main sources of imports are Vietnam, followed by the rest of ASEAN, the Philippines, Malaysia, Singapore and Thailand. However, India experiences a welfare loss due to both allocative inefficiency and negative terms of trade effect. India's allocative efficiency increases as countries move towards greater tariff liberalization, but the terms of trade effect continue to worsen and remain negative. This is arrested once the gain in allocative efficiency is used to improve productivity in the export-oriented sectors as well as achieve economies of scale. In the ASEAN region, Malaysia, Singapore and Thailand show positive welfare gains with the largest gain accruing to Singapore. The smaller countries all enjoy positive welfare gains except Cambodia, the Lao PDR and the Philippines. This welfare gain by ASEAN countries is primarily due to their improved terms of trade.

Mondal *et al.* (2012) did a quantitative assessment of the impact of AIFTA for dairy commodities in India. Using a SMART model to run simulations this study suggested that AIFTA will provide an additional scope for increasing dairy exports from India to ASEAN countries, while it will provide very less scope to the ASEAN countries for increasing their shares. Chandran and Sudarsan (2012) used simple revealed comparative advantage indices to assess the likely impact of AIFTA on India's fish trade by identifying the complementarity and competing product categories. The results of the simulation show that tariff reduction results in trade creation, improves welfare and reduces tariff revenue to some extent. However,

AIFTA may not lead to large import of marine products, and, hence, may not adversely affect the Indian fishermen.

It is important to note that each of these studies focussed on different aspects of AIFTA to analyse its impact on India and ASEAN nations. While some used the tariff schedule as agreed by India and ASEAN members to analysis the impact on the partner countries trade variables, others used simulation models to understand the impact of the final tariff commitments of the countries on the bilateral trade flow. Still others studied the impact of AIFTA on select products only as also on the overall economy and its welfare. However, so far there are limited attempts to analyse the impact of the phased tariff liberalizations by the countries on the trade and related variables for the Indian economy, particularly when the FTA has already been implemented by India and the three big ASEAN member countries. The present study seeks to fulfil this gap by using a general equilibrium methodology that will help to assess in detail the possible impact of this trade agreement on the trade and related variables exclusively for the Indian economy. Most importantly, it considers the current status of AIFTA, assesses its impact on India's trade and related variables and then goes on further to observe its likely impact when the implementation of the FTA is completed by all the partner countries. It also analyses the impact of reduction of trade cost on overall welfare gain and endowment.

Methodology

It is three years into the FTA and India, Malaysia, Singapore and Thailand have completed the tariff liberalization with respect to the products in their Normal Track1. To assess the impact of this tariff liberalization on the two-way trade between India and these countries, the total trade that has been taking place between India and each of these ASEAN members since 2006 is tracked (Figure 2).

ASEAN-India FTA has eventually created new trade opportunities. At the same time, firms taking shelters under protections still exist. While some firms are enjoying new market access, some are unable to compete due to barriers. Large firms can manage the business much faster than SMEs. An FTA should bring an inclusive development in the economy over time.

Figure 2

(Unit: US$ million)

(a): India's Trade with Brunei

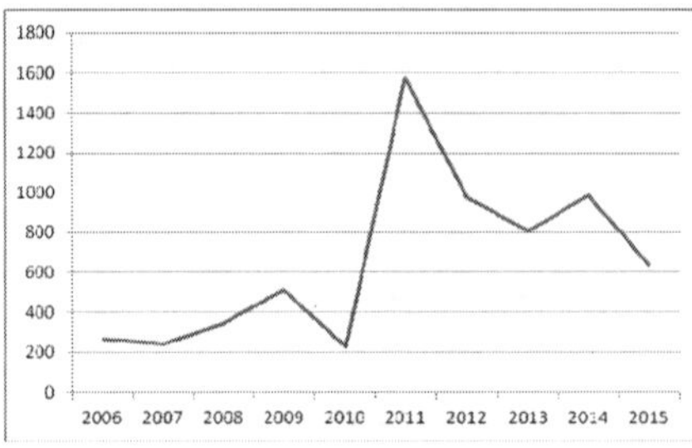

(b): India's Trade with Cambodia

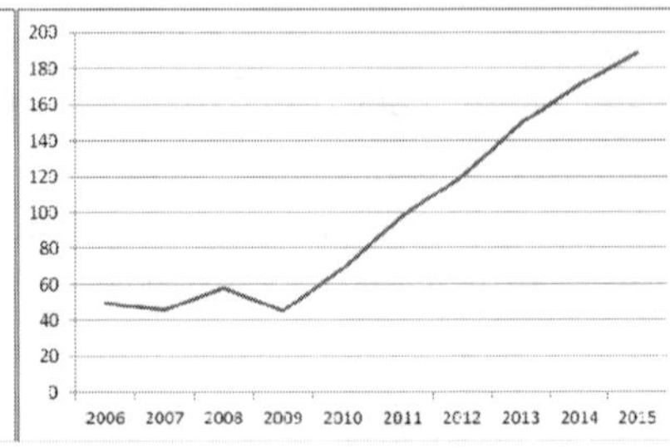

(c): India's Trade with Indonesia

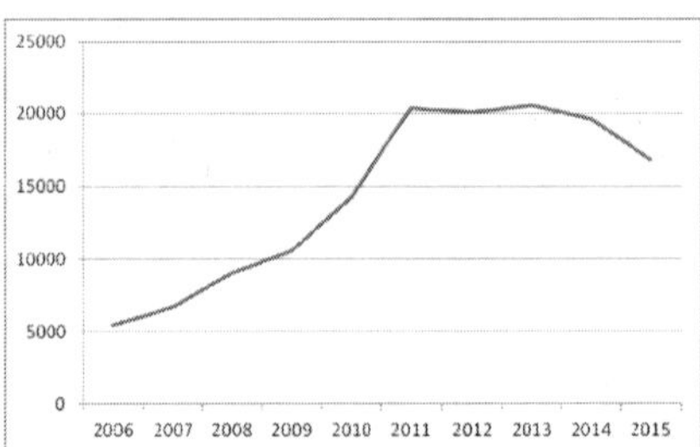

(d): India's Trade with Lao PDR

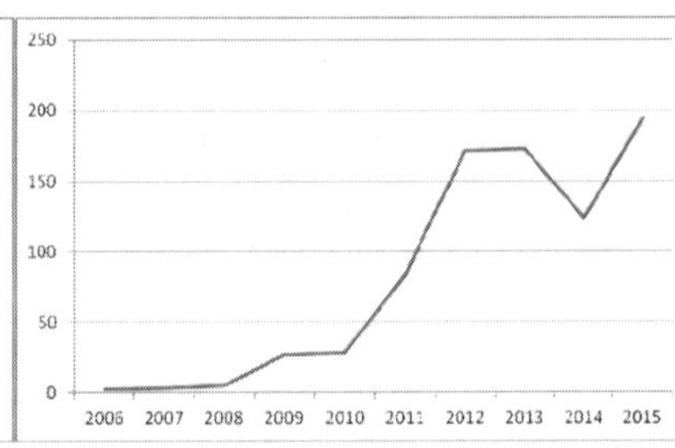

(e): India's Trade with Philippines

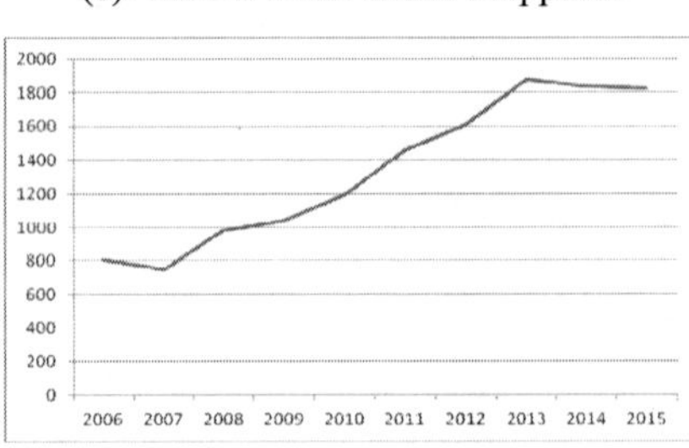

(f): India's Trade with Malaysia

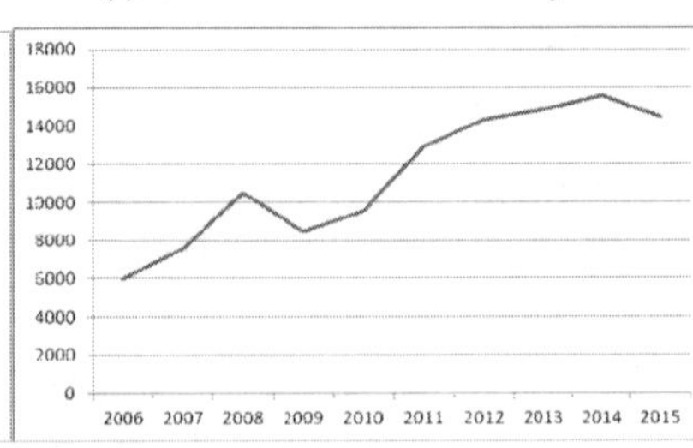

(g): India's Trade with Myanmar

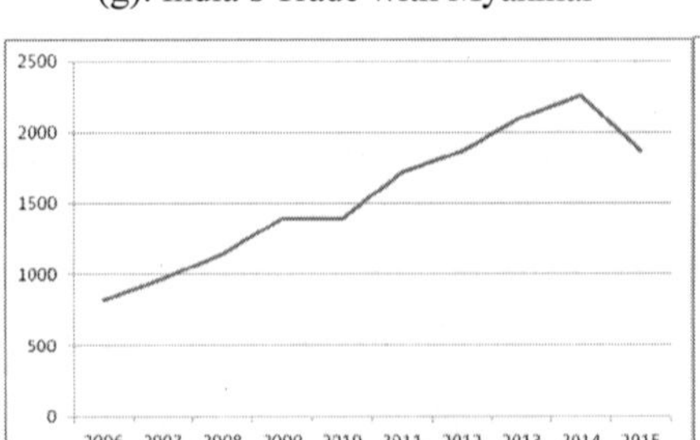

(h): India's Trade with Singapore

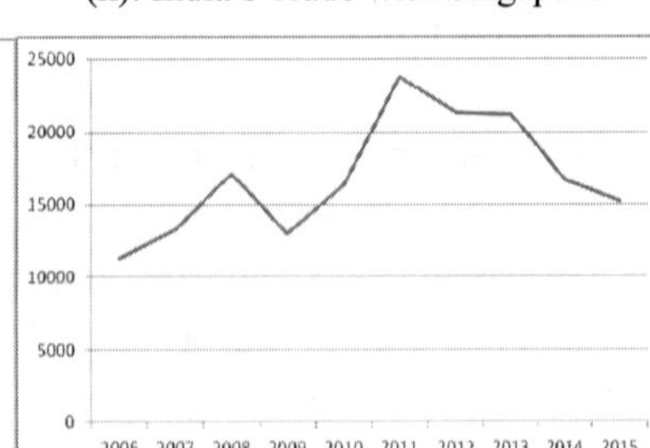

(i): India's Trade with Thailand

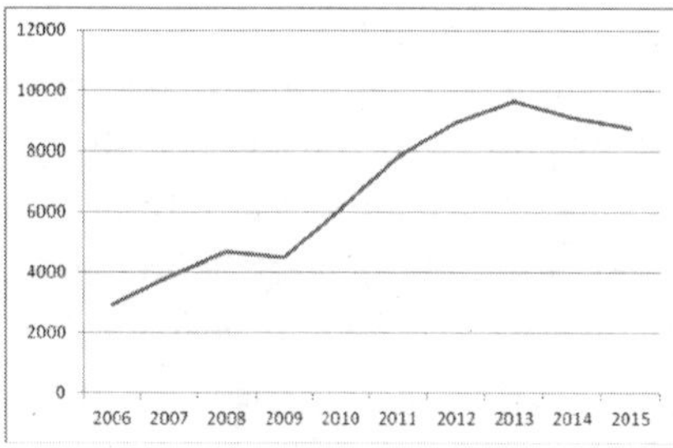

(j): India's Trade with Vietnam

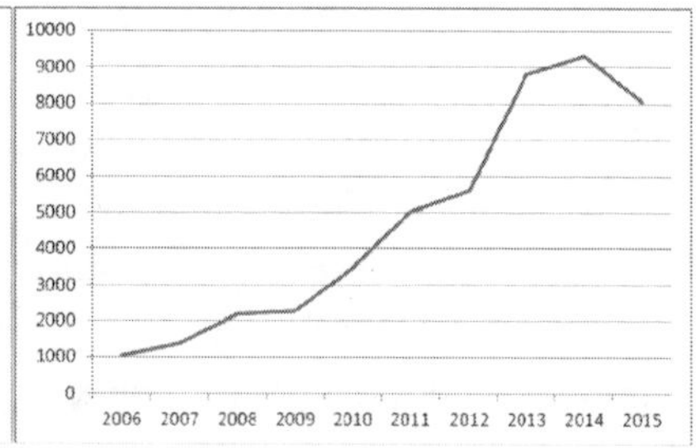

Source: Drawn based on UNCOMTRADE

As observed in Figure 2, the two-way trade between India and the ten ASEAN members increased steeply from or uniformly through 2009 to 2012, and then decreased from 2013 to 2015. Thus, it indicates that the increase in this bilateral trade is not specially limited to the countries in the ASEAN region, which have implemented the AIFTA. Hence, to understand if the FTA implementation explained the variation in this two-way trade a regression exercise is done, where the two-way trade between India and the ASEAN countries is regressed on two dummy variables – first, for countries which have implemented the FTA in the year 2010, and, a dummy variable for years greater than 2009. After this, the study proceeds for a further in-depth analysis of the trade impact of the AIFTA on its partners.

A complete analysis of trade and trade related issues require an analytical framework, which takes into account a holistic view of the economies across the world. This is because there are not only inter-linkages present between various sectors of an economy but also sectors in an economy are linked to rest of the world by the way of exports, imports of final products, intermediate goods, capital goods and so on. Thus, linkages are present at the national, regional and also at the global level both in product as well as in the input markets. The present study makes an attempt to integrate these linkages considering the Global Trade Analysis Project (GTAP) as the analytical tool. The computable general equilibrium (CGE) modelling framework of the GTAP is one of the best possible ways to analyze *ex ante* the economic consequences and trade implications of multilateral and bilateral trade agreements.

General equilibrium refers to the study of models that determine simultaneous equilibrium in more than one market. CGE models help to covert these theoretical general equilibrium models into practical tools for analysing policies. The optimizing behaviour of economic agents is explicitly built into the CGE models through the utility maximization conditions underlying the expenditure function and the profit maximization conditions underlying the production and cost functions. The conditions underlying the GDP and expenditure functions reflect the constraints applicable throughout the economy. The CGE modelling framework also explicitly captures the relationship between the various sectors of the economies. The demand and supply in each market is a function of relative price vector. To this basic CGE framework, the applied models often add many complexities to capture the features of the real world economies.

The following section provides a brief overview of the particular CGE model used in this study – the GTAP model

GTAP Model

Global Trade analysis Project (GTAP) is a multi-regional applied general equilibrium model which captures the economic activity across the world in 57 different sectors of 129 regions (Version 8 of GTAP data base). The system of equations underlying the GTAP model consists of two different types of equations. One set comprises of the accounting relationships which balances the receipts and expenditures of every agent in the economy. The other set comprises of the behavioural equations which is based on microeconomic theory and describes the behaviour of optimizing agents in the economy like demand function, supply function etc.

To understand the basic GTAP model framework, this section represents a graphical illustration (Figure 3) which explains the basic concept of GTAP by focusing on the accounting relationships involved in the model (Brockmeier, 2001).

An economy comprises of four economic agents:

i. Regional Household
ii. Producer
iii. Government
iv. the Rest of World

To understand the interactions between these four economic agents and the underlying accounting relationships between them, we look at the economy both from the demand side as well as the supply side.

Accounting Relations on the Demand Side

Each country or composite region as considered in the GTAP database consists of a regional household. This regional household earns all the income generated within the domestic economy, which is then spent on three forms of final demand: Private household expenditure (PRIVEXP), Government Expenditure (GOVEXP) and savings (SAVE). This expenditure is done on the basis of a Cobb-Douglas per capita utility function and any increase in regional income leads (roughly) to an equi proportional change in each of these expenditures.

The producers' hire endowment commodities from the regional household for production and hence pay the regional household the Value of Output at agents price (VOA). This VOA makes up the regional income. The regional household on the other hand, supply endowment commodities to the producer's in exchange for this payment/income received from the producers. Figure 3 does not show the flow of these endowment commodities as well as the flow of other commodities for the sake of clear presentation.

The private consumption expenditure by households represents the first component of final demand in the economy. This is referred to as Value of Domestic Private household purchases, evaluated at Agent's price (VDPA). The constrained optimizing behaviour of the private consumers is represented by a CDE (Constant difference of Elasticity) implicit expenditure function.

The second component of final demand are government purchases of consumption goods from firms which are denoted as Value of Domestic Government purchases, evaluated as Agent's prices (VDGA). A Cobb Douglas sub-utility function which represents the behaviour of government spending shows the government expenditure shares are constant across all commodities.

Savings is the third component of final demand, which as shown in Figure 3 is completely exhausted on investment (NETINV). Thus, demand for investment is savings driven.

Accounting Relations on Production Side of the Economy

The producers receive payments for selling consumption goods to private households (VDPA) and government (VDGA), intermediate inputs to other producers (Value of Domestic Firm Purchases, evaluated at Agents' prices, VDFA) and investment goods to the savings sector (NETINV). Under the zero profit assumption employed in GTAP, these revenues must be exhausted on spending for intermediate inputs (VDFA) and primary factors of production (VOA).

The nested production technology in GTAP shows constant returns to scale and every sector produces a single output. The profit maximizing firms decide on their optimal mix of primary factors independently of prices of intermediate inputs. Thus, the elasticity of substitution between any individual primary factor and different intermediate inputs is taken to be equal. This technology is even simplified by considering the Constant Elasticity of Substitution (CES) functional form in the aggregation of primary factors, as well as in the combination of value-added and intermediate inputs in order to produce output.

Accounting Relations with Policy Intervention

Further, to the demand and supply activities in an economy, every economy also includes government/policy interventions. This results in additional value flows. These are denoted as Taxes in Figure 3. These value flows include both taxes (TAXES) and subsidies and as such they denote net tax revenues.

Now the private households and the government do not only spend their income on consumption of goods, but also pay taxes to the regional household. Taxes paid by the government consist of consumption taxes on commodities. Taxes paid by the private household cover consumption taxes as well as income tax net of subsidies.

Producers, besides buying intermediate inputs and primary factors, also pay taxes to the regional household on account of taxes on intermediate inputs and production taxes net of subsidies.

In GTAP, tax revenues and subsidy expenditures are calculated by comparing the value of a given transaction at agents' and at market price. In case there is a difference between the two values, then this difference is equal to the tax or subsidy. In case of tax (subsidy) on demand side, agents' price is higher (lower) than market price. In case the tax (subsidy) is on the supply side, the relation between agents' price and market price is just the opposite

Accounting Relations in an Open Economy

The inclusion of Rest of the World in the framework represents a multi-region open economy. The new accounting relations that come in to the framework that has been developed so long are:

For Producers

On the production side, firms now earn additional revenues by selling commodities to the Rest of the World. These exports are denoted by VXMD. On the other side, the producers now also import intermediate inputs. This expenditure on imported inputs is denoted by VIFA. The firms also have to pay an additional consumption tax on imported inputs to the regional household. This tax is included in the Taxes flowing from the producer to the regional household.

The GTAP model employs the so-called Armington assumption and hence distinguishes imports by their origin. Thus, imported commodities are assumed to be separable from domestically produced goods and hence are combined in an additional nest in the production tree. The elasticity of substitution in this input nest is equal across all uses. Hence, the firms decide first on sourcing of the imports and based on the resulting composite import price, then work out their the optimal mix of imported and domestic goods

For Government and Private Households

Now, the government and private households spend their income both on domestically produced as also on imported commodities which are denoted as VIPA and VIGA, respectively. Both these agents also have to pay additional commodity taxes on imports to the regional household.

GTAP model includes conditional demand equations for commodities imported by government and private households. Imported commodities and domestically produced commodities are combined in a composite nest for both private household and government expenditures, respectively. The elasticity of substitution between imported and domestically produced goods in this composite nest of the utility tree is assumed to be equal across uses. Thus, firms and households import demand equations differ only in their import shares.

For Savings

In multi-region version of the GTAP model, savings (Global Savings) and investment are computed on a global basis, so that all savers in the model get a common price for this savings commodity. This implies that if all other markets are in equilibrium, all firms earn zero profits, and all households satisfy their budget constraint, then global investment must equal global savings and this Walras' Law is satisfied.

For Rest of the World

The Rest of the World receives payments for selling their goods to private households, government and firms. These revenues are spent on commodities exported from the single region to the Rest of the World, which is denoted as VXMD, and on import taxes, MTAX, and export taxes, XTAX paid to the regional household.

Using this GTAP modelling framework the present study seeks to estimate the impact of the India-ASEAN trade liberalization on important trade variables and trade related issues of the partner economies with special focus on India.

Figure 3: A Graphical Exposition of the GTAP Model

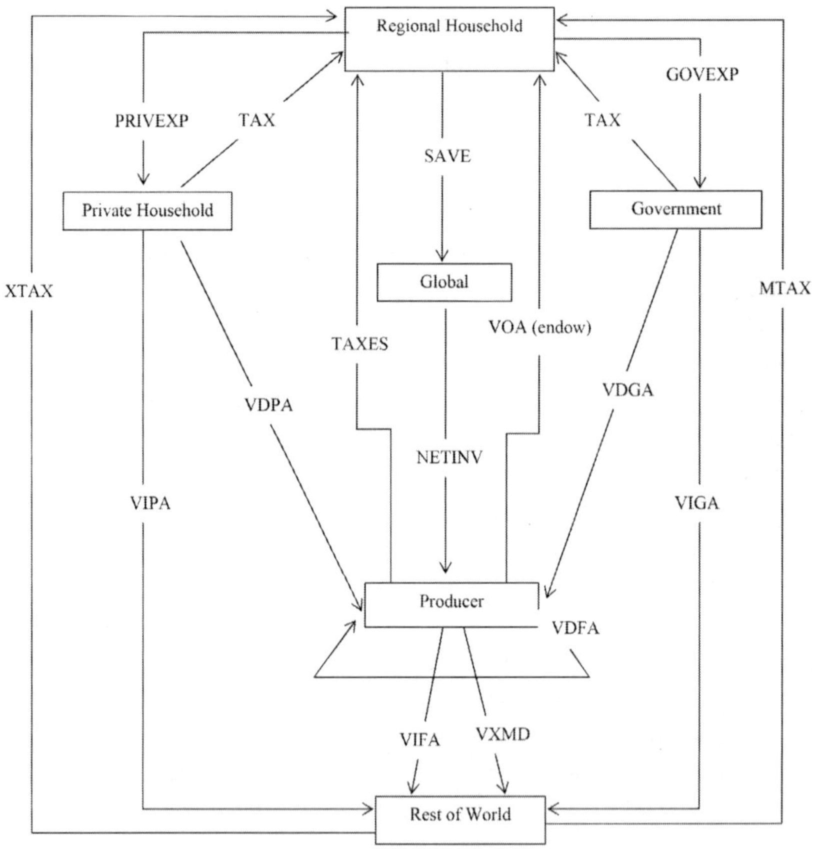

Source: Brockmeier (2001)

Closure in GTAP Model

One of the fundamental ways that a CGE model differs from the models of neoclassical general equilibrium models is that the exogenous variables of the model need to be selected at the outset. This is referred to as the closure. Simulations in most CGE models involve examining comparative static results i.e, most models consider the impact that changes in exogenous parameters (shocks) have on allocation of goods among consumers and resources among productive activities and also the consequences for economic efficiency. The models compare alternative equilibrium states without considering the path between the two states. Thus, the models do not have explicit time dimension. They represent different time frames by changing the microeconomic elements of the closure. The results of static simulations are often interpreted as representing how the economic system under study would look if the new policy had been in place in the base year, after relevant adjustments had taken place (Gilbert, 2001).

In this study, we adopt a microeconomic closure different from the standard closure defined by the CGE framework of the GTAP database. A standard GTAP closure considers full employment. This is a neoclassical approach whereby the endowments of the productive factors are fixed allowing the market prices to adjust so as to maintain full employment. But full employment is far from true in the real world, particularly for unskilled labour force and that too for developing countries. Thus, the simulations conducted in this paper replace this assumption of full employment with existence of unemployment for unskilled labour force in India as well as in all the ASEAN members. This is done by swapping the fixed endowment of unskilled labour in all of India and the ASEAN members with fixed real wage of unskilled labour. Thus, the endowment of unskilled labour which is otherwise fixed in a standard GTAP closure with the market prices adjusting so as to maintain full employment is now replaced with fixed real wage. Thus, market prices of unskilled labour no longer adjust to ensure full employment, but instead capture the unemployment with respect to unskilled labour in each of the economies.

Data

The database used here is the latest version 8 of the GTAP database, which has 2007 as the base year. This has been updated to reflect the world economy in 2010. The database is compiled for bilateral exports and imports and tariffs inclusive of other flows for 129 regions across the world and for 57 tradable commodities of the world. The present study does various simulations using this database, and accordingly, the 129 regions of the database is aggregated into 23 regions. Similarly, the 57 sectors have been aggregated into 36 sectors for all the simulations conducted (see Appendix 1 for details). The detailed schedule of tariff commitments of each of the member countries of the AIFTA is available. But, the commitments are not corresponding to product categories. They are corresponding to specific tariff lines at eight digit tariff classification of HS code. The tariff lines under same product category are often found to belong to different tracks. After having scrutinized the schedules for each country various categories of tariff commitments have been worked out for different commodities (as aggregated in GTAP) and then they have been converted into the 36 product categories (Appendix 1).

To capture the status of AIFTA at its various phases of liberalization by the different partner countries, the study does three simulations. They include situations as follows:

- **Scenario I**: Partial liberalization (tariff elimination for products in normal track, tariff reductions for the sensitive track products and no change in tariffs for products in the exclusion list) involving India and the three ASEAN members of Malaysia, Singapore and Thailand – a scenario which represents the status of the FTA after December 31, 2013.
- **Scenario II**: Partial liberalization (tariff elimination for products in normal track, tariff reductions for the sensitive track products and no change in tariffs for products in the exclusion list) involving all ASEAN members - a scenario which represents the status of the FTA as in December 31, 2021. This simulation is done in two stages – First a scenario of partial liberalization is simulated involving India and the three ASEAN members of Malaysia, Singapore and Thailand. This is a situation representing the status of AIFTA as on December 31, 2013 (this refers to the preceding scenario I). Then using this scenario I as the base/initial situation a further simulation is done whereby all other ASEAN members eliminate tariff on all normal track products, reduce tariff on their sensitive track products while keeping the tariffs on their exclusion list as before.

- **Scenario III**: Full liberalization (100 per cent tariff reduction from either side for all goods traded) involving all ten ASEAN members and India – a likely situation when eventually all tariff barriers between India and the ASEAN region are removed. This is done by starting with the GTAP scenario which represents the status of the AIFTA as in end of December 2021 and then reducing all the tariffs on the bilateral trade between India and each of these ten countries to zero.

Results: Impact of AIFTA on Total Trade Flows between India and ASEAN

Regression Exercise for Assessing if AIFTA Implementation Led to Rising Trade Flows between India and ASEAN

The results of the regression exercise which was done to assess if the AIFTA implemented by select countries did result in boosting the trade flows between the regions, show that that the FTA implementation was not an important reason explaining the variation in the two way trade between India and the region. The trade in general have been greater in years after 2009 irrespective of if the countries have implemented the AIFTA or not (Table 5).

Table 5: Results of the Regression Exercise to Determine the Impact of AIFTA Implementation on Total Bilateral Trade between India and ASEAN

Independent Variables	Coefficients
FTA implementation 2010	0.52 (.34)
Years >2009	1.15 (.187)*
Observations:	
Cross section	10
Total panel	80
F	21.13*
R^2	0.35

*Significant at 5 per cent level of significance. Standard errors are in parenthesis. Estimation is Random panel.

Thus, the statistical exercise at the outset does not indicate any notable change in the trade flow that AIFTA may have brought about. Thus to have a deeper understanding, the results of the simulations done using GTAP database are analysed.

Analysis of Results of the CGE Model using GTAP Database

Impact on Trade

Tariff liberalization under AIFTA proceeds in phases and accordingly this study looks at the impact of the FTA on trade variables of the partner countries, India in particular, at some of the crucial phases of the agreement. It first looks at the impact on the value of two way trade as it would be at the end of 2013, when India, Malaysia, Singapore and Thailand completes the tariff liberalization of normal track products. Then a scenario is simulated (taking end of 2013 as a base period) whereby all ASEAN countries eliminate tariffs on all normal track products and reduce tariff as per commitments on sensitive track products. The tariffs on products in the exclusion list continue to remain the same. This represents the situation expected to prevail by December 31, 2021. Additionally, a scenario of full tariff liberalization of all members are considered which considers elimination of all tariffs even for products on sensitive and elimination list to assess the additional gains/ losses that the partner countries are likely to have should they consider removal or pruning of their respective exclusion lists.

Two-way Trade in the Different Scenarios

The simulation results show that when initially only the bigger countries of the ASEAN region do the liberalization, India's two-way trade with the region increases by 37 per cent. When all other ASEAN countries complete the tariff liberalization in 2021 as per their commitments, there is a further but a much smaller increase of 12 per cent in this two-way trade. However, if the ASEAN members as also India consider downsizing their exclusion list, there could be substantial additional trade gains. In the ultimate if the exclusion lists are removed completely, the two way trade would jump by another 17.2 per cent from where it stands in December 2021. Figure 4 shows the value increase in these trade figures in the different liberalization scenarios.

Figure 4
Two-way Trade (US$ million) between India and ASEAN in Different Liberalization Scenarios

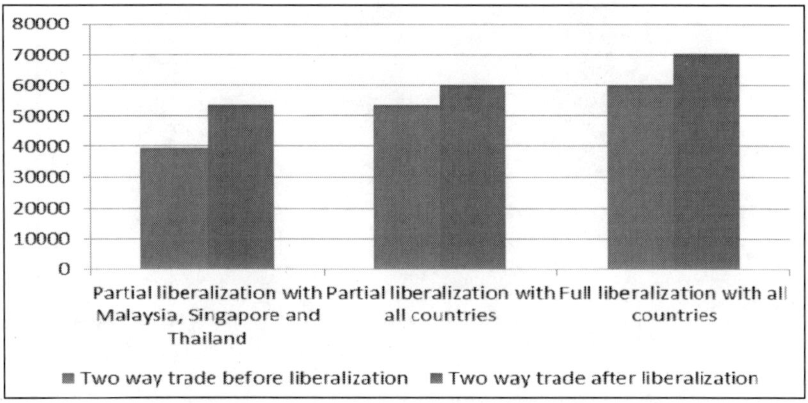

Source: Based on results from different simulation

Exports (US$ million) from India to ASEAN in Different Liberalization Scenarios

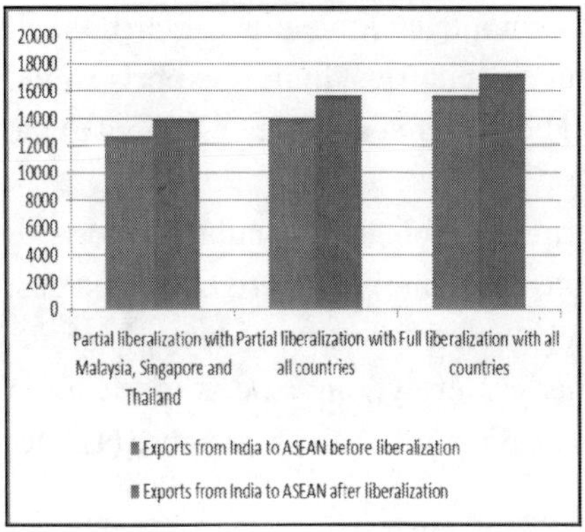

Imports (US$ million) into India from ASEAN in Different Liberalization Scenarios

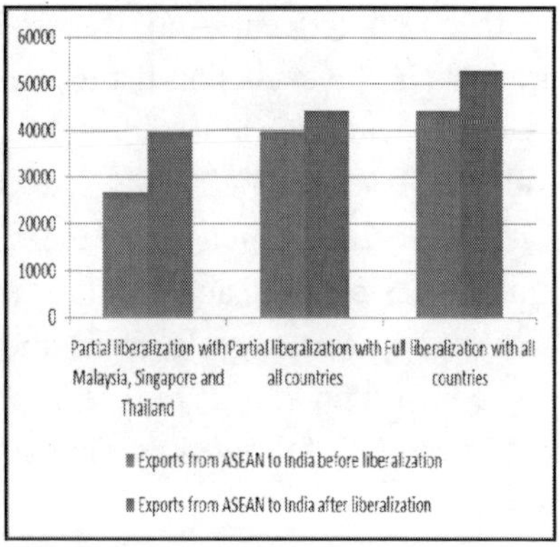

Source: Based on results from different simulation

India's Trade Balance (US$ million) with the ASEAN in Different Liberalization Scenarios

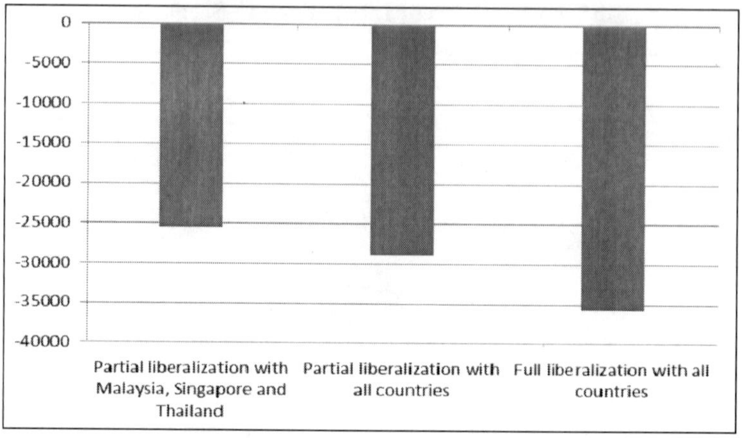

Source: Based on results from different simulation

India's Exports to the ASEAN Region under Different Scenarios

In the scenario of partial liberalization involving Malaysia, Singapore and Thailand, India's exports to the region show a small increase of 11 per cent while imports show a massive jump of 49 per cent. When the remaining seven members of the ASEAN region also complete their committed levels of tariff liberalization, then India's exports to the region would increase by another 11 per cent while imports from the region are likely to go up by another 12.5 per cent. And, if there is a complete elimination of tariff on all products in the exclusion list of the eleven countries, India's exports would be 11 per cent more and imports would be 19 per cent more compared to the end 2021 level.

The sectors which show the maximum increase in India's exports to Malaysia, Singapore and Thailand in scenario I are: other crops, oil and gas, textiles, apparels, cereals, fruits and vegetables, forestry products, oilseeds, vegetable oil and fat. It registers the highest growth in exports to Malaysia (32.5 per cent), followed by Thailand (25.4 per cent) and Singapore (1.9 per cent).

Table 6: Main Products in which Indian Exports to and Imports from ASEAN Increase with Partial Tariff Liberalization by Malaysia, Singapore and Thailand

Importing Countries	Liberalization involving Malaysia, Singapore, Thailand as in 2013	Liberalization involving entire ASEAN region and India as in 2021	Full liberalization involving ASEAN region and India (all tariffs eliminated)*
Malaysia	Other crops (-22.2), Oil and gas (-0.4), Textiles (-4.3), Apparels (-1.9), Cereals (-4.2), Dairy products (-1.2)	Coal (-3.7), Other crops (-0.28), Textile (-0.21), Paddy (-0.07), Leather (-0.19	Beverage and tobacco (-82.5), Paddy (-29.8), Motor vehicles (-15.6), Ferrous metal (-14.8), Apparels (-11.1)
Singapore	Wood (-0.2), Oil and gas (-0.4), Forestry products (-0.3), Metals other than ferrous metals (-0.2), Paper (-0.3) and Chemicals (-0.44)	Coal (-4.1), Other crops (-0.27), Textile (-0.21), Leather (-0.19), Animal products (-0.12)	Vegetable oil and fat (-5.8), Oilseeds (-6.5), Paddy (-1.8), Animal products (-2.5), Milk (-2.3)
Thailand	Apparels (-21.9), Vegetable oil and fat (-7.6), Fruits and vegetable (-28), Oilseeds (-22) and Forestry products (-15.4)	Coal (-3.9), Other crops (-0.28), Forestry (-0.02), Oil & gas (-0.05), Textile (-0.21),	Meat products (-18.8), Motor vehicles (-21.2), Apparels (-15.6), Beverage and tobacco (-33.7)
Cambodia	-	Apparels (-25.98), Machinery (-14.2), Electronics (-14.4), Leather (-10.4), Beverage and tobacco (-25.5)	Wheat (-5.7), Vegetable oil and fat (-6.3), Transport equipment (-5.02),Oilseeds (-7.2), Apparels (-4.7)
Indonesia	-	Motor vehicles (-21.3), Manufacturing (-8.05), Machinery (-7.5), Meat products (-4.9), Wood (-5.3),	Paddy (-15.9), Sugar (-19.6), Apparels (-13.2), Oilseeds (-6.5), Vegetable oil and fat (-5.9)

Lao PDR	-	Crops (other) (-27.5), Food products (-19.3), Leather (-9.5), Textile (-9.3), Transport equipment (-7.5)	Vegetable oil and fat (-6.4), Leather (-5.4), Transport equipment (-5.02), Oilseeds (-7.2), Other manufacturing (-5.)
Philippines	-	Transport equipment (-14.5), Apparels (-13.1), Wood (-10), Textiles (-8.02), Oilseeds (-10.7)	Sugar (-29.98), Paddy (-21.3), Motor vehicles (-20.7), Fruits & vegetables (-16.8), Vegetable oil and fat (-8.7)
Vietnam	-	Apparels (-27.9), Textile (-19.8), Oil and gas (-10.5), Wood (-18.9), Transport equipment (-9.3),	Motor vehicles (-21.4), Beverage & tobacco (-44.1), Sugar (-17.5), Paper (-13.3) Petroleum & coal products (-14.6)
Rest of ASEAN	-	Wood (-11.7), Coal (-8.2), Forestry (-9.3), Leather (-7.1), Textiles (-5.7)	Vegetable oil and fat (-7.9), Oil & gas (-4.6), Beverage and tobacco (-22.9), Paddy (-1.8), Oilseeds (-6.5)
India	From Malaysia: Transport equipment (-12.5), metals (-12.8), food products (-27.7), meat products (-23), leather (-12.4) From Singapore: Metals (-12.8), oil and gas (-8.8), other manufacturing (-12.7), meat products (-23.0), forestry products (-20.8)	From Malaysia: fall in imports of all products imported in scenario I. Singapore: fall in imports of all products imported in scenario I. From Thailand: fall in imports of all products imported in scenario I. From Cambodia: Apparels (-13.1), Manufacturing (-12.2), Machinery (-10.9), Crops (-23.4), Textiles (-7.0)	From Malaysia: Sugar (-49.6), Dairy product (-35.2), Fruits and vegetable (-42.1), Beverage & tobacco (-47.3), Vegetable oil and fat (-48.9), From Singapore: Motor vehicles (-48.8), Sugar (-41.1), Dairy products (-25.4), Beverage and tobacco (-46.6), Fruits & vegetable (-22.8) From Thailand: Paddy (-44.3), Sugar (-49.6), Dairy product (-30.6), Cereals (-41.3), Vegetable oil & fat (-49.3),

	From Thailand: meat products (-31.1), food products (-33.6), crops (other) (-16.4), leather (-11.8), apparels (-12.8), ferrous metals (-15.7), forestry products (-19.0)	From Indonesia: Crops (-28.5), Food (-12.5), Other metals (-15.8), Chemicals (-12.7), Forestry (-20.3) From Lao PDR: Electronics (-13.0), Forestry (-22.2), Chemicals (-13), Machinery (-7.4), Other crops (-18.3) From Philippines: Food products (-28.9), Transport equipment (-12.8), Other metals (-12.95), Machinery (-13), Forestry (-20.7) From Vietnam: Other crops (-39.5), Electronics (-12.4), Food (-25.7), Other metals (-12.8), Leather (-12.8)	From Cambodia: Vegetable oil & fat (-49.9), Oilseeds (-22.7), Textiles (-6.5) From Indonesia: Dairy products (-24.4), Vegetable oil and fat (-48.4), Beverage & tobacco (-35.7), Fruits & vegetable (-25.3), Fish (-22.3) From Lao PDR: Fruits & vegetable (-50), Textiles (-6.5) From Philippines: Vegetable oil & fat (-50), Beverage & tobacco (-25.6), Fish (-22.6), Motor vehicles (-13.1), Petroleum & coal products (-12.8)
		From Rest of ASEAN: Meat products (-24.8), Other manufacturing (-15.1), Oil & gas (-8.2), Chemicals (-16.4), Other metals (-12.6)	From Vietnam: Cereals (other) (-40.9), Oilseeds (-31.7), Vegetable oil & fat (-48), Fruits & vegetable (-23.5), Beverage & tobacco (-29.4) From Rest of ASEAN: Wheat (-47.2), Sugar (-39.2), Dairy (-24.4), Beverage & tobacco (-45.7), Cereals (other) (-40.9)

Note: *These are in addition to the other products that the countries are importing largely in the other two scenarios Figures in brackets show the percentage change in market prices of imported goods in the importing country. A minus sign denotes a reduction in price
Source: Based on simulation results

When the other ASEAN members implement the AIFTA and complete the tariff liberalization as per their commitments, the export basket continues to have more of the same goods as in the case of liberalization involving Malaysia, Singapore and Thailand only, but some other sectors too show significant export growth. These are leather, machinery, electronics, motor vehicles, wood, beverage and tobacco, meat products, food products, transport equipment, other manufacturing, coal and paddy. These goods are exported to the new smaller members who join in the tariff liberalization now. Thus, with entire ASEAN region implementing the FTA, India's export basket comprises more of manufacturing products (Table 6) as compared to the earlier scenario where it was mostly enjoying higher exports of primary products. The interesting feature to note is that post the joining of these seven members, most of the Indian goods which earlier had shown increase in exports to Malaysia, Singapore and Thailand actually get diverted to these smaller members thereby showing marginal increase in India's exports to these three bigger countries now. Lao PDR and the Philippines emerge as the most important markets for Indian products, followed by Cambodia, Vietnam and Rest of ASEAN.

In the full liberalization scenario, obviously the products which are mostly reserved in the exclusion list of the ASEAN members show tremendous increase in exports. These are vegetable oil and fat, oilseeds, paddy, beverages and tobacco, motor vehicles, sugar, fruits & vegetables, petroleum and coal products. The largest increase of Indian exports is recorded in Indonesia (18 per cent) and Malaysia (17.8 per cent), followed by the Philippines (12 per cent), Vietnam (10.3 per cent) and Thailand (10.2 per cent).

India's Imports from ASEAN under Different Scenarios

For imports into India in scenario I, Malaysia turns out to be the largest source, as imports from Malaysia increase by 103 per cent, followed by Thailand (88 per cent) and Singapore (40 per cent). The sectors registering largest imports into India from these three countries are: transport equipment, metals, food products, meat products, leather, oil and gas, other manufacturing, meat products, forestry products, crops (other), apparels and forestry products.

As the smaller ASEAN members also complete the FTA implementation on their part, the imports from Malaysia, Thailand and Singapore continues to be in the same products. But, the volumes of the imports fall from their 2013 level. In case of Malaysia, 78 per cent of products show decline in the volume of imports, while 67 per cent of the products imported from Singapore and 83 per cent of the products imported from Thailand show decline in imports. As a result, total imports from each of these three countries fall. Malaysia records a decline of 1 per cent, Singapore by 0.6 per cent and Thailand by 1.4 per cent. The smaller ASEAN countries now turn out to be bigger sources of imports for India. Vietnam emerges as the most important source of India's import from ASEAN region (172 per cent increase from 2013 level). This is followed by rest of ASEAN (90.6 per cent increase). The other important source is Indonesia (72 per cent increase) and the Philippines (34.5 per cent). Cambodia and Lao PDR in particular remain relatively less important import sources for India. The additional products in India's import basket from ASEAN region now are coal, paddy, leather, animal products, machinery, electronics, beverage and tobacco, motor vehicles, manufacturing (other), meat products, wood and wood products, food and transport equipment. Thus, with the smaller countries becoming important import sources, India now imports more of non-primary products from ASEAN region as compared to its import of more of primary products from Malaysia, Singapore and Thailand in scenario I.

In the ultimate scenario of complete tariff liberalization involving all countries, Indonesia becomes a major supplier to India recording a 65 per cent increase in goods supplied. Rest of ASEAN shows a 13 per cent increase. All other countries in the region including Malaysia, Singapore and Thailand show supply increases varying between 2.4 to 9.5 per cent. Lao PDR with an increase of 2.4 continue remain the least important source of imports for India. The additional products, which now get imported into India in large quantities from these countries are sugar, dairy products, fruits and vegetable, beverage and tobacco, paddy, oilseeds, fish, petroleum and coal products, wheat and other cereals. Almost all of these products are currently in the exclusion list of India. Interestingly, many of these products see increase in imports into India when the smaller ASEAN countries join in the tariff liberalization even though India continues to deny any tariff concession on these. But, moment India eliminates tariff on these products, these goods instead of coming into India from the smaller countries actually comes in from the bigger countries of the region. Thus, with tariff elimination of these products from the bigger countries become more competitive than the same from the smaller countries.

An additional feature to be noted about India's imports under all tariff liberalization scenarios is that most of imports are to meet input demand rather than final demand. For secondary products like metals, oil and gas, coal, other manufacturing, this share is almost 100 per cent. Only for textiles and apparels the final demand commands larger shares than producer's demand. For all primary products, consumer's share is larger in the total imports done by India.

The list of country-wise products, whose exports/import from/to India to/from the ASEAN increases the most in different scenarios, are listed in Table 6.

Change in Prices of the Traded Goods Post AIFTA Implementation

An important feature to be noted in the context of this increased trade between India and the ASEAN region in the three trade liberalization scenarios is the change in the prices of imports supplied by the ASEAN countries to India and those of the goods supplied by India to each of these ASEAN countries.

In scenario I, the prices of most goods that India sends to each of Malaysia, Singapore and Thailand falls. Around 92 per cent of goods imported from India to each of Malaysia and Thailand fall while for Singapore this falls for 83 per cent of the goods. Average reduction in prices is highest in Malaysia (5.5 per cent), followed by Thailand (4.4 per cent). In Singapore the reduction is very small (0.2 per cent). For the goods which record the highest imports to each of these countries from India, the price reductions are substantial in Malaysia and Thailand. This reduction is particularly high in Thailand, varying from 7.4 per cent to 28 per cent. The price reductions offered to Singapore continue to be very small (refer Table 6). This is because in Singapore the goods from India already enter duty free so that there is no further reduction in tariff which may bring down prices of Indian imports in Singapore. These tariff reductions on Indian imports are highest in Thailand (on an average 4.6 per cent). Malaysia offers an average tariff reduction of 2 per cent. As the ASEAN market is competitive, Indian companies need to reduce the price significantly for their market access. This is possible when India will be able to reduce the cost of production using better technology and cheaper labour.

On the other hand, only 75 per cent of goods arriving in India from Malaysia record reduction in prices. This figure is still smaller for goods from Singapore (53 per cent) and Thailand (56 per cent). However, the average price reductions on goods supplied by these countries to India are higher than the price reduction on Indian goods sold in these countries. Prices of goods from Thailand reduce the most (on an average by 10.3 per cent), followed by Malaysia (7.6 per cent) and Singapore (5.8 per cent). This is also the trend for the top imports from these countries into India. Thailand's highest reduction is as high as 33.6 per cent for food products and lowest is 11.8 per cent for leather and leather products. Malaysia offers the highest reduction of 27.7 per cent for food products and lowest of 12.4 per cent for leather. This is important to note that India being a large country offers significantly higher demand. This provides an opportunity to ASEAN members to keep their prices for many goods relatively higher. However, they will face competition from other countries as well. So, in Indian market number of goods on which the ASEAN region offers price reduction will be less for the goods imported from Southeast Asia.

Figure 5: Welfare Components for India in Different Scenarios (US$ million)

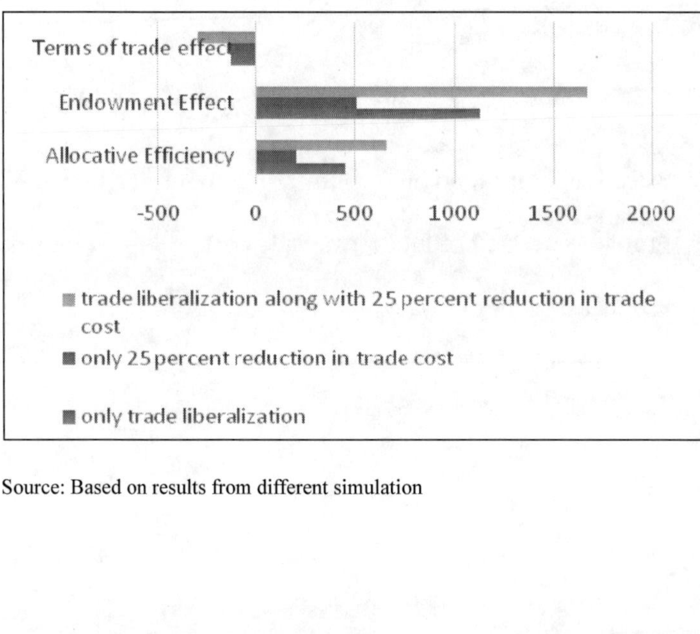

Source: Based on results from different simulation

Welfare Components for Singapore in Different Scenarios (US$ million)

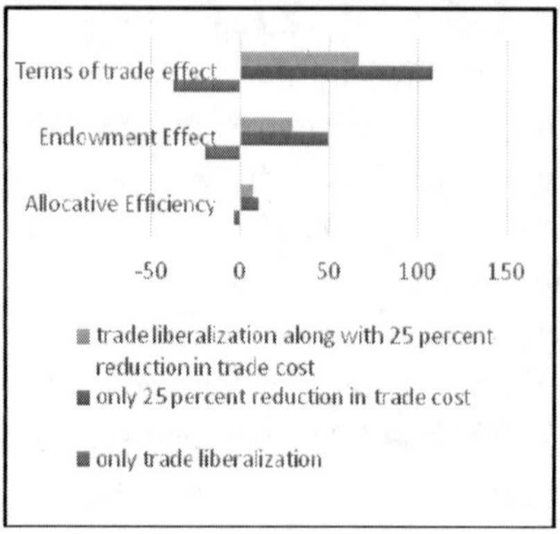

Welfare Components for Malaysia in Different Scenarios (US$ million)

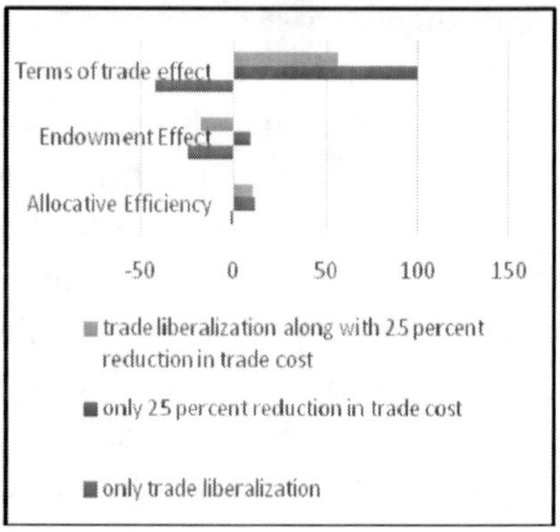

Source: Based on results from different simulation

Welfare Components for Indonesia in Different Scenarios (US$ million)

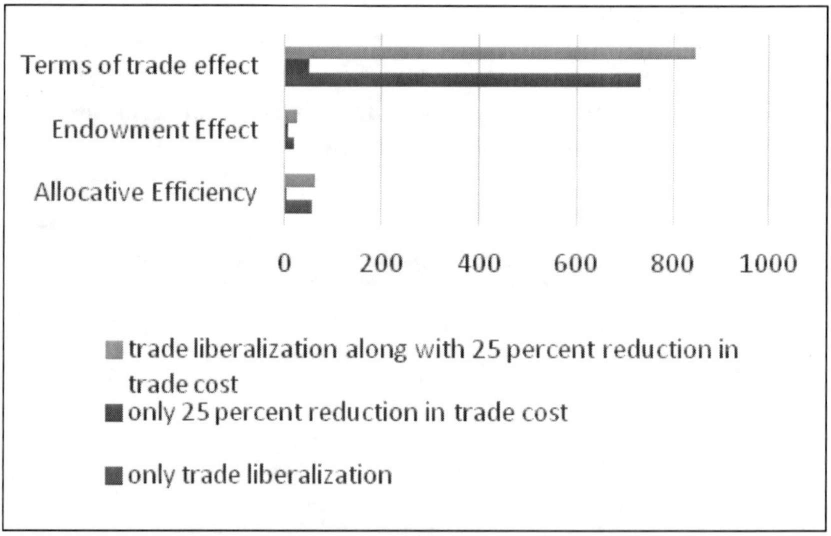

Source: Based on results from different simulation

Figure 6

Welfare Components of China, Japan and Korea in Different Scenarios (US$ million)

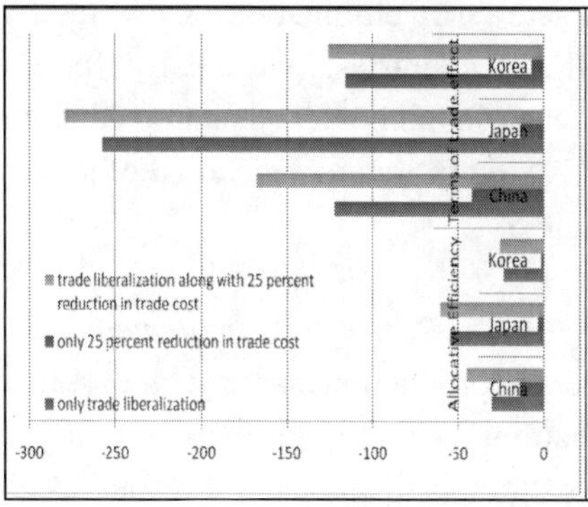

Welfare Components of Pakistan and Sri Lanka in Different Scenarios (US$ million)

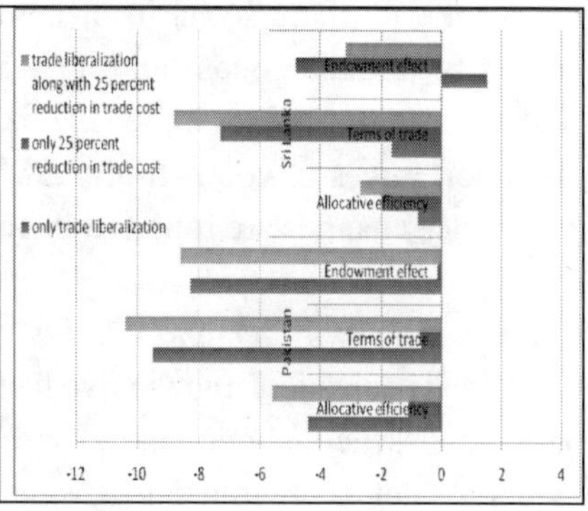

Source: Based on results from different simulation

But with all countries joining in the trade liberalization, the average reduction in prices of Indian goods is highest in Cambodia (7.2 per cent), followed by Vietnam (7 per cent), the Philippines (6.5 per cent) and Lao PDR (6.5 per cent). These price reductions are due to the tariff concessions offered to India by these countries. The largest average tariff reduction (8 per cent) is recorded in Vietnam with tariff on 26 products (out of 36 products considered in the study) reduced. Cambodia too reduces tariff on as many as 20 products and offers an average tariff cut of 5.2 per cent. The least fall in prices of Indian goods happen in Thailand (0.05 per cent) and Malaysia (0.07 per cent). Prices of Indian goods do not fall at all in Singapore. This is because these countries have completed almost all their tariff liberalizations by 2013. No additional tariff concessions are offered by these countries in this scenario. The fall in the market prices of goods in Malaysia and Thailand is due to the fall in the world price (cif) of the commodities supplied by India to these two countries.

For India's imports from each of Malaysia, Singapore and Thailand there are hardly any price reductions as India does not offer any further tariff reductions to these countries after December 2013. Among the smaller countries, imports from Indonesia, Vietnam and Rest of ASEAN is offered the maximum average tariff reductions (7.6 per cent, 7.3 per cent and 7.0 per cent, respectively). Accordingly, these are also the countries showing the maximum average price reductions of 7 per cent, 7.2 per cent and 6.5 per cent respectively. Imports from the Philippines also fall on an average by 6.4 per cent following an average tariff cut of 6.5 per cent. Goods originating in Cambodia and Lao PDR register the lowest average price reduction of 1.8 per cent each.

In the ultimate scenario of complete tariff elimination (scenario III), prices of Indian goods sold in ASEAN countries, particularly for the additional commodities traded in this scenario fall but less than the reduction in import prices of goods from ASEAN sold in India. A detailed of sector-wise price changes are reported in Table 6.

Change in Factor Demand and Factor Prices Post-AIFTA Implementation

GTAP data considers trade in five factors of production, namely, land, skilled labour, unskilled labour, capital and natural resources. Of these, the factors which do not easily transfer between sectors, land and natural resources are referred to as sluggish factors of production while skilled labour, unskilled labour and capital are termed the non-sluggish factors.

The only non-sluggish factor, the demand for which increases in all the three liberalization scenarios is unskilled labour. In scenario I, it increases by 5 per cent, in scenario II by 14.5 per cent and in scenario III it increases further by 11.7 per cent. Skilled labour demand increases in the first two scenarios by 1.96 per cent and 6.6 per cent respectively but falls in scenario III. As for capital the only time its demand increases (5.95 per cent) is in scenario II.

Generally, the demand for factors in an export intensive sector is expected to rise, while in an import competitive sector it is expected to fall. The increase in demand for the three non-sluggish factors- unskilled labour, skilled labour and capital for the top export sectors of India are reported in Table 7. The demand for these factors increases for most of them. The change in demand for a factor is made of two parts – namely, the **expansion effect,** which shows the expansion of an industry in the country, and **substitution effect,** which shows the substitution between the five factors of production in production of a particular industry. In all the three scenarios it is the expansion effect which dominates the substitution effect leading to the change in demand for a particular factor of production. Thus, in cases where the decrease in demand for a factor is observed, it is the negative expansion effect which dominates the positive substitution effect leading to a decrease in demand for the factor.

Table 7: Percentage Increase in Quantity Demanded of Non-sluggish Endowments (Unskilled Labour, Skilled Labour and Capital) in Different Liberalization Scenarios

Main export intensive sectors in different scenarios	Liberalization involving Malaysia, Singapore, Thailand as in 2013	Liberalization involving entire ASEAN region and India as in 2021	Full liberalization involving ASEAN region and India (all tariffs eliminated)
Paddy	-	0.07, 0.01, 0.01	0.88, 0.44, 0.49
Wheat	-	-	1.56, 1.12, 1.17
Cereals	0.05, 0.01, 0.01	-	-
Fruits & vegetable	-0.01, -0.04, -0.04	-	0.5, 0.03, 0.08
Oilseeds	0.22, 0.2, 0.2	0.59, 0.54, 0.53	-20.9, -21.3, -21.2
Other crops	0.6, 0.6, 0.59	-0.83, -0.89, -0.9	-
Meat & meat products	-	5.4, 5.1, 5.07	5.54, 3.5, 3.7
Milk	-	-	1.06, 0.6, 0.67
Dairy products	0.01, -0.09, -0.01	-	-
Animal products	-	0.31, 0.25, 0.24	0.43, 0.003, 0.04
Forestry product	-0.5, -0.5, -0.5	-0.3, -0.31, -0.32	-
Fishing	-	-	-
Coal	-	-3.28, -3.3, -3.3	-
Oil & gas	-0.19, -0.2, -0.2	-0.1, -0.12, -0.13	0.63, 0.28, 0.32
Minerals	-	-	-
Vegetable oil & fat	0.5, 0.4, 0.4	-	-45.9, -47, -46.8
Sugar	-	-	3.1, 1.14, 1.35
Food products	-	0.25, -0.004, -0.05	-
Beverage & tobacco	-	0.23, -0.03, -0.05	2.12, 0.16, 0.37
Textiles	0.5, 0.42, 0.41	1.09, 0.8, 0.78	-
Apparels	1.02, 0.91, 0.9	0.47, 0.18, 0.16	4.6, 2.4, 2.6
Leather	-	1.3, 1.01, 0.99	6, 3.7, 3.97
Wood	-1.5, -1.59, -1.59	0.17, -0.12, -0.15	-
Paper	-0.39, -0.5, 0.51	-	2.3, 0.09, 0.33
Petroleum & coal product	-	-	2.09, -0.11, 0.13

Chemical rubber & plastic	-0.23, -0.34, -0.35	-	-
Ferrous metals	-	-	3.2, 0.96, 1.2
Other metals	1.36, 1.24, 1.24	-	-
Non-metallic minerals	-	-	-
Machinery	-	0.5, 0.2, 0.19	2.7, 0.46, 0.7
Electronics	-	0.36, 0.06, 0.04	-
Motor vehicles	-	0.89, 0.6, 0.57	0.03, -2.13, -1.9
Transport equipment	-	1.05, 0.76, 0.73	3.09, 0.87, 1.1
Other manufacturing	-	0.40, 0.11, 0.08	2.59, 0.38, 0.61
Utility Consumption	-	-	-
Services	-	-	-

Note: (-) denote that the products do not feature among top five exports from India in the particular liberalization scenario
Source: Based on simulation results

Impact on Welfare

In GTAP modelling framework, regional household behaviour is governed by an aggregate utility function specified over per capita private household consumption, per capita government spending and per capita savings. Hence, the welfare change variable in this model, which estimates the change of utility due to any distortion is the percentage change in aggregate per capita utility for a region. It gives changes in the regional welfare due to a policy shock and is given in dollar values (US$ million). This welfare gain is decomposed into various components: allocative efficiency effect, endowment effect, terms of trade effect and investment–savings effect. In a comparative static applied general equilibrium model with population, endowment and technology being fixed, the only way to increase welfare is to reduce the excess burden arising from existing distortions. Any change in 'allocative efficiency' may be directly related to tax and/or tax changes interacting with equilibrium quantities changes. Thus, the components that result in changes in real income arising due to the policy simulation under study are – change in income due to change in endowments net of depreciation (this is normally zero in a comparative static situation), tax on output of any good, tax on use of any endowment in any industry, tax on use of intermediate input in any industry, tax on private household consumption and government consumption of any good, trade taxes (export and import) on any good, changes in regional 'terms of trade' (ToT) and changes in relative price of 'savings and investment' (Inv-Sav) (Huff and Hertel, 2000). Intuitively, it is welfare improving to increase the level of a relatively taxed activity since this involves the reallocation of a commodity or endowment from a low value use to a relatively high social marginal usage. The same is true for endowments and for goods traded. Any good that yields trade tax to the economy benefits the economy. The terms-of-trade for a region, which is defined as the ratio of export price index of the region to its import price index contributes positively to the society, if export prices post simulation rises more than import prices. Similarly, with less than full employment to begin with, an increase in demand for a factor in a given sector brings in positive contribution to the economy due to the income generation that it brings about. Saving-investment term does not contribute to welfare changes but both investment and savings appear in welfare decomposition. This is because investment sales generate income but do not enter into regional utility while savings enter regional utility, but does not generate current income.

Table 8 reports the welfare gain accruing to India and the ASEAN members in the different liberalization scenarios.

Table 8(a): Welfare Effect (US$ million) of the FTA on the Partners in Scenario I

Country	Allocative Efficiency	Endowment Effect	Terms of Trade Effect	Total Welfare
India	-0.36	518	-650	-132.7
Malaysia	119	120	856	1095
Singapore	62.1	379	720	1161
Thailand	63.8	192	333	589
Cambodia	-1.2	-1.06	-3.7	-5.96
Indonesia	-5.5	0.85	-75.5	-80.2
Lao PDR	-0.13	-0.26	-2.1	-2.5
Philippines	-1.53	-4.4	-11.4	-17.3
Vietnam	-2.23	-9.7	-13.8	-25.7
Rest of ASEAN	-1.54	-2.1	-7.23	-10.9

Source: Based on simulation results

Table 8(b): Welfare Effect (US$ million) of the FTA on the Partners in Scenario II

Country	Allocative Efficiency	Endowment Effect	Terms of Trade Effect	Total Welfare
India	455.4	1133.9	-125.8	1463.5
Malaysia	-1.7	-24.3	-41.7	-67.7
Singapore	-3.4	-19.1	-37.3	-59.8
Thailand	-17.8	-30.8	-68.0	-116.6
Cambodia	0.09	1.6	-3.3	-1.6
Indonesia	56.4	19.96	730.6	8097
Lao PDR	0.13	0.17	0.19	0.49
Philippines	8.9	15.0	-10.1	13.8
Vietnam	13.2	82.1	51.7	147
Rest of ASEAN	11.4	14.1	116.7	142.2

Source: Based on simulation results

Table 8(c): Welfare Effect (US$ million) of the FTA on the Partners in Scenario III

Country	Allocative Efficiency	Endowment Effect	Terms of Trade Effect	Total Welfare
India	4236.8	6796.1	-1809.5	9223
Malaysia	55.8	142.1	107.4	305
Singapore	19.7	40.3	136.8	196.8
Thailand	-1.05	12.8	35.05	46.8
Cambodia	-0.9	-0.9	-1.9	-3.7
Indonesia	32.9	4.3	1114.5	1152
Lao PDR	-0.04	-0.08	-0.09	-0.2
Philippines	-4.01	3.3	-8.7	-9.4
Vietnam	-2.4	17.7	41.15	56.5
Rest of ASEAN	-12.4	-30.4	121.3	78.5

Source: Based on simulation results

With tariff liberalization by India, Malaysia, Singapore and Thailand as in scenario I, all the three ASEAN countries have substantial positive welfare gains. The highest gain accruing to Singapore (US$ 1161 million) followed by Malaysia (US$ 1095 million) and Thailand (US$ 589 million). They have positive gains on account of all of improved allocative efficiency, endowment effect and better terms of trade. Thus, the ASEAN economies experience increased production and consumption which results in increased tax revenues, profits etc. The tariff liberalization also fetches endowment gains for them. But, in particular, the countries reap huge gains from improved terms trade. Thus, they enjoy relatively lower import prices from India as compared to the export prices they offer India. This is in line with the feature observed in the section discussing the change in market prices of imports supplied to a region. It has been noted that while each of Malaysia, Singapore and Thailand offers higher average price reductions to India, but the number of products imported to India from these countries whose prices fall are much lesser than the number of products on which India offers them price reductions. This results in substantial loss (US$ 650 million) to India from deteriorating terms of trade. The only gain that accrues to India from this tariff liberalization is significant endowment gain (US$ 518 million). But, with large loss in terms of trade and some loss in allocative efficiency, India registers a total welfare loss (US$ 132 million).

Table 9(a): Welfare Effect (US$ million) of the FTA with Reduced Transaction Costs on the Partners

Country	Only Trade liberalization involving all countries (Scenario II)	Reduction in total trade cost* before entering Indian market			Trade liberalization plus reduction in trade cost* before entering Indian market		
		10 per cent	20 per cent	25 per cent	10 per cent reduction in trade cost	20 per cent reduction in trade cost	25 per cent reduction in trade cost
India	1463.5	224	461	565.9	1686.6	1930.3	2040.2
Malaysia	-67.7	51	96.7	121.3	-18.6	25.4	49.2
Singapore	-59.8	64.8	131.9	167.8	1.6	67.3	102.6
Thailand	-116.6	21.8	42.2	52.5	-99.7	-81.2	-71.7
Cambodia	-1.6	-0.4	-0.7	-0.9	-2.03	-2.4	-2.7
Indonesia	809.7	24	48.3	58.8	881	918.2	934.3
Lao PDR	0.49	-0.04	-0.08	-0.1	0.5	0.5	0.46
Philippines	13.8	0.8	1.6	1.9	11.7	12.7	13.1
Vietnam	147	.99	1.9	2.4	152	155.4	156.9
Rest of ASEAN	142.2	4.9	9.97	12.4	151	159.6	163.7

*Reduction of export cost from individual ASEAN countries and import cost at the entry point of India

Source: Based on simulation results

Table 9(b): Welfare Effect (US$ million) of the FTA with Reduced Transaction Costs on Other Countries in East and South Asia

Country	Trade liberalization only involving all countries (Scenario II)	Reduction in total trade cost* before entering Indian market			Trade liberalization plus reduction in trade cost*before entering Indian market		
		10 per cent	20 per cent	25 per cent	10 per cent reduction in trade cost	20 per cent reduction in trade cost	25 per cent reduction in trade cost
Hong Kong	-22.6	-1.9	-3.8	-4.7	-24.7	-26.8	-27.9
China	-152.7	-22.2	-44	-56	-176.6	-200.3	-212.8
Japan	-312.6	-7.4	-14.3	-17.8	-323.8	-334.4	-339.8
South Korea	-139	-3.5	-6.9	-8.7	-144.1	-149.1	-151.6
Mongolia	1.12	0	0	0	1.13	1.14	0.15
Taiwan	-88.5	-1.4	-2.9	-3.7	-90.8	-93.1	-94.2
Rest of East Asia	1.11	0.02	0.01	0.01	1.15	1.16	1.17
Bangladesh	1.8	.08	0.16	0.22	1.95	2.09	2.2
Pakistan	-22.2	-0.8	-1.6	-1.98	-23	-24.2	-24.6
Sri Lanka	-0.94	-5.7	-11.6	14.1	-6.6	-12.4	-14.8
Rest of South Asia	-1.6	-2.8	-5.6	-6.8	-4.3	-7.1	-8.3

*Reduction of export cost from individual ASEAN countries and import cost at the entry point of India

Source: Based on simulation results

The welfare position reverses as the other ASEAN countries liberalize too. With tariff liberalization as in scenario II, India gains positive welfare not only on account of endowment effect, but also due to improved allocative efficiency. But, the terms of trade continues to be negative. However, now all of Malaysia, Singapore and Thailand end up with welfare loses. This is on account of all of allocative inefficiency, negative endowment effect and deteriorating terms of trade. This too is supported by the fact that in this scenario, Malaysia, Singapore and Thailand hardly experiences any price reductions for the Indian goods they import. For India, though the terms of trade continues to be negative, it improves as the smaller countries not only offer India similar price reductions as India does to them but also offer price reductions on larger number of goods than the bigger members were offering India in scenario I. For all the 36 goods taken together, India will be selling larger number of goods at a cheaper rate in ASEAN. This will be a market access strategy to survive the intense competition there. As a result of this, India's export oriented sectors will flourish leading to positive endowment effect back in the country. On the other hand, due to intense competition, domestic sectors in ASEAN members need to keep a check on the higher return to labour and capital. This indicates that endowment benefit will be smaller and in some cases the change will be negative.

For all the smaller ASEAN countries which are now actively participating in the trade bloc, welfare gain is positive excepting for Cambodia which though enjoys positive allocative efficiency and endowment effect, loses out on account of terms of trade loss. Lao PDR is the other country, which though manages to reap positive gains, has a welfare gain of only US$ 0.49 million. Indonesia has the highest welfare gain mainly due to large terms of trade gains. Vietnam and Rest of ASEAN also have substantial welfare gains. For Vietnam, this is primarily due to endowment effect while for Rest of ASEAN it is terms of trade which brings about the gain. A common feature of the welfare position of these countries is the positive allocative efficiency and endowment gains that accrue to all of them. Terms of trade are also positive except for Cambodia and the Philippines.

With the proposed full liberalization as the liberalization process intensifies, welfare becomes positive for all of India, Malaysia, Singapore and Thailand. India, in particular, will enjoy large gain owing mainly to endowment gain and also due to allocative efficiency. Its terns of trade continues to be negative and is bigger possibly due to the fact that Malaysia, Singapore and Thailand once again gets greater market access to India with the proposed complete tariff liberalization. This could also possibly explain the welfare loses to some of the smaller countries. While Cambodia's loss intensifies, the Philippines and Lao PDR which were earning small gains in scenario II now end up getting welfare loses. The welfares accruing to Vietnam and Rest of ASEAN come down as compared to scenario II. Indonesia is still the country which enjoys the largest gain and it actually manages to increase its welfare with full liberalization owing to the huge terms of trade benefit.

Thus, the welfare effect is widely varying among both ASEAN member countries and India. It is dependent on the nature of liberalization. At the initial stage with partial liberalization among selected members of the agreement, the welfare for smaller countries of the ASEAN region is entirely negative. Their welfare positions turn favourable as they also join in the liberalization. But, then again if the liberalization process intensifies with the proposed pruning of negative list by all the countries then, the larger ASEAN countries will earn large positive gains. In scenario I, Singapore has the largest welfare, while in scenario III, it is Malaysia which will gain the most. While Singapore gains due to large positive terms of trade, Malaysia gains due to positive endowment effect. Among the smaller countries, Indonesia is the maximum gainer while Cambodia always loses welfare due to worsening terms of trade.

For India, excepting scenario I, welfare gains are always positive. It gains both allocative efficiency and large endowment benefits in both the scenarios. Particularly, when the negative lists are removed, the endowment effect enjoyed by it is so large and positive that it enjoys a major welfare gain in spite of its terms of trade being negative. Endowment gain for India is also positive in scenario I even though its net welfare gain is negative. Thus, the most important positive component of welfare for India is the endowment effect. The important feature to note is that this large positive endowment gains at all stages of the FTA is mainly on account of increased demand for unskilled labour in the economy. It increases by 5 per cent in scenario I, by another 14.5 per cent in scenario II and if scenario III prevails then there is a further increase of 11.8 per cent. Demand for skilled labour increase too in scenario I and II but much lesser (1.96 per cent and 6.6 per cent respectively). In scenario III, the demand for skilled labour falls and so does it fall for capital and natural resources. Therefore, most of the positive endowment effect in this scenario is explained by increased demand for unskilled labour in the economy. India's terms of trade remains negative throughout and worsens whenever the larger ASEAN members, Malaysia, Singapore and Thailand become active members of the trade bloc. Thus, India is likely to benefit from the FTA as more of the smaller countries from the region intensify their process of tariff liberalization and the gain is mainly due to endowment gains.

Impact on Welfare when Reduction in Trade Cost is Considered

Trade between countries across the world has grown rapidly over the last five or six decades. This growth in trade has largely been due to the worldwide drop in average import tariffs on goods which fell from 8.2 per cent in 1960 (Clemens and Williams, 2002) to 2.88 per cent in 2012 (The World Bank). In spite of this drop in trade tariffs, trade has not grown and diversified at the same pace across the world. The trade share of least developed countries continue to lag behind those of high income countries and their trade basket is still largely made up of low value added primary products. This has led to the focus being shifted to non-tariff barriers of trade which are now thought to be the primary obstacles to trade between the countries. One such non-tariff barrier is the obstacles to movement of goods across borders. In the wake of reduced tariff barriers the world over, cross-border inefficiencies or trade costs are often cited as more important determinants of trade between countries. Thus, we turn to examine the welfare implications of reduced trade cost between India and ASEAN. We consider three different reductions (25 per cent, 20 per cent and 10 per cent) in trade cost with respect to goods entering India from ASEAN. Thus, the total trade cost is made up of cost of exports from individual ASEAN countries plus the cost of imports in India. The country and product specific trade costs associated with movement of goods from the ASEAN countries to India is calculated and converted into their corresponding ad valorem or tariff equivalents for all sectors considered in the present study and for all of India and the ASEAN countries. The detailed methodology for calculation of country specific and product specific trade costs and their conversion into ad valorem or tariff equivalents are discussed in the Appendix 1.

Using this data on tariff equivalents, the impact of reduced trade costs (25 per cent, 20 per cent and 10 per cent) on welfare of India and the ASEAN countries are estimated. The impacts on welfare of other non ASEAN countries are also examined. Two main scenarios are simulated:

- A reduction in trade costs (25 per cent, 20 per cent and 10 per cent)
- A reduction in trade costs (25 per cent, 20 per cent and 10 per cent) along with trade liberalization (scenario II mentioned in Section 5) between the countries.

India has positive welfare gain both from trade liberalization as also reduction in trade cost and as such the highest gain to the country is when trade liberalization happens with the entire ASEAN region as per the scheduled tariff commitments along side a 25 per cent reduction in trade cost. In all the scenarios, India's welfare gain is on account of employment benefits and allocative efficiency gains. Terms of trade remains negative throughout, implying that in spite of reduced trade cost and elimination of tariff barriers the import prices for products in India remain higher compared to the export prices India offers to the ASEAN countries. Prices of the imported intermediate goods in India will still remain high even after trade liberalisation and reduction of trade cost due to high domestic demand in India. Hence, in production process, substitution between capital and labour will allow a major gain in employment in most of the productive sectors in India.

Among the ASEAN countries, Malaysia, Singapore and Indonesia have notable positive welfare gains when trade costs are reduced and obviously these gains are highest when trade costs are lowered to 25 per cent along with the countries lowering the tariff barriers. While Indonesia experiences an increase in positive gains owing to all of improved allocative efficiency, endowment and terms of trade, Singapore and Malaysia actually starts earning positive gains compared to the negative gains they had when the countries just lowered the tariffs applied to the bilateral trade. This improvement in welfare position is due to improved terms of trade. Thailand continues to face welfare loss, but with reduced trade cost the magnitude of loss comes down primarily due to terms of trade improvement. The other countries of the region do not show much of extra welfare gain, when trade costs are reduced along with tariff barriers.

Table 9(b) shows the welfare implication of the trade liberalization and reduced transaction cost between India and the ASEAN region on other countries in East and South Asia. As seen from this table, in East Asia China, Japan and South Korea are most hit by the improvement in trade facilitation. All of them earn negative welfare and this loss deepens as trade liberalization is accompanied by reduction in trade costs. Worsening terms of trade is main reason for welfare loss to these countries (refer figures). In South Asia, it is Pakistan and Sri Lanka which experience welfare loss, again due to worsening terms of trade.

Thus, as is noted from the discussion above most of East and South Asian countries are likely to be negatively hit as trade opens up and trade costs come down between India and ASEAN.

Conclusion

The AIFTA involving India, Malaysia, Singapore and Thailand has been operational since January 1, 2010 and has been proceeding with the tariff liberalization happening in phases from both sides. But, as is indicated by the present study this opening up of trade between India and the ASEAN region did not quite explain the increase in the two-way trade between the regions. India's trade with these countries in general have been greater in years after 2009 irrespective of the countries implementing the FTA.

A further in-depth analysis using the computable general equilibrium (CGE) modelling framework of the GTAP indicates that India's two-way trade with the region is likely to increase substantially (almost 53 per cent) by December 2021, when the tariff liberalization as per the commitments of all the partner countries are complete. Increase in India's imports from the region would be much greater (around 68 per cent) than its exports to the region (23 per cent). A further complete liberalization with all exclusion lists eliminated would boost this trade by another 17 per cent, with India's exports to and imports from the region rising by 11 per cent and 19 per cent respectively. Initially, Malaysia and Thailand become the largest markets for Indian goods. But when the smaller ASEAN countries intensify their tariff liberalization, Lao PDR and the Philippines emerge as the most important markets, followed by Cambodia, Vietnam and rest of ASEAN. In fact, many of the goods, which earlier reach the bigger ASEAN countries, now head towards these countries. India's export basket, comprises more of manufacturing products now as compared to the exports basket, which is more intensive in primary products when only the larger ASEAN members open up. In case of India's imports too, initially Malaysia and Thailand are most important sources, but with smaller countries opening up, Vietnam, followed by Indonesia emerge as the most important source of India's import from the ASEAN region. As in case of exports, for imports too, India imports more of non-primary products from the smaller countries of the region as compared to its import of more of primary products from Malaysia, Singapore and Thailand.

Thus, as the FTA proceeds in phases, India's trade with the ASEAN region increases consistently, with imports rising more than exports and the trade basket gradually become more intensive in secondary than in primary products.

The welfare effect of AIFTA too varies widely for India. It is dependent on the nature of liberalization. At the initial stages of the opening up, India's welfare position is negative mainly due to worsening terms of trade. But as the scope of the FTA widens with smaller ASEAN countries joining in, India's welfare turns positive. It gains both allocative efficiency and large endowment gains. Particularly, if the negative lists are removed by all the partners in the ASEAN region, the endowment effect enjoyed by it will be so large and positive that it will enjoy a major welfare gain in spite of its terms of trade being negative. India's terms of trade remains negative throughout the course of the tariff liberalization and worsens whenever the larger ASEAN members, Malaysia, Singapore and Thailand become active members of the trade bloc. Thus, India is likely to benefit from the FTA as more of the smaller countries from the region liberalize their trade with India. Particularly, notable would be the endowment effect, which is likely to increase manifold as the phased tariff liberalization process proceeds. This is mainly brought about by the increase in demand for unskilled labour employment mostly in the expanding export intensive sectors in the country.

Earlier Sikdar and Nag (2011) have studied the effect of the phased liberalization process under AIFTA and found that India would gain from the AIFTA as the smaller countries join in the liberalization process. The present paper provides a different result especially in case of welfare change compared to Sikdar and Nag (2011). This is mainly due to the fact the current paper takes up more practical approach of unemployment closure compared to the earlier work which considered wage flexibility. Also, the new data (GTAP 8 as compared to GTAP 7 in Sikdar and Nag (2011)) has been used in the current study. Owing to fixed wage, overall benefit to skilled and unskilled workers increased substantially due to heightened economic activity leading to large exports from India to ASEAN members. This is important to note that though Terms of Trade remained negative other gains have outweighed the negativity. There is also substantial allocative efficiency gain, which is through tax collection by the government from private consumption, production process and trade. Hence, it can be argued that the ASEAN-India FTA will provide more internal benefit to India as it unfolds gradually. However, bilateral trade deficit of India will bound to rise and we should not have a myopic view towards the trade deficit only. The FTA is bound to increase economic activities within India leading to more employment and income generation. With reduction in trade cost alongside tariff liberalization the employment gains to India will increase further.

References

Ahmed, S. (2010). *India –ASEAN Free Trade Agreement: A Sectoral Analysis*. SSRN working paper. No.1698849. Retrieved on 4 November 2010, from http://ssrn.com/abstract=1698849.

Brockmeier, M. (2001). *A Graphical Exposition of the GTAP Model*, GTAP Technical Paper No. 8

Chandran, B.P.S. & Sudarsan, P.K. (2012). *India-ASEAN Free Trade Agreement*, EPW, Vol - XLVII No. 16, April 21, 2012.

Clemens, M. & Williamson, J. (2002). *Why Did the Tariff Rate-Growth Correlation Reverse after 1950?*. NBER Working Paper 1205, 2002.

Francis, S. (2011). *A Sectoral Impact Analysis of the ASEAN-India Free Trade Agreement*. Economic and Political Weekly, vol xlvi no 2, January 8, 2011.

Gilbert, J.P. (2001) *Appendix: GTAP Model Analysis: Simulating the effect of a Korea –US FTA using Computable General Equilibrium techniques in Free Trade Between Korea and the United States?*. Policy Analyses in International Economics 62, Institute for International Economics.

Harilal, K.N. (2010). *ASEAN-India Free Trade - Area Noises of Dissent from Deep South*. State Planning Board Occasional Paper. Kerala State Planning Board. Thiruvananthapuram.

Hertel, W. H., Walmsley, T. & Itakura, K. (2003). *Dynamic Effects of the New Age Free Trade Agreement between Japan and Singapore*. GTAP Technical Paper 823. Retrieved on 05 September, 2014 https://www.gtap.agecon.purdue.edu/resources/download/548.pdf

Huff, K.M. & Hertel, T.W. (2000). *Decomposing Welfare Changes in the GTAP Model*. GTAP Technical Paper. No. 5.

Hummels, D., Minor, P., Reisman, M. & Endean, E. (2007). *Calculating Tariff Equivalents for Time in Trade*. Review paper of United States Agency for International Development. Retrieved on 05 September, 2014, from http://www.nathaninc.com/sites/default/files/

Karmakar, S. (2005). *India–ASEAN Cooperation in Services – An Overview*. ICRIER Working Paper. No. 176. New Delhi.

Kawai, Masahiro & Wignaraja, G. (2007). *ASEAN+3 or ASEAN+6: Which Way Forward?*. ADB Institute Discussion Paper. No. 77. September 2007.

Lee, H. & Liew, V.K.S. (2007). *India-ASEAN -5 Economic Integration: Impact of Liberalization*. The IUP Journal of Applied Economics. VI (6), 7-20.

Minor, P. & Tsigas, M. (2008). *Impacts of Better Facilitation in Developing Countries*. GTAP Technical Paper 4036. Retrieved on 05 September, 2014 from https://www.gtap.agecon.purdue.edu/resources/download/4036.pdf

Mondal, B, Sirohi, S & Thorat, V. (2012). *Impact of ASEAN-India Free Trade Agreement on Indian Dairy Trade: A Quantitative Approach*. Munich Personal RePEc Archive.

Pal, P. & Dasgupta, M. (2008). *Does a Free Trade Agreement with ASEAN Make Sense?*. EPW. November 15. 2008.

Pal, P. & Dasgupt, M. (2009). The *ASEAN-India Free Trade Agreement: An Assessment*. EPW. XLIV (38). September 19. 2009.

Sasatra, S. & Prasopchoke, M. (2007). *Go with the Gang, ASEAN!*. ASEAN Economic Bulletin. 24 (3). ISEAS, 339–35.

Sen, R., Asher, M.G. & Rajan, R.S. (2004). *ASEAN- India Economic Relation: Current Status and Future Prospects*. ISEAS Working Paper. 2004.

Sikdar C & Nag B (2011). *Impact of India-ASEAN Free Trade Agreement: A cross-country analysis using applied general equilibrium modeling*. Asia-Pacific Research and Training Network on Trade Working Paper Series, No. 107.

Veeramani, C & Saini, G.K. (2010). *Impact of ASEAN-India FTA on India's Plantation Commodities: A Simulation Analysis*. IGIDR Working Paper. No. 2010-004.

WITS. The World Integrated Trade Solution. Retrieved on 15 June 2011, from http://wits.worlbank.org/wits/

World Bank (2012), *World Development Indicators: Tariff Barriers*. Retrieved 08 September 2014 http://wdi.worldbank.org/table/6.6

Appendix 1

Regional Aggregation

The 129 regions of the World as in GTAP database version 8 are aggregated into 11 regions for the purpose of this study. They are - Malaysia, Singapore, Thailand, Cambodia, Indonesia, Lao PDR, Philippines, Vietnam, & Rest ASEAN (comprising of Brunei Darussalam & Myanmar) - these 9 regions collectively is the ASEAN region; India and Rest of the World comprising of all other countries of the world. For estimating welfare implications of reduced trade costs for non ASEAN countries Rest of the World has been further disaggregated into: China, Hong Kong, Japan, South Korea, Mongolia, Taiwan, Rest of East Asia, West Asia, Bangladesh, Pakistan, Sri Lanka, Rest of South Asia and Rest of the World.

Sectors Undertaken in Simulations (Sectoral Aggregation)

The 57 sectors of the GTAP model have been aggregated into 36 sectors in this study considering the importance of these sectors in this agreement. The sectors are namely, Paddy, Wheat, Cereals (other),

Vegetable & fruits, Oilseeds, Other crops, Meat & meat products, Milk, Dairy products, Other animal products, Forestry, Fishing, Coal, Oil & gas, Minerals, Vegetable oil & fat, Sugar, Food products, Beverages & tobacco, Textiles, Wearing apparels, Leather & leather products, Wood & wood products, Paper & paper products, Petroleum & coal products, Chemical, rubber & plastic, Ferrous metals, Other metals, Non-metallic Mineral products, Machinery equipment, Electrical equipment, Motor vehicles, Transport equipment, Other manufacturing, Utilities and Services.

Relevant Data and Methodology for Handling Trade Cost

Cross border inefficiencies, or trade transaction costs (TTCs) are of two types:

- Direct costs- these include charges such as customs fees, port handling charges, and informal payments. These are directly assessed on each transaction.
- Indirect costs- these are costs that refer to the cost of time in trade. For an exporter these include the time required to complete all pre shipment requirements and also the loading of cargo. For an importer, it is the time taken to take possession of the shipments once the ship has arrived at the port

Data on both the direct and indirect cost of trade is systematically catalogued in The World Bank's Doing Business Report[2]. For the purpose of this study data on trade costs have been collected for all of India and the ASEAN countries considered in the study. And then applying 25 per cent, 20 per cent and 10 per cent reduction to this trade costs for goods reaching India from the ASEAN countries, the welfare implications are assessed for all the partner countries as also the other countries, particularly the immediate neighbours of India and the ASEAN region. The welfare impact of the reduced trade cost is estimated using the CGE modeling framework of GTAP database. To use a CGE modeling framework, the time costs of trade which are typically measured and recorded in days had to be converted into cost units in dollars. To do this, the study uses data by Hummels *et al.* (2007) on ad valorem tariff equivalents for the cost of one day in trade for India and the ASEAN countries. Following Hummels *et al.'s* (2007) methodology, the tariff equivalents of trade delays considered in this study counted time in three stages: inland transport, customs processing and port handling. These values are then trade weighted using the bilateral trade data between India and ASEAN countries as reported in GTAP database 8 (as updated earlier as part of the study). The bilateral trade flow corresponds to the direction of the trade i.e. export time is export weighted and import time is import weighted. Tariff equivalents of time are created for all the 36 products and for India and all the ASEAN countries.

To estimate the welfare implications of trade cost reductions on welfare of the regions we consider the standard GTAP model with unemployment closure as mentioned in Section 4. The reduction in trade cost is implemented as in Hertel, Walmsley and Ikatura (2003). In this approach the product and region specific Armington demand function is shifted by the advalorem tariff equivalent of the reduction of the number of days to cross borders. It can be shown that this shifting parameter has the desired effect of reducing the market price of imported goods by the percentage shift in the demand curve and with a corresponding change in the quantity demanded. As the reduction in market price is simulated as a technical shift, no rebalancing of the database is required. Following the standard analysis of Armington functions, changing import demand and supply is a function of change in relative prices, demand and substitution elasticities, supply constraints and trade shares (Minor and Tsigas, 2008).

2. Doing Business data are available online at www.doingbusiness.org

SIX

ASEAN ATTEMPTS AT THE INITIATIVES TO BROADEN FREE TRADE AGREEMENTS IN EAST ASIA

Suthiphand Chirathivat

Introduction

ASEAN's notable presence in the regional arena can evidently be discerned from its dynamic trade development and integration policy as well as from a number of enterprising collaborative efforts of trading arrangements in East Asia. In the early 1990s, ASEAN initiated its own trading area, known to many as ASEAN Free Trade Area (or AFTA), which was then extended to be the ASEAN Economic Community by the end of the following decade. ASEAN's own initiative like AFTA had given the attention to its dialogue partners for a better part. Many of the ASEAN members had been able to solve their problems resulting from the last Asian financial crisis in 1997-98, thus came the new era of ASEAN's trade development and integration with outsiders, since the early part of the new century. Since then, ASEAN members, individually and as a grouping, have embarked upon multiple bilateral, regional and sub-regional initiatives for the flourishing pursuit of trading arrangements, often known as free trade agreements (FTAs) or sometimes as comprehensive economic partnership agreements (CEPAs).

ASEAN's interests in broader trading arrangements are one of the momentous outcomes of such changing environment and challenges. ASEAN and its trading partners found the complexities related to the proliferation of bilateral FTAs as the 'Asian noodle bowl' situation (Baldwin, 2007), and as such, a need for a region-wide FTA would be a good solution to solve such problems (Chirathivat, 2004; Kawai 2005; Kawai and Wignaraya, 2009). However, the thinking behind a way to move forward and to achieve a region-wide FTA still differs at the regional level. On the one hand, there is a proposal to start from an East Asian FTA (known as EAFTA) among ASEAN+3 countries, and then extending it gradually to ASEAN+6 countries and others. On the other hand, another idea proposes to take the task involving all major countries from the start to cover ASEAN+6 countries with a region-wide FTA, or Comprehensive Partnership for East Asia (known as CEPEA). Finally, both proposals have been merged into the Regional Comprehensive Economic Partnership (RCEP) in August 2012, with which ASEAN is regarded both as the FTA hub and as the driving force of broader regional economic integration.

Until the development and conclusion of ASEAN+1 FTAs become clear and joint studies on region-wide FTA in East Asia among China, Japan and Korea assume an active role, competition and rivalries among the three Northeast Asian countries, which played a positive role up to ASEAN+1 FTAs, could turn into a stumbling block to the advancement of a region-wide FTA. This is known as ASEAN+3 versus ASEAN+6. This fundamental problem is due to the lack of FTAs between China, Japan and Korea. In this case, the role of ASEAN in forging broader trading arrangements in East Asia looks important and prominent, even with a view not quite coherent among ASEAN members, but subject to increasing pressure to respond to the growing and urgent needs of such region-wide trade agreement. With the existence of numerous obstacles and problems, ASEAN has to move forward to play an active role in helping to achieve a desirable and consistent region-wide FTA, now known as RCEP that suits well with the grouping interests and other countries as they are all moving deeper into different stages and playing fields of regional economic integration.

This chapter discusses the role of ASEAN in building a regional FTA in Asia, and analyses the implications from expansion of Trans-Pacific Partnership and East Asia Summit into ASEAN+8.

Modus Operandi in Economic Regionalism and Region Building

Region building in Asia started in Southeast Asia with the founding of ASEAN in 1967. At the beginning, confidence building was necessary among members as they had little experience of cooperation between them. No distinctive economic cooperation was marked between them or with outsiders during this period (Acharya, 2012). Only then, after ASEAN launched the ASEAN Free Trade Agreement (AFTA) in 1992 that ASEAN began to both deepen and broaden its economic cooperation. On the one hand, ASEAN needed to respond to the economic regionalism elsewhere, particularly in the EU and North America, with its own approach to regional economic integration. On the other, ASEAN started to expand and develop seriously the annual Post Ministerial Conferences (PMCs) between the ASEAN Foreign Ministers and the 10 dialogues partners.[1] ASEAN also proposed the idea of forming an ASEAN Regional Forum (ARF) in 1993 to promote dialogue on political and security issues and to contribute to confidence-building and preventive diplomacy in the Asia-Pacific region.[2]

It is in this spirit that ASEAN also started the ASEAN plus one Summits (with China, Japan, Korea, Australia and New Zealand). The Asian financial crisis of 1997-98 came to stimulate further the way ASEAN thought in favour of broader economic regionalism, starting with the regional monetary cooperation, known as the Chiang Mai Initiative (CMI), which gave birth to the process of ASEAN+3, including China, Japan and Korea. Under the initiative of Korea at the early part of the new century, this process was also expanded to cover other areas of economic cooperation, to cite here the most notable example of an East Asian Free Trade Area (EAFTA), with China acting as an important supporter at a later stage. In the meantime, ASEAN took further steps in 2005 when the first East Asia Summit was convened. By this turn, Japan took the advantage to propose another Comprehensive Partnership for East Asia (CEPEA, also known as ASEAN+6). As a result, ASEAN started to host ASEAN+3 and ASEAN+6, as key initiatives related to broaden regional economic cooperation in East Asia.[3]

As a result, ASEAN has a blend of institutionalism and networked regionalism. It moves closer to the institutional regionalism paradigm, since the adoption of the ASEAN Charter in November 2007, and the three pillars of the ASEAN Community in January 2009, all expcted to foster culture of greater reliance on law and legally binding agreements and respect for its deeper integration commitments, something that ASEAN members had never been subject to before. For its networked regionalism, the ASEAN Way of informality, consensus and consultation remains vivid in the ways

1. Australia, Canada, China, Japan, Korea, India, the European Union, New Zealand, Russia, and the United States.
2. The current participants in the ARF: Australia, Bangladesh, Brunei Darussalam, Cambodia, Canada, China, European Union, India, Indonesia, Japan, Democratic Peoples' Republic of Korea, Republic of Korea, Laos, Malaysia, Myanmar, Mongolia, New Zealand, Pakistan, Papua New Guinea, Philippines, Russia Federation, Singapore, Sri Lanka, Thailand, Timor Leste, United States, Vietnam.
3. ASEAN plus China, Japan, Korea, India, Australia, New Zealand (known as ASEAN+6). (At the time of this writing, EAS hosted its first summit with two new members: the United States and Russia, making ASEAN+8.)

of its working for its future. In other words, the informal ASEAN became formalised. The question that arises here is: What would be the implications of ASEAN's transition from networked to a nascent from of institutionalized regionalism for Asian regionalism? For the moment, this institutionalised idea has not yet translated into the way ASEAN worked as a networked regionalism in East Asia. Only time will tell about this transformation if that would take place and it also matters when that would take place.

Fundamentally, the strength of ASEAN over the past four decades has really been its flexibility, informality, and consensual way of reaching the decision. This was also not without problems as it projected the image of ASEAN to many as ineffective, slow to act, and pulled down any substantial progress to region building. With this perspective in mind, it is fair enough to conclude that for its future ASEAN needs to strike the right balance between its loosely networked structure and legalisation of its norms, which could really mean that ASEAN member states are pursuing more ambitious forms of community-building and regional integration. It is also interesting to observe how ASEAN will work out with its ASEAN way to broader trading arrangements in East Asia.

ASEAN Centrality Calling into Region-wide Trade Talks

ASEAN today is at a critical juncture where its centrality and *de facto* position in the wider region is seriously challenged by another round of region-wide trading talks in East Asia. There have been various proposals to enhance the cooperation in the region that require ASEAN to take a leading role. ASEAN members, individually are not important economic players, and yet have such a privilege role although they cannot be compared with the neighbouring Northern Asian countries. Indeed, ASEAN needs to think beyond the AEC and deliver the next preferred region-wide FTAs that would benefit ASEAN and other countries involved. The EAFTA (2009) and CEPEA (2009) are both modalities for taking the region forward that seems to be based on ASEAN centrality at the moment.

The Chairman's Statement of the 16th ASEAN Summit (9 April 2010) stated: "We noted the initiatives to take forward regional integration by considering the recommendations of both East Asia Free Trade Area (EAFTA) and Comprehensive Economic Partnership in East Asia(CEPEA) studies together. We look forward to receiving the progress report at the 17th ASEAN Summit in October 2010 and to discussing with our regional architecture with

ASEAN at its core". The determination was reaffirmed during 17th ASEAN Summit (28 October 2010) "by pursuing a two-pronged approach which gives priority to the acceleration of ASEAN integration while intensifying ASEAN's external relations." Therefore, ASEAN needs to rethink and prepare for such a move to build partnership with other participating countries to develop proper modalities that serve well the interests of ASEAN.

However, the fact that these competing proposals of economic regionalism, whether it is EAFTA or CEPEA, are emerging is reflection of concerns over ASEAN's lack of overarching coherence and doubts about its ability to drive the region-building agenda. In spite of its longstanding role that ASEAN has played in a "driver seat" of region-wide economic regionalism in East Asia, ASEAN is increasingly coming under pressure for its centrality being questioned. The issue is how ASEAN would manoeuver its "steering wheel" to maintain its central role. Its unique traits in consensus building and lack of historical rivalries and tensions make the grouping unique to play such a central role for region-wide trading talks. In a way, the development of EAFTA and CEPEA must take into consideration the institutional development of ASEAN +3 and ASEAN +6 processes. This is essential because realising of both proposals in parallel will require appropriate institutional structures and mechanisms that can realistically be developed.

Before the ASEAN Charter of 2007 and the ASEAN Community of 2009, ASEAN was notorious for being state-driven, based on soft institutionalism, with strong emphasis on non-binding informal institutions, and decision were normally reached through consensus and based on uniformity as a principle. How will this mechanism be transferred to the region-building in Asia that is "multi-layered" with several inter-related institutions from ASEAN to wider cooperation, is still a valid question? The region has to take serious view of the fact that many regional initiatives in the past have failed to materialise because of the lack and/ or weakness of institutional mechanisms to implement them.

In this case, the efforts that began with EAFTA and CEPEA should go much further and should aim at the creation of a stronger process that could lead to the development of an institutional arrangement that would come to existence once those modalities related to broader trading arrangements are implemented. This is a necessary development for ASEAN and East Asia as a whole and will provide the foundation for promoting a genuinely economic partnership arrangement involving such diverse and emerging economies as ASEAN plus China, Japan, Korea and Australia, India and New Zealand. This is what is roughly lacking in the region today and unless this situation is rectified, with ASEAN centrality, now viewed increasingly as vital and decisive; the region cannot hope to be able to embark on serious efforts towards deepening regional economic integration.

ASEAN's Role in the Formation of EAFTA and CEPEA and the Creation of RCEP

Progress from the Beginning

A view has often been advanced that new regional institutions and processes have been created because of ASEAN's needs to respond to the new issues and problems at the regional level. Apparently, the crisis-hit Asian economies in 1997-98 led the creation of an East Asian-only process, the ASEAN+3 (ASEAN plus Three (APT)), initially with the aim of developing regional self-help mechanisms to deal with financial crises. Within a relative short time, the APT process took off in 1997. It has an annual summit and has made progress in financial cooperation (the Chiang Mai initiative and the Asian Bond Market initiative) and few other functional cooperation areas. It has also indirectly led to the development of ASEAN+1 trade and economic agreements (with China, Japan, Korea, and Australia, India, New Zealand). The feasibility of an East Asian Free Trade Area (EAFTA) has been explored, but the governments decided not to start any negotiation of an EAFTA until the ASEAN+1 agreement takes proper shape.

Instead of going for broader economic integration in East Asia, APT leaders decided to move towards broadening of the East Asian process to cover a larger geographic area. The East Asia Summit (EAS), launched in December 2005, included the then APT members plus Australia, India, and New Zealand, making it ASEAN+6. The East Asia Summit is developed in parallel with the strengthening of the APT and will not replace it. Since then, the EAS has also developed its own platforms for leaders to discuss various issues, regional and global, that are related to the development of the region. It has back-to-back summits with the APT, only some major differences are the number of countries that have been participated and the kinds of issues they select to discuss. Overall, the two processes in East Asia have created real questions, if not great confusion, about the way the people look at the region, and have complicated the regional institutional landscape.

The question remains whether the two parallel processes can be developed effectively given the limited capacity and resources on the part of many regional countries. There is no such clear cut answer for enhancing the one process in favour of the other. As Soesastro (2007) pointed out:

> "Market-driven integration has been progressed at about the same speed within different groupings in East Asia, whether it is ASEAN, APT or EAS. All three groupings also share a common feature of strong and continued outward orientation of regional integration in East Asia. Therefore, there does not seem to be any qualitative difference between the three, particularly APT and EAS.
>
> No conclusive results could be drawn whether functional integration schemes would be better pursued in APT or EAS as it is probable that a smaller APT would be a more effective grouping, but with other consideration, like cooperation in energy and environment, the inclusion of other countries could be more beneficial.
>
> Nature of institutional integration will be the most important political decision for East Asia to make. As widely known, these countries have been extremely cautious in its approach to institutionalising the processes of regional integration. So will both APT and EAS, which are said to be driven by ASEAN, being the "least objectionable" party to lead the group."

According to Soesastro (2007): "The politics of China-Japan relations will determine how both the APT and the EAS will unfold. While this uncertainty exists, it appears that for some time to come deepening of integration will be a major challenge for both APT and EAS, but more so for EAS than counterbalance China's possible domination of the process".

Ideally from an economic perspective, if integration is pursued through the formation of regional trading arrangements, the larger the grouping the greater will be the gains to its members but this will come at the expense of non-members. According to the study results (Urata, 2008), the East Asian economies will benefit from EAFTA and CEPEA as they can expect their combined GDP to increase by 2.05 per cent and 2.11 per cent, respectively. The importance of economic cooperation can be observed by comparing the results from simulation 1 (trade facilitation and liberalisation) with those from simulation 2 (trade facilitation and liberalisation, and economic cooperation). GDP growth rates of developing members are supposed to increase substantially when economic cooperation is included in the programme. However, such formation of a region-wide trading arrangement will serve better the region if only greater discipline is observed than forming the web of bilateral trading arrangements. It remains true that most bilateral FTAs with possibly significant diversion effects could turn out to be undesirable for the dynamic development of regional and global production networks involving all East Asian economies.

The EAFTA and CEPEA Proposals

By the time the ASEAN Economic Ministers met in Thailand in August 2009, two reports had been submitted to them by their Senior Economic Officials (as ASEAN played in the "driving seat" to prepare such reports for the leaders meetings of both APT and EAS later in the same year[4]:

- Report of the Joint Experts Group on the EAFTA Phase II Study; and
- Track Two Study on Comprehensive Economic Partnership for East Asia: Phase II

In fact, both reports are recommendations in the study on the EAFTA vis-à-vis the study of CEPEA with the view to guiding Senior Economic Officials Meeting (SEOM) as it deliberated on possible recommendations to the Ministers. These recommendations arising from the Phase I and Phase II of EAFTA and CEPEA can be summarised as follows:

- For EAFTA Phase I, the East Asian leaders put the EAFTA on the economic cooperation agenda during the 10th ASEAN+3 Summit and an independent process to form an EAFTA. The EAFTA process firstly proceed within the ASEAN+3 framework because it has already established a solid foundation (this is not to make the EAFTA an exclusive grouping, according to the study, membership will be open to other East Asian economies as well as other members of the East Asia Summit). EAFTA will lead to further deepening of economic integration, enhancing the competitiveness of production networks and progressively reducing the development gaps among the East Asian countries. Economic development cooperation initiatives with specific

4. The author had much benefitted from a discussion paper prepared by Anna M.Rubeniol from the ASEAN Secretariat in writing this topic.

action plans must be adopted along with the EAFTA with a view to helping the less developed countries.

- For EAFTA Phase II, the East Asian leaders put the EAFTA as an important initiative in the economic agenda during the 13th ASEAN+3 Summit in 2009 and suggested that the process to form an EAFTA should follow immediately. A gradual and realistic strategy shall be pursued to achieve a desirable and feasible EAFTA. Initially the EAFTA be formed by consolidating the existing FTAs (AFTA and the 3 ASEAN+1 FTAs), and further work shall be undertaken to incorporate trade in services and investment into the EAFTA. Concrete trade and investment facilitation measures shall be implemented to enable all participating countries, especially less developed countries, to fully realise the benefits of an EAFTA. Two working groups shall be immediately created to pave the way for an EAFTA: (i) one to design a unified regime of ROOs for the EAFTA; and (ii) another one to look into tariff nomenclature and other customs-related issues.
- For CEPEA Phase I, the report stated the CEPEA's objectives as to deepen economic integration in the region, to help narrowing the development gap and to achieve sustainable development. The structure of CEPEA, that is to be composed of the three pillars of economic cooperation, trade and investment facilitation, and trade and investment liberalisation, be affirmed by the leaders. Discussions should be commenced among East Asian governments on cooperation and facilitation measures under CEPEA. Necessary decisions should be made regarding an FTA under CEPEA, i.e. whether to commence a government process immediately, provide a clear timeline for future negotiations or continue to further detailed study as a track two process. A mechanism shall be developed for enhancing the opportunity for regional business leaders to contribute to the CEPEA realisation process. For CEPEA Phase II, CEPEA's objectives and structure were reaffirmed at the Leaders' level Study and discussions on concrete steps to realise CEPEA, as a comprehensive framework that includes cooperation, facilitation and liberalization commence immediately among the governments of the member countries.

It should be noted that these two reports had happened at the high time of the global financial crisis, so both the EAFTA and CEPEA Phase II studies had incorporated in the introductory section an assessment of the global environment and the role that regional economic integration, such as the EAFTA and CEPEA, can play not only to cushion the region from such an impact, but also to make it more resilient, relevant and less vulnerable to future similar shocks.

Outcomes from Recommendations

It is true that recommendations in the Phase I studies for the EAFTA and CEPEA are not exactly far apart. To highlight a few points, both studies:

- Emphasise a high quality FTA to further deepen economic integration and narrow development gaps among the countries participating in the relevant FTA;
- Make the suggestion that the FTA shall be based on 3 pillars: (i) liberalisation of trade (goods and services) and investment; (ii) trade and investment facilitation; and (iii) development and economic cooperation. The EAFTA study went further suggesting that an institutional framework for broad-based policy dialogues among the members be put in place to support development cooperation. On the other hand, the CEPEA study specified environment, energy, logistics and facilitation issues covered by the AEC Blueprint as important areas for cooperation and facilitation;
- Suggest a consolidation of related existing FTAs, with CEPEA, recognising this consolidation may take a while, suggested voluntary liberalisation of barriers and regulatory reforms through information exchange and monitoring; and
- Advocate open regionalism.

The rationale behind the current global financial crisis gives countries in the region the impetus to broaden economic integration. Meanwhile, recognising the proliferation of FTAs in East Asia, consolidation and streamlining of these FTAs should be a good thing and will have to be undertaken at some point in time in order to get maximum benefits as in principle economic gains from an FTA would be much greater the bigger the FTA grouping is.

When it comes to the recommendations of the Phase II of both studies, it could be generally described as follows:

- Pursue broader regional economic integration in East Asia, realising that the grouping has a greater potential for generating welfare gains for all the partners in the region because of the inclusion of more developed and emerging economies.

- Consolidate the existing ASEAN+1 FTAs based on a more practical approach rather than to negotiate a whole new agreement in a way to alleviate concerns on the "noodle-bowl" effect of the often "overlapping" FTAs in the region. The Northeast Asian region which could be a factor in the EAFTA has to make substantial progress with some kind of FTA(s) between China, Japan and Korea, often known as China-Japan-Korea FTA (or CJK FTA). As for lesser developed ASEAN countries, in particular, CMLV countries (involving Cambodia, Myanmar, Laos PDR, and Vietnam), they might not be prepared to extend to the other East Asian countries the same tariff treatment they are giving to ASEAN. Therefore, the consolidation process into "ASEAN+3 FTA" must take into consideration some of these sensitive issues. Only when both "ASEAN+3 FTA" as "CJK FTA" are put in place, an EAFTA can be achieved by consolidating them together.
- Elevate the EAFTA and CEPEA Track Two process to a Track One process, which, in fact, was done to the AEM meetings in Thailand in August 2009, then followed by their leaders summits.

Finally, it is undeniable that East Asian economies have become highly integrated through market driven expansion of trade, investment and capital flows. More recently, public sector initiatives and institutional arrangements have been seen as necessary to support further market-led integration. For these reasons, governments in the region have started to explore new policy initiatives for formal economic integration through multi-layered bilateral, sub-regional and regional free trade agreements. However, these FTAs are wide ranging, complex, and often overlapping – differing in coverage, depth and regulations – thus, rather than boosting trade, they exhibit increasing transaction costs that are undesirable and unhealthy for firms conducting business in the region. Moving forward with an adoption of a gradual and incremental strategy would be a solution to achieve a feasible and desirable EAFTA or CEPEA in the region.

Track One process had declared to work in parallel on recommendations of both reports – EAFTA and CEPEA. The governments begun to set up working groups related to important issues like ROOs, customs procedures, economic cooperation and tariff nomenclature, to cite a few of them.

Figure 1: Conceptual Formation of a Regional Comprehensive Economic Partnership in Relation to an East Asian Free Trade Agreement and Comprehensive Economic Partnership in East Asia

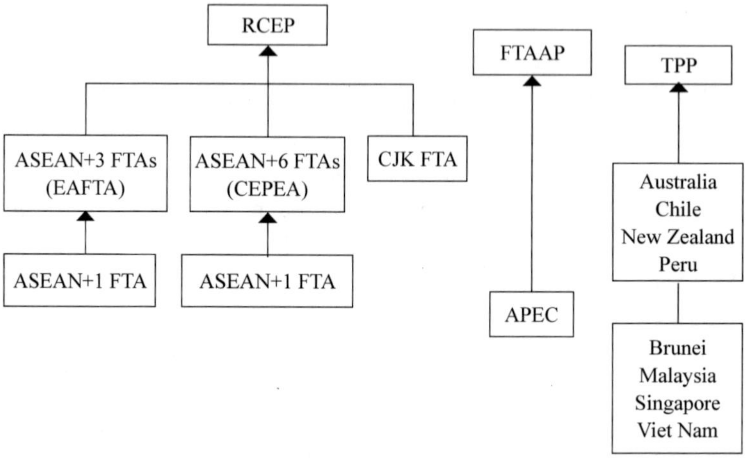

Note: FTA = Free Trade Agreement, EAFTA = East Asian Free Trade Agreement, CEPEA = Comprehensive Economic Partnership for East Asia, CJK FTA = China-Japan-Korea Free Trade Agreement, RCEP = Regional Comprehensive Economic Partnership, APEC = Asia-Pacific Economic Cooperation, FTAAP = Free Trade Agreement of Asia-Pacific, TPP = Trans Pacific Partnership.
Source: Authors' compilation.

However, the rationale in all of these related issues still depends upon a number of developments, which are explained below:

- An important task is to create a unified ROOs regime that is simple, liberal and trade facilitative.
- With regard to liberalisation in goods, instead of renegotiating tariff eliminations and schedules, it would be more reasonable to just focus on the reduction of discriminations arising from the implementation of multiple tariff concessions by, to the extent possible, harmonising tariff commitments made in AFTA and the existing ASEAN+1 FTAs.
- As for trade in services and investment, the agreements are feasible in light of similarities in the existing structure of agreements.
- Trade and investment facilitation measures as well as cooperation programmes are not regionally coordinated and to certain extend overlapped one and another, thus the grouping could focus on concrete facilitation and cooperation measures, particularly with a view to help those less developed countries such as CLMV.
- However, there is view that all these developments should be based upon a more realistic and achievable approach before moving forward

a high quality of trade and investment liberalisation, comprehensive facilitation and cooperation measures. The consolidation of the existing ASEAN+1 FTAs and the progress of CJK FTA become an important step towards broader regional trading arrangements in East Asia (see Figure 1). Differentiated approaches for less developed countries, particularly CMLV, should be allowed. The inclusiveness issue remains like the way the ASEAN+3 countries will work with India, Australia and New Zealand, and possibly more countries as the interest in the grouping is expanding rapidly with an emerging Asia in the global economy.

Regional Comprehensive Economic Partnership

While there is no one-size-fits-all template for ASEAN to broaden regional agreements in Asia, there are, however, persistent efforts to develop in parallel the EAFTA and CEPEA proposals. As shown from the EAFTA and CEPEA process and outcomes, ASEAN's attempt to broaden regional integration in Asia is starting to take shape, but is still far from complete. Since the beginning of 2010, officials from ASEAN, ASEAN+3, and ASEAN+6 have been working on issues related to rules of origin, tariff nomenclature, custom procedures, and economic cooperation. Several meetings have been held, with each working group making good progress on its agenda.

The crucial issue remaining to be settled is the "Asian noodle bowl" situation. For this reason, any future comprehensive and gradual approach to broaden regional integration, whether it is EAFTA or CEPEA, will need to tackle the complexity related to existing FTAs, in particular the ASEAN+1 and bilateral FTAs, which have hampered utilisation. As such ASEAN, with other interested partners, needs to find the best way to facilitate an early framework agreement to address at least the issues such as rules of origin and tariff nomenclature.

Fortunately, the idea of creating a regional comprehensive economic partnership (RCEP), following the 18th ASEAN Economic Ministers' Retreat in February 2011 in Nay Pyi Taw, was introduced and then gained momentum after the ASEAN Leaders Summit in Bali in November 2011. Since then, opportunities for ASEAN Senior Economic Officials to work on the scope of potential RCEP partners and its framework occurred during the 44th ASEAN Economic Ministers' Meeting in August 2012, where all ASEAN+6 countries agreed to RCEP by setting negotiations to start in early 2013 and be completed by the end of 2015.

For instance, the RCEP is a new ASEAN-led FTA linking Southeast Asia with all of the "plus six" countries, namely, Australia, China, India, Japan, the Republic of Korea, and New Zealand. In its design, ASEAN leaders have planned to adopt an open accession scheme that will allow other countries to join as new members provided they can comply with the grouping's rules and framework. In this sense, membership is open to other countries, although it will start with the ASEAN+6 countries. In principle, the RCEP will help ASEAN to cement its central role in the emerging broader regional integration architecture and seek to reduce the complexities of the "Asian noodle bowl" effect of all existing FTAs. In the longer run, this agreement will help to promote broader regional integration consistent with the multilateral trading system, while departing from the complexities of the small scope of other bilateral FTA arrangements.

Meanwhile, the RCEP is supposed to have a wider framework that includes trade in goods, trade in services, investment, trade and business facilitation, intellectual property rights, economic and technical cooperation, competition policy, and dispute settlement. Given the wide diversity among ASEAN countries, particularly the developing members such as Cambodia, Lao PDR, Myanmar, and Vietnam, the RCEP process would fall into a lowest-common-denominator trap of trying to accommodate all countries with a fare minimum level of liberalisation, and ASEAN must ensure this does not happen. On the other, a very strong position from ASEAN in the RCEP is needed to show a continuation of incremental efforts from the grouping in making a region-wide system, e.g., rules of origin to work with a view that this would also serve ASEAN's centrality and deeper integration of the AEC. The option for firms in ASEAN (whether local or foreign) to take advantage of regional trade and investment agreements will augment as these agreements will affect firm competitiveness. Helping to set up a truly borderless AEC is crucial to helping ASEAN firms position themselves better with firms in countries such as China and India. Also, the RCEP is potentially an important initiative for the region at a time when the United States continues to struggle with economic recovery and fiscal cliffs, and Europe still faces prolonged economic uncertainties.

The ASEAN Summit in Phnom Penh in October 2012 reaffirmed the stand of the ASEAN Framework for Regional Comprehensive Economic Partnership (RCEP), adopted in 2011. However, it remains for ASEAN to encourage all countries to deepen discussions towards a successful conclusion of the partnership. Steering such an important initiative into concrete action represents a very important challenge for ASEAN, given the past limitations of the grouping. It is important for ASEAN to play its central role in the formation of the RCEP, making sure of its success that will support implementation of the AEC and beyond. In the end, ASEAN needs to ensure that the RCEP becomes a key pillar in Asia's broader regional economic architecture.

Though considered a new but an important initiative for the region, there are, however, questions around future commitments to trade liberalisation among the countries involved. Some have even gone far to anticipate a low level of trade liberalisation for the RCEP. This is due to the so-called "ASEAN way" in which no member will adopt trade policies when there are disagreements and very often, due to different levels of development, some members would argue for protection of sensitive industries against increased competition. Although this flexibility may help to attract the less-developed countries to the grouping, a low level of trade liberalisation may leave further trade impediments and discourage greater and broader regional integration in the longer run.

Nevertheless, the main exercise for the RCEP, at least initially, remains the consolidation of all ASEAN+1 FTAs and bilateral trade agreements. In effect, members of the RCEP believe they will benefit from such an agreement as long as the scheme continues to develop. ASEAN countries are expected to streamline their existing FTAs and gain greater access to other non-ASEAN countries, whether they are ASEAN+3 countries – China, Japan, and Korea, or the ASEAN+6 countries – Australia, India, and New Zealand. At the same time, the RCEP is expected to encourage more investment flows from more-developed regions to less-developed ones and integrate them into regional production networks.

Implications from Expansion of Trans-Pacific Partnership and East Asia Summit into ASEAN+8

The region's major challenge is still the political will of their leaders and the geopolitical considerations in moving forward (Soesastro, 2006). The process of ASEAN+3 and ASEAN+6 and how their governments came closer in the formation of EAFTA and CEPEA and the creation of RCEP are clear example of this challenge. Alongside with this development, the debate for the 2011 leaders' summit involves the inclusion of Russia and the United States in the EAS, making an ASEAN+8, thus making a major turning point in the evolution of the EAS since its inception in 1995. In addition, the recent development of Trans-Pacific Partnership (TPP), an effort to tie economies along the Pacific into a free-trade zone, also poses a major concern for ASEAN, particularly, its centrality and driving force in regional economic integration. The issue remains how these latest developments could impact the RCEP, in particular, for its efforts to broaden regional trading arrangements as largely discussed in the former section.

To undertake such challenges for the future development of RCEP, it is important to understand the region building experiences in their recent historical context, which have impacted ASEAN strategy on broader regional trading arrangements. To anyone who was interested on the issue of region building in East Asia, Asia-Pacific Economic Cooperation (APEC) was the first product of the post-cold war era which evolves the East Asian economies since the early nineties. It is in East Asia's own interest to reach out and to engage with the United States. APEC provides a broader regional framework that included the US, apart from a smaller regional process of ASEAN. In fact, ASEAN and East Asian economies formed the core members of APEC. From the outset, East Asian participants recognised the importance of involving the US in the process. Although the US is not figured in East Asia, its critical role in the region's security earns it a legitimate place in East Asia. In fact, the term "Asia-Pacific" had been created to capture this geo-political and geo-economic reality, and was used to justify the incorporation of the US into this process.

However, when it comes to the APEC process of trade liberalisation, trade and investment facilitation and cooperation development, the Bogor Goals for achieving free and open trade and investment in the region[5] were limited and dwarfed due to the Asian financial crisis of 1997-98 which prevented those developing Asian economies to continue with such programmes. Indeed, the process is not like an FTA because of the liberalisation, in its design, and will not be discriminatory (but on an MFN basis) and nor does it involve a negotiation. Instead, a unique modality called "concerted unilateral liberalisation" had been adopted and this modality was supposed to work though peer pressure. Until recently, a more 'limited' version of the creation of a Free Trade Area of the Asia-Pacific (FTAAP) had been advanced.[6] Given different views and acceptance of the concept of region

5. In 2010 for the developed members and 2020 for the developing members.

6. For example, C. Fred Bergsten, Director of the Peterson Institute of International Economics in Washington D.C., is one of the main proponents of FTAAP.

building among its members, APEC still struggled with the implementation of such a concept. This is because APEC's main challenge has been to show that the "soft" approach of region building can produce concrete results.

As a result, the recent initiative known as the Trans-Pacific Partnership was advanced as an alternative to the Asia-Pacific trade and investment liberalisation. The TPP had been seen as a low-key effort with little economic impact on the US. There are four core members with small economies: New Zealand, Singapore, Chile and Brunei. The US already has free-trade pacts with Singapore and Chile, as well as with Australia and Peru, which are part of the TPP trade expansion talks Australia, Canada, Japan, Malaysia, Mexico, Peru, and Vietnam also joined the discussion, bringing the total number of participating countries to twelve. Indeed, this building momentum of TPP is seen as a way to counterweight China's economic influence in the region and the US government under President Barack Obama has taken new interests in region building and its role in East Asia although the US is not even yet figured in as member of TPP.

No matter on what one might like to express, TPP is seen as an expression to form a geo-political and geo-economic interest in a bloc that could serve as counterweight to the rise of China, which is now the largest trading partner with most Asian economies, and has been active in recent years in signing trade arrangements with its neighbours. Notable is ASEAN-China FTA, which came into full effect in 2010. Viewing from this angle, more ASEAN countries are likely to join TPP at the moment, with the exception of major economies like Indonesia and Thailand, which have not yet expressed their interests to join such partnerships. There also remain divergent perspectives among individual countries in ASEAN reflecting their motives and interests on TPP and it will do so for at least in the time to come.

Above all these recent developments, ASEAN strategy for the expanded East Asia Summit (EAS) is somewhat very different from the above mentioned region-wide trading arrangements, FTAAP and TPP, in the sense that this expansion is seen as reaffirming the ASEAN centrality in an emerging regional architecture. For this reason, ASEAN, as a whole, takes this as a serious challenge and looks at opportunities for the grouping and the evolving regional architecture in East Asia. With the participation of both, the US and Russia, the EAS would automatically turn from an ASEAN+6 to ASEAN+8 with implications that the meetings could be far more interesting and complex in addressing regional and global issues.

For the interests of broader trading arrangements in East Asia, it is interesting to see how an expanded EAS, now ASEAN+8, could impact the new arrangements of RCEP. In this connection, four issues had been identified for the ASEAN Foreign Ministers' discussion, namely, EAS priorities, EAS meeting format and agenda, the involvement of the heads of international institutes and the future expansion of the EAS. For the EAS priorities, it is outlined that unlike the ASEAN+3 process, the EAS is not meant to be a functional-based forum, but rather, representing a high level-strategic forum, with focus on key strategic issues that have global impact and have significant implications for the region, namely, global issues, on-going cooperation especially economic-financial, and political-security.

The possibility to involve the two new participants of the EAS to modalities for taking forward the RCEP was also discussed. It was also mentioned that the ASEAN needs to think the next preferred region-wide FTAs that would benefit ASEAN most. The FTAAP, proposed by APEC, currently joined by a number of ASEAN member countries could present an interesting approach with commitment of the US, the largest economy, but again this is not based on ASEAN centrality, and ASEAN should take into consideration on how that would impact ASEAN-led broader trading arrangement – RCEP. It is also suggested that with the inclusion of the US and Russia in 2011 the EAS will need some time to consolidate before further expansion. Therefore, the expansion issue of the EAS could take place upon the realisation of the ASEAN Community.

In sum, the inclusion of the US and Russia in the EAS represents an important step in the recognition of ASEAN-led arrangements as the center piece of the regional architecture. This is a key strategic development for ASEAN, but also leaves a lot of homework for ASEAN, in particular how the initiative with regard to the expanded EAS would interface with its existing structure and process like broader trading arrangements of RCEP. It also seems that ASEAN leaves the door open to these two new countries for RCEP if the confidence is placed in ASEAN and ASEAN centrality is not misplaced. However, on the other hand, ASEAN would let its members act freely upon their own interests in other region-wide trading arrangements such as FTAAP and TPP as long as these arrangements do not disturb the ASEAN strategy and centrality in conducting the emerging regional architecture.

Conclusion

The emergence of the idea for a broader regional economic integration in East Asia represents a real challenge for ASEAN. Indeed, the ASEAN experience in regionalism is traced as background to the ASEAN approach to concept of region building and economic regionalism in East Asia. And yet, ASEAN is subjected to criticism for its weakness of regionalism institutions, especially, the consensual way of ASEAN in reaching common decisions as well as enforcing rules and regulations. This is certainly true in a large part as the past construction of ASEAN is merely reflected in its loose organisational structure – networked regionalism, with strong emphasis on non-binding informal institutions, and decisions are generally arrived through consensus and based on unanimity as a principle. However, the implementation of the ASEAN Charter in 2007 and the ASEAN Community in 2009 marks a key step for ASEAN to recognise the importance of increasing institutionalisation in its future region building. In a way, it seems that ASEAN needs to look out for balancing its own networked regionalism by increasing the institutional pressure in order to move forward.

It is also interesting to understand the development of the ASEAN centrality that has been progressed over years, from the middle of 1990s when the ASEAN Regional Forum (ARF) was formed, to the launching of the East Asia Summit (EAS) in 2005, and its latest inclusion – the US and Russia in 2011. In between, the Asian financial crisis of 1997-98 encouraged the crisis-affected countries to cooperate closer, as they sought common ground to guard against future crises. In 2000, ASEAN along with China, Japan and Korea launched the multilateral arrangement of currency swaps, the Chiang Mai initiative. The process became ASEAN+3, the following year, when leaders decided to widen this monetary cooperation beyond to cover also other economic dimensions. In conjunction with the proliferation of multi-layered bilateral, sub-regional and regional FTAs in the "Asian noodle bowl" fashion, the creation of an EAFTA was proposed as a preferred form to consolidate the existing trend of FTAs. Only when the EAS was created, another preferred region-wide trade agreement, CEPEA, was advanced as an alternative. Here comes again into play the ASEAN centrality as ASEAN was put into the central role or "driver's seat" to bring about further region-wide trading arrangements.

Figure 2: Final Demand Composition of Asia's Exports in 2006

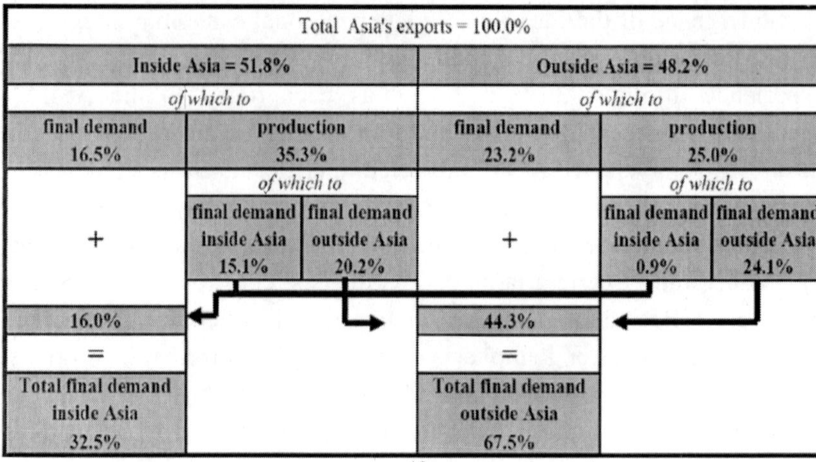

Source: ADB, Asian Development Outlook and Kawai (2010)

In discussing EAFTA versus CEPEA proposals up to the creation of RCEP, all national leaders acknowledge that East Asia is growing more interdependent, with the competitiveness of its intricate production networks, making East Asia an interesting example of regional integration. Intra-regional trade in East Asia climbed from a low level back then to over half today in many countries despite the fact that three-fifths of manufactured exports go to the Western countries, particularly the US and the EU (see Figure 2). Counting on important factors related to what is going on with regard to the global financial crisis causing more obstacles for their exports and the potential for future growth still bright in the region with a strong consumption of vibrant middle class, this is a better time than never to reinforce this kind of broader regional trading arrangements; the merit for such proposals cannot be deniable.

The rationale of these two parallel proposals, both aimed to be attained, is the consolidation of existing ASEAN+1 FTAs, by a high quality of region-wide FTA, though practical and sequential in its implementation, with unified rules of origin with facilitation and cooperation measures that suit the less developed countries, like CLMV countries in ASEAN. ASEAN welcomes for such a role as the two reports were recommended by the ASEAN process to EAS leaders and ministers, but the optimal approach for such cooperation has to be backed by national strategies and respective governments, both within and outside ASEAN. The biggest challenges for ASEAN and East Asia are still the political will and geo-political considerations in moving forward as witnessed by the latest approach of the EAS to include the US and Russia, making an ASEAN+8 and open a new consideration to the newly created RCEP, apart from other initiatives like FTAAP and TPP, which seem to challenge the ASEAN centrality indirectly. The uneasiness of the three Northeast Asian neighbours, viz. China, Japan and Korea and the strong competition from the US with regard to the rise of China in East Asia seem strong than ever before that ASEAN has to take into consideration. All these developments pose challenges directly to ASEAN to take this opportunity to accelerate the concrete discussion on the future desirable region-wide trading arrangement, with the lead by proposing possible "modality" to participating partners, based upon benefits and problems in the existing FTAs. ASEAN's regional integration will only be successful if linkages are broadened with regional and global partners through proper framework of region-wide trading arrangements. Only time will tell whether or not ASEAN will do utmost possible efforts to make all these East Asian projects a reality.

References

Acharaya, A. (2012). *The Making of Southeast Asia: International Relations of A Region.* Cornell University Press and Institute of Southeast Asia Studies.

Baldwin, R.E. (2007). *Managing the Noodle Bowl: The Fragility of East Asian Regionalism.* ADB Working Paper Series on Regional Economic Integration, No.7, February.

Bergsten, C.F. (2007). *China and Economic Integration in East Asia: Implications for the United States.* Policy Briefs in International Economics, no PB07-3, Peter G. Peterson Institute for International Economics, March.

Bhagwati, J.N. (2008). *Termites in the Trading System: How Preferential Agreements Undermine Free Trade.* Oxford: Oxford University Press.

CEPEA. (2009). *Phase II Report of the Track Two Study Group on Comprehensive Economic Partnership in East Asia*, 3 July, mimeograph.

Chia, S.Y. (2010). *Regional Trade Policy Cooperation and Architecture in East Asia.* ADBI Working Paper 191. Tokyo, Asian Development Bank Institute.

Chirathivat, S. (2004). *East Asia FTA: Economic Modalities, Prospects and Further Implications.* Journal of Asian Economics, Vol.15, 889-910.

Chirathivat, S. (2006). ASEAN's Role and Interests in the Formation of East Asian Economic Regionalism. In P.J.Welfens, F. Knipping, S. Chirathivat, & C. Ryan (Eds.) *Integration in Asia and Europe: Historical Dynamics, Political Issues and Economic Perspectives.* Heidelberg: Springer-Verlag.

Chirathivat, S. & Srisangnam, P. (2013). *The 2030 Architecture of Southeast Asia Free Trade Agreements.* ADBI Working Paper, No. 419, Asian Development Bank Institute, April.

EAFTA. (2009). *Final Report on EAFTA Phase II Study on Desirable and Feasible Option for an East Asia FTA.* 7 June, mimeograph.

East Asian Vision Group. (2001). *Towards an East Asian Community – Region of Peace, Prosperity and Progress.* Report Submitted to the ASEAN Plus Three Summit in Brunei Darussalam, 31 October.

Kawai, M. (2005). *East Asian Economic Regionalism: Progress and Challenges*. Journal of Asian Economics, Vol.16 (1).

Kawai, M. (2010). *Rebalancing Growth in Asia*. The World Economy Asia Lecture, University of Nottingham, Kuala Lumpur, 14 January.

Kawai, M. & Wignaraya, G. (2008). *EAFTA or CEPEA: Which Way Forward?*. ASEAN Economic Bulletin, Vol. 25, No.2, 113-139.

Kawai, M. & Wignaraya, G. (2009). Multilateralizing Regional Trade Arrangements in Asia. In Baldwin, R. and P. Low (Eds.) *Multilateralizing Regionalism*. Cambridge University Press. (pp.495-549).

Park, I. (2008). *Trade Agreements in East Asia: Will They Be Sustainable?*. Asian Economic Journal, Vol.23, Issue 2, 169-194. June.

Ravenhill, J. (2010). *The 'New East Asian Regionalism': A Political Domino Effect*. Review of International Political Economy, Vol.17, No.2, 178-208.

Soesastro, H. (2007). *The Regional Institutional Architecture for the Asia Pacific*. A PECC Study Project, Discussion Paper (First Draft), April, mimeograph.

Soesastro, H. (2006*). Regional Integration in East Asia: Achievements and Future Prospects*. Asian Economic Policy Review, Vol.1, Issue 2 (December), 215-238.

Urata, S. (2008). *CEPEA: Japan's New Regional Cooperation Initiative in East Asia*. Japan Spotlight, November/December, 12-13.

Zhang, Y. (2010). *China and Asian Regionalism*. Singapore: World Scientific.

SEVEN

INDIA-THAILAND PARTNERSHIP: WAY TOWARDS GREATER COOPERATION

Sineenat Sermcheep, Piti Srisangnam and Nuanpan Thamanovanish

Introduction

In the Vision Statement of the ASEAN-India Commemorative Summit 2012, the ASEAN and Indian leaders emphasized that in order to pursue sustainable development, people must know each other and develop a multicultural society. Apart from economic relations, it is seen that cultural understanding is fundamental for India to engage and strengthen economic and commercial ties with rest of the world.

The cultural relationships between India and Thailand could be traced back through histories. Symbols and structures used by the two countries are evidences of shared culture and civilisation. The Lion Capital of Ashoka the Great, a Buddhist king who brought Buddhism to Thailand, is the national emblem of India, where Hinduism is the religion of the majority of people, while Garuda, a birdlike mythological beast of the Hindu tradition, is the national emblem of Thailand, where the majority of the population is Buddhist. These cultural ties illustrate a key stepping stone to build efficient and seamless connections for a more competitive, prosperous and integrated region.

The Look East Policy (LEP) of India initiated in 1991 was implemented to promote economic integration among India, especially the eight Northeastern States of India, and Southeast Asia. With China's rising power in the region, Look East Policy (LEP) became an essential strategy for India to contain Chinese influence (Malik, 2012). India has recently unveiled the Act East Policy (AEP). India has been negotiating bilateral free trade agreements (FTAs) covering trade in goods, services, and investment among ASEAN+6 (ASEAN member countries plus China, Japan, South Korea, India, Australia, and New Zealand) as the regional framework for an

Asian Economic Community (AEC). In addition, in terms of socio-cultural aspects, India has forged cooperation at sub-regional groupings such as the Mekong-Ganga Cooperation (MGC) and the Bay of Bengal Multi-Sectoral Technical and Economic Cooperation (BIMSTEC). Such attempts in terms of both economic and socio-cultural relations, aiming at increasing India's international economic and commercial relations, are thus essential to bring Indian economy closer to neighbouring countries and to strengthen India's position as a competitive and effective global player.

This chapter reviews the India-Thailand partnership and discusses the way towards greater cooperation between ASEAN and India.

Look East – Act East Policy

Ever since the Sino-Indian War, China and India have been strategic competitors in South and East Asia. While China began cultivating extensive trade and economic relations with Asian nations, India sought to establish economic and commercial ties, increase strategic and security cooperation, and strengthen cultural links (Malik, 2012).

"Look East Policy" marked a shift in India's perspective of the globalization. It was developed and enacted during the government of former Prime Minister P.V. Narasimha Rao and rigorously pursued by the successive governments of Atal Bihari Vajpayee and Manmohan Singh. Since then India has been liberalising its economy and removing restrictive policies by reducing tariffs and relaxing controls over Foreign Direct Investment (FDI) in order to integrate itself into the global economy (Shahin, 2003).

According to Prime Minister Manmohan Singh, "*the Look East policy is not merely an external economic policy; it is also a strategic shift in India's vision of the world and India's place in the evolving global economy*" (Astarita, 2011, pp.55). The essential philosophy of "Look East Policy" is that India must find its Asian partners to engage with the rest of the world and that India's future and economic interests are best served by greater integration with East and Southeast Asia. Under the new leadership in Delhi, India's Look East Policy has morphed into a proactive Act East Policy, which envisages accelerated across-the-board engagement between the two growth poles of a vibrant Asia. This has been reflected in a spate of two-way visits in the first few months of the Modi government.

Look East – Act East Policy is an attempt to forge closer and deeper economic integration with its eastern neighbours as part of the new realpolitik as evidence in India's foreign policy, and the engagement of India with the Association of Southeast Asian Nations (ASEAN) is a part of the recognition on the part of India of the strategic and economic importance of the region to the country's national interests.

Regional Trade Agreement

Thailand-India Free Trade Agreement (TIFTA)

India is one of the top 10 trading partners of Thailand. The bilateral trade agreement between Thailand and India came into effect in the late 2004 and enabled Thailand to gain trade surplus with India since 2005. Thailand's trade value with India has risen significantly since 2009 to over US$ 7,800 million in 2015 (Figure 1). However, the investment between the two countries does not reflect the size of economies. It can be seen that the Indian investment in Thailand ranked 14th among other foreign investors in 2011, whereas Thailand's outward investment in India saw a slight increase, as compared to the previous year (Figure 2).

Figure 1: Thailand-India Trade (US$ million)

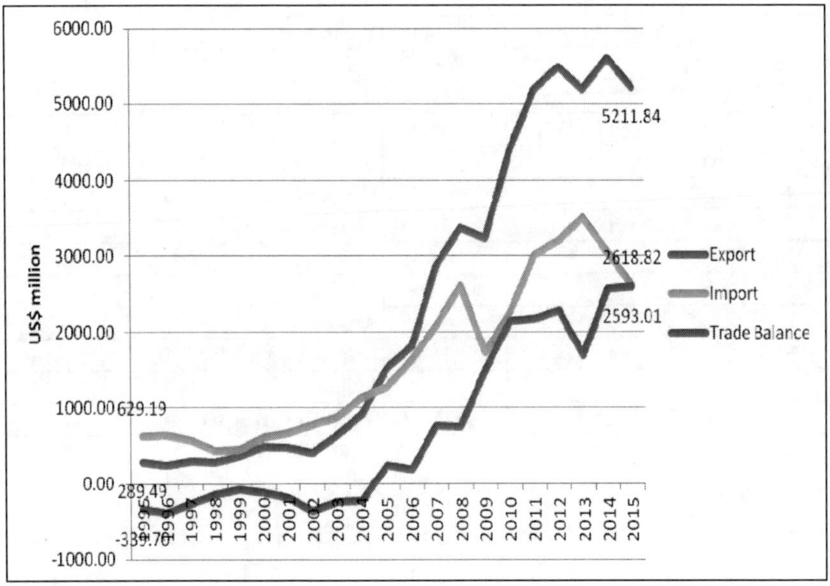

Source Authors

Figure 2: Thailand-India Foreign Direct Investment (US$ million)

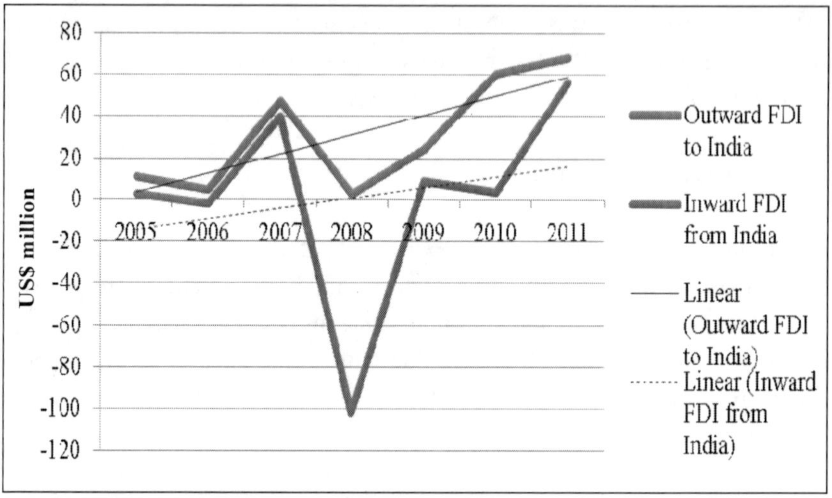

Source: Authors

Table 1: Thailand's Investment, 2011 (US$ million)

Sl. No.	Outward FDI		Inward FDI	
1	ASEAN	4231.45	Japan	4,548.25
2	Canada	2013.22	ASEAN	1,145.14
3	Hong Kong	1329.45	South Korea	728.18
4	USA	806.03	USA	473.60
5	Australia	699.46	Bermuda	375.38
6	British Virgin Islands	300.95	Cayman Islands	304.25
7	Switzerland	234.84	Switzerland	281.35
8	EU-27	194.77	Hong Kong	207.74
9	Cayman Islands	151.45	Mauritius	159.49
10	China	107.68	China	137.67
11	India	67.99	Taiwan	102.46
12	Japan	45.26	Australia	99.74
13			British Virgin Islands	76.16
14			India	56.12
	Total Outward FDI	**10625.33**	**Total Inward FDI**	**9,511.25**

Source: Authors

Trade in Goods

Thailand and India implemented an EHS (Early Harvest Scheme) covering trade in goods. The tariffs of 82 products under TIFTA EHS have been reduced to zero per cent since 2007. Thailand and India have been planning to expand the trade agreement for 5,000 non-EHS products. At the 21st

Meeting of Negotiating Committee of Thailand-India FTA in September 2011, about 900 Thai items categorized under "Product Specific Rules" (PRS) such as garments, electricity, agricultural products, and electronic devices were provided tax benefits. On 8 June 2012, Thailand and India had implemented the Second Protocol to amend the Framework Agreement for establishing free trade area between Thailand and India. The Second Protocol has added a total of 83 duty exempted products traded under the EHS from Thailand to India (Sabhasri *et al.*, 2012).

Trade in Services

The negotiations for trade in services agreement between Thailand and India are still continuing. Thailand and India have been exchanging information, regulations, and knowledge about service sectors of each other's interest areas (see Table 2) (Sabhasri *et al.*, 2012).

Table 2: Service Sectors of Thailand's and India's Interest

Thailand's Interest	India's Interest
• Construction • Tourism • Retailing	• Computer Service • Information Technology (IT) • Finance • Mechanism for ASEAN-Economic Community (AEC) -Protection of Thai national entrepreneurs -Free Movement in skilled labors

ASEAN-India Free Trade Agreement (AIFTA)

India became a sectoral dialogue partner with ASEAN in 1992, a full dialogue partner in 1995, a member of the Council for Security Cooperation in the Asia-Pacific and a member of the ASEAN Regional Forum in 1996, and a Summit level partner (on par with China, Japan, and South Korea) in 2002. The first India-ASEAN Business Summit was held in New Delhi in 2002, and the initial framework agreement was signed on 8 October 2003 in Bali, Indonesia. The final agreement was signed on 13 August 2009. The free trade area came into effect on 1 January 2010.

Trade in Goods

AIFTA aims for tariff liberalisation of over 90 per cent of products, including "Special Products" such as palm oil (crude and refined), coffee, black tea, and pepper. Tariffs on over 4,000 products will be eliminated by 2016.

Products that are not bound will be reviewed later. The benefits of AIFTA tend to be higher than the TIFTA because of more flexibility of the Rules of Origin (ROOs).

Trade in Services

ASEAN and India have signed ASEAN-India Trade in Services and Investment Agreement. ASEAN has agreed to develop an ASEAN-India Tourism Cooperation Arrangement and requested the ASEAN-India Tourism Working Group to further discuss and prepare the draft agreement.

The Services Agreement between ASEAN and India provides common definition of free movement of skilled labours. It includes business visitors, intra-corporate transferees, contractual service suppliers, articles on spouse and dependents agreement.

In exchange for the opening of the Indian services market, Thailand has purposed to open up trade in goods with India. However, India has preferred that Thailand should open up service sectors. Therefore, opening up of the services sectors between the two countries will be the best way forward.

Foreign Relations

India-ASEAN Relations

India has established strong commercial, cultural and military ties with the Philippines, Singapore, Vietnam, and Cambodia. India also signed free trade agreements with Sri Lanka, Malaysia and Thailand and stepped up its military cooperation with them.

It has forged numerous FTAs with the East Asian economies, including a Comprehensive Economic Cooperation Agreement (CECA) with Singapore and an Early Harvest Scheme (EHS) with Thailand, while it has signed Economic Partnership Agreement (EPA) with Japan and South Korea.

India-Myanmar Relations

India is the largest market for Myanmar's exports, and Myanmar is the fourth largest trading partner of India after Thailand, China, and Singapore. The Indian government has been working to strengthen air, land, and sea routes with Myanmar. It has also decided to establish a gas pipeline. While the involvement of India's private sector has been low and growing at a slow pace, both the governments are proceeding to enhance cooperation in agriculture, telecommunications, information technology, iron and steel, oil, natural gas, hydrocarbons, and food processing.

Even though India had traditionally supported Myanmar's pro-democracy movement for many years, India's policy changed in 1993, making friendly overtures to the military junta (Allison, 2001; Saptarsi, 2009). India signed trade agreements and increased its investments in Myanmar, although private sector activity remains low. Indian state corporations have been engaged for the construction of major roads and highways, pipelines, and upgrading of ports.

India has also increased its competition with China over harnessing of Myanmar's significant oil and natural gas reserves. Although China remains Myanmar's largest military supplier, India has offered to train Myanmar's military personnel, and has sought their cooperation in curbing separatist militants and the heavy drug trafficking affecting much of Northeast India (Allison, 2001).

India-China Relations

While India and China remain strategic rivals, India's "Look East Policy" has included significant rapprochement with China. Since 1993, India began holding high-level talks with Chinese leaders and established confidence-building measures. In 2006, China and India opened the Nathu La Pass for cross-border trade for the first time since the 1962 war.

On 21 November 2006, Prime Minister Manmohan Singh and the President Hu Jintao issued a 10-point joint declaration to improve ties and resolve long-standing conflicts. Trade between China and India is set to reach the US$ 100 billion target by 2018.

However, China's close relations with Pakistan and other South Asian countries have threatened the improvement of the bilateral relations (Hong'e, 2006).

India-East Asia Relations

There are numerous infrastructure projects serving to bring India closer to East Asia. India is participating in the UN Economic and Social Commission for Asia and the Pacific (UNESCAP) initiatives for an Asian Highway Network and the Trans-Asian Railway Network (Maps 1 and 2). Discussions are also going on reopening the World War II-era Stilwell Road linking India's Assam state with China's Yunnan province through Myanmar (Map 3) (Bajpaee, 2007; Bhaumik, 2013).

Map 1: Asian Highway Network

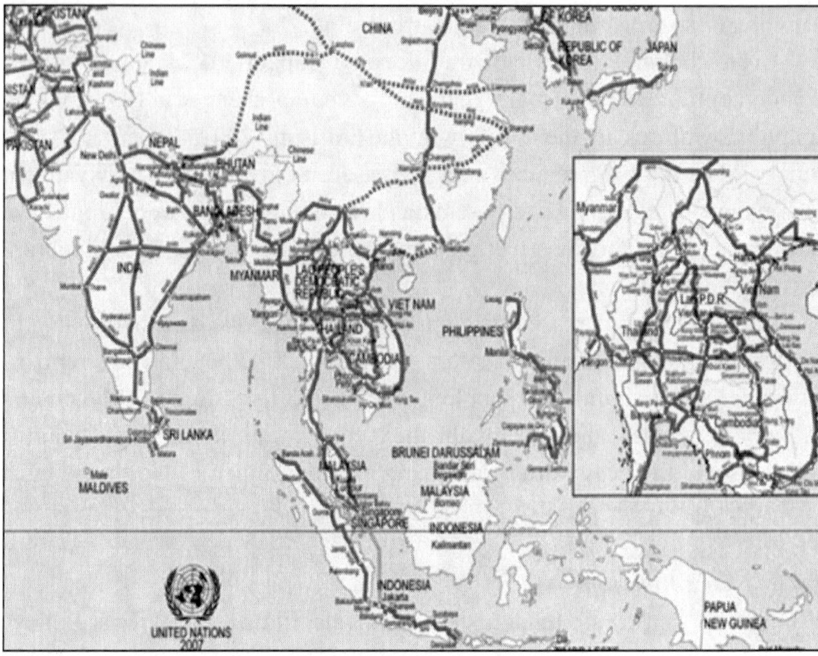

Source: UNESCAP

Map 2: Trans-Asian Railway Network

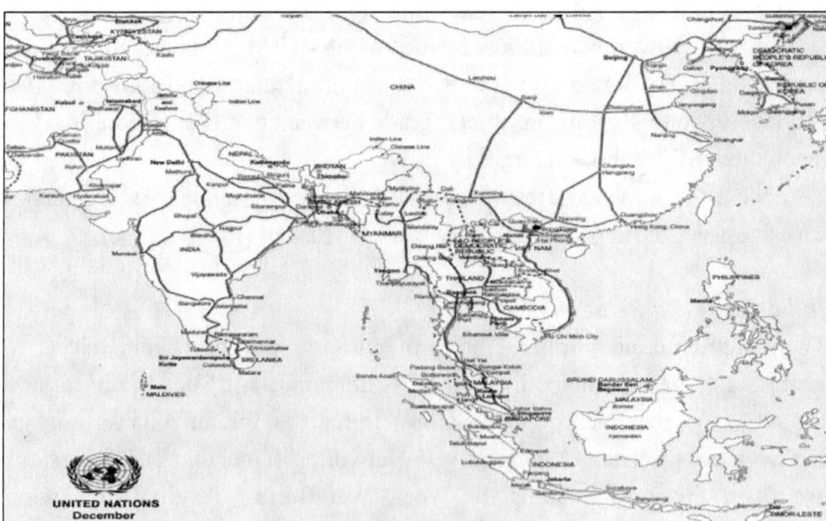

Source: UNESCAP

Map 3: Burma-Leo Stilwell Road

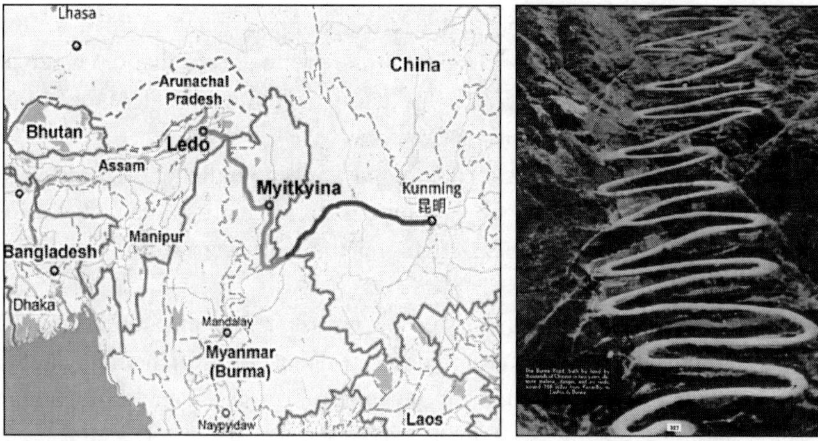

Source: Authors own

Regional Trade Agreements

ASEAN Plus Plus FTA

India's membership to forums such as AEAN, East Asia Summit (EAS) and the Asia-Pacific Economic Cooperation (APEC) has been a result of attempts by the region to balance China's growing influence in the region. Notably, Japan brought India into ASEAN+6 to dilute the ASEAN+3 process, where China is dominant, while Singapore and Indonesia played a significant role in bringing India into the EAS. The United States and Japan have been lobbying for India's membership in the APEC.

BIMSTEC

The Bay of Bengal Initiative for Multi-Sectoral Technical and Economic Cooperation (BIMSTEC) is an international organisation involving a group of countries in South Asia and Southeast Asia. The member countries of this group are Bangladesh, India, Myanmar, Sri Lanka, Thailand, Bhutan and Nepal.

On 6 June 1997, a new sub-regional grouping was formed in Bangkok and given the name BIST-EC (Bangladesh, India, Sri Lanka, and Thailand Economic Cooperation). Myanmar attended the inaugural meeting as an observer and joined the organization as a full member at a Special Ministerial Meeting held in Bangkok on 22 December 1997, upon which the name of the grouping was changed to BIMST-EC. Nepal was granted observer status by the second Ministerial Meeting in Dhaka in December 1998. Subsequently, full memberships have been granted to Nepal and Bhutan in 2004. In the first Summit on 31 July 2004, leaders of the group agreed that the name of the grouping should be BIMSTEC or the Bay of Bengal Initiative for Multi-Sectoral Technical and Economic Cooperation.

BIMSTEC provides an excellent opportunity to build a bridge between SAARC and ASEAN. The cooperation has great positive implications for development of India's Northeastern region transforming a security dilemma to India's gateway to the East.

BIMSTEC members have listed 13 priority areas of cooperation: (i) Trade and Investment, led by Bangladesh; (ii) Transport and Communication, led by India; (iii) Energy, led by Myanmar; (iv) Tourism, led by India; (v) Technology, led by Sri Lanka; (vi) Fisheries, led by Thailand; (vii) Agriculture, led by Myanmar; (viii) Public Health, led by Thailand; (ix) Poverty Alleviation, led by Nepal; (x) Counter-Terrorism and Transnational Crime, led by India; (xi) Environment and Natural Disaster Management, led by India; (xii) Culture, led by Bhutan; and (xiii) People-to-People contact, led by Thailand.

Other Trade Agreements

BIMSTEC and Asian Development Bank (ADB)

ADB has become BIMSTEC's development partner since 2005. ADB undertakes studies designed to help promote and improve transport infrastructure and logistics among the BIMSTEC countries. ADB has already completed the BIMSTEC Transport Infrastructure and Logistics Study (BTILS), which aims to strengthen the coordination of projects and activities under the BIMSTEC transport cooperation agenda, including the action plan and implementation programme.

BIMSTEC Free Trade Area Framework Agreement

BIMSTEC member countries have agreed to establish the BIMSTEC Free Trade Area in order to stimulate trade and investment among the member countries, and attract outsiders to trade with and invest in BIMSTEC at a higher level.

The Trade Negotiating Committee (TNC) was set up and had its first Meeting in Bangkok in 2004. TNC's negotiation areas cover trade in goods and services, investment, economic cooperation, as well as trade facilitations and also technical assistance for least developed countries (LDCs) in BIMSTEC. It was agreed that once negotiation on trade in goods is completed, the TNC would then proceed with negotiation on trade in services and investment. The last negotiation of TNC was held in Thailand in 2015.

Sub-Regional Cooperation

Mekong – Ganga Cooperation (MGC)

Mekong–Ganga Cooperation (MGC) was established on 10 November 2000 at Vientiane comprising six member countries, namely, India, Thailand, Myanmar, Cambodia, Lao PDR and Vietnam. MGC covers four areas, namely, tourism, culture, education, and transportation linkage in order to have strong foundation for future trade and investment cooperation among the people inhabiting these two major river basins – Mekong and Ganga.

The working mechanism for MGC consists of the Annual Ministerial Meeting (back to back with ASEAN Ministerial Meeting), the Senior Officials' Meeting (SOM), and the five Working Groups: (i) Working Group on Tourism (Thailand is the lead country); (ii) Working Group on Education (HRD) (India is the lead country); (iii) Working Group on Culture (Cambodia is the lead country); (iv) Working Group on Communication and Transportation (Lao PDR is the lead country); and (v) Working Group on Plan of Actions (Vietnam is the lead country).

India is committed to the completion of the India-Myanmar-Thailand Trilateral Highway and its extension to Lao PDR, Cambodia and Vietnam as well as the new highway project connecting North Eastern part of India to the Greater Mekong Sub-region or the so-called "Mekong-India Economic Corridor" (MIEC) (Ministry of External Affairs of India, 2013: ERIA, 2009).

At the Second MGC Ministerial Meeting held in Hanoi on 28 July 2001, the member countries adopted the Hanoi Programme of Action affirming their commitment to cooperate in four areas of cooperation, namely, tourism, culture, education, transport, and communications. The Hanoi Programme of Action set a six-year timeframe for implementation (2001-2007), and the progress of its implementation shall be reviewed every two years.

At the Third MGC Ministerial Meeting held in Phnom Penh on 20 June 2003, the member countries adopted the "Phnom Penh Road Map", introducing cooperation in the pharmaceutical sector, as a plan to accelerate the implementation of all MGC projects and activities (ASEANIndia.com, 2012).

Conclusions

India has been reverting to free market economy by undertaking massive economic reforms since 1991. Following the market-based reforms, India became one of the fastest-growing major economies. The opening up of Indian economy with the external countries has increased Indian competitiveness, innovation, and efficiency that are pulling factors for India to be a major player in the international business. To unlock the economic potential of the eight North Eastern states and gain the maximum utilisation of the ASEAN production network in Thailand and GMS countries, the international trading routes via India-Myanmar-Thailand Trilateral Highway and its extension to Lao PDR, Cambodia and Vietnam or, so-called "Mekong-India Economic Corridor (MIEC)" is inevitable. Hence, in order to achieve greater economic integration, economic, socio-cultural, and political-security are three essential aspects to take into account while implementing any measure. Finally, the sincere heart of the people in the participating countries is needed to ensure prosperous, peaceful, sustainable, and secure society.

References

Allison, T. (2001). *Myanmar shows India the road to Southeast Asia.* Special Report. Asia Times21 February. Available at: http://www.atimes.com/reports/CB21Ai01.html#top5. Accessed 8 August 2013.

ASEANIndia.com. (2012). *Vision Press Briefing: Transcript of The Joint Press Interaction following The 6th Mekong Ganga Cooperation Ministerial Meeting.* Available at: http://www.aseanindia.com/press-release/2012/09/04/press-briefing-transcript-of-the-joint-press-interaction-following-the-6th-mekong-ganga-cooperation-ministerial-meeting-sept-4. Accessed 8 August 2013.

Astarita, C. (2011). *The Contemporary Version of India's Look East Policy.* Turkish Policy Quarterly. Year 9, No.11, Summer.

Bajpaee, C. (2007). *India rediscovers East Asia.* Asia Times. 31 October 2007. Available at: http://www.atimes.com/atimes/South_Asia/IJ31Df02.html. Accessed 8 August 2013.

Bhaumik, S. (2013). *India Divided on Opening of Stilwell Road.* The Irrawaddy. 13 May. Available at: http://www.irrawaddy.org/archives/34418. Accessed 8 August 2013.

Department of Trade Negotiation. n.d. BIMSTEC (Bay of Bengal Initiative for Multi-Sectoral Technical and Economic Cooperation). ThaiFTA.com, Department of Trade Negotiation. Ministry of Commerce of Thailand [online]. Available at: http://www.thaifta.com/english/eng_bim.html. Accessed 8 August 2013.

ERIA (Economic Research Institute for ASEAN and East Asia). (2009). *Mekong India Economic Corridor Development*. ERIA Research Project Report 2008-4-2. March. Available at: http://www.eria.org/publications/research_project_reports/mekong-india-economic-corridor-development.html. Accessed 8 August 2013.

Malik, M. (2012). *China and India Today: Diplomats Jostle, Militaries Prepare*. World Affair. July/August. Available at: http://www.worldaffairsjournal.org/article/china-and-india-today-diplomats-jostle-militaries-prepare. Accessed 8 August 2013.

Ministry of External Affairs of India. (2006). *Activities Planned for India-China Friendship Year - 2006*. 23 January, New Delhi. Available at: http://web.archive.org/web/20071020114246/http://meaindia.nic.in/pressrelease/2006/01/23pr01.htm. Accessed 8 August 2013.

Ministry of External Affairs of India. (2013). *Mekong-Ganga Cooperation (MGC)*. May, New Delhi. Available at: http://mea.gov.in/Portal/ForeignRelation/Brief_on_MGC_for_MEA_website-Final.pdf. Accessed 8 August 2013.

Hong'e, Mo. (2006). *China, India raise national flags at border pass to restart business*. Xinhua. www.chinaview.cn 6 July [online]. Available at: http://news.xinhuanet.com/english/2006-07/06/content_4800709.htm. Accessed 8 August 2013.

Sabhasri C. *et al*. (2012). *Thailand FTAs Utilisation and the Future Trade Negotiation Policies: Thailand-India FTA, ASEAN – India FTA*. Presented to the Department of Trade Negotiation, Ministry of Commerce, Thailand.

Saptarsi, Nag. (2009). *Look East Policy*. Our World Our View. 8 October 2009. Available at: http://saptarshinag1.blogspot.com/2009/10/look-east-policy.html. Accessed 8 August 2013.

Shahin, S. (2003). *India's 'Look East' Policy Pays off*. Global Policy Forum. Asia Time. Available at: http://www.globalpolicy.org/component/content/article/162/27908.html. Accessed 8 August 2013.

EIGHT

INDIA-ASEAN PRODUCTION NETWORKS: WHAT IS THERE FOR INDIAN SMES?

Biswajit Nag

Introduction

Global Value Chains (GVCs) have become an important feature in modern international trade. Activities in the value chain are no longer confined within domestic borders and a single firm. Production now involves multiple countries and multiple firms with complex webs and layers of interaction. Empirical evidences suggest that the emergence of international production networks in East Asia results from market-driven forces such as vertical specialization and higher production costs in the home countries and institutional-led reasons such as free trade agreements. Kimura and Obashi (2011) have argued that the unprecedented development of international production networks in the region has made East Asia truly the "Factory of the World". They also have the observation that the pattern of international division of labor and international trade in East Asia is no longer adequately explained by traditional trade theories as the international division of labor in the region is not by industry, but by production process. What we observe is the fragmentation of production process and the formation of industrial agglomerations. The network among different players at various stages of production process has provided a new dimension in the Asian value chain development. Such networks are well developed in machines and auto-component sectors though they are also present in other industries. Machines typically consist of a large number of parts and components, each of which is produced by diversified technologies and inputs. Machinery industries are thus particularly suited to the fragmentation of production. The networks are initiated by lead firms, who are typically multinational corporations (MNCs) and they play the role of designers and coordinators. These MNCs are not just from Japan or South Korea, but are also from USA and Europe. ADB (2007) has reported that the increase in intra-Asian trade comes from the vertical integration of production networks among countries and more than 70 per cent of intra-Asian trade is in intermediate goods, while G3 countries are important markets for final goods. Authukorala (2010) has identified wage differentiation and lowering of trade transaction cost in Southeast Asia as major catalysts in enhancing and expansion of the network to ASEAN including countries like Vietnam and Indonesia.

Transaction costs have been reduced because of soft policies such as trade and investment regimes (FTAs and investment promotion) and trade facilitation measures, and hard policies such as the development of airports, seaports, domestic transportation systems, etc. Authukorala (2010) has also highlighted the importance of the 'second mover advantage', rather than the first mover advantage, as the key determination of production fragmentation and relocation in the region. Foreign investment, which came as part of the first wave, created the foundation for the second wave. Investors during the second wave have received the benefit of supporting industries from the earlier investment and learned from the first wave's experiences. They expanded their operations in neighbouring countries as well. Additionally, the investors in the second wave and particularly the third wave, which invested in Vietnam, enjoy the economic growth of Southeast Asia and benefit from its positive income effect. Needless to say, the investment activity has got accentuated due to proliferation of FTAs in the region in which ASEAN has been actively involved, and this includes India-ASEAN FTA also.

In post-implementation of India-ASEAN FTA, expectation and fear grew up rapidly about possible export opportunities and import threats. India has steadily reduced its tariffs since its implementation in 2010. This agreement has indirectly promised for an expansion of ASEAN production network in India with possible investment from Singapore, Malaysia, Thailand and Indonesia. It has also opened up huge market access opportunities in these countries along with Vietnam, Lao PDR, Cambodia, Myanmar and the Philippines. India's import of machinery products from ASEAN grew up substantially leading to higher trade deficit. Auto components, telecom equipments, automatic data processing equipments, mechanical and electrical apparatus are the main imported items by India from Southeast Asia. In this context, this chapter studies India's integration process especially in three sectors viz. machinery, electrical and optical products and automobiles including parts and accessories. Special attention on these sectors stem not only from the fact that they are among key trading sectors between India and ASEAN, but these are few important sectors among others where IPN building process as a result of FTA carries emphatic impact for SME's. Studies also suggest that production fragmentation in these sectors is relatively higher than other manufacturing sectors, and, hence, there is higher degree of internationalization. The present study begins with describing the distinction between global value chain and international production network and how these two are interwoven. In the following sections, the role of trade agreements in accentuating production network and role of SMEs have been discussed. In this context, India's SME policy have been analysed to comprehend how it is pushing small companies to get exposed internationally. To understand the trade aspect, the study makes an attempt to explore trade in value added (TiVA) database, based on the data prepared by OECD. Analysing the degree of foreign value added component in India's gross exports in selected sectors, the study has identified the emerging trend of IPN in India between 2000 and 2009. As post India-ASEAN FTA data on value added trade is not yet available, the significant opening up in last few years following the FTA has given us an indication for deeper integration. We have observed significant growth in trade along with marked drop in tariff rates especially in identified sectors.

Rest part of the chapter is organized as follows. Section 2 discusses the conceptual framework of global value chain and international production network. Section 3 presents Indian policies and achievements in engaging SMEs in IPN. Participation of Asian countries in international value chain is discussed in Section 4. Section 5 carries the analysis of value chain in selected industries among ASEAN and India. Prospects of IPN in ASEAN-India FTA are discussed in Section 6. Conclusions are drawn in Section 7.

Global Value Chain (GVC) and International Production Network (IPN): Conceptual Framework

Chain vs. Network Approach

The concept of value chain encompasses the set of activities related to production or services which firms and workers undertake to bring a product from its drawing board to its end use and beyond. This includes both manufacturing process and related services such as design, production, marketing, distribution, after sale support to the final consumer, etc. Due to fragmentation of production process, many firms get engaged in producing parts, components and accessories which is carefully managed by lead firms for generating higher values. Economic integration through trade agreements and WTO process has reduced the trade barriers, thereby helping firms to get linked with suppliers and buyers from other countries. The GVC literature makes an attempt to understand the value chains that are divided among multiple firms and spread across wide swaths of geographic space. GVC shows variety of structures starting from a simple format of buyer-seller relationship to more complicated formats such as relational value chain[1], or captive value chain,[2] which are close to 'network' type value chain. Because of increasing complexity value chain literature is now submerged into the broader concept of 'production network'.

A production network depicts connections within or among a group of firms in a particular value chain for producing specific products. The network is very much active in production process of products such as vehicle, apparel, computer or electronic goods. The main focus of the production network literature is how lead firms organize their particular networks of subsidiaries, affiliates and suppliers to produce a given product. Lead firms in a network control access to key resources and activities such as product design, international brands and access to final consumers, etc. This generally gives them leverage over the other enterprises (such as suppliers) in the production network. When the distribution and coordination of geographically dispersed activities within and/or among enterprises takes place across borders in multiple countries, production networks become 'international'. IPN has been identified in the literature as a major driver for international business. It creates a cobweb of production process connecting MNCs and SMEs. This leads towards more competition and innovation.

Apparently, GVC and IPN are used in the same context, but there exists a difference. The value creation in macroeconomic sense from one production facility to other is captured under GVC, which focuses on the competitive advantage of each location. On the contrary, firm specific issues are addressed under IPN literature. GVC is more concerned with relatively not so flexible one directional 'chain' approach, whereas 'network' concept, as conceived by IPN, deals with flexibility and back-and-forth value transmission among various players in the production process. This leads to

1. Based on pattern of dependency between the players in the chain
2. Based on governing pattern of smaller players in the chain

more 'open innovation' and provides an opportunity especially to mid-sized companies for creativity. Under this concept, economic actors are dynamic and reconfigured on an ongoing basis as claimed by Sturgeon (2000). The success of IPN is closely linked to business environment relating to intellectual property rights, technology transfer, FDI policies, Rules of Origin (RoO) under various trade agreements, etc.

Fragmentation vs. Agglomeration

The issues related to fragmentation and agglomeration of production processes has closely linked the concept of GVC and IPN. Agglomeration through industrial clusters hosting number of component manufacturers is an effort to develop a close knitted value chain. This is independent of any international dimension. Fragmentation of the process, on the other hand, has pushed the production location of components to get scattered, and, in many cases across the borders. These two dimensions simultaneously link the vertical and horizontal process. It is observed in recent time that many of the OEMs are reducing their vertical linkage by shredding off completely some of the operations. Ford and GM separated their component divisions as independent suppliers (Visteon and Delphi). Similarly, IBM Microelectronics was created separating IBM's logic division from the main company. As an extreme situation, Dell Computer has given up all internal manufacturing facility and does only in-house designing.

The concept of 'power centre' has occupied a principal position in the literature of IPN. It could be a 'lead firm', which governs the network. In manufacturing sector, generally OEMs act as power centre. However, when the chain gets extended, power centre may get shifted to other nodes in the network, and, for example, we can mention about large retailers like Walmart. These new dimensions have attracted many manufacturers to grab the retail space. Companies such as Nike and Gap who outsource large part of their production and invest resources to manage their brand are increasingly control the retail space by opening their own outlets. In general, as the production process is fragmented, contract manufacturers and turnkey suppliers are more in demand and these suppliers have also generated capacity of full-range of services without a great deal of input by lead firms. In several countries, the dynamism and vibrancy of SMEs have been accentuated by this force. With the influence of lead firms there are continuously attempts for intra- and inter- chain innovation. Intra-chain innovation refers to identification of new function and moving backward and forward from one node to other within the network. On the other hand, inter-chain innovation identifies firm's effort to discover competence in other or related sectors.

Role of Trade Agreements

IPN has become the main driving force behind trade integration among nations (Athukorala, 2008). The unbundling of the stages of production across borders can be traced to technological innovation in communication and transportation that has not only reduced physical distance, but also facilitated the establishment of services links, necessary for the efficient combination of various segments of the production processes. The literature highlights that IPN in Asia has developed from a simple North-South outward processing trade but has turned into a much broader phenomenon (Baldwin, 2008). To facilitate the trade in components, countries have gone beyond tariff liberalization and negotiated other issues such as FDI, technical barriers to trade, intellectual properties, etc. Thorbecke and Bhattacharyay (2012) has argued that production networks increase the productivity, thereby fuel economic growth.

In the midst of a huge literature linking IPN with faster economic growth, there are several economists who have raised doubts regarding the participation of low income countries in IPN. To secure the benefit in a sustained way, economies have to invest in necessary infrastructure, change regulations and harmonise several policies across the nations (Lawrence,1996). Antras and Staiger (2008) also have shown that production processes in multiple locations demand new forms of policies for smooth movement of intermediate goods, which eventually created pressure for deeper economic integration. Nag (2009) and Nag and De (2011) have argued that in an integrated production system, value created at each stage is small, and hence, component trade is more sensitive to trade cost. Orefice and Rocha (2011) have claimed that both deeper integration and production networks influenced each other but not in a symmetric way. Their works show that deeper trade agreements influence production network more, compared to the opposite flow of influence. Higher levels of initial trade in production networks raise a less likelihood of signing deeper agreements. In a separate study, Kimura (2012)[3] have argued that once the initial condition holds, network grows over the years and it gets accentuated when there is a sharp

3. Presentation by Fukunari Kimura on December 13, 2012, at KKC Interaction Programme, Tokyo

decline in network set up cost, service link cost and production cost. An FTA must be supported by other development agenda such as physical connectivity and infrastructure (electricity, water supply, EPZ). Any FTA can simplify policy, but other development issues are important to improve the efficient supply chain (Table 1).

Table 1: Enhancing Unbundling of Production Activities through FTAs

	Reduction in Network Set-up Cost	Reduction in Service Link	Reduction in Production cost
High Level FTAs	Investment Liberalisation IPR Protection Competition Policy	Tariff Removal Trade Facilitation Enhancing Institutional connectivity	Liberalisation of production supporting services Investment liberalisation
Development Agenda	Investment Facilitation/ Promotion	Enhancing Physical Connectivity (hard and soft logistics infrastructure development) Reduction of Transaction cost in economic activities	Upgrading infrastructure services such as electricity supply and EPZ Enhancing agglomeration effect through SME development Strengthening Innovation

Source: Presentation by Fukunari Kimura on 13th December, 2012 at KKC Interaction Programme, Tokyo

The discussion about India's potential gain through IPN has come up in the forefront as it has signed number of FTAs with Asian countries viz. Japan, South Korea, Thailand, Malaysia and ASEAN as a group. Although India has not been able to expand the market for manufactured goods following these agreements because of the low duty regimes in these countries, there is potential for gain in the services sector. India requires to increase its investments in infrastructure, R&D, human capital, etc. to derive more sustained gain from the Asian IPN.

Nag and Sikdar (2011) have pointed out that India's gain from ASEAN FTA will be mainly in terms of 'allocative efficiency' due to the import of cheaper and better quality industrial inputs from ASEAN members, which will improve the performance of India's industrial sector. However, balance of trade will remain negative with major ASEAN members. India can benefit through investment to achieve 'economies of scale' and specializing in sectors subject to 'imperfect competition'. Yamashita (2011) has pointed out that Japanese companies in India are increasingly having higher local purchase from Indian SMEs. Several companies have started exporting from India too. It can be argued that India's focus is mostly remained in the reduction in production cost, but infrastructure is yet to be developed in order to smoothen the production process. Hence, as described in Table 1, to reap the benefit from these FTAs, India needs to work on to reduce the service link cost and network setting costs.

SMEs and IPN: Indian Policies and Achievement so far

There is a strong debate about the benefits SMEs can derive through proliferation of IPN. Researchers have raised questions about the absorptive capacity of SMEs and possible exploitation by MNCs while procuring components at lowest possible price. Many observed that this can create an environment of 'race to the bottom', and small industries will face too severe a competition to survive.

The success of an IPN-driven industrialization for the benefit of SMEs depends on many conditions. Demand side conditions are dependent on the product life cycle of the existing products and nature of competitiveness at the end market. If there is high demand, automatically, the entire supply chain receives the benefit. In case of supply side, right kind of policies is needed to make the business environment conducive for SMEs to play. Proper infrastructure and improvement of trade facilitation augments the forward and backward linkage. Finally, technology spillover, capabilities of SMEs to upgrade their production system etc. are essential to receive the benefit of IPN. The enabling conditions to link IPN with SME benefits are as follows.

- End Market competitiveness: Opportunities for upgrading and sustainability of competitiveness (incentives, conditions, opportunities, etc.) depends on how the demand of final goods varies in the end market and how product life cycle moves.

- Trade Policy Environment: Identification of sectors, scope of liberalization (tariff and non-tariff issues), investment opportunities, capability of the identified sectors to exploit the incentives offered to them etc. are also important to make a sector ready for IPN.
- Trade Facilitation and Infrastructure issues: For fast movement among the production facility, it is necessary to have an efficient process. The reduction of transaction cost provides a natural reason to MNCs to get linked with SMEs in the sourcing countries.
- Capability of SMEs and Industrial Policy: Strengthening horizontal and vertical linkages, cluster development, empowerment of SMEs through scope of dialogues with various levels of governments, etc. are also extremely important. SMEs face major challenge in arranging finance and accessing technology. Existing industrial policy of the country is required to be tuned in this direction which can ensure an effective participation by SMEs in the IPN.
- Technology Absorption Capacity in the sourcing country: Along with the changing demand pattern of the final good how the technological flexibility and adaptability in the lower end of the value chain makes the SMEs to be more innovative is having an overwhelming impact on the sustainability of an IPN.

Historically, Indian SME policy has given focus more on employment generation and less on productivity growth including technology transfer. India requires to bring up a balanced focus on labour augmenting and labour replacing technology with due emphasis on skill development. In 2006, MSMEs Policies have been introduced with an emphasis on internationalization and inter-dependence among innovation, learning, marketing and business strategy. Despite an elaborate and dynamic policy, the progress of Indian SMEs continuously have been hindered by some basic constraints such as, poor credit availability, low level technology, lack of basic infrastructure etc. During the last 20 years, the growth of SME sector has been significant, yet volatile. It accounts for about 40 per cent of India's manufacturing output, 40 per cent of India's total exports, employs about 101 million people in more than 44 million units spread across the country providing 70 per cent of the employment opportunities. The major contribution in terms of SME output comes from sectors such as Apparel (14 per cent), Food Products and Beverages (14 per cent), Fabricated Metal

Products (9 per cent), machinery and equipment (5 per cent) etc.[4] Capital investment and employment in Indian SMEs grew quite fast along with country's overall growth. The fixed investments in the sector between 2001-02 and 2011-12 have grown at a CAGR of 22.53 per cent and employment has grown with a CAGR of 15.04 per cent.

It is also important to note that the share of exports from small enterprises to total exports has slowly been declining recently. According to the report of the Inter-Ministerial Committee for boosting exports from MSME Sector, the exports of gems and jewellery declined by 3.5 per cent in 2012-13, as compared to the previous year. Electronic items show a decline of 9.27 per cent in 2012-13. Readymade garments of all textiles show a decline of 5.76 per cent in 2012-13. Experts have identified the major constraints, which are mainly the lack of finance, technology and international exposure. Indian SMEs find problem to raise funds as banks are reluctant to provide loan with no collateral or high risk. The related serious issue is the growing sickness of the small scale sector as firms are unable to repay the loan. In addition to financial problems, infrastructure constraints, policy hindrances are identified by SMEs as major bottlenecks.

In 2006, government introduced landmark MSMED Act, which provides first step towards connecting Indian SMEs with IPN. It gives thrust on enhancing competitiveness, increasing link with multiple stakeholders and striving for larger market presence beyond India. The policy attaches importance to network with stakeholders both up-stream and down-stream in the network of global value chain, from raw material to procurement to processing/manufacturing to marketing to customer services. To enhance competitiveness, the Government of India has created the National Manufacturing Competitiveness Council (NMCC), which intervenes in upgrading technology, marketing and sales strategy and IPR protection, etc. In terms of promoting innovativeness, the Government has promoted Technology Absorption Schemes for SMEs. Though in certain sectors, FDI and technology have flown smoothly, but it did not happen in many sectors. As a result, the Government has recently created Technology Bureau for Small Enterprises (TBSE), aiming to help enterprises to strengthen their capabilities to develop, transfer, adopt and apply technology; improve the terms of technology transfer; etc. Government insists upon SMEs to obtain

4. Source: Government of India, MSME Annual Report 2012-13

ISO certificate with the provision of partly reimbursement of the cost. Advisory services are also made to SMEs to link them with global production network. In this context, E-commerce is being promoted aggressively. The Ministry of Commerce provides Market Develop Assistance (MDA) and also other assistance through their policy framework (for example Focus Product, Focus Country Scheme, etc). SMEs also enjoy number of schemes relating to exemption or reduction of duties (customs, excise, etc). Moreover, growth of special economic zones (SEZ) in last few years provides a great incentive to Indian SMEs to link them externally operating through the SEZs.

A recent study by Uchikawa (2011) has given indication that Indian firms' participation in Japanese IPN is steadily increasing. MNCs have a long history of procuring parts and accessories from Indian SMEs both in the organised and unorganised sector. This was started mainly to meet the targets of local content. Local suppliers have accumulated 'relations specific skills' through sub-contracting, which Uchikawa has identified as a major channel for technology spill-over in India. With the infusion of FDI in manufacturing sector of India, the sub-contracting activities increased substantially especially in post-2000. As the domestic demand expanded rapidly, many sub-contractors secured economies of scale. Unlike Southeast Asia, where capturing foreign market was the main target of manufacturing MNCs, in India they wanted to provide cost effective solutions to domestic market first. Uchikawa has shown that there are substantial gains of gross value added both in the organised sector as well as in unorganised sector in India, especially in machinery and electrical and chemical sectors, in which Japanese companies are more interested. Many establishments in the unorganised sectors are catering for replacement market or manufacturing the products that the organised sector is not doing. The several tiers of production structure, necessary for a network to develop is now well present in India, especially in industries such as automobile, textile, pharmaceutical, machinery and electronics and electrical goods. Automobile sector in India grew both due to high domestic demand and surge in exports. The total productivity growth in automobile industry from 2000-01 to 2005-06 was 13.9 per cent, in TV and communication equipment 18 per cent, electrical machinery 5.7 per cent, office and computing machinery 10 per cent, and other machinery and equipments 15.4 per cent. Annual growth of Gross Value Added (GVA) in several sectors also has produced encouraging picture. Yamashita (2011) has shown that there is a rise in requirement of medium and high skill workers in Japanese companies in India, indicating gradual introduction of sophisticated technology in production system. Exports from Japanese companies in India have increased steadily from 6 per cent in 2000-01 to 22 per cent in 2004-05. Yamshita has also claimed that this rate of growth of exports, compared to other MNC export platform economics such as Singapore, Taiwan and Thailand. In some sectors, export from Japanese affiliates is quite high in India. Around 50 per cent of sales by Japanese MNC affiliates in the machinery industry was exported to other countries (other than Japan) in 2005. In the transport equipment industry, while the bulk of sales went to local markets, around 23 per cent of sales was exported to third countries. Hence, there are signs that Japanese companies are gradually trying to make India an export platform. The study has also pointed out that the local purchase ratio by Japanese MNCs in India is quite high in chemicals (87 per cent of total purchases), computers and electronic products (64 per cent) and transport equipment (60 per cent), even though they also depend on imports from Japan. This clearly shows that the triangular pattern of IPN is slowly emerging in India and SMEs are engaged in the value chain. It is important to note that these statistics refer to the period before the CEPA was signed with Japan, and we expect this trend to grow in post-FTA period. As mentioned earlier, many Japanese players would like to take advantage of India-ASEAN FTA and procure accessories from their subsidiaries in Southeast Asia or their trusted suppliers from these countries. They may also want their vendors in India to get linked to these companies also and purchase required components.

Participation of Asian Countries in International Value Chain

Use of TiVA and GVC Database

One of the important aspects that ensues the discussion on global value chains is to segregate the role of various countries in the value chain ladder. Most of the trade databases and statistics available today present a gross analysis in so far as they record most of the items in gross terms and the problem of multiple counting also remains inevitable. As an example, one can mention about i-phone's value chain and multiple counting in trade statistics. I-phone is designed in USA, but before it reaches the final stage of assembly in China, its components are procured, some assembly operations are done in three countries viz. Germany, Japan and South Korea. Trade statistics take into account value of the products traded in each stage from one country to other country. Trade data also takes into account the full value when the final good is exported back from China to USA despite the case that actual value addition by China is only 3.6 per cent of the total value of i-phone (Xing, 2013). As the global production is increasingly fragmented, the current way of capturing the value of trade is quite misleading. OECD in association with WTO has brought out a database on trade in value added, popularly known as TiVA. The Inter-Country Input-Output (ICIO) tables of 58 countries accounting more than 95 per cent of world output has been linked with Bilateral Trade Database by Industry and End-Use Category (BTDIxE) to estimate the flows of intermediate inputs across countries and industries. The analysis is based on various economic assumptions, and, hence, it provides estimated value added information. Data are available for 1995, 2000, 2005, 2008 and 2009 (Backer and Miroudot, 2013). OECD has also its own database on global value chain. Together, with these two set of information, we are able to comprehend the position, contribution and the nature of involvement of a country in a particular value chain. This database includes emerging economies such as India, China, Brazil and most of the ASEAN members.

These database map the involvement of countries in value chains. This is done by analyzing several indices like Index of Production Stages, Participation Index and Index of distance to final demand, origin of value addition, domestic and foreign value addition in own exports and also foreign country exports, etc. The thrust amid this discussion, however, still centers on comparing and locating the possible production networks between India and ASEAN countries. Subsequently, more specificity are explored by focusing on IPN in certain key industries viz. electric, machinery and automobiles between these countries. A comparative analysis of aforesaid indices is also done for India, ASEAN and other leading Asian economies (like China, Japan and South Korea), who are key players in these industries to find out how they have evolved on the parameter of value addition. Box 1 presents recent development in India's engagement in GVCs.

Box1. India in GVC

- India has seen acceleration in its integration into global value chains over the last two decades with the foreign content of its exports more than doubling from less than 10 per cent in 1995 to nearly one quarter in 2011, which now puts it at the second highest rate among BRIICS economies.
- A specialisation in services has played a key role in India's integration with 57.5 per cent of the total value of exports reflecting services content in 2011. But the services content of manufacturing, at just over one-third of the total value of manufacturing exports, was relatively low in 2011.
- Although low compared to most economies, the export orientation of Indian manufacturers (27.1 per cent) in 2011 was the third highest among BRIICS economies and nearly double the rate in 1995.

Source: OECD-WTO TiVA Country Notes on India, October 2015

Integration Issues with an Analytical Approach

To start with, we would like to analyse the engagement of major Asian economies in GVC and how it has progressed over the years. We can compare India's position vis-à-vis ASEAN. The data upto 2009 reflects how India has been slowly integrated with the world economy and MSMED 2006 policy has given a boost to SMEs for international exposure. Also studies by Uchikawa (2011) and Yamashita (2011) have given indication that both forward and backward linkages of Indian industries are growing internationally.

Figure 1 provides a direction of how foreign value added are getting importance in the export of one country and how domestic value added embodied in foreign exports are changing over time. It takes into account few Asian players including India and ASEAN countries. Left panel illustrates that slowly domestic value added in the national export basket has been going down, thus indicating that backward integration has been increasing. It is important to note that there is a sharp decline between 1995 and 2008 in countries like Japan, South Korea, India, Malaysia, Thailand, etc., and then stabilized perhaps due to global recession. Right panel explains how forward linkages are increasing over the years. It shows that more and more domestic value added components become part of another country's exports. Japan, Indonesia, the Philippines are ahead in this context. It is also important to note that India's forward linkage is more than China and Thailand.

Figure 1: Importance of Domestic Value Addition in Exports: Asian Experience

Domestic Value Added Share of Gross Exports (%)

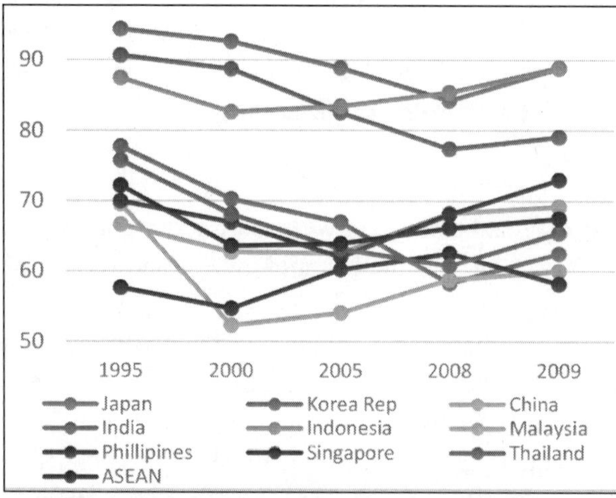

Domestic Value Added Embodied in Foreign Exports as Share of Gross Exports (%)

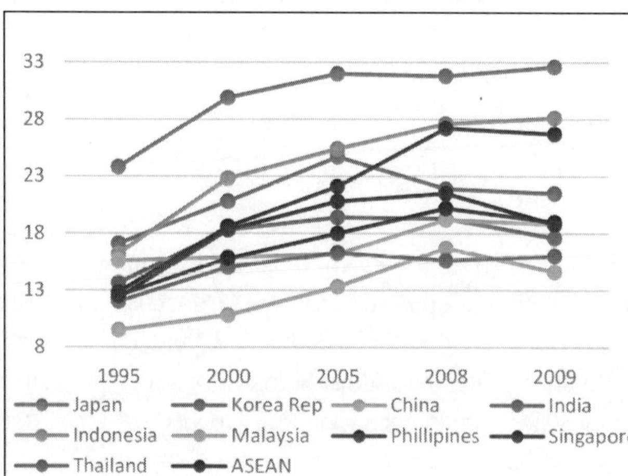

Source: TiVA Database

Participation index looks into this more rigorously. A country's involvement in production process can be said to have both forward and backward linkages. These could be understood in the sense that a country enters the value chains both as a recipient of foreign inputs for the items it exports as well as a supplier of intermediate products, which acts as inputs in third countries exports to which it has supplied. The index is expressed as a percentage of gross exports and indicates the share of foreign inputs (backward participation) and domestically produced inputs used in third countries' exports (forward participation). The calculation of the index is based on work suggested by Koopman *et al.* (2010). There is a decomposition of gross exports into value added shares by source country and the following matrix is calculated:

$$VBE = V.(I - A)^{-1}.E \qquad (1)$$

where V is the diagonal of a vector with value added shares in each country and industry, $B = (I - A)^{-1}$ is the Leontief inverse and E is the diagonal of a vector of gross exports.

When adding values in the columns of the VBE matrix (without the contribution of domestic industries), one obtains the contribution of foreign industries to exports (the import content of exports), which divided by gross exports in each country gives a vector of VS shares, as defined by Hummels *et al.* (2001). Summing over rows (and, omitting domestic industries), we get the contribution of domestically produced intermediates to exports in third countries. Divided by gross exports for each country, this calculation provides the VS1 shares defined by Hummels *et al.* (2001).

The GVC participation index (P_{ik}) simply adds the VS and VS1 shares for country *i* and industry *k* and can be expressed as:

$$P_{ik} = \frac{VS_{ik}}{E_i} + \frac{VS1_{ik}}{E_i} \qquad (2)$$

where VS_{ik} is an element of the vector obtained by summing the columns of the VBE matrix (without domestic industries), corresponding to the import content of exports in country *i* and industry *k*, and $VS1_{ik}$ is an element of the vector obtained when summing the rows of the VBE matrix (without domestic industries) and corresponding to exports of domestically-produced intermediates used in third countries' exports. VS and VS1 are values that are divided by E_i (gross exports in country *i*) in order to express the participation index as a share of gross exports (opcit).These two parts describes the backward and forward participation, respectively. The higher the foreign value-added embodied in gross exports and the higher the value of inputs exported to third countries and used in their exports, the higher is the participation of a given country in the value chain. The index is expressed as percentage of gross exports and hence the range of value is 0-100.

Table 2. Participation in GVC by Asian countries: Year wise Participation Index (%)

Participation Index	Year	India	China	ASEAN	Japan	South Korea
Total	2000	**31.84**	**32.57**	**54.96**	**36.00**	**52.06**
Forward	2000	19.06	13.75	18.38	26.09	19.13
Backward	2000	12.78	18.81	35.47	9.91	32.93
Total	2005	**42.78**	**48.63**	**61.77**	**43.39**	**63.94**
Forward	2005	23.27	12.25	23.55	29.64	26.22
Backward	2005	19.51	36.38	36.55	13.75	37.72
Total	2008	**46.07**	**47.62**	**62.09**	**50.05**	**68.40**
Forward	2008	22.34	14.35	23.94	30.70	24.98
Backward	2008	23.72	33.27	36.13	19.35	43.42
Total	2009	**42.27**	**46.06**	**57.63**	**47.75**	**65.03**
Forward	2009	20.35	13.43	22.45	32.95	24.39
Backward	2009	21.92	32.63	33.14	14.79	40.64

Source: OECD STATS, TiVA Indicators, May 2013

Table 2 indicates that participation of Asian countries in GVC have been rising steadily except 2009, which we may consider as an exception due to global recession. But, the increase in participation is not homogeneous for all the countries, and, further, translates into either higher use of foreign inputs in own exports or a rise in the contribution of exports of third countries. This is precisely the trend that gets corroborated from Table 2. India, for instance, has witnessed a rise in the participation index from 31.84 per cent to 42.27 per cent over the reference period, but within that rise the share of forward participation index has increased slightly from around 19 per cent in 2000 to 22 per cent in 2008, but came down to 20 per cent in 2009. In case of backward participation index, in 2000 it was only 13 per cent, but increased to 24 per cent in 2008, and then came down to 22 per cent in 2009. This implies that during the last decade India has been integrated more backwardly as increasing amount of foreign inputs are now used in its exports. This is more than our forward linkage in terms of supplying semi-finished goods to third country. Similar is the case for China, where the overall participation index has increased from around 32 per cent to nearly 46 per cent over the period, but within that there has been significant increase in backward participation index from nearly 18 per cent to around

32 per cent that has contributed significantly to the overall rise in the former. The share of forward participation index on the contrary has remained more or less same during this period with certain fluctuations. The Apple i-phone example, as discussed before, is corroborating the fact that China has come up as the final stage assembler of many products having significant backward linkage. ASEAN's participation index has shown relatively less growth. Backward index is more or less constant, where forward linkage increased marginally. ASEAN's overall participation index has been around 57.63 per cent in 2009, which is higher than India, China and Japan. South Korea's international linkage is much higher compared to other selected countries. The participation index for South Korea has increased from 52 per cent to 65 per cent over the period with the share of backward participation index reaching almost 40 per cent in 2009, compared to 32 per cent in 2000.This reflects the increasing reliance on foreign inputs for own exports for concerned countries. Japan has highest forward linkage, which has been around 33 per cent in 2009. Japan derives significant gain from exporting technology-based high valued components, which are used in other country's exports.

At the next level to gauge the India's engagement in IPN, we require to understand its position in the value chain in different industries. The distance to final demand, an indicator suggested by Fally (2012), gives an idea of this. It tells us about how upstream or downstream a country is located in a particular value chain. The index is calculated in the following way:

$$D = u.\ (I - G)^{-1} \qquad (3)$$

where D is a column vector with the indexes for all countries i and industries k, u is a column unit vector, I is the identity matrix and G a matrix of output coefficients, with $(I - G)^{-1}$ being known as the *output inverse* or *Ghosh inverse* in the input-output literature. The index is similar to the calculation of forward linkages in the context of an ICIO. As this is primarily an output inverse, it reflects how many production stages are left before the final delivery of the product. Thus a higher value is indicative of the fact that a country is involved in more upstream activities that lie at the beginning of the value chains (R&D, input oriented activities, etc). Lower value of the index indicates closer proximity to final consumers, and, thus, engagement in downstream activities.

The index is further drilled down at the industry level through the following method. For the industry 'I', the distance to final demand is the number of stages of production left to reach the final product. In other words, D reflects the number of stages that have yet to be achieved before reaching final demand.

$$D_i = 1+\sum_j \varphi_{ij} D_j \qquad (4)$$

In equation (4), $\varphi_{ij}=\frac{Y_j \mu_{ji}}{Y_i}$ and under open economy assumption is $\varphi_{ij}=\frac{Y_j \mu_{ji}}{Y_i+M_i-X_i}$, where Y_i stands for both the demand for good i and the supply of good i. In an open economy, part of the local demand is met by imports, while a fraction of the local production is exported. The share of production purchased by industry j is the same whether the good is internationally traded or not. In this expression Y_i stands for the value of production of good i, M_i for imports and X_i for exports. is the input-output coefficients (value of inputs from industry j used to produce one dollar of goods in industry i) φ_{ij} and is the fraction of that corresponds to intermediate input demand (D_j) from industry j to industry i. In the extreme case where the entire production of this good is used as final consumption, this measure of distance to final demand is one. If part of the production is used as an intermediate good, this index is greater than 1 and depends on the share of production used as intermediate good and as well as the number of stages separating the corresponding downstream industry from final demand. The industry level index is calculated for each of the selected countries.

Table 3 shows the comparative analysis of the index for India, China and some leading Asian countries for the years 2000 and 2009 for certain key industries. We have not included Japan and South Korea in this analysis as we have noted from the earlier index that they are in general ahead of most of the Asian countries. Also, selected countries in Tables 3(a) and 3(b) are close competitors to each other in many industries. A closer examination of the tables reveals that China's value has increased in almost all industries between 2000 and 2009, implying its increasing involvement in upstream activities. However, in contrast, for Indian industries such as machinery, chemicals, electrical and optical equipment, wholesale and retail trade, transport, storage & telecommunication, financial intermediation, etc. have experienced a rise in the index scores, reflecting their more engagement in upstream activities in international value chain. On the other hand, fall in the index scores is visible in industries such as textile, transport equipment, business services, etc., which indicates the move towards the downstream activities. In other words, companies in these industries operating from India are exporting products, which are close to final goods in the value chain. Among ASEAN members, Vietnam, the Philippines and Indonesia have experienced move towards downstream activities, where Singapore, Thailand and Malaysia has gone ahead with the upstream activities focusing more on technology development and critical component manufacturing. To summarize, countries such as Singapore, Malaysia, Thailand, along China have moved ahead towards upstream activities and have more control on the value chain and this trend is visible in some industries in India too. But Indonesia, the Philippines and Vietnam are at the lower end of the value chain and mostly concentrating on assembly shop activities. ASEAN FTA has reduced the duties on parts and accessories substantially. Along with this, streamlining the trade facilitation process, investment in infrastructure and reduction of trade barriers have helped the ASEAN value chain to spread across the region. Bigger and richer countries in the region are ahead in the value chain leaving basic assembling and non-critical activities in the hand of other countries such as Vietnam and Indonesia. Investment flow within the region has also accentuated the process. Also, due to economic growth, wage rates in Thailand, Malaysia and even in China have increased substantially, which is also one of the major reasons for pushing the basic manufacturing activities towards the countries with lower wage rate.

While discussing industry-wise scenario, it can be mentioned that in production of machinery China is more involved in upstream activities compared to all selected players in the Table 3(a) and India is ahead of Malaysia, the Philippines and Vietnam. In case of electrical and optical equipment, Singapore has the highest score in 2009, followed by Malaysia. India has also shown a rising trend and remains close to Vietnam level. In transport equipment, China experienced a fall along with India. India is still not involved much of upstream activities and mainly engaged in downstream activities, which are more related to final assembly in the production network.

Table 3(a): 'Distance to Final Demand Index' Reflecting Country's Position in Industry-wise Value Chain

Year: 2000	China	India	Indonesia	Malaysia	Philippines	Singapore	Thailand	Vietnam
Industry								
Food products and beverages	1.82	1.27	1.62	2.27	1.37	1.67	1.68	1.40
Textiles, leather and footwear	2.22	1.64	1.88	1.42	1.25	1.89	1.70	1.41
Wood, paper, paper products, printing and publishing	2.98	2.37	2.98	2.59	2.34	2.51	2.70	2.19
Chemicals and non-metallic mineral products	3.13	2.54	2.76	2.66	2.63	3.10	2.74	2.44
Basic metals and fabricated metal products	3.28	2.52	2.97	3.02	3.06	2.86	2.77	2.86
Machinery and equipment n.e.c	2.23	1.68	2.36	1.52	1.84	1.77	1.97	1.90
Electrical and optical equipment	2.29	1.72	1.87	2.57	2.56	2.44	2.20	2.33
Transport equipment	2.39	1.64	2.07	1.97	2.41	2.63	1.94	2.16
Wholesale and retail trade; hotels and restaurants	2.69	1.92	2.17	2.68	1.95	2.06	1.90	1.86
Transport and storage; post and telecommunications	2.84	1.93	2.27	2.38	1.91	2.51	2.27	2.34
Financial intermediation	2.85	2.39	2.43	3.41	2.46	2.77	2.69	2.32
Business services	2.08	1.69	2.19	2.24	2.02	2.22	2.00	2.68

Source: OECD STATS, TiVA Indicators, May 2013

Table 3(b): 'Distance to Final Demand Index' Reflecting Country's Position in Industry-wise Value Chain

Year: 2009	China	India	Indonesia	Malaysia	Philippines	Singapore	Thailand	Vietnam
Industry								
Food products and beverages	2.55	1.35	1.74	2.39	1.30	1.72	1.67	1.30
Textiles, leather and footwear	2.53	1.61	1.54	1.51	1.73	1.99	1.84	1.37
Wood, paper, paper products, printing and publishing	3.64	2.56	2.68	2.82	2.51	2.54	2.74	2.21
Chemicals and non-metallic mineral products	3.41	2.67	2.67	2.83	2.62	3.25	2.87	2.35
Basic metals and fabricated metal products	3.48	2.58	3.30	3.19	3.08	3.00	2.88	2.69
Machinery and equipment n.e.c	2.34	1.73	1.83	1.60	1.57	2.01	2.12	1.52
Electrical and optical equipment	2.55	1.89	1.63	3.08	2.82	3.10	2.39	1.89
Transport equipment	2.34	1.57	1.91	2.08	1.83	1.83	1.96	2.01
Wholesale and retail trade; hotels and restaurants	2.59	2.07	1.84	2.75	2.01	2.41	1.96	1.71
Transport and storage; post and telecommunications	2.97	2.17	2.18	2.54	2.01	2.61	2.39	2.13
Financial intermediation	3.27	2.55	2.03	3.62	2.53	2.48	2.76	2.12
Business services	2.24	1.62	2.07	2.27	2.09	2.42	2.03	2.52

Source: OECD STATS, TiVA Indicators, May 2013

At this juncture it is also important to take note of the fact that the participation index discussed earlier only gives an idea of the extent of vertical specialization of a country. It tells about the domestic content used in third countries exports or the foreign content used in home countries exports at a particular point. However, we are not able to estimate about the length of the value chains. It might be the case that, for instance, the higher value of forward participation index for a country may be driven by higher share of value added at the final stage. This means that there is a need of certain indicator to shed the light on the length of value chains and subsequently to tell how many production stages are involved before a product is finally delivered. One such index suggested in literature and incorporated in the TiVA database is the index of production stages. It measures the length of GVCs in each industry. The index takes the value of 1, if there is a single production stage in the final industry, and its value increases when intermediate inputs from the same industry or other industries are used in the production of the final good or service. Further, this indicator can be decomposed to reflect domestic production stages and foreign production stages. The index was proposed by Fally (2012), and calculated for the USA economy with a single country input-output matrix. Using inter-country inter-industry framework, OECD-TiVA calculate the index of the length of GVCs as follows:

$$N = u. \ (I - A)^{-1} \qquad (5)$$

where N is a column vector with the indexes (for all countries i and industries k),u is a column unit vector, I is an identity matrix and A is the matrix of technical coefficients in the ICIO. $(I - A)^{-1}$ is the Leontief inverse and the index is similar to the calculation of backward linkages in the input-output literature. In the ICIO matrix, we have the values of all inputs used by one industry in a given country. In addition, we can distinguish between domestic inputs and foreign inputs by calculating the index in the country and industry dimension. This is how we decompose the index according to domestic production stages and foreign production stages.

At the industry level, the index N_i can be interpreted as the average number of stages involved in the production chain, weighted by the value added at each stage. This corresponds to a weighted-average number of plants involved sequentially in the production of i. An input coming from a different plant (a supplier) counts as a different stage even if this input is classified in the same industry as the output.

The value of inputs from industry j, used to produce one dollar of goods in industry i, is denoted by μ_{ij}. The index N_i is measured through recursive method. The average number of production stages embodied in a good depends on how many stages are embodied in each intermediate good. In other words, it can be explained as follows.

$$N_i = 1 + \sum_j \mu_{ij} N_j \tag{6}$$

Further, dividing between foreign and domestic inputs, this index can be extended as the following

$$N_i = 1 + \sum_j (\mu_{ij}^D + \mu_{ij}^F) N_j = 1 + \sum_j \mu_{ij} N_j \tag{7}$$

where μ_{ij}^D and μ_{ij}^F are domestic and foreign shares of input j.

If production does not require any intermediate goods, the measure of fragmentation N equals one. If production relies on a particular intermediate good, the measure of production stages N depends on how important intermediate goods are in the production process and on how many production stages are needed to produce these intermediate goods.

For the selected industries the index of stages of production is given in the Tables 4(a) to 4(c). This will give an account of the how long are the value chains for a given industry, and also the fact that out of that how much indigenous or foreign oriented it becomes in terms of the number of production stages driven domestically or internationally. In case of machinery sectors, Asia has become the factory of the world and value chain has got elongated during the last decade. A comparison between 2000 and 2009 data reveals that among selected ASEAN countries, highest increase is visible for Vietnam. It has increased for other countries as well including that for India. However, in India's final demand index of international stages of production is still quite low. Similar result is observed for electrical and transport equipment. This is important to note that India's index of total production stages is quite close to ASEAN level, but it focuses mostly on domestic value addition.

Table 4(a): Index of Number of Production Stages in Selected Countries: Machinery and Equipment Sector

Country	Index of Production Stages in 2000			Index of Production Stages in 2009		
	Total	Domestic	International	Total	Domestic	International
India	2.45	2.12	0.33	2.56	2.09	0.47
Indonesia	2.50	1.36	1.13	2.55	1.56	0.99
Malaysia	2.40	1.10	1.29	2.58	1.14	1.44
Philippines	2.56	1.52	1.03	2.68	1.78	0.90
Singapore	2.52	1.63	0.89	2.65	1.33	1.33
Thailand	2.38	1.46	0.91	2.51	1.46	1.05
Vietnam	2.64	1.50	1.14	2.86	1.38	1.48

Source: OECD STATS, TiVA Indicators, May 2013

Table 4(b): Index of Number of Production Stages in Selected Countries: Electrical and Optical Equipment Sector

Country	Index of Production Stages in 2000			Index of Production Stages in 2009		
	Total	Domestic	International	Domestic	Total	International
India	2.42	2.08	0.33	2.51	2.04	0.47
Indonesia	2.48	1.83	0.65	2.41	1.71	0.70
Malaysia	2.47	1.12	1.34	2.62	1.16	1.46
Philippines	2.50	1.18	1.32	2.65	1.40	1.26
Singapore	2.71	1.41	1.30	2.83	1.33	1.49
Thailand	2.38	1.32	1.06	2.59	1.33	1.26
Vietnam	2.77	1.49	1.28	3.05	1.36	1.69

Source: OECD STATS, TiVA Indicators, May 2013

Table 4(c): Index of Number of Production Stages in Selected Countries: Transport Equipment Sector

Country	Index of Production Stages in 2000			Index of Production Stages in 2009		
	Total	Domestic	International	Domestic	Total	International
India	2.65	2.32	0.33	2.61	2.11	0.5
Indonesia	2.22	1.68	0.54	2.31	1.88	0.44
Malaysia	2.58	1.34	1.23	2.69	1.47	1.23
Philippines	2.72	1.65	1.08	2.8	1.92	0.88
Singapore	2.5	1.81	0.68	2.48	1.46	1.01
Thailand	2.56	1.45	1.11	2.62	1.47	1.15
Vietnam	2.66	1.57	1.09	2.84	1.47	1.37

Source: OECD STATS, TiVA Indicators, May 2013

Analysis of Value Chain in Selected Industries between ASEAN and India

TiVA country note on India[5] indicates that the country has witnessed a significant move to get itself integrated with GVC. Its domestic value added content for its exports has been around 78 per cent in 2009, which was close to 90 per cent in 1995. Business services, other manufacturing industry, chemicals, transport equipment, machinery, electronic equipments, etc. are the major sectors, which have higher foreign component in their exports. Contributions from many regions in India's gross exports rose during 1995-2009, with East and Southeast Asia, Europe and North America increasing their shares by 3.5 per cent, 2.5 per cent and 1 per cent, respectively. India has contributed significantly by providing value added services in other country's exports. In value added terms, over half of India's exports reflect services, which are slightly higher than even OECD in 2009. This has been mainly driven by increasing direct exports of services along with higher service content in manufacturing exports such as machinery, electronics and transport equipment.

Appendix Tables A1 to A4 describe the backward linkage in India's exports in selected products. In all these categories between 2000 and 2009, India's domestic component in its exports has come down. In machinery, it got reduced from 84 per cent in 2000 to 77 per cent in 2009. A careful observation reflects that share of value added component from EU and NAFTA was high in 2000, but it has come down by 2009 with a rising share of East Asia and ASEAN. Partner countries contributed mainly through supplying value added products from sectors such as basic metal, electrical equipments, etc and providing services such as trading, transport, financial services and business services. In case of India's exports of electronics and optical equipment, we have observed an increased contribution by East Asian and ASEAN countries. These countries are supplying value added components, which are used in India's exports of electronic products. It is also noteworthy that the contribution of western economies is slowly coming down. The value added components and services coming from EU, which are embodied in Indian exports include products like chemicals, basic metals, trading, storage, financial and business services. However, contribution from ASEAN is mostly limited to products, and not services, except trading. In case of transport equipment, a similar trend is also visible. India is now outsourcing almost 24 per cent of the value added

5. Refer, http://www.oecd.org/sti/ind/TiVA_INDIA_MAY_2013.pdf accessed on 5th August 2014

products and services, which are embodied in India's export of automobile and components. Share of EU has slightly come down whereas share of East Asia and ASEAN has increased significantly. It is important to note that share of NAFTA has also increased. Like other sectors, western economies are both supplying products and services, but Asian economies are mostly supplying components, which are embodied in India's exports. More strikingly, in case of manufacturing products (not elsewhere classified)[6], India's exports now contain almost 50 per cent of foreign value added components. All selected regions' contributions including those from ASEAN have experienced a big jump during 2000 to 2009.

Table 5 describes country-wise share of value added components and services in India's exports in different sectors. It can be identified that though India has become much closer to Asian countries, it is still importing major value added components from EU and United States for its exports of selected products. Among Asian countries, China and Japan are much above, compared to Southeast Asian countries. India's close economic relation with Russia is also noteworthy.

Table 5: Share of Value Added from Selected Trade Partners Embodied in India's Gross Exports: Industry-wise Scenario in 2009 (%)

Source Country	Machinery	Electrical	Transport	Manufacturing (nec)
France	0.45	0.47	0.57	1.12
Germany	0.92	0.98	1.09	3.55
Japan	0.65	0.76	0.84	2.66
South Korea	0.54	0.61	0.66	1.85
United Kingdom	0.6	0.59	0.69	1.08
United States	2.04	2.04	2.55	4.83
China	1.1	1.28	1.38	6.35
Indonesia	0.26	0.28	0.27	0.66
Malaysia	0.2	0.26	0.23	1.03
Philippines	0.04	0.07	0.05	0.19
Russian Federation	0.55	0.54	0.55	0.94
Singapore	0.32	0.38	0.41	0.91
Thailand	0.2	0.22	0.26	1.02

Source: OECD STATS, TiVA Indicators, May 2013

6. This sector is not among the selected three sectors. We have considered it as it has experienced a significant decline in domestic value added component in gross exports during 2000 and 2009.

Table 6 explains the foreign value added embodied in major ASEAN members' exports. Intra-ASEAN's trade has helped the region to become more integrated and competitive in other parts of the world. A significant amount of their exports are sourced from other countries in the region. This is very high for Indonesia. We have seen earlier that Indonesia has specialised in downstream activities, and, hence, large portion of its exports are originated in other countries, and, they come to Indonesia at the final stage of production to leverage the advantage of cheap labour. However, in terms of sourcing from India, countries such as Singapore, Malaysia and Vietnam are ahead of other countries in the region. India provides mainly business services, which are required in the manufacturing process. Apart from this, India also supplies metal products, machinery and other manufactured products. India's engagement in trading, transport, storage and telecommunication are also important for the exports from ASEAN region.

Table 6: Share of Foreign Value Added Embodied in ASEAN's Exports in Selected Sectors in 2009 (%)

Source Country	Destination Country	Machinery	Electrical	Transport	Manufacturing (nec)
India	Indonesia	0.56	0.59	0.28	0.33
	Malaysia	0.6	0.7	1.23	0.97
	Philippines	0.74	0.37	0.72	0.3
	Singapore	1.12	1.9	0.85	1.11
	Thailand	0.62	0.43	0.65	0.45
	Vietnam	0.82	0.86	0.63	0.75
Source Region	Destination Country	Machinery	Electrical	Transport	Manufacturing (nec)
ASEAN	Indonesia	66.67	77.07	86.19	88.19
	Malaysia	49.81	49.52	58.93	61.05
	Philippines	68.39	57.97	70.08	80.63
	Singapore	48.22	47.61	58.66	58.66
	Thailand	60.05	54.00	59.69	68.24
	Vietnam	50.22	44.19	51.14	48.34

Source: OECD STATS, TiVA Indicators, May 2013

India-ASEAN FTA and Prospect for IPN

The India-ASEAN Free Trade Agreement (AIFTA) came into effect on 1 January 2010 with selected ASEAN countries. Other countries were also scheduled to join in the due course. Both India's exports and imports with ASEAN have increased significantly in last few years. In 2010, India's total trade (export + import) with the region was around US$ 52 billion, and this has increased to US$ 80 billion by 2013, accounting close to 10 per cent of India's global trade. At the same time, India's trade deficit with ASEAN rose from US$ 6.6 billion in 2010 to more than US$ 10.4 billion in 2012. However, it has reduced substantially in 2013, registering a figure of US$ 4.42 billion. Figure 2 shows the trend of India's trade with ASEAN

Figure 2: India's Export and Import to/from ASEAN (US$ billion)

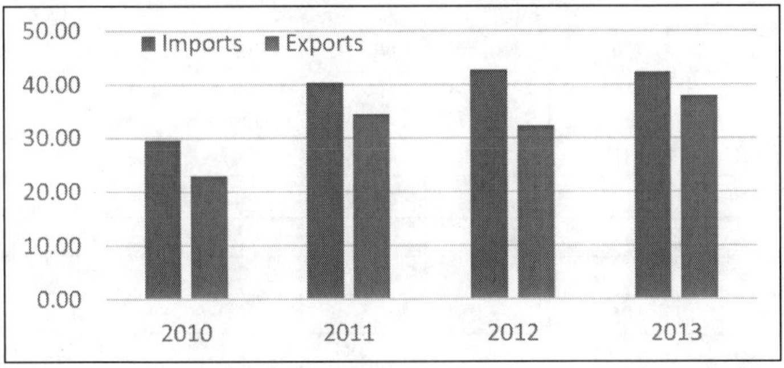

Source: Calculated from UNCOMTRADE

It was predicted that as India would reduce duties, its industries would get integrated with IPNs in ASEAN. Analysis in earlier sections showed that during 2000 and 2009, foreign value added component in India's gross exports from Southeast Asia was not only rising, it was also slowly replacing EU and USA. India-ASEAN FTA is expected to accentuate the process. Between 2010 and 2013, following the FTA process, India has slashed duties especially in the selected sectors substantially. Table 7 provides a snapshot of the changes in the preferential rates for three sectors (machinery (HS 84), electrical (HS 85) and automotive (HS 87)). In case of HS 84, in 2010 only 104 lines attracted zero duties, and in 2013 it increased to 128. In 2010, bulk of the products (1068) under this chapter heading was having 5 per cent duty, and now majority (930) of them has come down to only 2.5 per cent. In the 3 per cent category, number of lines increased from 6 to 172. In HS 85, tariff rates of the bulk of the products in 2010 were either 7.5 per cent or 5 per cent. Majority of them also came down to 2.5 per cent. Some products are in 3 per cent and 4 per cent category. The reduction of the tariff in the HS 85 category looks more steady and distributed. As far as the category HS 87 is concerned, it is evident from the table that most of the products in this category are in the exclusion list. This corroborates the common view that countries want to achieve high degree of localization in the automobile sector. Other observation that is revealed from this table is that there seems to be a major one shot decline in the number of those products which attracted higher duties earlier towards the lower category of 2.5 per cent. For all three sectors, India has substantially reduced number of products under higher duty category.

Table 7: Frequency Table of Sector wise Tariff Rates under India-ASEAN FTA

	HS 84		HS 85		HS 87	
Tariff Rates	No. of Lines on 1-Jan-10	No. of Lines on 1-Jan-13	No. of Lines on 1-Jan-10	No. of Lines on 1-Jan-13	No. of Lines on 1-Jan-10	No. of Lines on 1-Jan-13
0	104	128	146	147	1	1
2.5	0	930	0	331	0	58
3	6	172	0	50	0	0
4	20	7	1	72	0	6
5	1068	0	256	0	0	6
6	43	43	48	48	0	0
7.5	39	21	197	26	64	13
9	21	0	26	0	13	0
20	0	0	0	0	0	6
30	0	0	0	0	12	0
Exclusion List	35	35	20	20	92	92

Note: *Author's calculation using India-ASEAN (5+CLMV) Tariff Schedule

In continuation to the reduction of duties, India's import under these three categories increased significantly in last few years. Appendix Figures A1 to A3 shows the trend of India's export and import in these three sectors. India's machinery import jumped leaps and bound after 2009. The imported machineries are used for producing final goods both for domestic as well as international consumption. The rising trade deficit under this category has slightly tapered off in 2013 due to slowing down of imports. In 2013, India's export was around US$ 1.7 billion and it imported machinery under HS 84 approximately of US$ 3.4 billion. India's import of electrical and optical products from ASEAN rose steadily since last one decade. Increased purchasing power due to rising economic growth in India in post-2000 period has been responsible for higher imports. In HS 85, India's trade deficit has been rising continuously as India's exports to Southeast Asia has remained more or less stagnant with a slow rising trend. In 2013, India's export was merely US$ 878 million, while it imported goods worth around US$ 4.5 billion. Quite interestingly, in automobile sector under HS 87, India has small yet positive surplus. A production network in true sense with return trade is visible in this sector. Since the implementation of early harvest scheme under India-Thailand FTA in early 2000, Toyota has started exporting gear box and other critical components from India. India's trade balance in HS 87 has been positive from 2004 onwards. Now, India exports small passenger vehicles pick up vans, special purpose vehicles and large scale two wheelers in Southeast Asia. In 2013, its export has been more than US$ 1 billion, while it imported around US$ 414 million.

Concluding Remarks

The discussion so far made an attempt to analyse India's engagement with Southeast Asian value chain. It has highlighted that a trade agreement is only a catalyst for developing IPN. However, it depends on host of conditions ranging from infrastructure, conducive industrial policies, encouragement towards technological innovation, to absorptive capacity of SMEs and end market competitiveness. The analysis, though based on pre-FTA data, clearly revels that India's engagement is rising.

The IPN may be a producer driven or buyer driven or even it could be a hybrid of both. In case of parts and components, large lead players (MNCs) procure or outsource critical and non-critical components. Indian SMEs could be part of this outsourcing drive. It is already happening in some sectors such as auto components, but favourable policies are required for other sectors such as electronic goods, pharmaceutical, machinery, chemicals, etc. Buyer driven network is more prominent in consumer goods, where contract manufacturers produce the final good (or almost final) for their worldwide stores or markets. The sourcing strategies of IKEA, Walmart, etc. are good examples for this. Companies should have the capability to do process innovation as per the technical specifications given by the lead company. Firms in textile, furniture, processed food, other FMCG may be promoted for this purpose.

Policies are also required to synchronise the functions of Indian SMEs with IPN governance models. In 'Market' model price is the main driving force for between SMEs and MNCs. The main question is whether Indian firms are competitive enough to replace ASEAN or Chinese firms in terms of price and yet have a margin to sustain. As SMEs do not have internal economies of scale, government policies towards this should be driven by offering external economies of scale through common infrastructure, connectivity, subsidy for network building, etc. We need to identify few sectors in this connection, who can be promoted for 'Market' model. In 'Modular' governance model, suppliers make products according to the customer's specifications and take full responsibility for the process technology using generic machinery, thereby spreading investment across a wide customer base. A better investment regime, high productive efficiency and good logistics infrastructure are needed to fulfil the requirement of Modular kind of network. Indian government must choose areas where some flexibility can be offered for few specified products, which can be directly shipped to ASEAN and similarly some components can be imported. Eastern and Northeastern parts of India have natural advantage because of their geographical closeness to ASEAN. However, higher efficiency and better logistics facility are needed to complement the natural advantage. 'Relational' model works more for the mid-sized firms, who can take risk and have the capability to do some level of innovation. In this model, governance occurs when the buyers and sellers exchange complex information with the lead firms specifying what is needed from the buyer, thereby exerting some level of control over the supplier firms. Automobile, pharmaceutical, machinery are the sectors which can be promoted to develop relational model with the lead firms. Hence, to make Indian SMEs ready for taking the advantage from IPN, it is required to have layered policy (rather than a blanket policy) for different sectors.

The chapter establishes that Indian SMEs have already become part of GVC but its progress has been much less than their counterparts in other Asian countries. It is true that a majority of SMEs across different industries are not able to identify their competitive strengths within the value chain. They also lack understanding whether this identification is important to optimise their participation in global value chains. Indian SMEs are mostly concerned about availability of financial and managerial resources. They have poor capability to do some level innovation. The common logic we come across that SMEs are small and they do not have the critical dimension to support adequate R&D costs, training of personnel, which restrict their ability to grow further in the value chain. The culture of maintaining standards and quality still has not instilled properly. The fulfilment of strict product standards required for participation in GVCs is difficult and costly.

These warrant that SME support system from the government requires a complete overhauling to gear them for participating in the GVC. Strategic joint ventures with foreign firms should be encouraged for the mid-level firms, who will act as backbone to the resurgence of Indian industry.

Analysing data from TiVA, it has been observed that India is slowly but steadily getting integrated with the industries of Southeast Asia, especially in machinery, electrical products and automobile sectors. This also carries some ramifications for Indian SMEs because all the above mentioned industries are dominated by domestic SMEs, and, therefore, if SMEs could overcome technological, financial and other barriers, the IPN in these sectors might act as a growth stimulator. Commenting on TiVA analysis further, it is observed that so far, in India's exports of above mentioned products (viz. electric, machinery and automobile), contribution of Europe and USA has been higher than Southeast Asia and China, but the scenario is changing fast. India is mostly importing components and then engages itself in downstream activities. China has moved towards upstream activities, thereby has better control of the value chain activities. India is ahead of Indonesia, the Philippines and CLMV countries, but behind Malaysia, Singapore and Thailand in terms value addition capability in the production system. India's contribution in the global value chain is not only limited to downstream final assembly but also in various business services, which are required in the manufacturing process. India's engagement in trading, transportation, storage and telecommunication are also important for the exports from ASEAN region. It is noted that in post-FTA period, India has surged ahead with exports of automobile components, implying its strong presence in ASEAN IPN. On the other, in machinery, imports from Southeast Asia is used both in final goods production for domestic consumption as well as for international use. In case of electronic and optical equipment, India is still on the fringe with limited connectivity. India lacks attractiveness in terms of possible investment in these sectors especially in developing joint ventures with SMEs. Several policy documents indicated that India has a major skill gap, which is inhibiting productivity gain, thereby ability to link them with GVC. Coupled with this, as said earlier, most SMEs still face certain barriers in the form of lack of financing, exposure to new technology and ability to conduct small innovation. An effective handholding, proper policy support and awareness about global business strategy can help Indian SMEs to become more connected with emerging international production network.

References

ADB (2007). *Is Intra-Asian Trade Growth Driven by Independent Regional Demand?*. Asian Development Outlook.

Antràs, P., & Staiger, R. (2008). *Offshoring and the Role of Trade Agreements*. CEPR Discussion Papers 6966.

Athukorala, P. (2008). *China's integration into global production networks and its implications for export-led growth strategy in other countries in the region*. ANU working paper on trade and development, No. 2008/04, Australian National University, Canberra.

Athukorala, P. (2010). *Production Networks and Trade Patterns in East Asia: Regionalization or Globalization?*. ADB Regional Economic Integration Working Paper Series, No.56.

Baldwin, R. E. (2008). *Managing the Noodle Bowl: The Fragility of East Asian Regionalism*. Singapore Economic Review, vol. 53, No. 3, 449-478.

Fally, T. (2012). *Production Staging: Measurement and Facts*. University of Colorado-Boulder, May.

Gereffi, G. (1994). The Organization of Buyer-Driven Global Commodity Chains: How U.S. Retailers Shape Overseas Production Networks. In Gereffi, G. & Korzeniewicz, M. (eds.), *Commodity Chains and Global Capitalism*. Westport, CT: Praeger Publishers. (pp. 95-122).

Gereffi, G. and K. Fernandez-Stark. (2011). *Global Value Chain Analysis: A Primer*. Center on Globalization, Governance & Competitiveness (CGGC), Duke University, North Carolina, USA.

Government of India. MSME Annual Report 2012-2013.

Hummels, D., Ishii, J., & Yi, K. M. (2001). *The nature and growth of vertical specialization in world trade*. Journal of International Economics, Vol. 54, No. 1, 75-96.

Kimura, F., & Obashi, A. (2011). *Production Networks in East Asia: What We Know So Far*. ADB Working Paper, No. 320.

De Backer, K., & Miroudot, S. (2013). *Mapping Global Value Chains*. OECD Trade Policy Papers 159, OECD Publishing.

Koopman, R., Powers, W., Wang, Z., & Wei, S. J. (2010). *Give credit to where credit is due: tracing value added in global production chains*. NBER Working Papers Series 16426, September 2010.

Lawrence, R. Z. (1996). *Regionalism, Multilateralism and Deeper integration*. Washington DC: Brookings Institution.

Nag, B., & De, D. (2011). *Rules of Origin and Development of Regional Production Network in Asia: Case Studies of Selected Industries*. ARTNeT Working Paper Series, No. 101, May 2011.

Nag, B. (2009). *Auto-component Industry in Asia: Structure, Trade patterns and Potential for Further Upgrading*. International Journal of Technological Learning, Innovation and Development, Vol. 2, Nos. 1/2.

Nag, B., & Sikdar, C. (2011). *Welfare Implication of India-ASEAN FTA: An Analysis using GTAP Model*. IIFT Working Paper, EC-11-06, July. The bigger version of the paper was presented at the 14th Annual Conference on Global Economic Analysis during June 16-18, 2011 at Venice, Italy.

Rocha, N., & Orefice, G. (2011). *Deep Integration and Production Networks: an Empirical Analysis*. Staff Working Paper ERSD, WTO, July.

Sturgeon, T. J. (2000). *How Do We Define Value Chains and Production Networks*. MIT IPC Globalization Working Paper 00-010. Industrial Performance Centre, MIT.

Thorbecke, W., & Bhattacharyay, B. N. (2012). *Role of Production Networks in Sustaining and Rebalancing Asia's Growth*. CESIFO Working Paper No 3896, Category 8: Trade Policy, July.

Uchikawa, S. (2011). *Linkage between Organised and Unorganised Sectors in Indian Machinery Industry*. Economic & Political Weekly, vol XLVI, No. 1, January, 45-54.

Appendix

Table A1: Share of Value Added from GVC Partners Embodied in India's Gross Exports: Machinery Industries

(%)

	2000						2009					
Source Country	Total	India	EU15	East Asia	ASEAN	NAFTA	Total	India	EU15	East Asia	ASEAN	NAFTA
Source Industry												
Total	100	84.22	5.2	1.85	0.64	2.32	100	77.06	3.92	2.62	1.12	2.31
Chemicals and non-metallic mineral products	3.97	2.98	0.34	0.16	0.05	0.1	3.93	2.69	0.23	0.22	0.09	0.17
Basic metals and fabricated metal products	11.65	9.38	0.97	0.21	0.02	0.15	10.54	7.58	0.43	0.46	0.06	0.22
Machinery and equipment, nec	36.98	35.82	0.45	0.16	0.02	0.16	32.11	31.45	0.23	0.11	0.02	0.09
Electrical and optical equipment	2.18	1.4	0.19	0.17	0.07	0.25	1.45	0.79	0.12	0.22	0.06	0.1
Wholesale and retail trade; Hotels and restaurants	11.05	8.18	0.98	0.41	0.15	0.51	13.81	10.62	0.6	0.55	0.26	0.39
Transport and storage, post and telecommunication	6.46	4.93	0.56	0.18	0.06	0.27	6.53	5.26	0.34	0.19	0.07	0.15
Financial intermediation	7.09	6.21	0.2	0.11	0.04	0.17	8.79	6.74	0.5	0.14	0.09	0.27
Business services	4.7	3.07	0.71	0.15	0.03	0.41	4.11	1.75	0.83	0.18	0.05	0.55
Other Sectors including Services	15.92	12.25	0.8	0.3	0.2	0.3	18.73	10.18	0.64	0.55	0.42	0.37

Source: OECD STATS, TiVA Indicators, May 2013

TableA2: Share of Value Added from GVC Partners Embodied in India's Gross Exports: Electrical & Optical Equipment

(%)

Industry	2000						2009					
Source Country	Total	India	EU15	East Asia	ASEAN	NAFTA	Total	India	EU15	East Asia	ASEAN	NAFTA
Source Industry												
Total	100	84.39	4.87	2.28	0.94	2.59	100	77.9	4.08	3.06	1.3	2.34
Mining and quarrying	3.8	2.54	0.08	0.04	0.13	0.05	7.11	2.24	0.08	0.06	0.26	0.1
Chemicals and non-metallic mineral products	4.76	3.63	0.37	0.2	0.08	0.11	4.77	3.26	0.29	0.28	0.12	0.21
Basic metals and fabricated metal products	8.66	6.98	0.71	0.18	0.02	0.12	7.91	5.53	0.38	0.4	0.06	0.18
Electrical and optical equipment	42.56	40.21	0.53	0.52	0.24	0.72	34.8	33.1	0.29	0.54	0.16	0.24
Electricity, gas and water supply	3.21	2.75	0.11	0.06	0.02	0.03	1.93	1.54	0.08	0.08	0.02	0.02
Wholesale and retail trade; Hotels and restaurants	10.87	8.08	0.93	0.45	0.18	0.49	15.2	12.1	0.61	0.58	0.28	0.37
Transport and storage, post and telecommunication	8.9	7.42	0.53	0.19	0.08	0.26	9.94	8.52	0.42	0.22	0.09	0.17
Financial intermediation	5.3	4.49	0.18	0.13	0.06	0.15	6.01	4.25	0.46	0.16	0.09	0.23
Business services	3.42	1.8	0.69	0.18	0.04	0.4	3.53	1.24	0.84	0.22	0.05	0.5
Other Sectors including Services	8.52	6.49	0.74	0.33	0.09	0.26	8.86	6.06	0.63	0.52	0.17	0.32

Source: OECD STATS, TiVA Indicators, May 2013

Table A3: Share of Value Added from GVC Partners Embodied in India's Gross Exports: Transport Equipment

(%)

	2000						2009					
Source Country	Total	India	EU15	East Asia	ASEAN	NAFTA	Total	India	EU15	East Asia	ASEAN	NAFTA
Source Industry												
Total	100	84.7	4.91	1.95	0.67	2.46	100	76	4.52	3.31	1.31	2.88
Mining and quarrying	4.52	3.2	0.08	0.04	0.11	0.05	7.03	2.3	0.07	0.07	0.24	0.1
Chemicals and non-metallic mineral products	5.05	3.9	0.37	0.19	0.06	0.12	4.52	3	0.28	0.29	0.11	0.22
Basic metals and fabricated metal products	9.92	8.02	0.78	0.17	0.02	0.14	7.78	5.4	0.39	0.4	0.06	0.21
Machinery and equipment, nec	2.41	1.67	0.29	0.09	0.02	0.11	2.52	1.9	0.25	0.12	0.02	0.09
Electrical and optical equipment	1.89	1.14	0.17	0.17	0.07	0.25	1.52	0.7	0.14	0.28	0.07	0.14
Transport equipment	31.3	30.8	0.22	0.2	0.01	0.05	31.1	30	0.14	0.37	0.03	0.22
Electricity, gas and water supply	4.8	4.28	0.12	0.06	0.01	0.03	2.59	2.2	0.08	0.08	0.02	0.03
Wholesale and retail trade; Hotels and restaurants	11.5	8.7	0.93	0.41	0.16	0.52	13.2	9.7	0.7	0.65	0.32	0.46
Transport and storage, post and telecommunication	6.86	5.32	0.55	0.19	0.07	0.3	6.6	5.3	0.38	0.21	0.08	0.18
Financial intermediation	8.92	8.02	0.2	0.12	0.04	0.22	10.5	8.2	0.65	0.17	0.12	0.35
Business services	5.28	3.65	0.68	0.16	0.03	0.44	3.56	1.1	0.88	0.22	0.05	0.58
Other Sectors including Services	7.51	6.01	0.52	0.15	0.07	0.23	9.07	6.3	0.56	0.45	0.19	0.3

Source: OECD STATS, TiVA Indicators, May 2013

Table A4: Share of Value Added from GVC Partners Embodied in India's Gross Exports: Manufacturing Products (not elsewhere classified)

(%)

	2000						2009					
Source Country	Total	India	EU15	East Asia	ASEAN	NAFTA	Total	India	EU15	East Asia	ASEAN	NAFTA
Source Industry												
Total	100	79.9	6.47	3.29	0.97	2.62	100	50.9	10.3	12.98	4.08	5.67
Mining and quarrying	4.67	2.92	0.11	0.06	0.16	0.06	6.51	0.62	0.14	0.26	0.68	0.18
Chemicals and non-metallic mineral products	5.09	3.55	0.51	0.3	0.08	0.14	6.00	2.1	0.77	1.21	0.34	0.51
Basic metals and fabricated metal products	10.4	8.23	0.91	0.24	0.02	0.13	3.8	0.99	0.61	0.88	0.07	0.29
Manufacturing nec; recycling	33.2	31.8	0.45	0.33	0.01	0.1	32.6	26.4	1.66	1.57	0.54	1.06
Electricity, gas and water supply	3.23	2.66	0.14	0.09	0.01	0.03	1.33	0.5	0.19	0.3	0.05	0.05
Wholesale and retail trade; Hotels and restaurants	14.1	9.6	1.56	0.87	0.26	0.76	13.4	5.28	1.66	2.58	0.89	0.93
Transport and storage, post and telecommunication	8.29	6.39	0.68	0.29	0.09	0.31	6.89	4.3	0.7	0.71	0.19	0.28
Financial intermediation	6.86	5.83	0.23	0.22	0.06	0.13	8.61	6.29	0.46	0.58	0.18	0.28
Business services	3.59	1.62	0.86	0.27	0.05	0.4	5.37	0.77	1.76	0.86	0.15	0.91
Other Sectors including Services	10.7	7.28	1.02	0.62	0.23	0.56	15.5	3.63	2.34	4.03	0.99	1.18

Source: OECD STATS, TiVA Indicators, May 2013

Figure A1: India's Exports and Imports to/from ASEAN (HS84)

(US$ Million)

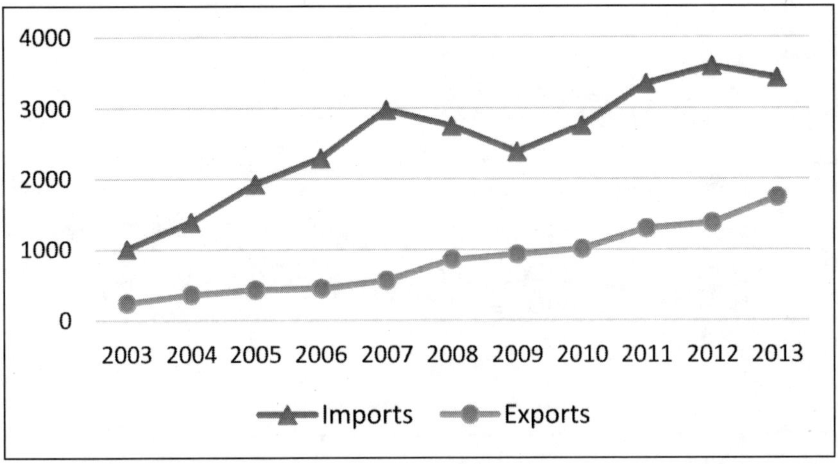

Source: UNCOMTRADE

Figure A2: India's Exports and Imports to/from ASEAN (HS 85)

(US$ Million)

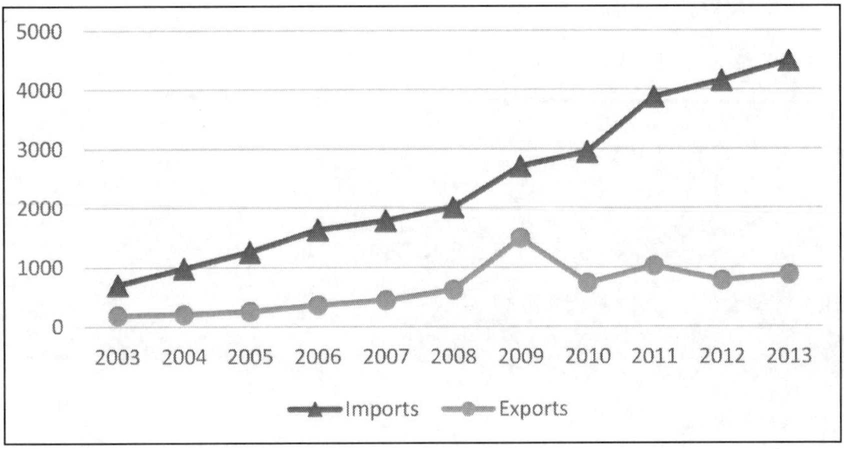

Source: UNCOMTRADE

Figure A3: India's Exports and Imports to/from ASEAN (HS 87)

(US$ Million)

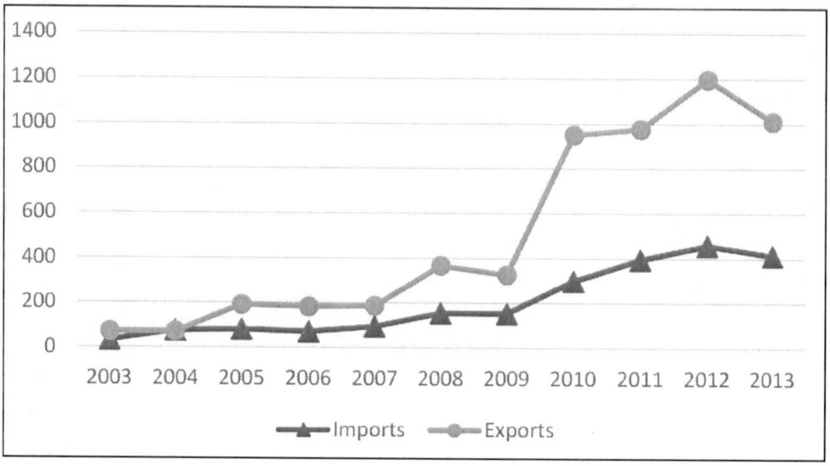

Source: UNCOMTRADE

NINE

TRADE IN SERVICES IN ASIA-PACIFIC: ASSESSING BARRIERS AND IMPLICATIONS FOR SERVICES TRADE FACILITATION IN INDIA

Durairaj Kumarasamy and Imdadul Islam Halder

Introduction

Trade in services has gained immense importance in recent years as advances in technology have permitted new means of providing services across borders. It has been increasing faster than goods trade in the last one and half decades, and has become an important means of conducting international economic activities, besides goods trade and foreign direct investment (FDI) (Urata and Kiyota, 2003). Almost two-third of World's GDP is presently contributed by services sector, and trade in services accounted for 21 per cent of total international trade in 2014 (WTO, 2015). With the technological advancement, many opportunities have become available for cross-border trade that supports for higher trade in services in coming years.

Initially, services were not included in the trade negotiations. However, the growing role of services and their increasing importance in trade flows motivated the countries to sign the General Agreement on Trade in Services (GATS) in 1995. This Agreement governs the rights and obligations of the World Trade Organization (WTO) member countries in the area of services trade. In the recent years, several countries have been showing interests to include services in bilateral as well as regional trade agreements.

Services trade is more prominent in developing countries and is rising fast. The shares of services sector to GDP of the developing economies of the Association of Southeast Asian Nations (ASEAN) and South Asian Association for Regional Cooperation (SAARC) were 47 per cent and 52 per cent, respectively, in 2014. In case of share of services export to total export of goods and services, SAARC holds 44 per cent and ASEAN holds about 20 per cent in 2014, which have been relatively higher than the developed countries of Asia-Pacific. The increasing share of services in economic activities is attributed to increase in the services trade to the world. There has been an increasing demand of the business communities to improve the competitiveness of the services sector, since there are supply side barriers within countries and trade restrictions that hinder the growth of services exports.

This chapter attempts to examine the determinants of services export and its barriers to trade. By analysing the cross-country experiences in the Asia-Pacific, our purpose here is to understand the macro perspective of performances of services export, and also to assess whether the supply-side barriers have any effect on the growth of services export in developing economies of the Asia-Pacific. Furthermore, at disaggregated level using bilateral services trade data, we also attempt to examine the factors determining services export in India. Since most of the developing countries of Asia-Pacific do not have bilateral services export data, we have considered the case of India to study the services exports at the disaggregated level. Although factors determining services export may differ across countries in Asia-Pacific, we specifically study how the supply side barriers have been addressed by the Asia-Pacific countries in general and India in particular.

The rest of the chapter is organised as follows. A brief discussion on literature is provided in Section 2. Section 3 presents an overview of services trade in Asia-Pacific. The role of services trade in India is provided in Section 4. Section 5 presents the determinants of services export and its barriers in the Asia-Pacific and explores the relations between services exports and the barriers in the case of India based on gravity model in Section 6. Finally, the conclusions are provided in Section 7.

Literature Review

The trade in services has been found growing faster than trade in goods over the span of last twenty years with developing countries playing a significant role in it. Expanding the importance of services in the economy has got greater attention in recent studies, especially, with the improvement in information and communication technology (ICT), transportation and other business services. Several studies have used traditional comparative cost theories of either Ricardo or Heckscher-Ohlin to prove that liberalization of trade in services is welfare improving for both the source as well the recipient countries (De, 2013). Studies have used gravity model extensively in international trade services to estimate the determinants and its barriers to trade in services.

The first papers on the gravity model to services trade are by Francois (2001) and Francois *et al.* (2003). They have used GTAP database on services trade and estimated the factors determining services trade and barriers to services trade. Grunfeld and Moxnes (2003) have applied the gravity model to the bilateral export of services and FDI flow using data from the OECD. They have found that the standard gravity model applies to services trade too. Trade between two countries is positively related to their size and negatively related to the distance between them and barriers to services in place in the importing country.

Kimura and Lee (2004) have applied the standard gravity framework to services trade with the aim of comparing the results with the estimates for trade in goods. They used the OECD statistics on trade in services. They have estimated the gravity equation using a mixture of OLS and time-fixed effects. The major difference reported by them is that distance between countries is more important in services trade than in goods trade. They have also found that common language between the importer and the exporter is not significant.

Walsh (2006) has examined the determinants of trade in services and barriers to trade in services using gravity model. He has collected data from OECD database for both total services imports and sub-sectors, such as travel, transport, government and commercial services. He has applied Hausman-Taylor model and found that wealth of countries and a common language were the most important determinants of services trade. To measure the services trade barriers, he has followed tariff equivalent measures developed by the Australian Productivity Commission (APC), and found that services trade barriers were weakly significant for total services trade.

Shepherd and Marel (2010) have explored the determinants of services trade for APEC member countries based on gravity model. They have found that market size, members in regional trade agreements, distance, regulation, and language are major determinants of services trade. They have also suggested that reducing transaction cost and improving infrastructure development would boost trade in both services and goods. Francois and Hoekman (2010) have done an extensive literature survey on services trade and policy. They have argued that services liberalization is a major potential source of gains in economic performance and is also an important determinant in trade volume.

Eichengreen and Gupta (2012) have examined the determinants of the services export performance of 60 developing countries, including India, over the period 1980 to 2008. They have found that per capita income of exporting country, market size, and world demand of services exports, infrastructure development and FDI, and human capital are important factors explaining services export. Nasir and Kalirajan (2013) have examined the determinants of modern export performance of South Asian and East Asian countries and have shown that the performance of emerging economies of South Asia and Southeast Asia in terms of the realization of export potential is considerably lower than that of North America and Europe.

In case of India, Sahoo *et al.* (2013) have analyzed the factors responsible for India's performance in services export. They have found that India's aggregate services exports are determined by the world demand, exchange rate, manufacturing exports, human capital, infrastructure and financial development. They have also found that institutions, FDI and financial development have significant impact on the export of modern services than that of the traditional services. De (2013) has performed an empirical analysis of the linkages between India's services trade flows and probable barriers to services trade. To measure the trade barriers, he has generated services trade facilitation index (STFI) and has found that trade facilitation would help unlock the trade potential, and, therefore, there is need of effective policy approaches towards improved services and trade infrastructure.

Trends and Patterns of Services Trade in Asia-Pacific

Services are much greater part of both output and trade in Asia-Pacific. Table 1 show that services account for nearly 40 to 50 per cent of GDP in both ASEAN and SAARC countries, whereas, developed countries in Asia-Pacific holds the share of 50 to 70 per cent of GDP. Thus, services sector has a very important role to play in all economies of the region.

Over the last two decades, services export has registered remarkable growth in Asia-Pacific. Among ASEAN countries, the share of services export in total export has increased considerably in Cambodia, Indonesia, the Philippines, Thailand, Malaysia and Singapore. The overall services export in ASEAN has increased to 19 per cent in 2014 from 14 per cent in 2000. Travel, Transport and other business services are the major components of services export in ASEAN region (see Figure 1a). Singapore's services export is very large relative to the size of its economy, with services export accounting for 36 per cent of total export of goods and services. A large share of Singapore's services export comes from travel and transport services, followed by financial services. Services exports of the Philippines are similar to India's services export, where information and technology services export is the main component of services exports.

Table 1: Trends of Services Sector and Services Export in Asia-Pacific

Country	Share of Services Sector in GDP (%)			Share of Services Export in Total Export of Goods and Services (%)		
	2000	2005	2014	2000	2005	2014
Brunei	35.20	27.60	32.86	4.89	9.21	4.59
Cambodia	37.14	39.08	39.97	23.53	27.72	36.43
Indonesia	42.14	44.26	42.25	0.00	13.35	11.18
Lao PDR	36.62	38.43	41.14	33.71	21.86	16.15
Malaysia	46.51	44.20	49.29	12.40	12.19	16.80
Myanmar	33.07	35.80	37.66	-	-	-
Philippines	51.55	53.46	57.51	8.11	18.11	31.24
Singapore	59.99	64.55	70.87	15.75	16.11	25.62
Thailand	54.57	52.17	52.67	16.92	15.38	19.76
Vietnam	38.73	34.43	43.38	16.07	11.62	6.82
ASEAN	**43.55**	**43.40**	**46.76**	**14.60**	**16.17**	**18.73**
Afghanistan	19.79	34.13	49.43	-	-	-
Bangladesh	47.47	50.49	53.64	12.37	14.55	9.63
Bhutan	35.83	38.08	36.93	15.66	13.28	17.51
India	40.53	42.55	50.79	27.41	32.45	33.39
Maldives	84.61	71.50	69.42	62.38	66.64	90.84
Nepal	43.79	45.83	48.58	39.56	32.07	59.16
Pakistan	50.04	51.23	50.81	13.88	21.33	19.33
Sri Lanka	46.91	57.99	56.33	14.73	19.52	33.48
SAARC	**46.12**	**48.98**	**51.74**	**26.57**	**28.55**	**44.70**
Australia	64.16	63.67	65.62	24.67	24.35	17.84
China	39.35	40.52	47.30	12.21	10.26	11.33
Japan	67.10	70.19	69.92	13.46	15.59	20.00
South Korea	51.63	53.56	54.19	16.04	15.34	15.80
New Zealand	61.81	64.31	64.57	26.64	31.28	25.71

Source: UNCTAD Database

Figure 1(a): Share of Major Components of Services Export in Total Services Export in ASEAN (%)

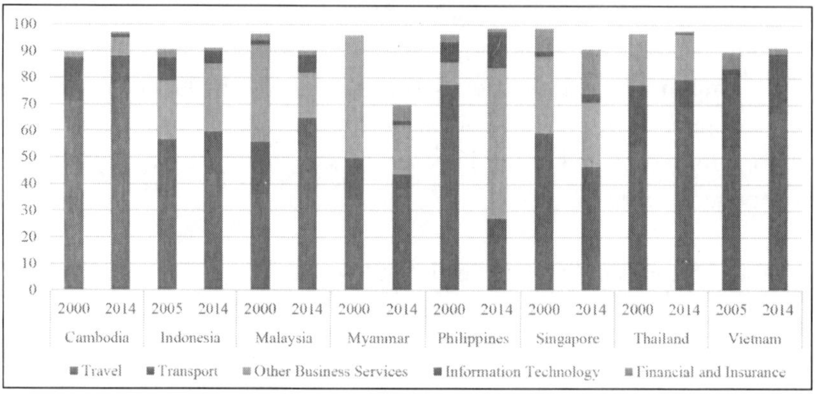

Source: Drawn based on UNCTAD Database

SAARC region has seen significant rise in services exports in recent years. In 2014, the share of services exports to total exports of goods and services has increased to 45 per cent (Table 1). The pattern of services export is not similar in SAARC (see Figure 1b). For instance, Bangladesh exports government services, while Maldives exports travel services. The major services exports of Nepal, Pakistan and Sri Lanka are travel, transport and other business services, respectively. In case of India, information technology services is the largest and one of the fastest growing services exports, followed by export of transport and travel services.

In the case of other Asia-Pacific countries, the share of services export to total goods and services export is relatively low, compared to ASEAN and SAARC regions. New Zealand is having the highest share of about 25 per cent, whereas China has the lowest share of about 11 per cent of services export to total export of goods and services in 2014 (see Table 1). The major components are travel, transport, other business services and financial services. China, Japan and Korea hold the major export share in construction services (see Figure 1c).

Figure 1(b): Share of Major Components of Services Export in Total Services Export in SAARC (%)

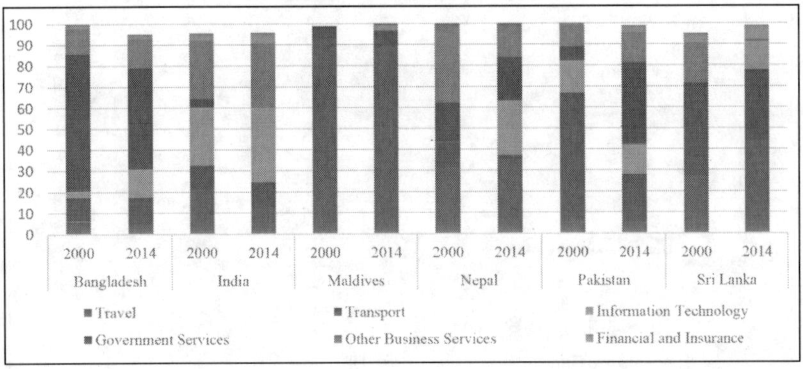

Source: Drawn based on UNCTAD Database.

Figure 1(c): Share of Major Components of Services Export in Total Services Export in Other Asia-Pacific Countries (%)

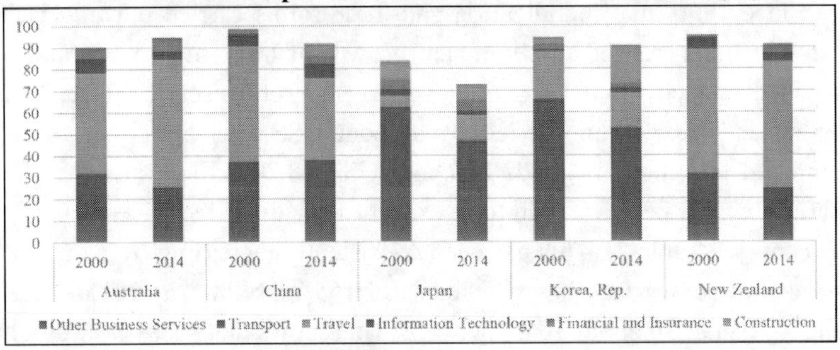

Source: Drawn based on UNCTAD Database

Trends in Services Trade in India

In the last two decades, the services sector has been a major contributor to the higher GDP growth rate in India. For instance, the share of service sector to GDP has increased from 45 per cent in 1990 to about 61.35 per cent in 2014. At the same time, share of services export in country's total export has increased from 21 per cent in 1990 to 32 per cent in 2014. As a result, India's share in global services exports has increased from 0.5 per cent in 1990 to over 3 per cent in 2014 (see Figure 2).

Figure 2: Trends in India's Services Sector Contribution to GDP and Share of India's Services Export in Total Trade and in World Services Export

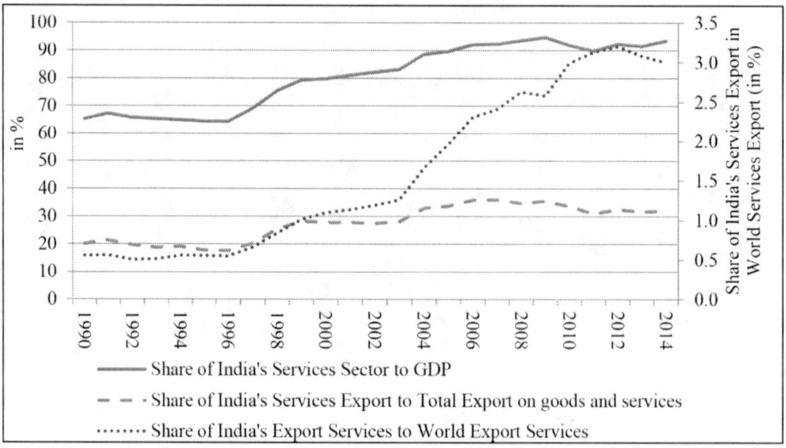

Source: Drawn based on World Bank Database and RBI Database on Indian Economy

Since 1990, the liberalization and the reforms carried out in services sector in India has led to significant growth of trade in services and has provided an access to the growing overseas market for services (De, 2013). For instance, export in services was about US$ 4.63 billion in 1990 as compared to export in goods of about US$ 18.29 billion, and therefore, share of export in services in total export of goods and services was 20.19 per cent (see Table 2). This has been consistently increasing over the years, and export in services has reached US$ 155.84 billion in 2015, thereby holding a share of about 36.41 per cent. This shows that services export has grown more rapidly than the country's merchandise exports. Due to such rapid growth in services exports, India has succeeded in raising its position in global markets more rapidly for services than for goods. Services trade has contributed over 12 per cent of India's GDP in 2015 from a mere 3 per cent in 1990 when India embraced the globalization process. Services export has grown faster than services import in the last two decades and thus has generated a growing trade surplus. For example, the share of import of services in total imports of goods and services remained almost constant to about 25 per cent between 1990 and 2015, whereas, the share of export in services to total export of goods and services has grown from 20.19 per cent in 1990 to 36.41 per cent in 2015 (see Table 2).

Table 2: Trends in India's Goods and Services Trade

	Export of Goods			Export of Services		
	Value	Share in Total Export	Share in GDP	Value	Share in Total Export	Share in GDP
	(US$ billions)	(%)	(%)	(US$ billions)	(%)	(%)
1990	18.29	79.81	5.60	4.63	20.19	1.42
2000	43.25	72.16	9.07	16.69	27.84	3.5
2005	102.40	66.25	12.28	52.18	33.75	6.25
2010	230.77	66.34	13.51	117.07	33.66	6.85
2015	272.16	63.59	13.13	155.84	36.41	7.52
	Import of Goods			Import of Services		
	Value	Share in Total Import	Share in GDP	Value	Share in Total Import	Share in GDP
	(US$ billions)	(%)	(%)	(US$ billions)	(%)	(%)
1990	23.44	79.38	7.18	6.09	20.62	1.86
2000	53.89	73.74	11.31	19.19	26.26	4.03
2005	134.69	74.06	16.15	47.17	25.94	5.65
2010	359.98	75.83	21.07	114.74	24.17	6.72
2015	409.45	76.88	19.75	123.11	23.12	5.94

Source: Calculated based on UNCTAD Database

Given the performance of India's services sector, almost all the components of India's services export have shown double digit growth rate per annum (see Table 3). Telecommunication, computer and information services registered the highest export in services, which has increased from US$ 16.86 billion in 2005 to US$ 57.66 billion in 2015, and has grown at an annualised growth rate of 13.08 per cent per annum during 2005 and 2015. It has contributed to almost 40 per cent of India's total services export in 2015. This shows that due to consistent demand from developed countries and comparative advantage in offering IT-enabled services, India is the fastest growing information technology market in the world. This is followed by exports in travel and transportation services, which has contributed 9 and 13 per cent in India's services export in 2015, respectively. India's services export is directed mostly to the USA, Japan and European countries such as Belgium, Denmark, France, Italy, the Netherlands, Sweden and the United Kingdom (see Table 4).

Table 3: Composition of India's Services Exports

Category	2005		2010		2015		CAGR (2005 -2015)
	Value	Share in Total Services Export	Value	Share in Total Services Export	Value	Share in Total Services Export	
	(US$ billion)	(%)	(US$ billion)	(%)	(US$ billion)	(%)	(%)
Transport	6.54	12.53	13.28	11.34	14.34	9.20	8.18
Travel	7.49	14.36	14.49	12.38	21.01	13.48	10.86
Construction	0.35	0.66	0.53	0.45	1.49	0.95	15.70
Insurance and pension services	0.94	1.80	1.78	1.52	1.99	1.28	7.76
Financial services	1.14	2.19	5.83	4.98	5.33	3.42	16.65
Charges for the use of intellectual property	0.21	0.39	0.13	0.11	0.46	0.30	8.45
Telecommunications, computer, and information services	16.86	32.32	40.51	34.60	57.66	37.00	13.08
Other business services	18.21	34.90	34.53	29.49	48.61	31.19	10.32
Personal, cultural, and recreational services	0.11	0.21	0.98	0.83	1.26	0.81	27.51
Government goods and services	0.33	0.63	0.49	0.41	0.55	0.35	5.32
Goods-related services					0.32	0.20	
Total Services Export	52.18	100	117.07	100	155.84	100	11.56

Source: UNCTAD Database

In the case of services import, about 43 per cent and 12 per cent of India's services import came from the transport and travel services, respectively, in 2015 (Table 5). This shows that India imports more of transportation services and travel services, followed by other business services, financial and insurance services.

Table 4: Composition of India's Services Imports

Category	2005		2010		2015		CAGR (2005-2015)
	Value	Share in Total Services Import	Value	Share in Total Services Import	Value	Share in Total Services Import	
	(US$ billion)	(%)	(US$ billion)	(%)	(US$ billion)	(%)	(%)
Transport	20.89	44.28	46.53	40.56	52.29	42.48	9.61
Travel	6.19	13.12	10.49	9.14	14.85	12.06	9.15
Construction	0.60	1.28	0.99	0.87	0.97	0.78	4.84
Insurance and pension services	2.33	4.94	5.01	4.36	5.30	4.31	8.58
Financial services	0.87	1.84	6.79	5.92	3.10	2.52	13.56
Charges for the use of intellectual property	0.67	1.42	2.44	2.13	5.01	4.07	22.24
Telecommunications, computer, and information services	1.47	3.13	3.62	3.15	3.78	3.07	9.87
Other business services	13.57	28.78	25.50	22.22	29.91	24.29	8.22
Personal, cultural, and recreational services	0.10	0.22	4.18	3.64	1.39	1.13	29.47
Government goods and services	0.47	0.99	0.70	0.61	0.89	0.72	6.62
Goods-related services					0.29	0.23	
Total Services Export	47.17	100	114.74	100	123.11	100	10.07

Source: UNCTAD Database

Table 5: India's Services Export by Major Countries and Sectors

(US$ billion)

Country	Computer and Information Technology		Financial Services		Transpor- -tation Services		Travel Services		Other Business Services		Other Services		Total Services	
	2007	2012	2007	2012	2007	2012	2007	2012	2007	2012	2007	2012	2007	2012
Belgium	0.04	0.11	0.003	0.004	0.06	0.20	0.02	0.03	0.08	0.14	0.02	0.07	0.24	0.55
Denmark	0.06	0.03	0.000	0.000	0.29	0.37	0.01	0.02	0.08	0.08	0.01	0.03	0.46	0.54
Finland	0.03	0.14	-	-	-	-	-	0.00		0.43	0.23	0.08	0.26	0.65
France	0.01	0.36	0.001	0.045	0.31	0.49	0.28	0.23	0.16	0.56	0.12	0.12	0.88	1.81
Italy	0.01	0.01	0.001	0.001	0.07	0.08	0.24	0.27	0.14	0.20	0.04	0.04	0.49	0.60
Japan	0.09	0.12	0.022	0.021	0.10	0.05	0.08	0.17	0.12	0.35	0.14	0.04	0.56	0.75
Netherlands	0.24	0.23	0.002	0.005	0.09	0.00	0.06	0.10	0.25	0.46	0.09	0.25	0.73	1.04
Sweden	0.03	0.26	0.000	0.001	0.01	0.01	0.00	0.00	0.11	0.43	0.02	0.06	0.17	0.77
United Kingdom	-	-	-	-	0.68	0.37	1.67	1.33	-	-	1.20	1.93	3.55	3.63
United States	4.20	10.25	0.232	0.300	0.28	0.42	2.11	2.32	-	-	3.07	5.29	9.89	18.58

CAGR (2007-2012)

Country	Computer and Information Technology	Financial Services	Transpor- -tation Services	Travel Services	Other Business Services	Other Services	Total Services
Belgium	20.05	7.09	26.06	2.79	10.74	23.01	17.79
Denmark	-12.14	-	4.84	12.52	0.70	31.63	3.43
Finland	37.80	-	-	-	-	-19.39	19.84
France	96.66	101.06	9.50	-3.41	28.89	-1.04	15.38
Italy	14.04	-18.63	3.76	2.32	8.29	-0.02	4.28
Japan	7.96	-0.52	-14.52	14.58	23.17	-21.96	6.16
Netherlands	-0.93	19.25	-	10.43	12.74	22.31	7.17
Sweden	56.61	37.91	0.40	-	31.31	31.83	35.74
United Kingdom	-	-	-11.61	-4.41	-	9.93	0.42
United States	19.56	5.28	8.29	1.90	-	11.52	13.45

Source: Computed based on OECD Database

Liberalisation of Services Sector

The reason for the dynamism in the services sectors is mainly attributable to factors such as the income elasticity of demand for services, cost-reducing and variety-enhancing technological advances, and changes in the method of organising production favouring increased outsourcing. In addition, access to a growing external market for services and gradual liberalisation of the domestic economy have also played a significant role in growth in India's service sector.[1] A study by the World Bank (2004) shows how the reforms combined with access to the global market have helped in increasing the growth rate of services sectors. The highest growth segments have been business and communication services, followed by banking and life insurance services, which are also classified as significantly liberalised sectors. Storage, postal and railways services have registered the lowest growth rates, and are classified as non-liberalised or more-restricted sectors. Several services that have experienced moderate growth rates have generally undergone moderate liberalisation.

Overall, India's services export has grown strongly over the past two decades. India has been playing a proactive role in liberalization of services trade since the Doha Round of multilateral trade negotiations under GATS. Cross-border supply (GATS mode 1) and the presence of natural persons (GATS mode 4) are the two key modes of service delivery in which India has comparative advantages[2]. India has embarked on several regional and bilateral level trade agreements that incorporate services trade. The major features of India's services trade in bilateral and regional trade arrangements include trade complementarities and opportunities; trade facilitation to expand the bilateral trade flow; market access and national treatment obligations; and GATS plus outcomes in provisions relating to domestic regulations and recognition[3]. However, India's services export has both internal and external challenges. Internal challenges are related to infrastructure constraints, whereas the external challenges relate to international competitiveness in services and ways to overcome barriers to trade in services.

1. See, for example, the World Bank (2004).
2. See, for example, the World Bank (2004) for the policy implications on accessing foreign markets and counter present and potential protection on India's services sector.
3. See, for example, Raychaudhuri and De (2012) for extensive collection on literature review

Determinants of Services Export in Asia-Pacific

Model and Data

In this section, we formulate a framework of analysis to determine the factors affecting services exports in developing economies of Asia-Pacific. Based on several empirical studies given in Section 2, we find that determinants of services exports are broadly influenced by internal and external factors. Internal factors or supply side factors include GDP, skilled labour force, FDI inflows, infrastructure development and the quality of institutions. External factors or demand driven factors include world income, world demand for services imports and relative prices of services products. We started with the list of all countries of Asia-Pacific (as defined by the World Bank), but had to eliminate many countries as they did not have adequate (or any) data, and finally we have screened down to 20 countries in Asia-Pacific. The list of selected countries is given in Appendix 1. Thus, the study has covered a panel of 20 countries over the period 2000-2015. The definitions of the variables and data sources are given in Appendix 2.

In our study, we have followed the single equation approach of Chinn (2003), where both demand and supply equations are solved together to present equilibrium volume of exports. The empirical model for our panel data estimation is given as follows:

$$\begin{aligned} &Ln\ Real\ Services\ Export_{it} \\ &\quad =\alpha+\beta_1 LnRGDP_{it}+\beta_2 LnSkilledLabour_{it}+\beta_3 LnRER_{it}+\beta_4 LnRFDI_{it} \\ &\quad +\beta_5 STFI_{it}+\beta_6 Institution\ Index_{it}++\beta_7 LnReal\ World\ Demand_{it}+\varepsilon_{it} \end{aligned} \qquad (1)$$

Ln Real Services Export denotes the log of real services export to the world from respective selected countries for our analysis. The subscript *i* and *t* represent country and year, which is the random error term. *LnRGDP* is the supply side factors, implies that higher the level of economy output, higher would be the services export, as surplus of output can be exhausted in international markets (Majeed *et al.*, 2006). So, we expect positive impact of GDP on services export.

Ln Skilled Labour is to capture the level of skilled and educated labour force in a country. Countries which have highly skilled labour force is likely to contribute to productivity, competitiveness, absorbs the technology transfer effectively that would lead to promote services export. As we have seen from the Figure 1a to Figure 1c, the main components of services export in Asia-Pacific are Travel, Transport, IT and Financial services. To promote these services, the countries should focus on providing adequate skills and training for the labour, to face the competitiveness in services export. Therefore, we expect to have positive relation with services export. We used Barro-Lees (2013) average years of schooling as a proxy for skilled labour[4].

RER is real exchange rate, measures the fall in the relative domestic prices due to exchange rate depreciation, which makes exports cheaper in international markets, leading to increase the services export, and, therefore, we expect the positive impact of real exchange rate on services export. Real exchange rate is important for the services export particularly for information and communication technology (IT) and financial services, where many of the Asia-Pacific countries are engaged in business process outsourcing and other IT related services, mostly for the developed countries like USA and European countries. Therefore, given the international competitiveness and diversification in the products of services, any changes in exchange rate would have huge impact on services export.

Ln Real World Demand is the log of real world import of services to capture the world demand for services export from the selected countries. The services export market is influenced by the condition prevailing in the world market. The demand for services exports increases in response to the income of the rest of the world. For instance, higher the level of foreign real income, larger the demand for services exports from the host country. In the literature, measures like GDP, industrial production, and world demand for real imports of services are used to estimate the income elasticity (Huang and Viana, 1995; Deardoff *et al.*, 2000; Sahoo, 2013). In this study, we consider world import for services import to measure the world demand for services.

Institution Index is to measure the quality of Institutions. We have used Kaufmann *et al.* (2010) worldwide governance indicators, which cover six dimensions of governance such as Voice of Accountability, Political Stability and Absence of Violence, Government Effectiveness, Regulatory Quality, Rule of Law and Control of Corruption. Institutional Index has been estimated using Principal Component Analysis (PCA). The quality of

4. As a proxy for skilled labour, we tried to use secondary enrolment ratio and labour force participation with secondary education. However, the continuous data is not available for all sample countries.

institutions is highly correlated with trade (Francois and Manchin, 2006). They have found that export performance and the propensity to participate in the trading system depend on Institutional quality. Kimura and Lee (2006) also have suggested that trade in services is positively influenced by the quality of institutions. Institutions also indirectly affect trade via strengthening investment and productivity (Meon and Sekkat, 2008). Therefore, we expect the institutional index to have a positive effect on services export.

Assessing Services Trade Barriers: Methodology

Unlike trade in goods, measuring restriction on trade in services is more difficult. International trade in goods involves an exchange of a product between a producer and consumer, and restriction on such trade usually takes the form of a tariff. Whereas, trade in services involves a less tangible exchange between the producer and the consumer, restrictions usually take the form of domestic regulations. There are several studies, which have extensively studied the service trade restrictions.[5] However, quantitative estimates are not feasible for such restrictions. Hence, we have estimated service trade facilitation index, following De (2013) that captures some important trade facilitation elements, which influence the services trade flow between countries. From the measure of STFI, supply side bottlenecks are specifically captured, which are equally important to address and removal of trade barriers, leading to increase the services trade flow.

The STFI is comprised of five indicators, viz. (i) internet users (per 100 people) (ii) international internet bandwidth (bits per person), (iii) electric power consumption (kWh per capita), (iv) air transport passengers carried (per 100 people), and (v) fixed line and mobile phone subscribers (per 100 people). Each of the five services trade facilitation indicators is normalized for the size of the economy so that it is not affected by the scale. STFI has been estimated with the help of Principal Component Analysis (PCA). The weights are calculated by dividing the rotated factor loading of any variable by the sum of rotated factor loadings. Thus, weights make intuitive sense since they express the contribution of each variable to the total variance of the common factor. The data for measuring services trade facilitation index are all collected from the World Development Indicators, World Bank Database.

5. See, for example, Raychaudhuri and De (2012) for an extensive collection on literature review

Generalized Method of Moment (GMM): Econometric Estimation Procedure

We have used GMM estimation procedure to estimate the determinants of services export in Asia-Pacific. This method takes into consideration the dynamic structure between the dependent and independent variables (Baltagi, 1995). The use of panel data in estimating ensures control for missing or unobserved variables, while relationships allow identification of country-specific effects (Arellano-Bond, 1991). The dynamic panel data model allows dynamic effects to be introduced into the model and feedback from current or past shocks by using the first differences of the variables as instruments. The dynamic panel data model estimates an equation such as:

$$y_{it} = \delta y_{t-1} + \beta x_t + u_t \qquad (2)$$

where y_i is the dependent variable for i=1,2,…,n different countries in the panel and t=1,2,…,t refers to the (yearly) time period. δ is a scalar, x is k x1 vector of explanatory variables, μ_i denotes the country effect for country i and u_{it} is the error term of regression.

The inclusion of the lagged dependent variable along with the fixed effects can cause estimations to be biased. The GMM estimation procedure uses the first differences of explanatory variables as instruments to minimise bias effects. The Sargan test is used to check the suitability of the instruments and that they are not correlated with the error term, while the Arellano-Bond (AB) test is used to check that a serial correlation problem does not affect estimates. The GMM procedure has the advantage that potential endogeneity of variables usually does not significantly affect the estimated parameters.

Results and Discussions

In this section we report the empirical results based on panel data for 20 Asia-Pacific countries over the period 2000 to 2015. The results of GMM estimation are given in Table 6. We have carried out the analysis for different country groups, in order to understand how within a sample country, different country groups differ in the estimation. Thus, we have done the analysis for 20 sample countries of Asia-Pacific, 15 countries of developing economies of Asia-Pacific, ASEAN and SAARC. The list of countries in different groups is given in Appendix 3.

Table 6: Determinants of Services Export in Asia Pacific

Country Group	Model 1	Model 2	Model 3	Model 4
	Asia-Pacific	Developing Economies of Asia Pacific	ASEAN	SAARC
Log of RGDP	0.93 (0.23)***	0.66 (0.35)**	0.44 (0.24)**	1.57 (0.66)***
Log of Real World Services Import	0.59 (0.06)***	0.68 0.09***	0.69 (0.13)***	0.26 (0.13)***
Log of Schooling	0.57 (0.36)*	-0.40 (0.56)	-0.12 (0.84)	1.71 (0.64)***
Log of Real Exchange Rate	0.33 (0.08)***	0.44 (0.12)***	0.42 (0.19)***	0.39 (0.15)***
STFI	0.06 (0.03)***	0.15 (0.06)***	0.15 (0.08)*	0.10 (0.23)
Institution Index	0.13 (0.06)***	0.17 (0.08)***	0.15 (0.11)*	-0.002 (0.09)
Log of RFDI inflows	0.002 (0.01)	0.009 (0.02)	0.03 (0.02)	-0.002 (0.03)
Constant	-26.55 (5.03)***	-20.10 (7.99)***	-15.44 (10.71)	-39.76 (15.16)***
Wald test of joint significance	5153.99***	6389.81***	3329.10***	1646.81***
Sargan test (p-value)[1]	0.14	0.08	0.86	0.48
AB test (p-value)[2]	0.55	0.55	0.37	0.57
Observations	209	161	106	62
Period	2000-2015	2000-2015	2000-2015	2000-2015
Countries	20	15	9	6

Notes: [1]The Sargan test's null hypothesis is that the instruments are not correlated with the residuals. [2]TheAB test's null hypothesis is that there is no serial correlation. Parentheses show standard error. ***/**/* imply significance at 1 per cent, 5 per cent and 10 per cent confidence levels, respectively.

The effect of GDP is highly significant, having positive sign. The rise in level of economic activities can be utilized at domestic and international level at the same time. Moreover, larger size of economic activities would bring more investment in the services sector that in turn would promote services export. The regression results also reveal that real exchange rate is positive and significant in all the models. The depreciation of the real exchange rate increases export, thus showing positive link between the depreciation of real exchange rate and services export. The variable schooling is positive and significant only in whole sample of Asia-Pacific and SAARC regions. In case of ASEAN region, it is negative and insignificant.

The coefficient of real world services import is consistently positive and significant, thus implying that higher the global demand for services, higher will be the services export from the Asia-Pacific. In particular, the coefficient is slightly higher around 0.70 for the developing economies of Asia-Pacific and ASEAN countries, compared to SAARC region for which it is about 0.26. This shows that every one per cent increase in the world demand for services import leads to increase of about 70 per cent of services export from the developing economies of Asia-Pacific and ASEAN regions. It reflects that ASEAN services export depends on the growth of the world demand.

The coefficient of service trade facilitation index is positive and significant for Asia-Pacific as a whole. In case of ASEAN, the coefficient is positive, but significant at 10 per cent level, whereas, for the SAARC region, it is positive, but not insignificant. The result suggests that supply side endowment factors facilitate services export in Asia-Pacific and ASEAN regions. In case of SAARC, the variable has come out as statistically insignificant.

The institutional index is positive and significant in all the country groups except for SAARC region. Better institutional factors such as government regulation, rule of law, control of corruption do promote services export in ASEAN region. The result also supports the previous studies like Kimura and Lee (2004) and Francois and Manchin (2006).

The coefficient of FDI inflows is found as consistently positive and insignificant in all the models. This indicates that the success stories of increasing inflows of FDI in Asia-Pacific are not necessarily needed to promote the services export. Moreover, the role of FDI in many developing countries may not contribute to export growth, if the motive of FDI is to capture the domestic market. Kolstad and Villanger (2008) have argued that many services related industries are not tradable or costly to trade, and some of the services to large extent cannot be subjected to cross-border trade. Therefore, tapping domestic demand for services require physical presence of foreign investment, when services are difficult to trade, thereby implying that FDI in services is likely to be market seeking. However, the interpretation of the results has to be taken cautiously since we have taken aggregate FDI inflows, instead of FDI inflows in services.

Determinants of India's Services Exports and Barriers to Trade in Services

Model and Data

It is evident that the Asia-Pacific as a whole shows that the coefficients are with expected signs and significant. Developing economies of Asia-Pacific show mixed results because it includes the developing countries of ASEAN (excluding Singapore), all SAARC countries and China. Therefore, any difference in the results of ASEAN and SAARC might have an effect in this model. However, the core determinants are consistent in all the models except for the case of schooling and STFI. ASEAN region has a high potential to benefit from the services export, given that STFI and institutional index are positively promoting services export, and also ASEAN reacts favourably towards the world import of services. It is evident that SAARC has to concentrate on infrastructure development, which would facilitate the services export. However, given that India's higher performance in services sector, compared to other SAARC countries, India has gained comparative advantage in information technology and financial services. Therefore, it is worth investigating the performance of services export of India. We need to investigate whether the services trade facilitation factors positively promote services export in India. In this section, we intend to examine the factors, which are responsible for India's services export. Particularly, our interest is to analyse the determinants of India's services export in a gravity model framework and also to assess the trade barriers that are impediments to trade in services.

To empirically estimate the model, we have used an augmented gravity model. The baseline equation is as follows:

$$ln\, EXP_{ij}^{t} = \alpha + \beta_1 TGDP_{ijt} + \beta_2 SGDP_{ij}^{t} + \beta_3 DGDPPC_{ij}^{t} + + \beta_4 DIST_{ij} + \beta_5 Language_{ij+} + \beta_6\, STFI_i + \beta_7\, STFI_j + Other\ Controls + \epsilon_{ij}^{t} \quad (3)$$

The dependent variable is export of services from country i to country j at time t. We have also estimated the model for major components of services exports, namely, computer and information technology, transportation, travel and financial services as dependent variables.

In the literature on gravity models, three variables are used as a measure of the size of a country - GDP, GDP per capita and population for both origin and destination countries. The present study has used three different measures developed based on new trade theory such as TGD_{ij}^{t}, $SGDP_{ij}^{t}$ and $DGDPPC_{ij}^{t}$ to assess the sizes of the origin and destination countries that determine bilateral trade[6].

$TGDP_{ij}^{t}$ is the log of sum of origin and destination countries GDP. The coefficient β_1 is expected to be positive. A higher level of income in the importing country should indicate a higher level of demand for services (produced domestically or imported), whilst a higher income level in the exporting country should be positively related to that country's ability to produce more services for export. Mirza and Nicoletti (2004) have shown that the supply of services to foreign markets is strongly linked to the availability of inputs in both domestic and foreign markets.

$SGDP_{ij}^{t}$ is the similarity index computed as $\left[1-\left\{\frac{GDP_i^t}{GDP_i^t+GDP_j^t}\right\}^2-\left\{\frac{GDP_i^t}{GD_i^t+GDP_j^t}\right\}^2\right]$. The similarity index reflects that similar in terms of size (GDP) determines trade. Higher the similarity, higher will be the trade (Helpman and Krugman, 1985).

$DGDPPC_{ij}^{t}$ is the dissimilar per capita income level measured as absolute difference of log of GDP per capita of origin and destination countries, i.e. $|lnGDPPC_i^t - lnGDPPC_j^t|$. Similarity of per capita income levels enhance trade because of Linder hypothesis. For example, the more similar the demand structure of two countries, the more intensive potentially is the trade between these two countries (Linder 1961). Linder assumes the per capita income as the most important determinant of the demand structure. The most common approach of testing the Linder Hypothesis has been to include a variable in the gravity model, which has a negative and significant supporting the Linder hypothesis. On the other, the variable is also used to test the Hecksher – Ohlin – Samuelson (H-O-S) factor endowment model. A dissimilar per capita income level would signify difference in factor endowments, which should promote trade. It is interesting to assess whether India's services trade follows H-O-S model or Linder hypothesis, which one is more relevant. Linder even states that his theory is not applicable to developing countries. Hence, he had believed that his hypothesis is only valid for developed countries trade and would not work for South-South and South-North trade.

6. For further details, refer Stark (2009) and Stack and Pentecost (2011).

Our study has used ($DIST_{ij}$) population weighted distance between two countries i and j i.e. ($\ln\left[\sum_{k\in i}\left(\frac{popk}{popi}\right)\sum_{k\in j}\left(\frac{popt}{popj}\right)D_{kl}\right]$). It is interesting to see whether the physical distance matters for service trade. In view of speed of communication, many services delivery would not depend on distance, and it is worthy to see whether in service sector distance puts barrier to trade. Although distance between the importer and exporter ($DIST_{ij}$) is typically expected to have a negative impact on trade in goods, it is not clear from the review of the existing literature that this is necessarily the case for services. Depending on the nature of the service, in some cases it requires movement of physical persons. But, in others, it may be communicated electronically. Consequently, the importance of distance in services trade may be low or even insignificant. Kimura and Lee (2004) have found that geographical distance is consistently more important for services than for goods trade. They have argued that the cost of transport for tradable services is higher than that for goods. They have also emphasized the need of further investigation using the disaggregate services trade data to find out why distance is more important for the flow of services trade.

The dummy variable indicates whether the exporting country shares a common official language ($Language_{ij}$) and it is expected to be positively related to the level of trade. India's official language is English. India's skilled and semi-skilled labours have privilege to service trade with those countries, which have English as an official language. Language has been found to be significant in gravity model assessing the goods trade flows, and this effect could be expected to be particularly strong in services as common language would greatly facilitate many transactions. There is evidence to suggest that a common language variable may also capture other effects such as cultural or institutional similarities between countries.

In most of the gravity model, particularly goods trade, it is common to include a variable measuring the impact of FTA. But, it is not clear whether this is appropriate for services trade as the majority of such agreements focus on the free movement of goods rather than services. Walsh (2006), however, has included the European Union (EU) in his model. He has argued that though EU is not fully liberalized in terms of trade in services, but some of the elements of EU policy promote or facilitate trade in services and FDI, as opposed to European Free Trade Association (EFTA). Grunfeld and Moxnes (2003) have found that the presence of the FTA is not significant in the case of services. Recent study of De (2013) on linkages between India's services trade flow and its barriers has found that the coefficient of FTA is not statistically significant. We have also included FTA in our estimated model, and found insignificant.[7]

$STFI_{it}$ is service trade facilitation index to measure the supply side barriers in services trade. We have expected positive sign of STFI from both partner and reporter countries. However, the exporting country's service trade is more important than that of importing country to access the supply side barriers in services exports in India.

Data Source

We have used OECD database, to collect India's services export to OECD, and non-OECD partner countries, for the period 2000 to 2013. The OECD database covers bilateral services trade between 34 OECD and other non-OECD countries and up to 50 of their trading partners. Since the present study focuses on India's services export to all major economies, which is already listed in the OECD database, we have considered import of services from 30 OECD and 3 non-OECD countries to India. The list of countries selected for the analysis is given in Appendix 4. Gravity model related variables like distance, common language and landlocked are collected from CEPII database. The detailed variables and their corresponding data sources are given in the Appendix 5.

The Gravity Model: Poisson Pseudo-Maximum Likelihood Method

The origin of the gravity model can be traced back to Tinbergen (1962). The aim was to undertake an econometric exercise to determine the normal or standard pattern of international trade that would prevail in the absence of trade impediments. In 1979, Anderson proposed a theoretical explanation of the gravity equation based on a Armington (1969) type of demand function with constant elasticity of substitution (CES), where each country produces and sells goods in the international market that are differentiated from the products of every other country. Further, Anderson and van Wincoop (2003) developed a model based on Anderson (1979) that has made a significant contribution related to the multilateral dimension of the gravity model. They have shown that the

7. In our estimated models, among 30 OECD and 3 non-OECD countries, only Japan and South Korea are having FTA with India, whereas Mexico is having PTA with India.

flow of bilateral trade is influenced by both trade obstacles that exist at the bilateral level (bilateral resistance) and by the relative weight of these obstacles with respect to all other countries (multilateral resistance). The other issue is the selection bias associated with the presence of heterogeneous firm operating internationally, which is contrary to the Krugman (1979) model on monopolistic competition that not all existing firms operate on international market.

Firms are generally active only in a subset of countries. Thus, the matrix of bilateral trade flows may have zero values. The occurrence of zero values happens at both aggregate and disaggregated level. Therefore, the standards OLS estimation of the gravity equation would be inappropriate if the zero entries are the result of the firm choice of not selling specific goods to specific market. Zero observations are dropped from the OLS model because the logarithm of zero is undefined. However, they are relatively common in the trade matrix since not all countries trade all products with all partners. To deal with zero observed trade value, the present study use poisson pseudo-maximum likelihood estimation (Silva and Tenreyro, 2006). The poisson regression model is defined by:

$$\Pr(y_i = _j \mid x_i) = \frac{\exp(-\lambda)\,\lambda^j}{j!}, j = 0,1,2,\ldots\ldots \tag{4}$$

where λ is generally specified as $\lambda = \exp(x\beta) = \exp(\beta_0 + \beta_1 x_{1i} + \ldots\ldots)$

With this formulation, the vector of parameters of interest, can be estimated by maximizing the log-likelihood function given by

$$lnL(\beta) = \sum_i^n [-\exp(x_i{}'\beta) + (x_i{}'\beta)y_i - \ln(y_i{}^!)] \tag{5}$$

The Poisson estimator has a number of additional desirable properties. The reduced form of the gravity equation derived from Anderson-Wincoop-Armington type of theoretical model, typically coexists with multiplicative error term which is prone to be heteroskedastic. This kind of heteroskedasticity cannot be removed by using simply robust covariance matrix estimator and calls for other non-linear estimation procedure[8].

8. Readers are refer to user guide by Shepherd (2013)

Results and Discussions

The estimated results for total services export are presented in Tables 7a and 7b. Table 7a presents the augmented gravity model by estimating both pooled OLS and PPML models. The extension of the Table 7a by including STFI for India and other partner countries is given in Table 7b. The differences in column (1) to (8) are due to the inclusion of with and without country effect in the model. The heteroscedasticity problems discussed in previous sections suggest that the multiplicative error term in model presented in column (1) suffers from heteroskedasticity.[9] However, using Poisson Pseudo Maximum Likelihood (PPML) estimation, the problem is resolved in column (3). In column (4), we have removed both heteroskedasticity and heterogeneity across countries using country dummy. The model shows that $TGDP_{ij}$, $SGDP_{ij}$, Distance, Landlocked and Language estimators are with expected signs and statistically significant. This shows that the augmented gravity model is fitted well for the India's services export.

The coefficients of both $TGDP_{ij}$ and $SGDP_{ij}$ are positive and strongly significant across the models. This shows that a higher level of income in both exporting and importing country indicates a country's ability to produce more services for export and also higher level of demand for services. Mirza and Nicoletti (2006) have shown that the supply of services to foreign markets is strongly linked to the availability of inputs in both domestic and foreign markets.

The coefficient of $DGDPPC_{ij}$ is positive, but insignificant in most of the models. This shows that in case of India's services export, Hecksher – Ohlin – Samuelson factor endowment model works well. Dissimilarity in the per capita income level, signify difference in factor endowments, thus promoting trade.

Overall, the results reveal that size of GDP of both reporter and partner countries jointly determine the demand for India's services export. As India's major export partners are from the developed countries, it signifies that richer countries demand for more services that India can potentially offer to enhance the services trade.

9. A Breusch-Pagan / Cook-Weisberg test for heteroskedasticity is conducted when robust standard error and clustering is not applied, and p value (0.0655) rejects the Homoskedastic null hypothesis.

Table 7(a): Regression Results for Total Services

	(1)	(2)	(3)	(4)
Estimator	OLS	OLS	PPML	PPML
$TGDP_{ij}$	2.306***	2.175***	1.884***	2.160***
	(11.68)	(9.17)	(7.92)	(12.17)
$SGDP_{ij}$	0.942***	0.737**	1.072***	1.560***
	(6.63)	(2.10)	(3.98)	(4.72)
$DGDPPC_{ij}$	0.905***	0.121	0.168	0.220
	(4.61)	(0.45)	(0.69)	(0.94)
Ln(Distance)	-1.146**	-2.439	-0.559	-2.280***
	(2.46)	(1.09)	(0.88)	(7.19)
Landlocked	-0.369	-3.096***	-0.170	-3.653***
	(1.25)	(5.41)	(0.52)	(5.28)
Language	0.957***	1.126	1.273***	-2.341**
	(3.29)	(1.12)	(5.04)	(2.05)
Constant	-52.110***	-34.134**	-42.632***	-31.602***
	(9.11)	(2.34)	(8.38)	(8.90)
Country Effect	NO	YES	NO	YES
Observations	345	345	345	345
Adjusted R^2	0.856	0.950		

Notes: (i) Absolute *t* statistics in parentheses are based on robust standard error (except column 3, 4, 6 and 8). (ii) Clustering is around Country. (iii) The level of significance is indicated as follows: * p<.10, ** p<.05, *** p<.01. (iv) For the OLS estimation dependent variable is natural logarithm of total value of India's service export (in US$ million). (v) For Poisson Pseudo-Maximum Likelihood Estimation (PPML) value of service export is taken as dependent variable.

The analysis here shows that common official language is positive and statistically significant in most of the models. A shared language will increase trade between two countries. It is reasonable to expect a common language to have a positive impact on trade in services than on goods trade. Many services transactions rely on the movement of physical persons and person to person communication, both of which will be greatly facilitated by a common official language.

Distance is negative and significantly influences services trade flows in India in most of the models. This shows that the physical distance matters for services trade even in the era of technological advancement, where many services could be done electronically. Kimura and Lee (2004) have also found that geographical distance is consistently more important for services than for goods trade. Besides, India's services export is negatively affected when destination of services export is a landlocked country.

Table 7(b): Regression Results for Total Services

	(5)	(6)	(7)	(8)
Estimator	OLS	PPML	OLS	PPML
$TGDP_{ij}$	1.484***	1.373***	2.044***	2.153***
	(7.73)	(5.88)	(4.95)	(5.53)
$SGDP_{ij}$	1.272***	1.066***	0.733*	1.618***
	(11.17)	(6.56)	(1.82)	(4.59)
$DGDPPC_{ij}$	0.503**	0.509**	-0.065	0.177
	(2.72)	(2.18)	(0.21)	(0.70)
Ln(Distance)	-1.307***	-0.957*	-1.555	-2.403***
	(4.42)	(1.93)	(0.67)	(5.60)
Landlocked	-0.386	-0.425*	-3.193***	1.162*
	(1.54)	(1.89)	(5.61)	(1.84)
Language	0.749***	0.979***	0.684	2.346***
	(4.30)	(5.37)	(0.70)	(3.78)
STFI India	-0.039	-0.012	-0.029	-0.023
	(1.44)	(0.40)	(0.74)	(1.22)
STFI Reporter	0.387***	0.349***	0.055	0.040
	(6.95)	(5.87)	(0.49)	(0.37)
Constant	-25.698***	-25.845***	-37.541**	-34.871***
	(5.97)	(6.09)	(2.18)	(3.88)
Country Effect	NO	NO	YES	YES
Observations	273	273	273	273
Adjusted R^2	0.912		0.963	

Notes: (i) Absolute *t* statistics in parentheses are based on robust standard error (except columns 3, 4, 6 and 8). (ii) Clustering is around country. (iii) The level of significance is indicated as follows: * p<.10, ** p<.05, *** p<.01. (iv) For the OLS estimation dependent variable is natural logarithm of total value of India's service export (in US$ million). (v) For Poisson Pseudo-Maximum Likelihood Estimation (PPML) value of service export is taken as dependent variable.

In the case of service trade facilitation index, the stock of India's *STFI* is negative and insignificant. For the present analysis, the exporting country's service trade is more important than that of importing country. In the case of STFI for importing country, the result shows positive and significant in columns (5) and (6), when country effect is not included in the analysis. However, when the country effect is included in columns (7) and (8), it becomes insignificant. Therefore, the result has to be interpreted cautiously since estimated coefficient of *STFI_reporter* is not significant in columns (7) and (8).

Table 8: Regression Results for India's Services Export: Major Components

	Computer and Information Service		Financial Services		Transportation Services		Travel Services	
	OLS	PPML	OLS	PPML	OLS	PPML	OLS	PPML
	(1)	(2)	(3)	(4)	(5)	(6)	(7)	(8)
TGDPij	2.26**	2.65**	2.44*	5.985***	3.013***	1.888***	0.110	1.019**
	(2.18)	(2.05)	(2.10)	(3.19)	(3.24)	(3.70)	(0.16)	(1.99)
SGDPij	1.01	1.15	4.31***	4.135***	0.528	0.052	0.360	1.372***
	(1.42)	(1.40)	(4.12)	(2.63)	(0.73)	(0.23)	(0.92)	(5.13)
DGDPPCij	2.06***	0.13	-1.50	1.057	-0.158	0.323	0.537	0.952**
	(2.81)	(0.23)	(0.86)	(0.74)	(0.31)	(1.20)	(1.41)	(2.53)
Ln(Distance)	1.72	1.25	-1.07	-9.057***	-7.235*	-4.485	6.768*	4.808
	(0.31)	(0.20)	(0.53)	(2.72)	(1.90)	(1.51)	(1.90)	(1.39)
Landlocked	-2.19	1.52	4.94	11.914**	1.350	2.866***	-3.776**	-1.772***
	(0.77)	(0.49)	(1.32)	(2.01)	(0.74)	(3.56)	(2.35)	(2.76)
Language	1.05*	2.39*	8.18**	3.863*	1.920	5.707***	-0.915	-0.260
	(1.22)	(1.45)	(2.41)	(1.73)	(0.53)	(5.99)	(0.72)	(0.22)
STFI India	0.20*	0.06***	-0.15	-0.304**	-0.107**	-0.063	0.022	-0.072***
	(1.95)	(2.58)	(0.72)	(2.51)	(2.28)	(1.34)	(0.42)	(3.42)
STFI_Reporter	0.11	-0.06	0.003	0.147	-0.200	0.081	0.257	0.294**
	(0.47)	(0.26)	(0.01)	(0.47)	(0.82)	(0.75)	(1.37)	(2.26)
Constant	-81.69***	-84.7***	-53.1***	-90.626***	-17.013	-15.796	-60.747***	-70.021***
	(3.58)	(3.82)	(3.11)	(3.30)	(1.01)	(1.09)	(4.23)	(3.92)
Country Effect	YES	YES	YES	YES	YES	YES	YES	YES
Observations	200	211	153	190	237	241	206	223
R^2	0.912	0.998	0.864	0.919	0.947	0.942	0.972	0.986
Adjusted R^2	0.897		0.840		0.938		0.967	

Notes: (i) The level of significance is indicated as follows: * p<.10, ** p<.05, *** p<.01. (ii) For the OLS estimation dependent variable is natural logarithm of total value of India's service export (in US million Dollar). (iii) For Poisson Pseudo-Maximum Likelihood Estimation (PPML) value of service export is taken as dependent variable.

To understand the sectoral differences in the determinants of India's services export and the intensity of trade barriers, the standard gravity model estimation is conducted for major components of India's services exports. The results are reported in Table 8. The result reveals that GDP of importing and exporting countries is positive and significant in all services sector. Distance is positive and insignificant for computer and information services, whereas it is negative and significant for other services like financial and transportation services. In case of travel services, distance is positive and significant in pooled OLS model, but not on PPML model. This shows that there are mixed results for the distance coefficient at the sectoral level analysis.

Landlocked country coefficient is negative and strongly significant for travel services indicating that the countries which are not landlocked have high potential for India's services export on travel services. For transportation and financial services, landlocked country dummy is found to be positive and significant, thereby showing the partner countries which are geographically landlocked and closer to India, have positive trade transportation and financial services. For computer and information services, estimated coefficient is found to be insignificant. The coefficient of language is positive and significant in all three sectors except for travel services.

Further, to understand the trade impediments for services trade, the study includes services trade facilitation index (STFI) for both India and partner countries. The study also includes individual services trade facilitation variable in the analysis, and the results are given in Appendix Table 3. The services trade facilitation index for computer and information services is positive and significant, whereas, for financial, transportation and travel services, it is negative and significant. This shows that India's services trade facilitation benefits more in case of trade in computer and information services than other services. The result also shows that improved services trade facilitation may unlock the unrealized trade potential in these sectors.

Conclusions

This paper attempts to examine the determinants of services export and its barriers to trade. We have looked at the cross-country experiences in developing economies of Asia-Pacific such as Southeast and South

Asia, in general, and India, in particular. To investigate the cross-country analysis, we have used GMM panel data model for the period 2000 to 2015. We find that determinants of services export such as GDP, real exchange rate, quality of institutions, skilled labour and service trade facilitation are the important determinants for a sample of 20 Asia-Pacific countries. However, we find mixed results for developing economies of Asia-Pacific, ASEAN (excluding Singapore), all countries in SAARC and China. We find that the core determinants are consistent with all the other models except for the case of schooling and STFI. We also find that ASEAN region has a high potential to benefit from the services export, given that STFI and institution index are positively promoting services export, and also ASEAN reacts favorably towards world import of services. SAARC has to emphasis on infrastructure development that facilitates the services export.

At disaggregated level using bilateral services trade data, we have examined the factors determining services export and its barriers in India. We have employed PPML gravity model approach on OECD database for the period 2000 to 2013. The result has found that standard gravity framework explains the determinants of India's export services well. The GDP of the importing and exporting countries, a common language and distance are found to be the most important determinants of services trade. The study has found that the services trade facilitation index (STFI) for India is negative and insignificant for total services. However, when services export is disaggregated, STFI is negative but significant for financial, transportation and travel services, which suggest that improved service trade facilitation would help unlock the unrealized trade potential in these sectors. In case of computer and information technology services, our estimated models indicate that STFI has been facilitating services export from India.

To conclude services trade facilitation is the key factor affecting services export in Asia-Pacific, ASEAN and India. However, the results have to be interpreted cautiously in view of quality of data. Barriers to services trade and facilitation are wide ranging and reflect the heterogeneous nature of services. Therefore, getting quantitative data on assessing services trade barriers is challenging task, which may limit the present study to understand potential barriers to India's services export.

[**Acknowledgement:** We thank Prof. Prabir De, Coordinator, ASEAN-India Centre, Research and Information System for Developing Countries (RIS) for his constant encouragement, valuable comments and guidance on this paper. We would like to thank Ms. Sreya Pan and Ms. Opinder Kaur for excellent research assistance in writing the paper. Any errors that remain are the sole responsibility of the authors.]

References

Anderson, J. E. 1979. "A Theoretical Foundation for the Gravity Equation." *American Economic Review,* Vol. 69, pp. 106-116.

Anderson, James E. and Wincoop, Eric van. 2003. "Gravity with Gravitas." *American Economic Review,* Vol.93, pp.170-92.

Arellano, M. and Bond, S. 1991. "Tests of Specification for Panel Data: Monte Carlo Evidence and an Application to Employment Equations." *The Review of Economic Studies*, Vol.58, No.2, April, pp.277-297.

Armington, P. S. 1969. "A Theory of Demand for Products Distinguished by Place of Production." IMF Staff papers, No.16, pp.159-76.

Baltagi, B. H. 1995. *Econometric Analysis of Panel Data.* New York: John Wiley & Sons.

Barro, Robert and Lee, Jong-Wha. 2013. "A New Data Set of Educational Attainment in the World, 1950-2010." *Journal of Development Economics,* Vol.104, pp.184-198.

Bernard, A. B, Jensen, J. Bradford, Redding, Stephen J. and Schott, Peter K. 2007. "Firms in International Trade." NBER Working Papers 13054, National Bureau of Economic Research (NBER), Cambridge.

Chinn, Menzie D. 2003. "Doomed to Deficits? Aggregate U.S. Trade Flow Re-Examined." *NBER Working Paper 9521*. National Bureau of Economic Research, Cambridge.

De, Prabir. 2013. "Assessing Barriers to Trade in Services in India: An Empirical Investigation." *Journal of Economic Integration*, Vol.28, No.1, p. 108-143.

Eichengreen, B. and Gupta, P. 2012. "Export of Services: India Experiences in Perspective." *India Growth and Development Review,* Vol. 6, No. 1, pp. 35 – 60.

Francois, J. 2001. "The Next WTO Round: North-South Stakes in New Market Access Negotiations", Centre for International Economic Studies, Adelaide.

Francois, J. and Hoekman, B. 2010. "Services Trade and Policy", *Journal of Economic Literature,* Vol. 48, pp. 642 – 692.

Francois, J., and Manchin, M. 2006, "Institutional Quality, Infrastructure, and the Propensity to Export" World Bank, Washington, DC. pp.1-32.

Francois, J., van Meijl, H. and van Tongeren, F. 2003. "Economic Benefits of the Doha Round for the Netherlands." Agricultural Economics Institute, The Hague.

Ghani, E. and Kharas, H. 2010. "The Services Revolution in South Asia" in E. Ghani (ed.) *The Services Revolution in South Asia.* New Delhi: Oxford University Press.

Grunfeld, L. and Moxnes, A. 2003. "The Intangible Globalisation: Explaining Patterns of International Trade in Services." Norwegian Institute of International Affairs Paper # 657, Oslo.

Huang, J.H., and S. Viana. 1995. "Modelling US Services Trade Flows: A Cointegration ECM Approach." Federal Reserve Bank of New York Research Paper No. 9518.

Haveman, Jon and Hummels, David. 2004. "Alternative Hypotheses and the Volume of Trade: the Gravity Equation and the Extent of Specialization." *Canadian Journal of Economics*, Vol.37, No.1, pp.199-218

Helpman, E. and Krugman, P. 1985. Market Structure and Foreign Trade: Increasing Returns, Imperfect Competition, and the International Economy. Cambridge, Massachusetts, London and England: MIT Press.

Kimura, F. and Lee, H.-H. 2004. "The Gravity Equation in International Trade in Services." Paper presented at the European Trade Study Group Conference held on 9-11 September in Nottingham later the paper was printed in *Review of World Economics*, Vol. 142, pp. 92-121.

Kaufmann, D., Kraay, A. and Mastruzzi, M. 2010. "The Worldwide Governance Indicators: Methodology and Analytical Issues", Policy Research Working Paper No. 5430, The World Bank.

Kolstad, Ivar and Espen, Villanger. 2008. "Determinants of Foreign Direct Investment in Services." *European Journal of Political Economy*, Vol.24, pp. 518-533.

Kox, Henk, and Lejour, Arjan M. 2005. "Regulatory Heterogeneity as Obstacle for International Services Trade." CPB Discussion Paper 49. CPB Netherlands Bureau for Economic Policy Analysis.

Krugman P. 1979. "Increasing Returns, Monopolistic Competition, and International Trade." *Journal of International Economics,* Vol.9, pp.469–479.

Lejour, A. and Verheijden, J.W. de Paiva. 2004. "Services Trade within Canada and the European Union: What do They Have in Common ?" CPB Discussion Paper # 42. CPB Netherlands Bureau for Economic Policy Analysis.

Linder, S. B. 1961. *An Essay on Trade and Transformation*. New York: Wiley and Sons.

Majeed, Muhammad Tariq, Ahmad, Eatzaz and Khawaja, M. Idrees. 2006. "Determinants of Exports in Developing Countries." *The Pakistan Development Review*, Vol.45, No.4, pp. 1265-1276.

Mirza, D. and Nicoletti G. 2004. "What is so Special about Trade in Services?" Research Paper 2004/02, Leverhulme Centre for Research on Globalisation and Economic Policy.

Nasir, S., and Kalirajan, K, 2013. "Export Performance of South and East Asia in Modern Services." ASARC Working Paper 2013/07.

Nicoletti, G., Golub, S., Hajkova, D., Mirza, D. and Yoo, K.-L. 2003. "Policies and International Integration: Influences on Trade and Foreign Direct Investment." OECD Economics Department Working Paper No. 359. Organisation for Economic Cooperation and Development (OECS).

Raychaudhuri, Ajitava, and Prabir, De. 2012. *International Trade in Services in India: Implications for Growth and Inequality in a Globalizing World*. New Delhi: Oxford University Press.

Sahoo, P., Dash, R. K. and Mishra, P.P. 2013. "Determinants of India's Services Export." IEG Working Paper No.333, Institute of Economic Growth (IEG), New Delhi.

Shepherd, B., and Marel, E. Van Der. 2010. *Trade in Services in the APEC Region: Patterns, Determinants, and Policy Implications*. APEC Policy Support Unit.

Shepherd, Ben. 2013. *The Gravity Model of International Trade: A User Guide*. ARTNeT and UNESCAP.

Silva, JMC Santos, and Tenreyro, S. 2006. "The log of gravity." *The Review of Economics and Statistics*, Vol.88, No.4, pp.641-658.

Stack, M. 2009. "Regional Integration and Trade: Controlling for Varying Degrees of Heterogeneity in the Gravity Model." *The World Economy*, Vol.32, No.5, pp.772-789.

Stack, M.M. and Pentecost, E.J. 2011. "Regional Integration and Trade: A Panel Cointegration Approach to Estimating the Gravity Model." *Journal of International Trade and Economic Development*, Vol.20, pp.53-65.

Tinbergen, Jan. 1962. *Shaping the World Economy: Suggestion for an International Economic Policy.* New York: Twentieth Century Fund.

Urata, Shujiro and Kiyota, Kozo. 2003. "Services Trade in East Asia", in Takatozhi Ito and Anne O. Krueger (eds.) *Trade in Services in the Asia Pacific Region*. NBER East Asia Seminar on Economics (EASE), Vol.11, pp. 1-51. Available on: http://www.nber.org/chapters/c10165

Walsh, Keith. 2006. "Trade in Services: Does Gravity Hold? A Gravity Model Approach to Estimating Barriers to Services Trade." IIS Discussion Paper, No. 183, pp.1-41, Institute for International Integration Studies.

World Bank. 2004. *Sustaining India's Services Revolution: Access to Foreign Markets, Domestic Reform and International Negotiations*. World Bank, Washington, D.C.

WTO. 2015. *International Trade Statistics 2015*. World Trade Organisation (WTO), Geneva, Switzerland.

Appendix 1: List of Selected Asia-Pacific Countries

Sl. No.	Country	Sl. No.	Country
1	Australia	11	Malaysia
2	Bangladesh	12	Nepal
3	Brunei Darussalam	13	New Zealand
4	Cambodia	14	Pakistan
5	China	15	Philippines
6	India	16	Singapore
7	Indonesia	17	Sri Lanka
8	Japan	18	Thailand
9	South Korea	19	Vietnam
10	Lao PDR	20	Maldives

Appendix 2: Data Sources and Descriptions

Data Description	Sources
Real services export is defined as total services export in US$ as measured by the GDP deflator.	UNCTAD Database
Real world import is defined as World Import of Services in US$ as measured by the GDP deflator	
GDP (constant 2010 US$)	World Development Indicators, World Bank Database
Real Exchange Rate is defined as nominal exchange rate by multiplying with US Consumer Price Index divided it by domestic CPI	
Services Trade Facilitation Index (STFI) comprising (i) air transport passenger, (ii) air transport freight (million ton-km), (iii) electric power consumption (kwh per capita), (iv) fixed broadband subscriptions (per 100 people), (v) fixed telephone subscriptions (per 100 people), (vi) internet users (per 100 people), (vii) mobile cellular subscriptions (per 100 people), and (viii)secure internet servers (per 1 million people)	
Real FDI inflows is defined as Foreign direct investment, net inflows (BoP, current US$) as measured by GDP deflator	
Institutional Index comprising: (i) Control of Corruption, (ii) Government Effectiveness, (iii) Regulatory Quality, (iv) Rule of Law and (v) Voice and Accountability.	Worldwide Governance Indicators, World Bank Database
Schooling is defined as Barro-Lee: Average years of total schooling, 15+, total is the average years of education completed among people over age 15.	Education Statistics, World Bank Database

Appendix 3: Country Group in Asia-Pacific

Sl. No.	Developing Economies of Asia-Pacific	ASEAN	SAARC
1	Brunei Darussalam	Brunei Darussalam	Bangladesh
2	Cambodia	Cambodia	India
3	Indonesia	Indonesia	Nepal
4	Philippines	Philippines	Pakistan
5	Malaysia	Malaysia	Sri Lanka
6	Thailand	Singapore	Maldives
7	Vietnam	Thailand	
8	Lao PDR	Vietnam	
9	Bangladesh	Lao PDR	
10	India		
11	Nepal		
12	Pakistan		
13	Sri Lanka		
14	Maldives		
15	China		

Appendix 4: List of India's Partner Countries Selected for the Study

Sl. No.	Country	Sl. No.	Country
1	Australia	18	Japan
2	Austria	19	Korea
3	Belgium	20	Luxembourg
4	Canada	21	Netherlands
5	Czech Republic	22	New Zealand
6	Denmark	23	Norway
7	Estonia	24	Poland
8	Finland	25	Portugal
9	France	26	Russia
10	Germany	27	Slovak Republic
11	Greece	28	Slovenia
12	Hong Kong, China	29	Spain
13	Hungary	30	Sweden
14	Iceland	31	Turkey
15	Ireland	32	United Kingdom
16	Israel	33	United States
17	Italy		

Appendix 5: Data Sources and Description

Data Description	Sources
Service Export and its major components such as Transportation, Travel, Information and Technology and Financial services	Statistics on International Trade in Services, OECD
GDP and GDP per capita	World Development Indicator, World Bank
Services Trade Facilitation Index (STFI) comprising (i) air transport passenger, (ii) air transport freight (million ton-km), (iii) electric power consumption (kwh per capita), (iv) fixed broadband subscriptions (per 100 people), (v) fixed telephone subscriptions (per 100 people), (vi) internet users (per 100 people), (vii) mobile cellular subscriptions (per 100 people), and (viii)secure internet servers (per 1 million people)	World Development Indicator, World Bank
Financial Openness Index	Chinn-Ito index, http://web.pdx.edu/~ito/Chinn-Ito_website.htm
Distance between exporter and importer	CEPII Gravity Data Base (Geo_dist)
Landlocked	
Common official Language	

Appendix 6: Regression Results for Major components of India's Services Exports

	Computer and Information Service		Financial Services		Transportation Services		Travel Services	
	OLS	PPML	OLS	PPML	OLS	PPML	OLS	
	(1)	(2)	(3)	(4)	(5)	(6)	(7)	(8)
TGDPij	2.43***	2.58**	1.28	2.55***	2.28***	1.90***	0.81	1.55***
	(2.84)	(2.05)	(1.67)	(4.26)	(6.26)	(7.78)	(1.06)	(4.09)
SGDPij	1.06**	1.16	3.10***	0.84*	0.22	0.03	0.79*	1.60***
	(2.37)	(1.33)	(3.16)	(1.70)	(0.52)	(0.15)	(1.93)	(5.32)
DGDPPCij	2.31**	0.08	-0.87	-0.09	0.54	0.68**	0.35	0.97***
	(2.67)	(0.14)	(0.75)	(0.11)	(1.24)	(2.51)	(0.77)	(3.10)
Ln(Distance)	4.30	3.57	0.00	-3.23**	-2.71	-3.78***	4.35	2.23
	(0.81)	(0.70)	(.)	(2.37)	(1.11)	(2.78)	(1.08)	(0.87)
Landlocked	-5.18	-3.74	-2.99***	-0.71	2.19***	2.02**	-1.38	-0.40
	(1.08)	(1.41)	(5.19)	(0.64)	(3.92)	(2.08)	(0.70)	(0.38)
Language	4.52*	3.21*	3.30	3.25***	3.11*	4.96***	2.32*	0.47
	(1.96)	(1.58)	(1.21)	(6.24)	(1.80)	(6.27)	(1.73)	(0.46)
Broadband_India	1.66**	-0.03						
	(2.09)	(0.11)						
Broadband	0.05	0.01						
	(1.57)	(0.35)						
Electricity consumption_India	-0.00	0.00						
	(1.05)	(0.32)						
Electricity consumption	-0.00*	-0.00						
	(1.85)	(1.59)						

Financial openness India			0.00					
			(.)					
Financial openness			1.62	-1.25				
			(0.70)	(0.45)				
Air Freight India					-4.56e+05	91481.66		
					(0.84)	(0.31)		
Air Freight					38.91**	51.08		
					(2.22)	(0.64)		
Air passenger India							6.85	-1.89
							(0.41)	(0.25)
Air passenger							0.24	0.43*
							(1.29)	(1.90)
Constant	-101.00***	-96.15***	-29.24	-41.34***	-41.90***	-23.64***	-61.22***	-62.73***
	(3.81)	(4.58)	(1.34)	(6.57)	(2.79)	(3.22)	(3.36)	(4.22)
Country Dummy	YES	YES	YES	NO	YES	YES	YES	YES
Observations	236	248	171	250	275	279	240	260
R^2	0.92	1.00	0.86	0.88	0.95	0.94	0.96	0.98
Adjusted R^2	0.91		0.84		0.94		0.96	

Note: The level of significance is indicated as follows: * p<.10, ** p<.05, *** p<.01. For the OLS estimation dependent variable is natural logarithm of total value of India's service export (in US$ million), for Poisson Pseudo-Maximum Likelihood Estimation (PPML) value of service export is taken as dependent variable.

TEN

ASEAN-INDIA CONNECTIVITY: PROGRESS SO FAR

Suthiphand Chirathivat and Anupama D. Masali

Introduction

Southeast Asia and India share a strong civilizational link, which dates back to history. The cultural and historical ties happened through inter-regional exchanges of people, trade, language and culture, which contributed to the richness and development of India and Southeast Asia. Such exchanges in the past made our borders not only meaningless but also provided a solid foundation for today's contemporary relations. From this perspective, both Southeast Asia and India are regionally integrated and also globally connected.

Although they form an integral part of Asia, Southeast Asia and India were distant neighbor as a result of divided and fragmented political regime during the 19th and the first half of the 20th century. The end of the Cold War and the new episode of "re-emerging" Asia have, however, encouraged once more renewing of contact between Southeast Asia and India.

In particular, Southeast Asia, also known as ASEAN, is strategically located to link the whole region with India and beyond. India has announced its "Look East" policy in 1991, which represents a major shift from its recent past, and has been pursued consistently. These new settings and environment have had many positive impacts, which were followed by several new initiatives. ASEAN and India saw the opportunities to renew their ties, and, thus, they came together to conclude the sectoral dialogue partnership in 1992.

The new partnership is evolving with time, and both the partners are working towards deeper integration. The celebration of 20th year of this enhanced partnership in 2012 had served not only to review the past two decades of relationships, but also helped to lay down an important blueprint for a strategic partnership between them. Both are committed to work closely in the future on common regional and international issues and support each other's role. A special feature of the Vision Statement of the ASEAN-India Commemorative Summit is the importance given to the ASEAN-India connectivity.

In order to understand the progress of ASEAN-India connectivity, and how it holds the future relationships, this chapter illustrates the rationale behind the ASEAN-India connectivity (Section 2), in particular the motivations for ASEAN-India connectivity. Section 3 discusses the trade flows between ASEAN and India and how they have helped in economic development of both sides as well as how these will cement further such connectivity in the future. The understanding of the ASEAN-India connectivity will not be completed without reviewing the recent ASEAN-India physical connectivity initiatives. Therefore, this chapter looks at the progress so far made in Section 4. The challenges are analysed in Section 5, whereas Section 6 presents the conclusion.

Rationale for ASEAN-India Connectivity

The concept of ASEAN connectivity received a major institutional fillip during the15thASEAN Summit in Cha-am Hua Hin on 24 October 2009. During the Summit, the ASEAN Leaders held discussions on the imperative for well-knit ASEAN with reference to its advantageous position – bound by India to the west, China, Japan and South Korea to the Northeast, and Australia and New Zealand to the South. This reflects the potential for ASEAN to transform itself into transportation, Information and Communication Technology (ICT) and tourism hub of Asia.[1]

As a follow up to the statement issued in Cha-am Hua Hin in 2009 towards enhancing intra-regional connectivity, the Leaders continued to exhibit their commitment at the 16thASEAN Summit in Hanoi, Vietnam on 8-9 April 2010 by emphasising on the need for designing the Master Plan on ASEAN Connectivity (MPAC), with well-defined targets and specific measures/actions, and subsequently adopted the Master Plan on the occasion of the 17thASEAN Summit in Hanoi on 28 October 2010.

Connectivity reduces distance, cuts trade costs, facilitates exchanges and promotes interactions at the institutional level and brings people closer. Though MPAC has primarily envisioned intra-regionally well-connected ASEAN, connectivity with the economies beyond the region is also critical to the success of ASEAN. Having a future perspective and in recognition

1. Refer, the Master Plan on ASEAN Connectivity, 2011

of the importance of connecting with the nations beyond the region, the Sixth East Asia Summit (EAS) on ASEAN Connectivity, held in Bali, Indonesia on 19 November 2011, declared to include ASEAN Connectivity as an additional area of cooperation in the EAS, together with the existing five priority areas of cooperation.[2] On the other, one of the significant developments in international trade and foreign direct investment (FDI) in Asia during the recent years has been the rapid growth of international production networks, largely driven by multinational corporations (MNCs) leading to increased intra-regional trade in parts and components and outsourcing in bulk (Athukorala and Yamashita, 2006). This phenomenon is facilitated by the revolutionary growth in transportation and communication networks triggered by technological advancement. As a response and a strong fundamental to this new wave in trade theory, a well-knit region – in terms of physical, institutional and people-to-people connectivity, has become very vital for deeper integration.

Motivations for ASEAN-India Connectivity

Market Size: With a combined market of 1.84 billion people, a combined GDP of US$ 3.50 trillion and a total labour force of almost 0.8 billion[3], ASEAN-India connectivity offers a huge potential for increased business and economic interactions contributing to increased intra-ASEAN and extra-ASEAN trade. The mutual trade complementarity between ASEAN and India stood at 58 per cent and 63.69 per cent, respectively, in 2009 (see Table 1). Trade complementarity saw a significant increase of 17.11 per cent and 17.38 per cent for ASEAN and India, respectively, over the previous decade.[4]

2. Refer, Chairman's Statement of the Sixth East Asia Summit (EAS), November, 2011.

3. Source, UNCTAD Stat.

4. Trade complementarity is a type of overlap index. It measures the degree to which the export pattern of one country matches the import pattern of another. A high degree of complementarity is assumed to indicate more favourable prospects for a successful trade arrangement. Changes over time may tell us whether the trade profiles are becoming more or less compatible.

Table 1: Trade Complementarity between Selected ASEAN Countries and India

Country	Trade Complementarity Index (%)			
	India as a reporting country		India as a partner country	
	2000	2009	2000	2009
Indonesia	55.26	59.99	45.79	57.64
Malaysia	37.33	52.89	35.38	48.67
Philippines	24.75	36.26	37.34	52.35
Singapore	40.59	59.32	32.07	46.51
Thailand	35.96	46.25	42.54	57.45
Vietnam	44.57	44.45	43.77	55.13
ASEAN	46.31	63.69	40.89	58.00

Source: APTIAD Interactive Trade Indicators, UNESCAP.

Table 2: Selected Economic Indicators of ASEAN Countries, 2014

Country	Population (million)	GDP (US$ million, 2005 prices)	GDP per capita (US$ million, 2005 prices)
Brunei Darussalam	0.417	9952.445	23516.842
Cambodia	15.328	11484.943	745.375
Indonesia	254.455	475404.084	1880.463
Lao PDR	6.689	5386.085	781.260
Malaysia	29.902	220194.765	7294.141
Myanmar	53.437	26325.793	490.065
Philippines	99.139	165126.079	1649.669
Singapore	5.507	200676.569	36373.547
Thailand	67.726	252349.413	3753.916
Vietnam	92.423	92780.691	1002.515

Source: Based on UNCTAD Stat (2014)

Development Gap: Economic growth and developmental levels vary drastically among the ASEAN member nations. It can be seen from Table 2 that Myanmar, Brunei Darussalam, Cambodia and Lao PDR have registered much lower GDP size and per capita income compared to other high performing members in 2014, and this variation has been a trend over three decades consistently. One of the driving forces of the ASEAN connectivity is to bridge this gap by sharing the benefits of increased trade growth and its welfare effects with poorer member nations, groups and communities.

ASEAN's Centrality and Looking Beyond the Region: Economic interdependence has grown rapidly all over the world due to increasing trade and investment, especially since 1990. The same holds true at the regional level. In the Asia-Pacific region with the emergence of ASEAN as one of world's highly integrated production networks, its centrality in the region remains unquestioned among the major powers of Asia. In recognition of the ASEAN-led efforts towards the resurgence of Asian people, the 'ASEAN Way' has been accepted as a prime and strong proposition in search for Asian identities and values.[5] With the constantly evolving regional architecture entailing rising competition in global trade, changing political equations, the task of maintaining ASEAN's centrality poses a major challenge towards which strengthening connectivity within and beyond the region would be a vital and positive move.

Trade Flows between ASEAN and India

ASEAN's total trade with India was very low in 1990s. It has grown enormously since end of 1990s (see Figure 1). Adoption of *Look East Policy* by India in 1990s and the signing of successive regional, sub-regional and bilateral trade agreements have spurred the trade and investment flows. Total trade volume of Singapore, Indonesia, Malaysia, and Thailand with India is much higher than the CLMV. Singapore is one of the leading investors and trading partners of India.[6] Total trade growth[7] of ASEAN with India stood at 20.96 per cent in 2000, 37.73 per cent in 2010 and -0.29 per cent in 2014, while that of India with ASEAN was 2.18 per cent in 2000, 27.55 per cent in 2010 and -2 per cent in 2014.[8]

Likewise, during the last decade, export and import growth[9] of ASEAN with India were positive except in 2001, 2009, 2012, 2013 and 2014, when the growth came out negative (see Table 3). Export and import shares[10] have increased, though insignificantly.

5. Refer, Devare, Singh and Marwah (2012).
6. Singapore is the second largest investor in FDI equity inflows which is equal to 10 per cent of total inflows (Department of Industrial Policy and Promotion of Singapore).
7. Total trade growth is the percentage change in the value of total trade (exports plus imports) relative to the previous year.
8. Source: IMF Direction of Trade Statistics, retrieved at Integration Indicators, ARIC, ADB.
9. Export growth and import growth are the percentage changes in the value of exports relative to the previous year.
10. Export share and import share are the percentage changes in the value of exports and imports from a partner to a total exports and imports, respectively, of a country/region.

Figure 1 : Total Trade of ASEAN Countries with India

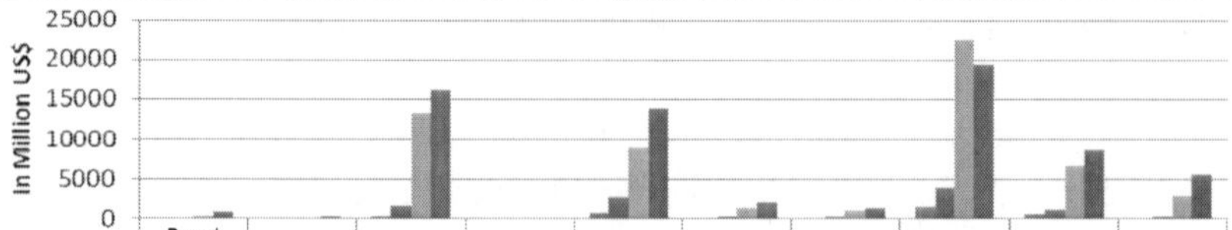

	Brunei Darussalam	Cambodia	Indonesia	Lao PDR	Malalysia	Myanmar	Philippines	Singapore	Thailand	Vietnam
1990	1.27	1.44	211.08	0.42	692.90	45.65	89.43	1477.55	607.33	24.63
2000	3.97	9.43	1676.11	5.50	2649.62	215.74	230.51	3945.68	1185.82	225.58
2010	211.96	60.48	13209.8	27.27	9002.11	1319.67	1001.36	22574.4	6674.55	2753.66
2014	903.37	183.85	16201.0	124.05	13843.0	2229.60	1350.12	19399.8	8603.26	5593.24

Source: IMF Direction of Trade Statistics, retrieved at Integration Indicators, ARIC, ADB.

Table 3: ASEAN's Trade with India – Selected Export and Import Indicators

Year	Export Growth (%)	Export Share (%)	Import Growth (%)	Import Share (%)
2000	11.92	1.59	44.54	0.91
2001	-7.37	1.63	7.00	1.06
2002	4.68	1.62	12.67	1.14
2003	30.49	1.82	11.65	1.14
2004	25.64	1.89	61.73	1.46
2005	37.96	2.28	17.91	1.48
2006	28.45	2.49	24.48	1.61
2007	30.04	2.89	27.62	1.81
2008	26.90	3.20	47.67	2.15
2009	-14.47	3.33	-29.46	1.95
2010	36.38	3.52	40.29	2.08
2011	23.92	3.70	47.18	2.54
2012	-6.79	3.40	-4.42	2.28
2013	-0.62	3.35	-6.38	2.10
2014	3.36	3.36	-6.12	1.98

Source: IMF Directions of Trade Statistics, retrieved at Integration Indicators, ARIC, ADB.

Leading ASEAN+6 members such as China, Japan, South Korea, Singapore, Australia and Malaysia are the major contributors to the intra-regional trade in the ASEAN+6 region. Illustrated in Figure 2, share of their contributions to the intra-regional trade were 27.6, 13.7, 12.8, 10.8, 8.2 and 6.6 per cent in 2014, respectively. However, India's share, on a relative term, is low (2.6 per cent). These numbers itself indicate the degree of regional integration in the region and propose the ample scope for India's active participation.

Figure 2: Intra-regional Trade Share of ASEAN +6 Countries

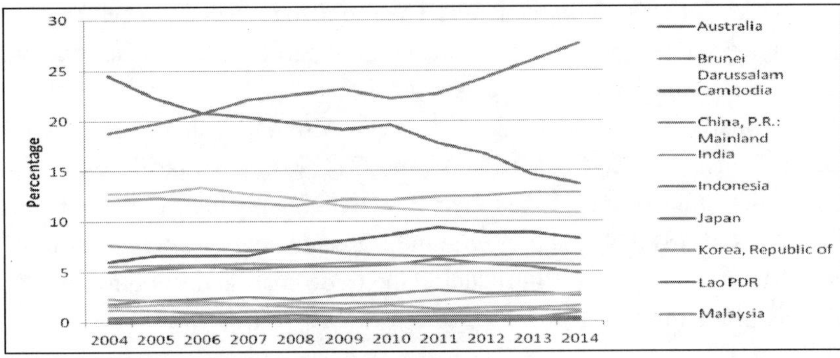

Source: Direction of Trade Statistics (DOTS), IMF

Table 4: Trade Facilitation Provisions in ASEAN and ASEAN+1 FTAs

Trade Facilitation coverage/RTA	ASEAN	ASEAN-Australia-NZ	ASEAN-China	ASEAN-India	ASEAN-Japan	ASEAN-South Korea
Customs procedures and co-operation	✓	✓	✓	✓	✓	✓
Technical regulations, standards and SPS measures	✓	✓		✓	✓	✓
NTBs, especially administrative fees and charges	✓	✓	✓	✓	✓	✓
Transparency of laws, regulations and administrative rulings	✓	✓	✓		✓	✓
Use of ICT and E-Commerce	✓	✓	✓		✓	✓

Note: "✓"indicates the presence of provisions.
Source: Wong and Pellan (2012)

Trade Facilitation: Current Status

Institutional connectivity, especially trade facilitation, is found to be limited. In a comparative analysis of trade facilitation provisions in ASEAN and ASEAN+1FTAs (see Table 4), Wong and Pellan (2012) have found that the coverage of trade facilitation in the ASEAN-India Agreement on Trade in Goods (AITIGA) is "fairly general". The provisions are said to be "broadly formulated and aspirational and do not commit parties to undertake concrete action or to achieve specific targets or goals".

Comparison of India and selected ASEAN countries' bilateral Comprehensive Trade Costs (CTC)[11] and CTC excluding tariff costs (NT-CTC) with China (see Table 5) reflect how significantly higher bilateral non-tariff costs of ASEAN countries with India are and how important the role of trade facilitation measures in reducing the trade costs and smoothening the bilateral trade flows is.

Table 5: Comparison of India and Selected ASEAN Countries' Comprehensive Trade Costs (CTC) and CTC Excluding Tariff Costs (NT-CTC) with China

	CTC				CTC Excluding Tariff Costs			
	India		China		India		China	
Country	2005	2010	2005	2010	2005	2010	2005	2010
Indonesia	168.45	158.73	146.63	129.85	125.86	118.11	136.23	127.42
Malaysia	132.04	127.77	111.66	114.96	101.84	94.23	101.91	109.50
Philippines	274.49	265.94	172.85	187.74	223.97	215.27	148.52	170.45
Singapore	168.48	165.01	139.87	137.43	131.03	130.99	127.92	135.30
Thailand	195.63	178.68	128.12	110.25	127.96	120.65	98.13	84.79
Vietnam	180.31	-	120.26	-	123.60	-	100.94	-

Source: UNESCAP Trade Cost Database (2011).

ASEAN-India Physical Connectivity Initiatives: The Progress So Far

In order to ensure seamless movement of goods, increase trade, and intensify participation in international production networks (IPNs), quality infrastructure and competent information and communication

11 Comprehensive trade costs (CTC) refer to all costs involved in trading goods internationally with another partner (i.e. bilaterally) relative to those involved in trading goods domestically (i.e. intra-nationally). It captures trade costs in its wider sense, including not only international transport costs and tariffs but also indirect costs associated with differences in languages, currencies as well as cumbersome import or export procedures.

technology (ICT) are vital. Master Plan on ASEAN Connectivity (MPAC) defines specific initiatives and sets clear targets. We explain the ASEAN-India physical connectivity initiatives in connection with the MPAC strategies.[12]

Complete the ASEAN Highway Network (AHN)

One of the key actions under this strategy is to upgrade the extension of AHN[13] to China and India, particularly sections from Ha Noi via northern Lao PDR through Myanmar to the border with India.[14] The Thailand-Myanmar-India Trilateral Highway is under construction. This Trilateral Highway (TH) runs through the following route: Mae Sot (Thailand)-Myawaddy-Kawkareik-Hypaan-Thaton-Theinzayat-Payagyi-Oktwin-Taungoo-Meiktila bypass-Kyaukpadaung-Bagan-Pakokku-Lingadow-Kyadat-Pale-Yinmabin-Chaungma-Kalewa-Tamu-Moreh (India).[15] The project, funded by the governments of Myanmar, Thailand and India, will open up Southeast Asia to India's Northeastern states. To support Myanmar, governments of India and Thailand have agreed to extend credit at concessional terms to Myanmar for financing specified sections of the TH.[16]

The TH, started in 2005, is a three-phased project. It was reported that the slow progress of the TH is due to lack of institutional support and government commitments.[17] The 1360 km TH, linking Thailand, Myanmar and India, is said to become a reality by 2018.[18]

---

12. The MPAC contains 19 strategies and 84 key actions under three dimensions, viz. physical, institutional and people-to-people connectivity. Under physical connectivity seven strategies and 32 key actions were drawn up with the view to expanding and improving road, rail, inland waterways, maritime and air linkages. 10 strategies and 32 key actions were outlined under institutional connectivity to facilitate free flow of goods, services and investment in the region. Under people-to-people connectivity, 2 strategies and 20 key actions were formulated to promote deeper intra-ASEAN social and cultural interaction and understanding by way of progressive relaxation of visa requirements (MRA) and promotion of tourism related activities, among others.
13. ASEAN Highway Network is one of the two flagship land transport infrastructure projects within ASEAN, the other project is Singapore Kunming Rail Link (SKRL).
14. Refer, MPAC strategies listed under the dimension of physical connectivity.
15. Refer, India Country Study, ASEAN-India Connectivity Report, RIS (2012).
16. Refer, De and Ray (2013)
17. Ibid.
18. Times of India, 13 August 2012.

Complete Implementation of Singapore-Kunming Rail Link (SKRL) Project

The SKRL project aims to build a railway link between Singapore and China (via Kunming). This requires building the missing links in ASEAN. The missing link sections include (a) Thailand: Aranyaprathet-Klongluk (6 km); (b) Cambodia: Poipet-Sisophon (48 km); (c) Cambodia: Phnom Penh-LocNinh (254 km); (d) Vietnam: LocNinh-Ho Chi Minh (129 km); (e) Vietnam: Mu Gia-Tan Ap-VungAng (119 km); (f) Lao PDR: Vientiane-Thakek-Mu Gia (466 km); (g) Myanmar: Thanbyuzayat-Three Pagoda Pass (110 km); and (h) Thailand: Three Pagoda Pass-Nam Tok (153 km).

Some of these missing links when constructed can also provide for extension of rail link to India. As noted in De and Ray (2013), Indian government's plan to establish Delhi-Hanoi Railway Link in two specific routes[19] that will connect Hanoi through Myanmar with different rail links. Diphu-Karong-Imphal-Moreh rail link in India, which is under construction, will connect India with ASEAN, and we need to build about 238 km missing links in Myanmar. This in turn would open up possibilities of establishing extended railway links to rest of the ASEAN member countries.

Establish Integrated and Seamless Multimodal Transport Systems to Make ASEAN the Transport Hub in the East Asia Region

Mekong-India Economic Corridor

Promotion of the Mekong-India Economic Corridor (MIEC) is important in order to strengthen the connectivity between ASEAN and India.[20]

MIEC is said to be an extended version of Southern Economic Corridor (SEC), where the SEC is one of the three major economic corridors in GMS. MIEC connects Myanmar, Thailand, Cambodia and Vietnam with India. Starting at Ho Chi Minh City in Vietnam, the MIEC passes through Phnom Phenh (Cambodia) and Bangkok (Thailand) and ends at Chennai in India. In order to establish a linkage between Bangkok and Chennai, an access route

19. Route–I will connect Hanoi via Myanmar, Thailand and Cambodia. In Route-II, it is diverted to Bangkok via Ye and newly constructed portion of Ye and Dawei in Myanmar, then to Hanoi through Thailand and Lao PDR (De and Ray, 2013).

20. Consists of (a) Construct the Mekong Bridge in NeakLoung (National road No. I in Cambodia); (b) Develop the Dawei deep sea port (by 2020); (c) Build the highway between Kanchanaburi and Dawei (by 2020); and (d) Conduct a feasibility study and preliminary design for the railway spur line between Kachanaburi and Dawei.

from Bangkok to the Andaman Sea is proposed to be opened by constructing a highway connecting Kanchanaburi (Thailand) and Dawei (Myanmar). The comprehensive Dawei projects include a deep sea port, special economic zones, power plants and so forth. It was noted that a deep sea port would open up opportunities for firms operating in Bangkok in particular and the region in general along the MIEC by opening up a new shipping route to India, and, on the other hand, firms in Chennai in particular and India in general are expected to have alternative access to ASEAN.[21]

The ERIA simulations have revealed the importance of MIEC; the percentage increase in real GDP in 2020 vis-à-vis the base line scenario is 0.32 per cent for East-West Economic Corridor (EWEC), 0.14 per cent for North-South Economic Corridor (NSEC) and 1.19 per cent for MIEC and the percentage reductions in Gini coefficients (a measure of income inequality) are 0.07 per cent for EWEC, 0.13 per cent for NSEC and 0.23 per cent for MIEC.[22]

Kaladan Multimodal Transit Transport Project (KMTTP): Connecting Myanmar-Northeast India-Rest of India

Due to weak connectivity between Myanmar and Northeast India, and between Northeast India and the rest of India, the vision of well-connected ASEAN-India remains blurred. Because of the geographical setting (most of lengthy borders are mountainous and porous), huge development gaps and prevalence of conflict-ridden atmosphere, especially separatist tendencies, along the borders, the progress of connectivity initiatives has been very slow.

Three routes between Myanmar and Northeast India are identified to be critical in enhancing connectivity between ASEAN and India, viz. Moreh/Tamu route, Zokhawthar/Rhi route, and Nampong/Pangsu route, which is known as Stilwell Road. Four land customs stations (LCSs), viz. (a) Moreh in Manipur/Tamu in Sagaing, (b) Zokhawthar in Mizoram/Rikhawdar in Chin (c) Avakhung in Nagaland/ Layshi in Saging, and (d) Nampong in Arunachal Pradesh/Pangsu in Sagain have been identified to serve the border trade with Myanmar.[23]

Similarly, Northeast India is remained underdeveloped (De, 2008) on account of very poor connectivity with the rest of India. However, the

21. Refer, ERIA (2011).
22. Refer, ERIA (2010).
23. Refer, Kimura, and Umezaki, 2011.

Government of India has taken up a number of initiatives to bridge this gap by encouraging investment in infrastructure. Kaladan Mulitmodal Transit Transport Project is one of such initiatives designed to open an alternative access route connecting Northeast India and the rest of India through Chin and Rakhain states in Myanmar.[24] The project, entirely funded by the Government of India, aims to connect Indian ports and Sittwe port in Myanmar, and road and inland waterways links from Sittwe to India's northeastern region of India.[25]

Accelerate the Development of ICT Infrastructure and Services in Each of the ASEAN Member States

One of the major challenges in building a strong ICT infrastructure for ASEAN has been bridging the existing digital divide within its member countries. ASEAN and India have established cooperation in the field of ICT at regional and bilateral level. Some of the activities taken up include:

Regional Level Cooperation: A workshop on Information Security for System Administrators of ASEAN nations was held at Manesar, Haryana in August 2006 with the objectives to strengthen expertise relating to the information systems security among system administrators of ASEAN countries and establish a network between system administrators and national Computer Emergency Response Teams (CERTs) from India and ASEAN countries. Two days seminar on e-Learning and e-Learning technologies was held in November 2006 in Hyderabad with the objectives of providing a platform to share the experiences of e-Learning, e-Learning technologies and its implementation between India and ASEAN. A seminar titled "Shruti Drishti" was organised to share India's expertise in assistive technologies in January 2007 in Pune with the objectives of establishing new bonds between India and ASEAN countries in the sector of assistive technology and doing more R&D in this field. These are promoting awareness about assistive technology for visually impaired people and making easy availability of this technique at low cost to them.

India-ASEAN IT Ministerial and IT Industry Forum was held in New Delhi in May 2007 with the aim that Industry Forum will provide inputs to IT Ministerial to propel IT industry in forward direction among ASEAN

24. Ibid.
25. Refer, De and Ray (2013).

nations and India. The IT Ministerial Forum is part of India-ASEAN-Telecommunications and IT Ministers Meeting (TELMIN).[26]

Bilateral Level Cooperation: At bilateral level, Myanmar, Vietnam, Thailand, Brunei Darussalam, Lao PDR and Malaysia have signed Memorandum of Understanding with India. The common areas of cooperation include electronic commerce and multimedia development, e-governance, information security and cyber-crime, research and development, human resource development, IT education and training, among others.[27]

Connectivity Challenges Ahead

Given the progress so far on ASEAN-India connectivity initiatives, it is interesting to note that these initiatives have become a full part of a new elevated strategic partnership between ASEAN and India. Both ASEAN and India look forward to the successful implementation of the ASEAN-India partnership for peace, progress and shared prosperity, with the plan of action for the period 2010-2015. More importantly, the latest political change in Myanmar has helped mainland Southeast Asia and India to focus on greater prospects for increasing connectivity and integration. With a proper understanding of the initiative of individual country like the case of Thailand, which also has its "Look West" policies linking to South Asia, the whole new landscape of mainland ASEAN and India will be taking a new shape in the near future. In this regard, a new dynamics of mainland Southeast Asia's connectivity plan could not be fully understood without scrutinizing the connectivity plan that each ASEAN country has and how it could interface with the overall ASEAN-India connectivity plan in coming years.

Connectivity as Promising Area for Further Integration

Without substantive improvements, ASEAN-India economic relations might not be able to develop that far and integrate more forcefully. For this, improving physical connectivity between ASEAN and India has become an important step for enhancing the ASEAN-India economic integration. Given the diverse geography and range of possible transport modes involving rural and urban and less and more developed areas, assessment and planning of transportation require regional and multimodal dimensions that include

26. Refer, The Hindu, 2 May 2012, New Delhi.

27. Refer, Department of Electronics and Information Technology, Government of India.

road, rail, and sea transport. For instance, works like ADB (2012) and ADBI (2013) have reviewed bottlenecks with regard to physical infrastructure between South Asia and Southeast Asia. More than half of the total length of the Asian Highway in South and Southeast Asia are class III or below roads, indicating much scope for further improvement needed in order to make a proper cross-subregional road network. In addition, transshipment will be required even after rail links are developed within the country due to incompatibility of gauges (track widths) between India, Myanmar and Thailand.

Within this perspective, key physical barriers or hindrances to cross-subregional trade are mainly in Myanmar. Questions remain how to fill these gaps of infrastructural bottlenecks in the years to come in order to improve physical connectivity, which will facilitate new trade linkages and opportunities between ASEAN and India. Fortunately, with the recent change in Myanmar, the country has recognised the importance of connectivity issues and has started to work from within and also with neighbouring countries, in particular with both India and Thailand, which are very active also in engaging with Myanmar for connectivity improvement.

Connectivity as Strategic Consideration

In their report to the leaders (AIEPG Report, 2012), ASEAN-India Eminent Persons Group had advanced further strategic partnership through enhanced connectivity. India represents one of the two ASEAN Dialogue Partners that shares both sea and land borders with ASEAN. Given such a linkage, there is definitely much potential for ASEAN and India to be more connected than the recent past. For this to happen, India should support the implementation of the Master Plan on ASEAN Connectivity (MPAC), with the view of expanding such connectivity and bringing South Asia and Southeast Asia closer.

ASEAN-India Eminent Persons Group also wishes to see regular exchanges between ASEAN and Indian Inter-Ministerial Group on ASEAN connectivity to explore ways and means to support the MPAC as well as come up with new practical initiatives to further deepen regional integration between ASEAN and India. The emphasis has been placed on promoting and upgrading regional infrastructure and inter-connectivity between ASEAN and India, combined with enabling policy framework to facilitate and promote goods in transit, multi-modal transport and inter-state transport, which would benefit both sides and will result in a wider free trade zone.

Indeed, references had been made for the proposed extension of the India-Myanmar-Thailand Trilateral Highway to Lao PDR and Cambodia as well as the development of Mekong-India Economic Corridor (MIEC) connecting mainland Southeast Asia with South Asia on the eastern part of India through the Andaman Sea. Such strategic considerations require greater attention from all sides in order to gain greater momentum to the growing trade and investment linkages between ASEAN and India.

As for the development of ICT, India has also expressed to support the ASEAN efforts to realise the ASEAN ICT Master Plan, drawing upon its expertise and capabilities in the sector and through sharing of best practices in policy, regulations and technological development and capacity building programmes (AIEPG, 2012). It has also suggested to establish an ASEAN-India broadband high speed optical fibre network to enhance virtual connectivity, with the aim of establishing an ASEAN-India broadband corridor.

Interestingly, the issue of connectivity has been highly regarded by the Vision Statement at the ASEAN-India Commemorative Summit in 2012. As such, it was recommended for the ASEAN Connectivity Coordinating Committee (ACCC) to work closely with India's Inter-Ministerial Group on ASEAN connectivity to enhance air, sea and land connectivity between ASEAN and India. The Vision Statement also put forward the commitment of leaders to the completion of connectivity projects as recommended by the ASEAN-India Eminent Persons' Group.

Conclusions

ASEAN and India are neighbours with a long history of friendly relations. These links, with their proximity and position, make both very important partners for each other. In recent years, significant and broad-based progress has been realized in all areas of relationships, paving the way for India to play a constructive role for ASEAN as a Dialogue Partner. With a combined population of 1.8 billion people and a sizable GDP, it would be wise for ASEAN and India to work together to manage the common challenge. For this to happen, greater connectivity in all aspects, be it trade, services, investment, and movement of people, is very important for both sides.

Master Plan of ASEAN Connectivity (MPAC) was initiated and adopted in 2009. At present, MPAC has been updated till 2025. Such an initiative has become a key strategic objective of ASEAN as it seeks to reinforce the building of the ASEAN Community as well as the development of an ASEAN-centered regional architecture. India had very well responded to such an initiative all along these years, in particular, at the ASEAN-India Leaders' Summit 2012 hosted by India in Delhi to commemorate the 20th anniversary of ASEAN-India partnership. The Vision Statement of ASEAN-India Commemorative Summit expressed and confirmed a strong support for promoting and enhancing ASEAN-India connectivity to a further level.

As such, the latest summit represented a crucial "take-off" for connectivity between ASEAN and India, in particular, the way in which mainland Southeast Asia could productively link to South Asia and India. As discussed, several ASEAN-India physical connectivity initiatives are consistent with the MPAC such as completion of the ASEAN Highway Network, establishment of integrated and seamless multimodal transport system linking South and Southeast Asia, or acceleration of ICT infrastructure development and services in the near future. These are some important initiatives to strengthen connectivity between them.

The opening up of Myanmar represents a beginning of the partnership. Myanmar represents an important gateway for India to Southeast Asia. The new relations will contribute to regional growth and development, which will benefit Northeast Asia and inner part of the Greater Mekong Subregion (GMS). The Trilateral Highway is for sure a clear example of cooperation between India, Myanmar and Thailand, which will be operational in 2018. It is expected that ASEAN-India partnership will cover a broad range of initiatives, including border area development, connectivity, capacity building, institutional development and infrastructure.

References

ASEAN-India Eminent Persons Group (AIEPG). (2012). *ASEAN-India Eminent Persons' Report to the Leaders* (mimeograph).

Association of Southeast Asian Nations (ASEAN). (2010). Master Plan on ASEAN Connectivity, Jakarta.

Asian Development Bank (ADB). (2012). *Initial Assessments of Road Transport Infrastructure and Logistic Services for Trade Facilitation on the GMS Countries.* Draft Final Report, Regional Investment Framework Sector Report for the 18th GMS Ministerial Meeting, Nanning, 11-12 December.

Asian Development Bank Institute (ADBI). (2012). *Connecting South Asia and Southeast Asia.* Interim Report, A Joint Study of the ADB and the ADBI.

Athukorala, P., & Yamashita, N. (2006). *Production Fragmentation and Trade Integration in a Global Context.* North American Journal of Economics and Finance, Vol.17.

Ishida, M. (2012). *Emerging Economic Corridors in the Mekong Region.* Bangkok Research Center, IDE-JETRO, Bangkok.

De, P. (2008). Infrastructure Development in India. In Kumar, N. (ed.), *International Infrastructure Development in East Asia – Towards Balanced Regional Development and Integration*, ERIA Research Project Report 2007-2, Chiba: IDE-HETRO. (pp. -105-130).

De, P., & Ray, J.K. (2013). *India-Myanmar Connectivity, Current Status and Future Prospects*. New Delhi: KW Publishers.

Devare, S.T., Singh, S., & Marwah, R. (eds). (2012). *Emerging China, Prospects for Partnership in Asia*. New Delhi: Routledge Publications.

Economic Research Institute for ASEAN and East Asia (ERIA). (2010). *The Comprehensive Asia Development Plan (CADP)*.

Kimura, F., & Umezaki, S. (2011). (eds). *ASEAN-India Connectivity: The Comprehensive Asia Development Plan, Phase II,* Economic Research Institute for ASEAN and East Asia (ERIA).

Vision Statement, ASEAN-India Commemorative Summit (2012), (mimeograph).

Wong, M. H., & Pellan, M. I. (2012). Trade Facilitation: The Way Forward for ASEAN and Its FTA Partners. *Policy Brief,* Economic Research Institute for ASEAN and East Asia (ERIA).

ELEVEN

LOOK EAST TO ACT EAST: CONNECTIVITY CHALLENGES TO INDIA'S NORTHEAST

Prabir De and P K H Singh

Introduction

The North Eastern Region (NER) of India is the bridgehead of India's connectivity with Southeast and East Asia. The NER is also central to India's Act East Policy (AEP). However, in relative terms, the NER is one of India's most economically laggard regions, contributing only 3 per cent to the country's gross domestic product (GDP).[1] At the same time, no other region in India can outperform the NER in terms of availability of natural resources and in benefiting from its location as the international border. About 98 per cent of the NER's borders forms India's international boundaries; on one hand, it shares borders with South Asian countries like Bangladesh, Bhutan, and Nepal, and with growing Southeast and East Asian countries like Myanmar and China, on the other (Table 1).

Table 1: International Borders of the Northeastern States of India

State	Bangladesh	Bhutan	China	Myanmar	Nepal	Total
	(km)					
Arunachal Pradesh		217.0	1080.0	520.0		1817.0
Assam	263.0	267.0				530.0
Manipur				398.0		398.0
Meghalaya	443.0					443.0
Mizoram	318.0			510.0		828.0
Nagaland				215.0		215.0
Sikkim		32.0	220.4		97.8	350.2
Tripura	856.0					856.0
Total	1880.0	516.0	1300.4	1643.0	97.8	

Source: Government of India.

1. GDP and GSDP are taken at the current price for the year 2012-13, sourced from Central Statistical Organisation (CSO).

In the past, transportation facilitated international trade of the NER, particularly in Assam. However, with the partition of the Indian sub-continent in 1947, the NER became isolated, at least economically, from the rest of India, and gradually surrendered to an inward-looking economic regime with broken transportation networks. Today, the NER's high transportation cost negates its advantages of having international borders. As Brunner correctly noted, isolation plus high transaction costs equal low growth for the NER.[2]

The reality is that the NER suffers from economic isolation. The region imports almost every consumer goods from outside the region. The absence of adequate institutional and physical infrastructure, both national and international, coupled with political disturbances and insurgency in part have slowed down the NER's development process.[3] Nevertheless, given its strategic location, the NER can be developed as a base for India's growing economic links, not only with Southeast Asia but also with Bangladesh and China.

Several studies posit that the NER has the potential to grow faster than its current pace, provided the region builds cross-border production links, particularly with Bangladesh, Myanmar and other Southeast and East Asian countries such as Thailand, Malaysia, China and Indonesia.[4] However, the bottlenecks to cross-border production links are many, of which inadequate connectivity, logistics and trade facilitation, more particularly at the border areas, are the major ones. The trade between the NER and Bangladesh, China and Myanmar, its immediate neighbours, significantly suffer from not only infrastructure related bottlenecks but also regulatory burdens associated with customs, security, standards and certification.

In recent years, India's trade with Bangladesh and Myanmar witnessed an increase in growth, which indirectly suggests the existence of a large trade potential. However, supply-side constraints, among others, inhibit the two-way trade across the borders with India's two neighbours (RIS, 2011). Enhancing the NER's existing level of trade and economic linkages between Bangladesh and Myanmar would need infrastructure and institutional support, which would facilitate growth and remove the region's economic isolation (see Figure 1). Removing the status quo, therefore, means the NER

2. Refer, Brunner (2010)
3. Refer, for example, NEC (2007), Bhattacharya and De (2006), De (2008), to mention a few.
4. Refer, for example, RIS (2012).

has to invest heavily in building physical and institutional infrastructures, which would in return lead to a higher production, both within and across borders, and enhance the growth of the region.

Figure 1: Removing the Economic Isolation: Development Cycles for NER

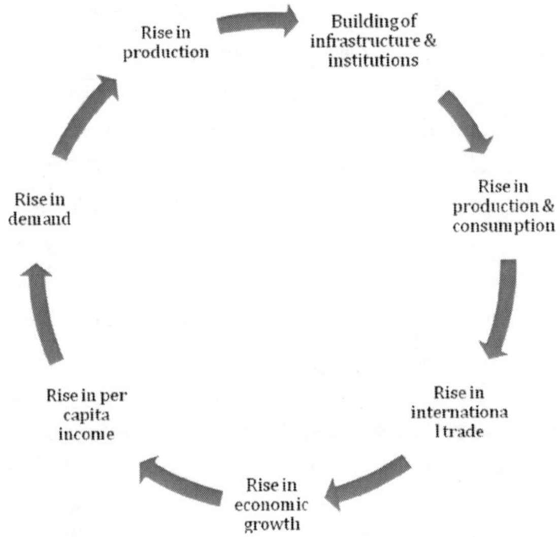

Source: De and Majumdar (2014)

In view of the above, the major objectives of this chapter are to analyse current scenario of NER's domestic infrastructure (also known as backend infrastructure), discuss the challenges faced by the region, and finally present policy implications. Rest part of the paper is arranged as follows. Section 2 presents the profile of the NER's domestic infrastructure, followed by a quick overview of select cross-border connectivity projects between India and Southeast and East Asia in Section 3. A discussion on cross-border infrastructure is important since we need to understand the links between cross-border connectivity and domestic connectivity. Concluding remarks are then drawn in Section 4.

Profile of Domestic Infrastructure of the NER

The NER comprises eight Indian states, namely, Arunachal Pradesh, Assam, Manipur, Meghalaya, Mizoram, Nagaland, Sikkim and Tripura. These eight states together cover an area of 2,62,179 sq. km., constituting 8 per cent of the country's total geographical area, and accounting for around 4 per cent of country's total population.[5] The region shares a long international boundary of around 96 per cent with its neighbouring countries, with China and Bhutan in the north, Myanmar in the east, Nepal in the west and Bangladesh in the south and west. Most of the hill states in the region like Arunachal Pradesh, Meghalaya, Mizoram and Nagaland are largely inhabited by tribal people with a fairly high degree of diversity even within the tribal groups. There is considerable uniformity among the NER states, but, at the same time, they carry distinctive differences.

The NER has a number of logistics handicaps. Physical infrastructure such as electricity, communication, transportation, and banking and finance are very sporadic and unevenly distributed among urban and rural areas. Amenities are limited in nature, and the lack of economic opportunities encourages migration, particularly that of skilled resources to work and live in better developed and developing parts of India.

Compared to the other regions of India, the NER as a region suffers more from inadequate infrastructure. Barring air and road density, the NER's performance is worst among the regions of India in transport infrastructure (Table 2). However, performance in infrastructure varies across the NER states since it comprises a heterogeneous group and is characterized by wide gaps in logistics and infrastructure. Table 3 presents basic infrastructure and logistics indicators of the NER for the year 2012. The profile suggests that the NER states are relatively better endowed with roads, airports, land custom stations (LCSs) and tele-density, where the variation across the NER states is not very high except for the road density in Tripura. However, the NER suffers from an availability of electricity; many of the NER states are yet to have an adequate supply of electricity. Next to electricity is the railway, where barring Assam and Tripura, the remaining states have either no railway lines or have very negligible railway presence such as in Arunachal Pradesh and Manipur. Similarly, only three of the NER states use inland water transport (IWT), among which Assam has the highest density of IWT in the NER. The remaining NER states are yet to utilize the inland waterways for the transportation of goods and passengers. In what follows the NER has gained tele-density, but lacks much in the form of physical infrastructure and logistics.

5. While population refers the year 2011, area refers the latest year, sourced from Census of India.

Table 2: Comparison of Transport Infrastructure, 2012

Region	No. of operational airports	Airport Density (per 1 lakh sq.km)	Rail length (km)	Rail density (per 1000 sq km)	Road length (km)	Road density (per 100 sq km.)
East	17	3.03	12944	23.04	640567	114.03
North	27	2.65	19311	18.92	662395	64.91
Northeast	11	4.20	2452	9.35	335237	127.87
South	24	3.77	13360	21.00	989300	155.48
West	22	2.70	15948	19.55	546485	66.99
National	101		64015		3173984	

Source: Authors

Table 3: Infrastructure Indicators of NER, 2012

States	Road*	Rail*	IWT*	Airport**	LCS**	Tele-density^	Electricity$
Arunachal Pradesh	24.12	0.02		6.34	1.87	33.56	1.93
Assam	37.91	31.08	33.04	9.87	18.65	49.60	0.65
Manipur	43.11	0.06		6.20	6.12	39.32	0.61
Meghalaya	37.08			5.12	51.10	44.03	1.03
Mizoram	44.18	0.07	6.87	5.03	15.33	33.34	1.45
Nagaland	30.54	0.78	22.93	6.83	7.31	39.94	0.76
Sikkim	9.48				15.11	38.34	3.98
Tripura	811.25	14.49		10.93	78.74	43.11	0.83

Notes: *km per 1000 sq. km. of area. **Number per 100,000 sq. km of area. ^Per 100 population. $Installed electricity per 10,000 population.
Source: Calculated based on various issues of Statistical Abstract, Government of India.

Roads and Highways

Roads are of particular importance in the NER because they provide access to inland parts of the NER. However, geographic constraints make the construction of roads an expensive endeavour in the NER. Till 2013, NER had a total length of National Highway (NH) of 9800 km, much lower than other regions of India. Government of India has taken steps to strengthen road network in the NER under the National Highways Development Project (NHDP) and Special Accelerated Road Development Programme in Northeast (SARDP-NE) schemes (Table 4). It is expected that by 2020, around 5744 km of NH will be added (see Table 4). Of this, SARDP-NE Phase A and Arunachal Package will add 3687 km of NH in NER. SARDP-NE aims to (i) upgrade National Highways to 2/ 4 lanes; (ii) provide connectivity of all 88 District Headquarters by 2-lane road (47 connected already); (iii) establish connectivity to backward and remote areas of NER; (iv) improve roads of strategic importance; and (v) improve connectivity to neighbouring countries.

Table 4: Improvement of National Highways at NER under Specific Programme

East West Corridor (NHDP-II) by NHAI (4 lane From Srirampur in Assam Border to Silchar in Assam) - (PDC 2015)	670 km
Under Phase A & Arunachal Package of SARDP-NE by NHAI, MoRTH, BRO and PWDs (2 lane Highways) (PDC 2018)	3687 km
NHDP-III by NHAI (2 lane Highways) (PDC 2016)	102 km
Under SARDP-NE, Phase B (yet to be approved for implementation)	1285 km
Total	5744 km

Source: Authors based on NEC

Railways

The presence of railways in the NER is more than 125 years old; originating around when the first passenger railway system came into operation in 1881 between Assam's Dibrugarh and Sadiya. Unfortunately, the railway system in the NER was severely disrupted with the division of India in 1947. However, the creation of a new railway zone in 1958 for the NER, the Northeast Frontier Railway (NF Railway) helped in further development of the railway system in the NER.[6] There are at present five divisions which serve these eight North Eastern states, viz. Katihar, Alipurduar, Rangia, Lumding and Tinsukia. Today, the NF Railway directly or indirectly serves all the eight NER states alongside parts of West Bengal and Bihar. The present rail network in the NER comprised of about 2602.35 km route (as of 31 March 2011), out of which 1454.16 km is broad gauge and the remaining 1148.19 km is metre gauge.[7] Out of the 1148.19 km remaining on the metre gauge, 1130 km has already been sanctioned for conversion to broad gauge.

6. NF Railway was carved out of the North Eastern Railway with headquarters at Maligaon, Guwahati.
7. Sourced from Annual Report, Indian Railway.

Table 5: Railway Projects Scenario in the NER

Sr. No.	1990	2014	2020
1	Broad Gauge (BG) Line upto Guwahati. All lines beyond Guwahati were Meter Gauge (MG) lines.	Broad Gauge Line upto Dibrugarh and Tinsukia – Gauge Conversion of Guwahati – Tinsukia – Dibrugarh completed including Furkating – Jorhat – Mariani and Simaluguri – Sibsagar – Moranhat Branch Lines. BG line to Dudhnoi-Mendhipathar ready, linking Meghalaya to rail map.	All the State Capitals will be on Broad Gauge.
2	Only One route between New Jalpaiguri to Guwahati. No alternative in case of disruption due to floods, accidents, bandhs, strikes, etc.	A complete alternative BG route from New Jalpaiguri to Guwahati commissioned by Gauge Conversion of Siliguri-New Jalpaiguri-New Bongaigaon MG Line and Jogighopa – Guwahati New Line.	A third alternative BG route from New Maynaguri to Jogighopa will be commissioned.
3	Mostly single BG Line beyond Katihar and Malda.		Doubling of New Jalpaiguri – Samuktala will be completed.
4	Most Express Trains take 40 to 48 hrs up to Guwahati from Delhi. Time taken to reach Dibrugarh/Tinsukia – up to 65 hours from Delhi.	Rajdhani Express introduced which takes 28 hrs up to Guwahati from Delhi. Time taken to reach Dibrugarh/ Tinsukia – 40 hours from Delhi.	
5	Only one Railway Bridge across River Brahmaputra – Rail-cum-Road Bridge at Saraighat (Guwahati) .	Second Railway Bridge across River Brahmaputra – Rail-cum-Road Bridge at Jogighopa opened.	Third Railway Bridge across River Brahmaputra – Rail-cum-Road Bridge at Bogibeel will be completed.

6	Along North Bank of Brahmaputra – MG Line from Rangiya to Murkongselek.		Entire North Bank of Brahmaputra will be on BG network and will get connected to South Bank at Dibrugarh through Bogibeel.
7	No connectivity to Capital city of any State except Assam.	Capital of Tripura (Agartala) connected by MG line. Naharlagun, Arunachal Pradesh connected with BG line.	Capital of Tripura (Agartala) connected by BG line. Capital of Manipur will be connected with BG line.

Source: Authors based on NEC.

Seventeen projects with the goal of new lines, gauge conversion, doubling rail track and railway electrification are currently in progress with a total estimated cost of Rs. 16,153 crore. Out of these, ten projects have been declared as National Projects where up to 75 per cent of the funding for the project is met by the Central Government and 25 per cent by the Ministry of Railways.[8] Table 5 presents major railway projects and compares projects under implementation for 1990, 2014 and 2020. Apparently, the Railways' investment in the NER has been going up.

At present, the backward links in railways are poor. Projects for rail connectivity to state capitals of Sikkim, Meghalaya, Mizoram, Manipur and Nagaland have been sanctioned by the Indian Railways. On 4 January 2014, the first Broad Gauge (BG) train from Guwahati to Tezpur via. Rangiya was started. The train has started operating between Naharlagun to Delhi.

Following projects shall be completed by 2018: (i) railway lines between Harmuti-Itanagar and Dudhnai-Mendipathar, which will provide rail connectivity to all North Eastern States except Sikkim; and (ii) railway line from Jiribum to Imphal to Moreh.

Inland Waterways

The NER has many large and small rivers providing facilities for water transport. The Brahmaputra and Barak rivers have been commonly used as

8. Sourced from NTDPC (2012)

the medium of transport for a long time.[9] It is estimated that the NER has about 1,800 km of river routes that can be used by steamers and larger country boats. At present, the river stretch from Sadiya to Dhubri (891 km) along the Brahmaputra River has been declared as National Waterways 2, since 1988. At present, we have inland water port at Pandu (Guwahati) with low- and high-level jetties, two warehouses, railway siding and open storage, etc. Floating terminals at Dhubri, Jogighopa, Tejpur, Silghat, Bishwanath ghat, Neamati, Bogibil, Dibrugarh, Panbari and Oriumghat are being maintained with berthing pontoon and gangway. Floating terminal can be provided at other locations on a need basis. Two shore cranes and five floating cranes are available for loading/unloading of cargo at the terminals. However, shallow drafted barges can only ply along the NW 2 due to low navigability. On top, night navigation is not possible in some parts along this stretch. However, night navigation aids have been installed between Dhubri (Bangladesh-India border) and Silghat (440 km).[10] DGPS stations set up at Dibrugarh, Silghat, Jogighopa and Dhubri. These DGPS stations will aid safe navigation using electronic charts.

To encourage inland waterways, some recommendations are as follows: (i) declaration of Barak river as National Waterway, particularly the stretch from Lakhipur to Bhanga (121 km), (ii) long term agreement of Indo-Bangladesh Trade and Transit Protocol, (iii) setting up RO-RO terminals at Dhubri and Hatsinghmari (Phulbari), (iv) development of ship repair facility at Pandu (Guwahati), (v) development of a multimodal terminal at Jogighopa, (vi) construction of approach road to Pandu port for heavy/ container traffic, (vii) develop Ashuganj terminal in Bangladesh with road links and custom facilities for transit cargo to NER via. Akhaura land border, and (viii) link Chittagong terminal in Bangladesh with road links and custom facilities for transit cargo to NER via. Sabroom land border.

9. With the growth of the tea industry these rivers became important carriers of trade. The East India Company started the water route along the Brahmaputra River from Kolkata to Dibrugarh in 1844 and steamships were introduced by the Joint Steamer Company in 1847. At about the same time, Silchar was linked with Kolkata along the Barak-Surma-Meghna navigation channel. However, with the partition of India in 1947, water transport in the NER faced slow progress.

10. Day navigation aids have been installed on the entire waterway from Dhubri to Sadiya/ Oriumghat (891 km).

Airways

In popular term, the NER is connected with the rest of India by air. NER's air density is highest among all the regions of India (Table 2). As noted in Table 6, Assam is the only state which has highest number of operational airports (6) in the NER, whereas Arunachal Pradesh is the only NER state which has the highest number of non-operational airports. Currently, 12 airports in NER are served by airlines such as Agartala, Lengpui, Bagdogra (CE), Dibrugarh, Dimapur, Guwahati, Imphal, Jorhat (CE), Lilabari, Shillong, Silchar (CE), and Tezpur (CE). While more airports are now connected by civil airlines, there has been a deceleration in the movement of aircrafts and freights in 2013-14, compared 2010-11 (Table 7). However, the volume of passenger flows has gone up over time, thereby showing a huge potential of air transportation in the NER and investment opportunities in airlines and aviation infrastructure.

Table 6: Airports in the NER

State	Operational	Non-Operational
Assam	6 3 IAF, 3 AAI	2
Arunachal Pradesh	-	5
Manipur	1	-
Meghalaya	1	1
Mizoram	1	1
Nagaland	1	-
Tripura	1	3
Sikkim	-	-
West Bengal	1	-
Total	11+1	12

Source: Authors based on NEC

Table 7: Movement of Aircraft, Passengers and Freight from the NER

	Aircraft Movements	Passengers	Freight
	(No.).		(tonnes)
2004-05	33019	1447453	10304
2010-11	67395	4590271	24087
2013-14	58839	5065733	21116

Source: Authors based on NEC.

Trade Facilitation and Border Infrastructure

Trading Across Borders (TAB) is most popular indicators of trade facilitation.[11] While the number of documents needed to be able to export and import has been static, both in Bangladesh and India since 2006, exporters and importers in Bangladesh submit relatively fewer documents, compared to India. At the same time, India and Bangladesh have been successful in reducing the time taken to export and import goods during 2006 and 2013. Today, India takes 16 days to export a container load of goods and Bangladesh takes about 25 days, a marked improvement from 27 and 35 days, respectively, for India and Bangladesh in 2006. Export and import times in India are consistently lower than that of Bangladesh. However, we witness a completely different scenario regarding the costs to export and import goods. The export cost is relatively high in India as compared to Bangladesh, whereas Bangladesh witnesses relatively higher import costs than India. However, traders in both the countries face a little over US$ 1000 per container as costs to export or import, witnessing a rising trend since 2008. If we compare the NER with Bangladesh in TAB in 2013, the NER outperforms Bangladesh in time and cost to export and import (Table 8). In other words, exports from and imports to the NER face lower costs and time than to and from Bangladesh. Contrary to popular belief, the NER's performance in TAB is better than the South Asian average (Table 8). Among major Indian cities, Guwahati ranks 7th in TAB in 2013, placed much higher than Bangalore or Delhi NCR (Table 9). NER's advantage lies in cost competitiveness in export and import.[12]

While the number of trade documents is not very high, the NER's major disadvantage is that these documents have to be filled in manually, particularly in the case of trade with Bangladesh and Myanmar, whereas the same process is conducted electronically for most of export and import procedures in Bangladesh.

---

11. Trading across Borders is a major part of World Bank's Doing Business database. Refer World Bank (2013) for its detailed methodology of calculation.

12. It is imperative to interpret this data cautiously. We have to keep in mind that the NER at present handles a relatively lower volume of trade, compared to Bangalore or Delhi NCR. Lower export and import costs appear due to low trade volume. Therefore, the NER's rank may change with the rise in trade volume.

Table 8: TAB Indicators in 2013: NER vis-à-vis Other Countries / Regions

Indicator	NER*	India	Bangladesh	South Asia	OECD
Documents to export (number)	8	9	6	8	4
Time to export (days)	22	16	25	32	10
Cost to export (US$ per container)	713	1,120	1,025	1,603	1,028
Documents to import (number)	9	11	8	9	5
Time to import (days)	28	20	34	33	10
Cost to import (US$ per container)	794	1,200	1,430	1,736	1,080

Note: * Refers Guwahati only.
Source: Drawn based on Doing Business Database, The World Bank.

Table 9: TAB Indicators for the NER, 2013

City	Rank	Documents to export (number)	Time to export (days)	Cost to export (US$ per container)	Documents to import (number)	Time to import (days)	Cost to import (US$ per container)
Bhubaneshwar	1	8	17	834	9	16	833
Chennai	2	8	25	541	9	19	593
Ahmedabad	3	8	17	946	9	18	978
Mumbai	3	8	17	945	9	21	960
Kochi	5	8	28	432	9	21	480
Kolkata	6	8	20	644	9	31	710
Guwahati	7	8	22	713	9	28	794
Ranchi	8	8	21	678	9	36	717
Bengaluru	9	8	25	783	9	25	1,024
Patna	10	8	19	941	9	32	985
Indore	11	8	21	912	9	35	981
Ludhiana	12	8	21	1,105	9	25	1,154
Hyderabad	13	8	26	1,012	9	23	1,084
Jaipur	14	8	22	1,289	9	22	1,384
New Delhi	14	8	25	1,077	9	28	1,158
Noida	16	8	25	1,077	9	27	1,187
Gurgaon	17	8	25	1,077	9	28	1,184

Source: Drawn based on Doing Business Database, The World Bank.

The inland transportation and handling costs associated with major export and import procedures in the NER are lower than that of Bangladesh. The completion of documentations for export and import procedures also takes relatively less time in the NER than in Bangladesh. While in importing goods, the NER does tend to take more time in completing (i) customs clearance and technical control, (ii) ports and terminal handling, and (iii) inland transportation and handling forms as compared to Bangladesh. The costs associated with inland transportation and handling for international trade in the NER can account for up to 2/3rd of the total costs of export or import, while it is the cost of ports and terminal handling procedures which contributes to almost 50 per cent of the total cost of export or import. Thus, document preparation takes a longer time than any other procedure in both export and import in the NER and Bangladesh.

Table 10: Availability of Border Infrastructure

Facilities/ LCS	Dawki	Sutarkhandi	KSFS	Agartala	Moreh
Electricity	Yes	Yes	Yes	Yes	Yes
Telephone	Yes	Yes	Yes	Yes	Yes
Internet	No	No	No	Yes	No
EDI	No	No	No	No	No
Weighbridge	No	Yes	No	Yes	Yes
Warehouse	No	Yes	No	No	No
Cold storage	No	Yes	No	No	No
Parking yard	No	Yes	Yes	No	Yes
Transshipment platform/ transit sheds	No	Yes	Yes	No	No
Dumping sheds	No	No	Yes	No	No
Drinking water	Yes	Yes	Yes	Yes	Yes
Drivers rest room	No	No	Yes	No	No
Passengers rest room	Yes	No	No	Yes	No
Health centre	No	No	No	Yes	No
Hotels and restaurants	No	No	No	No	No
Separate entry and exit gates	No	No	Yes	No	No
Banks	Yes	Yes	Yes	No	Yes
Courier/ Post office	No	Yes	Yes	Yes	No
Servicing centre/ Vehicle repair shops	No	Yes	Yes	No	No
Food testing laboratory	No	No	No	No	Yes*
Container handling yard	No	No	No	No	No
Container handling equipment	No	No	No	No	No
Currency exchange	No	No	No	No	No

Source: De and Majumdar (2014)

Some export and import procedures are bit lengthier in the NER and also in Bangladesh. The more time-consuming the export or import process, the less likely it is that a trader in the NER will be able to compete in the international markets.

In general, the NER is much more competitive than Bangladesh in completing export and import procedures. However, the trade cost incidence to the NER and Bangladesh is nonetheless very high compared to other developing countries. The removal of these trade costs would be important in easing the trade in the region and removing NER's economic isolation.

Infrastructure at the border is also not adequately available (Table 10). Therefore, trade at border faces high transport cost and time at the border. Electricity is available in all the LCSs, but the quality of electricity varies. Most of the LCSs face frequent power-cuts all throughout the day such as in Moreh, where electricity is available only for 4 to 5 hours in a day. The telephone facility (landline) is not available in many of the LCSs. Mobile communication facility except BSNL does not work at the Moreh LCS.[13] Internet is also not available, except perhaps in Agartala. The absence of consistently good quality electricity has de-motivated Customs from using the EDI facility. Virtually, the EDI facility is completely missing in LCSs in the NER. Therefore, trade is being handled manually. Unfortunately, facilities like weighbridges, warehouses, cold storage, etc., which are essential for trade, are not available except at Sutarkandi in Assam and Agartala in Tripura (and even then, it is only the weighbridge). There are also wide gaps in the availability of supporting facilities such as health centres, rest rooms, hotels and restaurants, etc., across the LCSs. The Karimganj Steamer and Ferry Station (KSFS) LCS atleast provides a driver's rest room, a facility that the others do not have. The Agartala LCS has a health centre, unlike other LCSs. However, hotels and restaurants are not available near any of the LCSs. Except for KSFS, none of the LCSs has a separate entry and exit gate for the export and import of goods. The availability of banks and testing laboratories are necessary for trade at the border. While banks are available at some LCSs such as Moreh, KSFS, Sutarkandi, and Dawki, but there are no food testing laboratories at the border except at Moreh, where the testing is conducted at Imphal, which is located 110 km from the border.

Therefore, the NER should pay greater attention to the improvement of logistics, both on trade infrastructure and also on human capital. The bottom line that comes out from this study is that logistics improvement unambiguously

13. Noticed at the time of survey in 17-19 April 2013

increases trade. Therefore, stronger connectivity would be important in order to facilitate trade and production networks across borders in the NER.

Backend integration with regional connectivity projects is essential in order to reap the benefits of growing economic linkages between India and Southeast and East Asia. Domestic connectivity has to be planned to link emerging development centres and nodes (see Figure 2). Annexure 1 presents a list of cross-border connectivity projects and current status of backend linkages that have been drawn in order to strengthen NER's connectivity – both domestic and cross-border.

Figure 2: New Development Centres and Nodes

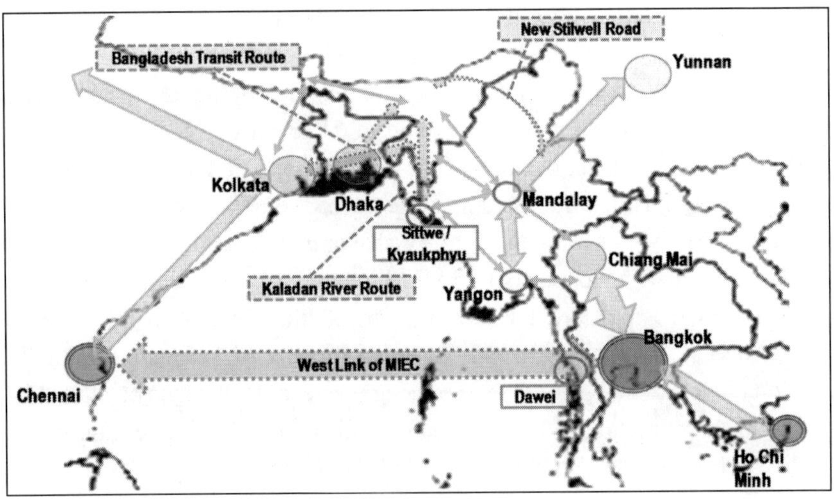

Source: ERIA (2012)

India's Cross-border Connectivity Projects with Southeast Asia

The corridors considered for linking up of the NER with the Southeast Asia are (i) Trilateral Highway, (ii) Kaladan Multimodal Transit Transport Project, (iii) Lawngtlai-Saiha-Rhi-Mandalay Road. ASEAN-India physical connectivity in the present form comprises two important projects, namely, (i) India-Myanmar-Thailand Trilateral Highway, and (ii) Kaladan Multimodal Transit Transport Project. The development has been started in most of the areas on the Indian side, container enabled connectivity is the missing link which needs to be included. Some of the projects worth considering are: Development of the Rhi-Tidim road sector, strengthening of the bridges under the Trilateral Highway and the Zoringpui-Paletwa road in Myanmar under the Kaladan project. Apart from these corridors, the NER states are demanding further developing the links via. the old Stillwell road which has been completed up to Pangsau pass and Meluri-Awankhu-Layshi from Nagaland. Lumla-Tashigong road on the Bhutan side also needs to be taken up. The linking of the Chittagong Port from Sabroom in Tripura will open up an effective link for the NER. Besides, Mekong-India Economic Corridor (MIEC) and Sittwe Economic Zone are two important projects which would facilitate multimodal connectivity and investment.

Trilateral Highway

On the Trilateral Highway, the Tamu and Kalewa friendship road is being constructed with India's assistance. About 132 km has been completed and handed over to Myanmar. Work on other 28 km is under progress. India has also undertaken the task of repair/upgradation of 71 bridges on the Tamu-Kalewa friendship Road, and upgradation of the 120 km Kalewa-Yargyi road segment to highway standard, while Myanmar has agreed to undertake upgradation of the Yargyi-Monywa stretch to highway standard. This project would help in establishing trilateral connectivity from Moreh in India to Mae Sot in Thailand via. Myanmar. Separately, the Government of India had taken initiatives to prepare Detailed Project Report (DPR) for construction of Chaungma-Yinmabin section (30 km); and upgradation from single lane to double lane of Yinmabin-Pale-Lingadaw section (50 km). India has also announced extension of the Trilateral Highway to Cambodia, Lao PDR and Vietnam.

Kaladan Multimodal Transit Transport Project

One of the objectives of Kaladan Multimodal Transit Transport Project is to provide an attractive access to the Bay of Bengal to landlocked Northeastern part of India. The Ministry of External Affairs (MEA), Government of India entered into a Framework Agreement with the Government of Myanmar in April 2008 to facilitate implementation of the project. The components of this project include: (i) construction of an integrated Port and Inland Water Transport (IWT) terminal at Sittwe including dredging; (ii) development of navigational channel along river Kaladan from Sittwe to Paletwa (158 km); (iii) construction of an IWT - Highway trans-shipment terminal at Paletwa; and (iv) construction of six IWT barges (each of 300 tonne capacity) for transportation of cargo between Sittwe and Paletwa. Framework Agreement and two protocols

(Protocol on Transit Transport and Protocol on Maintenance) were signed by India and Myanmar on 2 April 2008. Construction of integrated Port cum IWT jetty at Sittwe is substantially completed. Construction work of IWT terminal at Paletwa has been started in April 2013. The India-Manipur Border to NH 54 (Lawngtlai) Road on the Indian side in Mizoram is in progress under the Ministry of Road Transport and Highways, Government of India.

Sittwe Economic Zone

Sittwe Economic Zone (SEZ) is proposed to be located at Ponnar Kyun, 18 km upstream of Sittwe port. Situated at the mouth of Kaladan river, the Sittwe port is being developed by India as a part of the Kaladan Multimodal Transit Transport Project. Myanmar government has identified about 1833 acres of land at Ponnar Kyun for setting-up this industrial park. Kaladan river provides easy maritime connectivity with the region. Agro and fisheries are likely to have a good development potential in the region. This economic zone may accommodate industrial projects which will cater to the local and larger Indian market.

Mekong – India Economic Corridor (MIEC)

Another important cross-border connectivity project is the Mekong-India Economic Corridor (MIEC). MIEC involves integrating the four Mekong countries, namely, Myanmar, Thailand, Cambodia and Vietnam with India. It connects Ho Chi Minh City (Vietnam) with Dawei (Myanmar) via Bangkok (Thailand) and Phnom Penh (Cambodia) and Chennai in India. The major investment will be required for the development of a port at Dawei and SEZ. This corridor, when completed, is expected to augment trade with India by reducing the travel distance between India and MIEC countries and removing supply side bottlenecks. The emphasis of the corridor is on expanding the manufacturing base and trade with the rest of the world, particularly with India. The corridor will enable economies of ASEAN and India to integrate further and collectively emerge as a globally competitive economic bloc.

Delhi – Hanoi Railway Link

Railways do a bulk trans-national movement of goods and services among the neighbouring countries. Needs are four-fold—(1) to link India's Manipur with India's main railway corridor, (2) to link Imphal with Kalay in Myanmar (about 212 km), (3) to link Thanbyuzayat with Three Pagoda Pass in Thailand (110 km), and (4) to re-establish and renovate railway networks in Myanmar. Harmonisation of railway tracks in the region is essential. Without having a compatible and strong railway system inside Myanmar, closer communication would be difficult. RITES completed a preliminary study to establish Delhi–Hanoi railway link in 2006. Although Railways are in service in major parts of these routes, about 238 km are missing links, which have to be built in Myanmar in order to have Delhi-Hanoi railways in operation. Renovation of railway network systems in southern (Yangon to Dawei) and northern (Mandalay to Kalay) Myanmar is essential.

Concluding Remarks

With the region lagging behind rest of India in terms of growth for decades, the local market is not a large one. To look for markets beyond the NER under the new Act East Policy (AEP), weak connectivity with rest of India and lack of access to bordering countries are serious deterrents. Nevertheless, investment potential considerably goes up in the NER when one considers its geographical proximity to Southeast and East Asian markets. In order to reap this benefit, NER has to improve its 'backend' infrastructure, which would not only help the region to raise its competitiveness but also narrow the development gaps.

The major challenges faced today in order to strengthen the internal connectivity in the NER are lack of awareness of the common people about benefits of greater economic engagement between the NER and Southeast Asia. Sensitizing ground level executives of the procedures, participatory role of population and urgency are the challenges we need to overcome. The NER is prone to natural calamities. Therefore, we have to develop technology or source to suite the climate, terrain and need of the region for expediting the construction. About 50 per cent of the land mass in the NER has been covered with forest. Suitable amendments in the Acts may be considered to accommodate the developmental needs. At the same time, we need to digitize the land records of entire NER. Low private investment is another big challenge to overcome. Providing enabling environment for private investment would pave the way for engagement with Southeast and East Asia.

Some of the projects which can be undertaken are as follows: (i) all 95 district headquarters (HQs) should be connected by double lane road by 2018, (ii) all the State capitals of the Region should be connected by Broad Gauge Rail line and four lane roads by 2020, (iii) priority shall also be given to the important SARDP-NE Phase B and inter-state road projects,

(iv) the States should be provided with sufficient funds for maintenance and rehabilitation of its assets, (v) all the National Railway projects must be completed as per schedule by providing necessary funds in time, (vi) the Government of India shall fund the development of airports in the NER, (vii) air connectivity of the region has to be improved by making the short takeoff and landing (STOL) Aircrafts and Helicopter services more attractive for the private companies, and (viii) Guwahati should be developed as a hub for air connectivity and both Imphal and Guwahati shall be connected with neighbouring countries.

Stronger connectivity across the NER will build a stronger network of cross-border production chains, particularly with Southeast Asia and Bangladesh. Inadequate backward links in rail, water and road will continue to hamper the economic integration. The present institutional linkages are no doubt improving, but these have to be strengthened further to support the connectivity projects between India and Southeast Asia. Once connectivity projects start attracting investment, engages into the development of the region and improves the quality of life of the local people through generation of employment and reduction of poverty, it becomes a truly public good and then turns to be an economic corridor.

References

Bhattacharyay, B., & De, P. (2006). *Promotion of Trade and Investment between People's Republic of China and India: Toward a Regional Perspective*. Asian Development Review, Vol. 22, No. 1.

Brunner, H. P. (ed.). (2010) *North East India: Local Economic Development and Global Markets*. Sage. New Delhi.

De, P. (2008). *Reassessing Transaction Costs of Trade at the India-Bangladesh Border*. Economic and Political Weekly, Vol. 43, No. 29.

De, P., & Majumdar, M. (2014). *Developing Cross-Border Production Networks between North Eastern Region of India, Bangladesh and Myanmar: A Preliminary Assessment*. Research and Information System for Developing Countries (RIS), New Delhi.

Economic Research Institute of ASEAN and East Asia (ERIA). (2012). *ASEAN-India Connectivity Report*, ERIA, Jakarta.

North Eastern Council (NEC). (2007). *Northeastern Region: Vision 2020*, NEC, New Delhi.

National Transport Development Policy Committee (NTDPC). (2012). *Report of the Working Group on Improvement and Development of Transport Infrastructure in the North East*. NTDPC, New Delhi.

Research and Information System for Developing Countries (RIS). (2011). *Expansion of North East India's Trade and Investment with Bangladesh and Myanmar: An Assessment of the Opportunities and Constraints*, New Delhi.

Research and Information System for Developing Countries (RIS). (2012). *ASEAN – India Connectivity Report: India Country Study*, RIS, New Delhi.

Annexure 1: Backend Linkages

	Railway	Highway	Waterway	ICP
India -Bangladesh	• Railway infrastructure at India-Bangladesh border posts has to be upgraded in terms of doubling of railway lines, electrification, warehouses, customs and security, etc., particularly at Tripura and West Bengal.	• Strengthening of highways connecting India-Bangladesh border in Northeast India, particularly Assam, Mizoram and Meghalaya, is needed. • Mizoram government is implementing state road development projects including border road with support of World Bank.	• Setting-up / expansion of IWT jetties in Assam under various stages of implementation. • Cargo handling capacity at IWT jetties has to be upgraded.	• ICP at Agartala is completed already. ICP at Petrapole is almost ready. ICP in Dawki is yet to be ready. • Need to undertake another phase of ICP projects in Northeast India and West Bengal such as Hilli, Changrabandha, Karimganj, etc.
India – Bhutan	• Railway infrastructure has to be upgraded at Hashimara (N F Railway)	• NH 31 and 31C (East – West Corridor) already completed. • The road, Phuentsholing (Bhutan)-Jaigaon (India)-Hasimara (India)-Changrabandha (India)-Burimari (Bangladesh) (115 km), has to be upgraded into international standard.		• Border infrastructure at Jaigaon in West Bengal has to be upgraded.

India -Myanmar	• Projects for rail connectivity to state capitals of Sikkim, Meghalaya, Mizoram, Manipur and Nagaland have been sanctioned by Indian Railways and various stages of development. Following projects shall be completed: ▪ Railway lines between Harmuti-Itanagar and Dudhnai-Mendipathar, which will provide rail connectivity to all Northeastern States except Sikkim; ▪ Railway line from Jiribum to Imphal.	• All Highways (54, 39 in particular) leading to border of Bangladesh, Myanmar have to be upgraded to international standard. • Under SARDP-NE, highway projects are various stages of implementation. Following projects have to completed urgently: ▪ Highway from Aizal to Lawngtlai till Mizoram-Myanmar border ▪ Highway from Imphal to Moreh.	• Government of India has sanctioned development of a new port at Sagar (West Bengal) recently. • India – Myanmar IWT links and coastal shipping may be explored.	• Implementation of ICP at Moreh is moving slowly. • Border infrastructure at Champai has to be upgraded. • CHAs in Northeast, particularly in Manipur and Mizoram, have to be trained on EDI system.

Source: Authors, compiled from various secondary sources.

TWELVE

EDUCATION AND KNOWLEDGE INSTITUTIONAL COOPERATION WITH SPECIAL REFERENCE TO SCIENCE, SOCIETY AND INNOVATION FOR SUSTAINABILITY

Lawrence Surendra

Introduction

Globalisation in its wake has created both negative impacts as well as new ways in which "the knowledge economy" plays an important role in global, regional and national activity (Dunning, 2000b). While there has been much work done on how regions have specialised through intensification of knowledge in specific industries, the Indian IT industry being cited as an example, there is not much work done or cross-border alliances forged with regard to the role of knowledge institutions that create and provide the infrastructure for the penetration, continuance and sustainability of knowledge industries.

"Over the last three centuries the main source of wealth in market economies has switched from natural assets (notably land and relatively unskilled labour), through tangible created assets (notably buildings, machinery and equipment, and finance), to intangible created assets (notably knowledge and information of all kinds) which may be embodied in human beings, organisations, or in physical assets" (Dunning, 2000a).

With the advent and advancement of technology, the knowledge economy has gained a growing importance of innovation, not only competitiveness enhancing features but also innovation for coping with the impacts, social, ecological, environmental and economic of increasing cross-border trade flows and ties. This chapter explores the possibility of and the enabling conditions needed for knowledge institutional cooperation in the Asia regional context specifically between India and ASEAN.

India-ASEAN Cooperation in Science and Technology

Historically, ASEAN was created as a result of the Cold War. Some of the original founding countries of ASEAN were dependent and greatly influenced by big powers such as the USA. ASEAN as a grouping initially had reservations in extending ties with India, though many of the individual countries have historically maintained good, warm and mutually beneficial relations with India. However, the changing realities of the Indian economy and the ups and downs of the global economy have led to desire need for greater ties between India and ASEAN, and great ambitions have been placed for this relationship.

Indians and Indian institutions have always been more inclined to look west though our national leaders like Jawaharlal Nehru placed much value to our relations with Asia. He was instrumental in taking the initiative to organise the Asian Relations Conference just close to India's Independence in 1947 and then in 1949. Of course the Cold War had a role in India first moving towards Non-Alignment and then globalisation and the pressure that the west, especially the US, brought to bear on India, both in economic (trade and investment) and strategic matters. Altogether these changes made India incline more towards the west. However, the successive global economic crises, especially that of 2007-08, the one from which much of the west is still recovering, is gradually bringing India closer to Asia in terms of economic relations and cooperation. It is important that academics and industry play close attention to the developments and trends in our relations with our Asian neighbours and beyond the shores of South Asia, which we often tend to be obsessed with when our own self-obsession with our country needs a diversion. We need to train our younger academia especially our students, particularly in their own interest and the country's interest to cast their gaze eastwards and not the west alone.

India's Look East – Act East Policy

India launched the Look East Policy during the government of Prime Minister P.V. Narasimha Rao in 1991 after the end of the Cold War and break up of the Soviet Union as well the balance of payments crisis that India faced during the period of instability caused by Rajiv Gandhi's assassination. Successive Prime Ministers after Rao have built upon it. In Narasimha Rao's perspective the Look East Policy was part of a larger effort to enhance strategic cooperation with the USA. In 2014, India unveiled the Look East

Policy version 2, which is also popularly known as Act East Policy (AEP). Fortunately for India and other Asian countries, today the Look East – Act East Policy has gained a certain autonomy of its own and not tied to strategic politics of superpowers. India in the early decades of its economic growth missed on reaping the gains of the "Asian Miracle" and the Asian economic boom. The Look East – Act East Policy has helped in making the Asian region India's largest trading partner, especially in the context of the global economic crisis. It is clear that even in the medium term Asia will continue to be a dynamic growth region and a vibrant part of the world economy.

Beyond Trade and Investment

Globalisation hastened the speed of global economic integration albeit in a way that is not always beneficial to developing countries and weaker nations, thus accelerating inequality between and within nations. This together with the crisis of global capitalism has led to many trans-regional arrangements such as BRICS and closer regional cooperation within regional associations such as ASEAN and between ASEAN and India. There have been several Agreements and high level statements towards strengthening cooperation between India and ASEAN. For example, we find the Vision Statement of the ASEAN-India Commemorative Summit of 20 December 2012 held at New Delhi and ASEAN–India Eminent Persons Group Report, November 2012. Other major document is the Plan of Action to Implement the ASEAN-India Partnership for Peace, Progress and Shared Prosperity (2010-2015).

Apart from the efforts made by India and the ASEAN countries to foster cooperation, both bilaterally and regionally, there have also been movements of students from some of the ASEAN countries to India to study and to some lesser extent in the reverse direction from India to the ASEAN. In 1960s and 1970s, Malaysian students received training in Indian medical institutions as doctors. During the latter period, about 30,000 Malaysian students were said to be studying in India, though the number is likely to be much less now. Given that India as a non-aligned country continued to maintain relations with Vietnam during the Vietnam War as also maintained close relations with Lao PDR, after the Vietnam War India also encouraged students from Cambodia to study in India. Students from these countries have studied in Indian higher educational institutions and returned to occupy high positions in their governments.

Even three or four decades ago, in places like Mysore University, it was a common sight to see Thai Buddhist monks coming to study at Mysore University. Today, not only Thai monks but also students seeking higher education in different disciplines are coming to India to cities like Pune and Bangalore and states like Tamil Nadu and Karnataka. Given the number of Thai students pursuing higher studies, especially engineering, in Bangalore, the Royal Thai Consulate in Chennai has even facilitated the formation of a Thai Student Association Bangalore (ThaiSAB) with over 200 student members.

Students from Thailand have come to India to pursue academic and research studies and vice versa, though the number of Indian students studying in Thailand may be smaller. At the school level, while in the past, Thais have sent their wards to study in boarding schools in India in hill stations mostly in the North and East of India. However, number of Thai school going children have increased in Southern India too. These Thai students have accustomed themselves to the Indian social and cultural environment, and thus many of them are returning to study in higher education institutions in India. In the case of countries like Malaysia, considering that there are a large number of people of Indian origin in Malaysia, India has initiated a number of steps in terms of cooperation in education. Private educational institutions have set up campuses in Malaysia and many Malaysian Universities have set up twinning programmes with Indian higher education institutions especially with regard to medical degrees.

Other than students from Thailand coming to India for studies, cooperation between India and Thailand is of a longer vintage and standing. India and Thailand have had strong mutual links for decades, which have been periodically strengthened by agreements between the two countries in various fields. The trade agreement signed in 1968 was followed up, a year later by a bilateral air services agreement, which could be said as the first initiative for "connectivity". Equally of interest is the 'knowledge cooperation' that has been on the radar of India and Thailand relations, and, in 1986, a Protocol was signed for S&T Cooperation between Thailand Institute of Scientific and Technological Research (TISTR) and Council of Scientific and Industrial Research (CSIR) of India. This was followed by two more agreements—one on Scientific, Technical and Environmental Cooperation and Transfer of Technology, and, the other, namely, Agreement on Cooperation in the Exploration and Use of Outer Space for

Peaceful Purposes. This was followed up in 2003 with a Memorandum of Understanding (MoU) on Cooperation in the Field of Agricultural Science, Technology and Economy. In 2005, an MoU on Cooperation in the Field of Education was signed.

Ambitions or Pious Hopes for the Future of India-ASEAN Relations

India became a sectoral dialogue partner of ASEAN in 1992, and a full dialogue partner in 1996. Annual Summits with ASEAN have been held from 2002 with a special summit in 2012 to celebrate 20 years of India-ASEAN relations. The cooperation between ASEAN and India is fairly diversified and includes trade, science and technology, human resource development, health and pharmaceuticals, space sciences, agriculture, new and renewable energy, information and communication technology, telecommunications, transport and infrastructure, and tourism and culture. India has also contributed to several funds, beginning with the US$ 50 million fund for cooperation between India and ASEAN in 2009, the Science and Technology Cooperation Fund has been enhanced from US$ 1 million to US$ 5 million w.e.f. 2016 and the ASEAN-India Green Fund in the context of Climate Change with an initial corpus of US$ 5 million. In 2014-15, trade between India and ASEAN stood at US$ 68 billion. In 2012 during the visit of the Thai Premier, an agreement was signed with regard to the Programme of Cooperation in Science and Technology for 2012-14. Some of the cases for knowledge cooperation in Thailand-India are presented below to illustrate the areas in which India-ASEAN knowledge cooperation is evolving and has potential to evolve further.

In terms of the building blocks of strengthening cooperation between India and ASEAN, whatever has been said above may be good starting points. Yet, it must be stated that the long term vision and ambitions are still at a pedestrian level with not much imagination, especially from the Indian side and consequently an inability to leverage India's strengths, while complementing ASEAN needs and strengths in various areas. Like India's relations with many other Asian countries, India's relation with ASEAN is full of good sentiment but lacks strategic vision and most agreements are meek and built around the myopia and lack of real appreciation and knowledge of Southeast Asia. The same thing happens at the youth exchange, eminent persons platforms and so forth. However, if new creative initiatives are to come, they will not come from state bureaucracies, but they have to come from collaboration and cooperation between knowledge institutions and institutions of higher learning. Towards this, research institutes and higher learning institutions in India and ASEAN countries have to actively see ways of shaping cooperative and collaborative research and joint intellectual production. However, such collaborations need to be done on well articulated frameworks and preferably normative and shared frameworks that add value to relations between countries and also act as a critique and mirror of the problems that arise from market processes that may affect livelihoods or ecology or have wider social implications.

Prospects

There is a need to examine the prospects for creating shared frameworks for collaboration and cooperation between knowledge institutions and institutions of higher learning in India and Thailand (ASEAN). To begin with, one must recognise that in spite of shared cultural heritage, natural, cultural and historical ties, the relations between the two have been interrupted by the Cold War. The latter has definitely left an intellectual baggage that includes a legacy of old and new suspicions and alienated relations produced as a result of the Cold War. In the wake of growing positive relations in terms of economic relations in the area of trade, investment and heightened economic cooperation, it is difficult to say whether Cold War history and its baggage will be kept suspended or will permanently disappear. At the same time, the other issue is how permanent these economic ties will be. Will shifts happen once the global economy is out of its problems and Europe and the US start witnessing growth?

Crystal ball gazing to predict or shape the future of India-ASEAN relations, while it might take us nowhere, it is clear that growing economic relations is bound to have its own momentum, thereby also creating its own ripples in the fields of culture, tourism and educational exchanges and all of this hopefully contributing to and enhancing the quality of India-ASEAN relations in the future. As we had already mentioned, cooperation on the spheres of knowledge can not be left to evolutionary economic trends and positivist perspectives. They need normative goals and nurturing. It may be necessary to look at some of the ground realities especially in the context of cooperation between institutions of higher learning.

Problems and Ground Realities

Specifically in relation to institutions of higher learning like universities, many problems can be listed but problems common to both sides are as follows:

- Lack of common frameworks for educational cooperation and exchange;
- Little or no cooperation with regard to multilateral and international education standard setting processes, common certification, joint degrees and so forth; and
- No coherent strategy in evolving and promoting educational exchange and cooperation which can in turn lead to networking among knowledge institutions that can foster productive collaboration that adds value to both participating countries and their societies.

With reference to the problems and ground realities on the Indian side, till recently one of the major problems has been that Indian decision making has always been very centralized and the attitude of the Indian states is more akin to old empires, and, therefore, not encouraging or supportive of institutions outside Delhi building international partnerships of collaboration. This has changed, but still old bureaucratic habits cling on. However, as a result of the opening of markets and growing economic relations, some bilateral cooperation has begun between institutions of higher learning in Southeast Asia and India, mostly around conventional academic activities.

Creating Normative Frameworks for Cooperation – Potentials and Limitations

The International Conference to commemorate the 20th Anniversary of ASEAN-India Cooperation titled, 'Seamless Integration into the Third Decade – Building on Two Decades of ASEAN-India Partnership', organised by the Chulalongkorn University on 20th and 21st September, 2012, devoted one session for examining the knowledge production and its application, governance of science and technology probing systems of innovation in looking for partnerships with Indian institutions. It was also seen as a way of envisioning Chulalongkorn University's future as it prepared to celebrate its centennial anniversary and the restructuring of the University towards interdisciplinary and research-policy platforms and the creation of a 'research university'.

Science and Technology (S&T) is seen as the main driver of progress. In the discourse about S&T that is widely held, there are many claims made for S&T and the benefits it confers on society such as creating a 'knowledge society' and so on. Furthermore, innovation is treated as a cutting edge for national competitiveness. Indeed, while the gap between science and technology and social science and humanities have been widening (knowledge fragmentation), it seems that science and technology activities are much more complex and multi-layered social activities than ever before (large amount of investment, research-corporate nexus, etc.).

Going beyond the ambitions of the Chulalongkorn University Conference the session on 'Education, Knowledge and Institutional Cooperation' (especially in areas of science, society and innovation for sustainability) pointed to the potential areas for cooperation as also being part of building the normative framework for cooperation between India and Thailand or between India and ASEAN. Basically, what constitutes the core of the cooperation in terms of knowledge domains is science and technology and key focus of such cooperation is innovation.

It is in this context that it is important to remind ourselves of, as we have already referred to earlier, the Cold War history and intellectual legacies that kept us tied to the west and did not give us fresh perspectives to look within Asia. A major influence that is part of that intellectual legacy is positivist international relations (IR). Positivist IR and much of the academic discourse on Asia, has been a major constraint in enabling and providing creative environments that contribute to evolving normative frames and models for knowledge cooperation.

If we are to break out of the shackles and Eurocentric perspectives of positivist IR in the context of Asia and look at the possibilities for vibrant synergetic cooperation within Asia and between India and Asian countries, we have to look at enabling environments and pre-conditions for strengthening partnerships for knowledge cooperation especially in areas such as Science and Technology. Normative frameworks to promote cooperation in areas such as Science and Technology between higher learning institutions in India and Thailand also need to factor in society and sustainability. Cooperation in the area of Science and Technology in general requires perspectives that can draw from disciplines such as public policy and not just IR. Already one can see that India and ASEAN are including areas such as bio-diversity for cooperation with an agreement to work in this area. Normative perspectives are vital for not only laying the foundations for such cooperation and collaboration but also for the very survival of such cooperation when it comes to fields relating to science, society and sustainability not to mention innovation. Knowledge society debates that influence public policy decisions in Science and Technology must inform and influence such cooperation between societies. These debates cannot be done, when there is censorship and restrictions placed on assessments of technology from a technology and society perspective. Knowledge censorship also interferes with innovation especially of a trans-border kind.

The great interest in S&T also lies on the assumption that Science and Technology and Innovation is often equated as technology somehow automatically leads to a better quality of life. The history of technology and 'progress' as we know seems to give rise to the popular view and assumption that technology equals to innovation, which in turn equals to quality of life. There is also a confusion between innovation and invention. They are not same or related, and there is a fundamental difference them. Innovation relates to organisation and teamwork and most importantly to knowledge as opposed to invention, which is individual and more related to information. Innovation is not only about Science and Technology but also involves a range of organisations and social institutions. The causal link made especially in the lay mind about technology and innovation erases the fact that innovation is closely linked to knowledge and practice as mediating factors. These can be referred as knowledge and innovation life cycles. Often these linkages tend to be missed. Innovation takes place not only in scientific laboratories, but also everywhere. The conventional notions of innovation, mostly revolves around investment in science. The vital issue related with innovation is the quality of life, especially in the context of a society as ours, where poverty is still a major scourge and generally in Asia, where gross income inequality not only persists but also is growing and where societies are beset by severe environmental and health issues.

Knowledge and Innovation

Here, we cite two examples about how industry develops and innovation takes place when the basis for knoweldge and practice is laid. The first is from India with regard to the development of the IT industry in the South. Information technology that bloomed in South India (though later it become a phenomenon that extended beyond South India), which we now take for granted, was a result of the strong foundations in mathematics that were laid at school and college education level much earlier. In our opinion, this has happened due to the special quality of mathematics teachers and their excellence in mathematics teaching or the continuous investment made in mathematics as a discipline and a knowledge area. Therefore, today when engineering colleges and fancy courses mushroom to reap the profits of a growing new information technology sector, they are mostly oblivious to the early foundations laid by mathematics teaching, learning and even textbooks. Related to this were the investments in education and educational institutions that philanthrophists, missionaries and far sighted rulers made very early in South India. Madras (now known as Chennai) had some of the earliest educational institutions that were established more than a century ago and now are considered among the top ten colleges in India. Similar is the case of Karnataka and Bangalore, which is now called IT capital of the country. The success of IT industry in Bangalore is built on an earlier history of investments in knowledge institutions and capital. Scholars like Dunning (2000) and geographers have shown how industry clusters have developed and globalisation happened in different parts of the world including South India and Bangalore. Referring to South India and its growth in terms of educational institutions and the priority given to education in India, it is often said that South India has been known for its emphasis on mathematics and music and South India is also famous for its contributions to Indian classical music. Talking of music the other example of how investments in providing a knowledge base contribute to ripple effects that have larger contributions to the economy, technology and innovation cycles is of music and Sweden.

There is an assumption and rather crude functionalist assumption that sees the growth of industry and new markets, purely in terms of markets, liberalisation and greater investment in functionalist branches of education than education per se. This is one of the malaise we are facing in the discussion on education and how to improve the quality of our education system not only in India but also in countries like Thailand. The arrival of General Agreement on Trade in Services (GATS) and the need to open up the education sector also has brought in very crude market functionalist perspectives on education.

It can be said that "Innovation and the Knowledge Society is linked to three dimensions of knowledge in society - Informal Knowledge, Formal

Knowledge and the way the State, Markets and Society mediate this 'knowledge", where we do not give special privilege to any one aspect over the other, especially where tendencies to privilege the market are prevalent. We may and could inform normative frameworks leaders and innovators in higher learning institutions who take the lead in establishing cooperation between Indian and Thailand (ASEAN) higher educational institutions.

Science, Technology and Formal Knowledge Institutions

Against the background of creating partnerships that can promote 'Education and Knowledge Institutional Cooperation with special reference to Science, Society and Innovation for Sustainability', there must be joint and collaborative re-look at the present system of education in the Sciences and Humanities. Simply linking institutions for cooperation or forging partnerships between different faculties between Universities in Thailand (for example) and India will not provide any real basis for long term partnerships especially from a creative and innovative perspective. Special programmes on the lines of the United Nations Environment Programme (UNEP) like the Global Universities Partnership for Education for Sustainability (GUPES) can serve as examples.

The reputed international scholar of Science and Technology Policy, Sheila Jasanoff of Harvard University, in her works referring to formal knowledge institutions talks about 'The Social Contract for Innovation'. In her view, conventional notions, relating to Innovation, can be simply equated as: 'more science = more innovation and more innovation in science = more welfare'. As a consequence, she is of the view that National Governments have a duty to foster Science and Technology (S&T) and here they take the view that S&T institutions are self-regulating institutions and should be left to their own agendas. Governments trying to harness science, create programmes of 'Mission Oriented Science' assuming that this will address social needs and contribute to welfare.

Jasanoff has argued for the need of a new social contract especially on the changing face of techno-science and mission oriented science. She also cites disasters such as Bhopal and Chernobyl, which had created a crisis of confidence in S&T. Then, there are new convergent technologies such as nanotechnology with their promise as well as dangers. In the context of the developments in science and technology, we are witnessing the necessity of managing risk to managing ignorance and uncertainty. In managing risk and uncertainty, the precautionary principle has to be central. The view that "Government Knows Best" has to be avoided. There is a need for discussions on new technologies, whether it is Nano, GMOs or other areas, and government can not simply avoid public on these issues. The science, technology and society must go in unison; otherwise, there is the new danger of a new rhetoric innovation. Innovation should be firmly rooted in society. There is a need to recognise that innovation is a socially driven process and not just that of State or Markets. We are aware of the phenomena of "Bubble Companies" riding the wave of innovation, both real and rhetorical and creating a whole new class of venture capitalists, who have threatened the very fundamentals of global capitalism and almost took down with them major economies of the globe.

Another way of making innovation rooted in society and sustainable is to ensure that innovation does not mean only Science and Technology. Innovative societies bring together far more dimensions than just innovations in science and technology. Then there is the issue of separating completely the two spheres of Science and Knowledge and Science as Knowledge. Viewed from a knowledge perspective, science, technology and society must be seen as an ensemble and is an essential condition for providing the proper base for innovation and for a society to move consistently and sustainably on the path of innovation and not in spurts in case of sudden haphazard events. Binding science, technology and society is democracy and only S&T that is democratic and accountable can provide the sustainable basis for innovation. There is a very symbiotic link between innovation and democracy and Democratic Accountability must be built into activities for innovation. It is interesting that in the European Union (EU), the Seventh Framework Programme (the largest EU research programme), which ended in 2013, took upon itself the task of making the process of knowledge production more open, democratic and accountable. ASEAN-India knowledge cooperation can fruitfully draw from the EU's Seventh Framework Programme. Innovation is not about the sudden brilliance of a single actor, or some group of people or enterprise, society has to create the base and broad conditions in an open and democratic manner to let innovations take place. Innovation is very much part and parcel of society. It is about engaging society, it is interdisciplinary, involving - knowing, learning and acting. All of this in the context of innovation relate to quality of life and democratic accountability in a synergetic sense.

A key element of innovation in higher education in such a background is, "re-orienting education for sustainability". The tasks we have to look at in "reorienting higher education for sustainability" are how knowledge about sustainability can be extended and for that what role higher educational institutions can play.

Conclusion

Tremendous possibilities and potential exist for building long term cooperation between institutions of higher learning in India and ASEAN, which are of long term values to both countries and societies. However, these ties for cooperation can not be built just by trailing the evolutionary trend of growth in economic and market ties, or ad hoc cooperation arrangements built on conventional academic enterprises and existing educational approaches. Innovative cooperation can be built and it can contribute to virtuous cycles of innovation and social benefit through a process of mutual learning, if priority is given in such cooperation not purely in an inward looking institutional sense, but looking outward to society and forward to the future, anticipating the challenges that our societies commonly face in terms of ecological sustainability, economic growth with justice and equity and a quality of life for all citizens in our nations.

References

Balasubramanyam, A., & Balasubramanyam, V. N. (2000). The Software Cluster in Bangalore. In John H. Dunning (ed), *Regions, Globalization and the Knowledge Based Economy*. Oxford: Oxford University Press.

Dunning, J. H. (ed). (2000a). *Regions, Globalization and the Knowledge Based Economy*. Oxford: Oxford University Press.

Dunning, J. H. (2000b). *Regions, Globalization and the Knowledge Economy*. op. cit.

Goodland, Robert. (1992). The Case that World Has Reached Limits. In Goodland, R. J., Daly, H. E., & El Serafy, S. (eds), *Population, Technology, and Lifestyle: The Transition To Sustainability*. USA: Island Press.

Jasanoff, S. (2013). *A World of Experts: Science and Global Environmental Constitutionalism*. Boston College Environmental Affairs Law Review, 40(2): 439-452.

Jasanoff , S. (2012a). *Science and Public Reason*. London: Routledge.

Jasanoff, S. (2012b). *The Public of Public Reason* (Sarton Chair Lecture). Sartoniana 25: 17-36.

Jasanoff, S. (2012c). Taking Life: Private Rights in Public Nature. In Rajan, K. S. (ed), *Lively Capital: Biotechnologies, Ethics, and Governance in Global Markets*. Duke University Press, (pp. 155-183).